THE FIVE NIKĀYAS

Discourses of the Buddha
An Anthology

Book One

THE FIVE NIKĀYAS

Discourses of the Buddha
An Anthology

Book One

Translated by
the editors of *The Light of the Dhamma*

Edited by the English Editorial Board

DEPARTMENT OF RELIGIOUS AFFAIRS
RANGOON, BURMA

MPA Pariyatti Editions
an imprint of
Pariyatti Publishing
www.pariyatti.org

First printed and published in 1978 by U Chit Tin, Deputy Director for the Department of Religious Affairs at the Department of Religious Affairs Press, Rangoon, Myanmar.

First Pariyatti Edition 2025

ISBN: 978-1-68172-816-2 (paperback)
ISBN: 978-1-68172-821-6 (PDF)
ISBN: 978-1-68172-822-3 (ePub)
ISBN: 978-1-68172-823-0 (Mobi)
Library of Congress Control Number: 2025938068

Preface

In the year 1950, the Union Buddha Sāsana Council decided to bring out a periodical in English in order to disseminate the Theravāda Buddhist thought within the country and the world outside. The idea became a reality in 1952 when in October of that year, the first issue of *The Light of the Dhamma* came out. The Council decided to publish it once every three months and successfully did so till mid-1963.

As the idea of bringing it out was to spread the Theravāda Buddhist thought, the Council decided to incorporate in the periodical, translations of selected suttas from the five Nikāyas.

The Department of Religious Affairs of the Ministry of Religious Affairs continued the work of compiling and publishing the Buddha-Dhamma.

The present publication, *The Five Nikāyas, Discourses of the Buddha, An Anthology, Book One* is just a compilation of the translation work done by the editors of *The Light of the Dhamma* consisting of discourses, the analyses of the Suttas and compilations from Vinaya Piṭaka.

The work is divided into five parts, of which the first one is devoted to the Anthology of Dīgha Nikāya (Collection of Long Discourses): three discourses from it are included.

The second is a selection of four discourses from the Majjhima Nikāya (Collection of Middle-Length Discourses).

The third is a selection of twelve discourses from the Saṃyutta Nikāya (Collection of Kindred Sayings).

The fourth is a selection of sixty-two discourses from the Aṅguttara Nikāya (Collection of Discourses from Gradual Sayings).

The fifth is a selection of two discourses, two analyses as in Suttas (Suttantabhājanīya) and two compilations from Vinaya Piṭaka and Commentaries of Khuddaka Nikāya (Collection of Minor Anthologies).

It should be remembered that the translations included in the present compilation are the Texts par excellence to devout Buddhists. As such, every word actually belonging to it deserves to be brought within the reach not only of every Buddhist but also of anyone who is interested in Buddhist thought.

The energy put forth for bringing out the compilation will be considered fruitful and amply rewarded if the publication serves the purpose of enabling students and scholars to have an insight into the theory and practices of Buddha's Teachings.

Contents

DĪGHA NIKĀYA

Discourse on the Supreme Net....3
Discourse on the Advantages of a Samaṇa's Life....53
Ambaṭṭha Sutta....88

MAJJHIMA NIKĀYA

Great Discourse About Cowherds....131
Questions and Answers on Sakkāya, Sakkāya-diṭṭhi, the Noble Eightfold Path and Latent Tendencies....145
Discourse on Jīvaka the Doctor....153
Ānāpānassati Sutta....157

SAṂYUTTA NIKĀYA

Discourse on "Dependent Origination"....165
Sermon on the Untaught....167
Discourse on the Wandering Ascetic Susima....169
Discourse on What the Clinging Turns On....177
Discourse on the Seven Aspects....182
Discourse on the Characteristic of Anattā....187
Discourse to Anurādha....190
Mahākaccāna's Discourse with Lohicca Brahmina on Guarded and Unguarded Sense Doors....194
Simile of the Virulent Serpents....199
Discourse on the Similitude of the Log of Wood....204
Discourse on the Dhamma-way to Compare Oneself with Another....207
The Discourse on Setting the Wheel of the Doctrine in Motion....212

AṄGUTTARA NIKĀYA

Rūpādi-Vagga (Sight and the Rest)....219
Nīvaraṇappahāna-Vagga (Abandoning of Hindrances), Suttas 1–6....228

Nīvaraṇappahāna-Vagga (Abandoning of Hindrances), Suttas 7–10 247
Akammanīya-Vagga (Unadaptable) 253
Adanta-Vagga (The Untamed) 257
Paṇihitaaccha-Vagga (The Mind) Well-Directed 259
Discourse on Nibbāna 267
Discourse on Heretical Views 269
Discourse on Living Together as Husband and Wife 276
A Housewife's Fivefold Duty 279
Discourse on Hell 282
Discourse on Self-Confidence 283
Discourse on the Five Things Which Are Dangers and Enemies 284
Discourse on the Great Reflections of Venerable Anuruddha 296
Discourse on Bad Effects of Evil Deeds 302
Discourse on Observing the Precepts in Brief 304

KHUDDAKA NIKĀYA

Tirokuṭṭa Sutta 309
Commentary on Tirokuṭṭa Sutta 312
Āmagandha Sutta 326
Sacca-Vibhaṅga Suttantabhājanīya (The Four Noble Truths) 328
Analytical Exposition of the Dependent Origination
(Analysis as in Suttas) 340
Introduction to the Two Hundred and Twenty-Seven Rules of Vinaya 357
The Two Hundred and Twenty-Seven Rules of Vinaya 363

Index 398

DĪGHA NIKĀYA

SĪLAKKHANDHA

1. Brahmajāla Sutta

Discourse on the Supreme Net

THUS I have heard. On one occasion the Bhagavā was journeying along the high road between Rājagaha and Nālanda with a great company of monks, numbering about five hundred, and Suppiya, the wandering religious mendicant was also journeying along the high road between Rājagaha and Nālanda with his disciple, the young Brahmadatta.

Of these two persons - the teacher and his pupil, Suppiya the mendicant spoke in many ways in dispraise of the Buddha, the Dhamma, and the Saṅgha, whereas the youth Brahmadatta, his pupil, spoke in many ways in praise of the Buddha, the Dhamma, and the Saṅgha. Thus, they two - the teacher and the pupil, giving utterance to diametrically opposite views, were following, step by step, the Bhagavā and the company of monks.

2. Now the Bhagavā together with the company of monks approached the royal rest house in the Ambalatthikā garden for the purpose of spending a night there and so also did Suppiya and his young disciple Brahmadatta.

3. And in the early dawn a number of monks assembled, as they rose up, in the pavilion, and this was the trend of the talk that sprang up among them, as they were seated there.

> "How wonderful a thing it is brethren, and how strange it is brethren! That the Knower of the worlds, the Seer of the worlds, the One worthy of veneration, the Omniscient Buddha, should have so clearly perceived how various are the dispositions of sentient beings. Suppiya the mendicant speaks in many ways in dispraise of the Buddha, the Dhamma, and the Saṅgha, whereas the disciple, young Brahmadatta, speaks in many ways in praise of the Buddha, the Dhamma, and the Saṅgha. So do these two, the teacher and his pupil, follow step by step, after the Bhagavā and the company of monks, uttering words which directly contradict one another."

4. Now the Bhagavā on realizing, what they were talking about, went to the pavilion and having sat down on the appointed seat, said: "What are you talking about while you are sitting here, and what is the topic of your conversation?" They all then addressed the Bhagavā: "Lord, this was the

trend of the talk that sprang up among us, who rose in the early dawn and assembled here:

> 'How wonderful a thing it is brethren, and how strange a thing it is brethren! That the Knower of the worlds, the Seer of the worlds, the One worthy of veneration, the Omniscient Buddha, should have so clearly perceived how various are the dispositions of sentient beings. Suppiya the mendicant speaks in many ways in dispraise of the Buddha, the Dhamma, and the Saṅgha, whereas the disciple, young Brahmadatta, speaks in many ways in praise of the Buddha, the Dhamma, and the Saṅgha. So do these two, the teacher and his pupil, follow step by step after the Bhagavā and the company of monks, uttering words which directly contradict one another." This was what we were talking about, and before we concluded our conversation, the Exalted One arrived here.'"

5. And the Bhagavā said: "Monks, if others speak against me, or the Dhamma or the Saṅgha, you should not on that account either have a grudge against them or suffer heart-burning or feel ill-will. If you, on that account could be angry and hurt, that would become a danger to yourselves. If, when others speak ill of me, or the Dhamma or the Saṅgha, you feel angry at that and displeased, would you then be able to judge how far that speech is good or bad?"

"That would not be so, Lord."

"But when others speak ill of me, or the Dhamma or the Saṅgha, you should rebut their statement by saying: 'For this or that reason, this is not the fact, that is not so, such a thing does not exist among us, is not in us.'

6. "But also, monks, if others should speak in praise of me, in praise of the Dhamma, in praise of the Saṅgha, you should not be filled with pleasure and gladness, or be lifted up in mind, on that account.

"Monks, if others should speak in praise of me, in praise of the Dhamma, in praise of the Saṅgha and you, on that account, be filled with pleasure or gladness, or be lifted up in mind, that also would become a danger to your own selves.

"Monks, when others speak in praise of me, or the Dhamma or the Saṅgha, you should admit the fact as right, saying: 'For this or that reason this is the fact, that is so, such a thing exists among us, is in us.'"

CŪLA SĪLA (The Minor Morality)

7. "If a worldling desires to praise the Tathāgata, he would speak only things of small value, of mere morality. And what are those qualities of morality that are of insignificant value and that he speaks of a little?

8. "'Having abstained from taking the life of any living being, the monk Gotama refrains from the destruction of life. He has laid the stick and the weapon aside; he has moral shame and dread; shows kindness toward all beings and is full of solicitude for the welfare of all sentient beings.' It is thus the worldling, when speaking in praise of the Tathāgata, might speak.

"Or he might say: 'Having abstained from the taking of what is not given, the monk Gotama refrains from taking what is not given to him. He takes only what is given to him; appreciates the giving by others and lives in honesty and purity of heart.'

"Or he might say: 'Having abstained from unchastity, the monk Gotama practices chastity. He refrains from the vulgar practice and also from the sexual act which is the practice of the country folk.'

9. "Or he might say: 'Getting rid of lying words, the monk Gotama refrains from falsehood. He speaks the truth and nothing but the truth; faithful and trustworthy, he does not break his word to the world.'

"Or he might say: 'Getting rid of slander, the monk Gotama refrains from calumny. What he hears here, he does not repeat elsewhere to raise a quarrel against the people here; what he hears elsewhere, he does not repeat here to raise a quarrel against the people there. Thus, he binds together those who are divided, encourages those who are friends, makes peace, loves peace, is impassioned for peace, a speaker of words leading to peace.'

"Or he might say: 'Getting rid of the rudeness of speech, the monk Gotama refrains from using harsh language. He speaks only those words that are blameless, pleasant to the ear, lovely, reaching to the heart, polite, pleasing to the people, and beloved of the people.'

"Or he might say: 'Getting rid of frivolous talk, the monk Gotama refrains from vain conversation. At the appropriate time he speaks, in accordance with the facts, words full of meaning, on the Doctrine, on the Vinaya. And at the right time, he speaks words worthy to be noted in one's mind, fitly illustrated and divided according to the relevancy of the facts.'

10. "Or he might say: 'The monk Gotama refrains from causing injury to seeds and plants.

He takes only one meal a day, not eating at night and refrains from taking food after midday.

He refrains from dancing, singing, playing music, and witnessing shows with dances, singing, and music.

He refrains from wearing, adorning, or ornamenting himself with garlands, scents, and ointments.

He refrains from the use of lofty and spacious resting places.

He refrains from accepting gold and silver.

He refrains from accepting uncooked grain.

He refrains from accepting raw meat.

He refrains from accepting women or young girls.

He refrains from accepting slave servants of either sex.

He refrains from accepting sheep or goats.

He refrains from accepting fowls and pigs.

He refrains from accepting elephants, cattle, horses, and mares.

He refrains from accepting agricultural or wastelands.

He refrains from acting as an ambassador or messenger.

He refrains from buying and selling.

He refrains from cheating with scales or coins or measures.

He refrains from the cunning ways of bribery, cheating, and fraud.

He refrains from causing physical injury to anyone, murder, putting in bonds, highway robbery, dacoity, and plunder.'

"Such are the things, monks, which a worldling when praising the Tathāgata, might say."

Here ends the Cūḷa Sīla (The Minor Morality).

MAJJHIMA SĪLA (The Medium Morality)

11. "Or he might say: 'Whereas some recluses and Brahmins while living on food provided by the philanthropic and generous, cause injury to seedlings and growing plants whether propagated from roots or stems or joints or buddings or seeds, the monk Gotama refrains from causing such injury to seedlings and growing plants.'

12. "Or he might say: 'Whereas some recluses and Brahmins while living on food provided by the philanthropic and generous, use hoarded things—foods, drinks, clothing, conveyances, bedding, scents, and any eatables, the monk Gotama refrains from storing such things up.'

13. "Or he might say: 'Whereas some recluses and Brahmins while living on food provided by the philanthropic and generous, visit shows; which are these shows? They are:

niccaṃ (dances);
gītaṃ (singing of songs);
vāditaṃ (playing instrumental music);
pekkaṃ (theatrical shows);
akkhānaṃ (telling stories with a mingling of doggerel and rhymes);
pāṇissaraṃ (music attended by clapping);
vetāḷam (playing music by means of cymbals);
kuṃbhathūṇaṃ (playing drums);
sobhanakaṃ (art exhibitions);
caṇḍāla-vaṃsa-dhovanaṃ (acrobatic feats on the top of a hoisted bamboo pole);
combats of elephants, horses, buffaloes, bulls, goats, sheep, cocks, and quails;
exercising self-defence with quarterstaff, boxing, wrestling;
sham fights, roll-calls, manoeuvres, troop inspection.

The monk Gotama refrains from visiting the above-mentioned shows.'

14. "Or he might say: 'Whereas some recluses and Brahmins while living on food provided by the philanthropic and generous, indulge in the following games and recreations:

aṭṭha padaṃ (games on chess boards or boards with eight rows of squares);
dasa padaṃ (games on chess boards or boards with ten rows of squares);

ākāsaṃ parihāra-pathaṃ (such games played by imagining such boards in the air);
santikaṃ (games somewhat akin to hopscotch; or drawing diagrams on the ground, in which one steps only where one is allowed to do so);
khalikaṃ (throwing dice);
ghaṭikaṃ (hitting a short stick with a long one; games akin to tip-cat);
salākahatthaṃ (a play where the hand is dipped in dye and used as a brush);
akkhaṃ (games with balls of all sizes);
pangacīraṃ (blowing through toy pipes made of leaves or papers);
vankakaṃ (ploughing with miniature ploughs);
mokkhacikaṃ (turning somersaults);
cingulikaṃ (playing with paper wind-mills);
pattāḷakaṃ (playing with toy measures);
rathakaṃ (playing with toy chariots);
dhanukaṃ (playing with toy bows);
akkharikaṃ (a game where one has to find out the missing letter or letters);
manesikaṃ (guessing others' thoughts);
yathāvajjaṃ (games involving mimicry of deformities).

The monk Gotama refrains from such games and recreations.'

15. "Or he might say: 'Whereas some recluses and Brahmins while living on food provided by the philanthropic and generous, use high and luxurious resting places such as:

an extra-long chair or spacious couch;
thrones with animal figures carved on the supports;
carpets or coverlets with very long fleece;
patchwork counterpanes of many colors;
white blankets;
woolen coverlets richly embroidered;
quilts stuffed with cotton wool;
coverlets embroidered with figures of lions, tigers, etc.;
rugs with fur on both sides or with fur on one side;
coverlets embroidered with gold threads or silk coverlets;
carpets woven with furs;

elephant, horse, or chariot rugs;
rugs of antelope skins sewn together;
carpets with awnings overhead;
sofas with red pillows for the head and feet.

The monk Gotama refrains from using such high and luxurious resting places.'

16. "Or he might say: 'Whereas some recluses and Brahmins while living on food provided by the philanthropic and generous, use means for adorning and beautifying themselves, such as:

rubbing scented powder on one's body, massaging with oil, and bathing with scents;
massaging or patting the limbs so as to develop muscles;
the use of mirrors, eye-ointments, garlands, rouge, cosmetics, face powders, make-up, bracelets, top-knot, walking sticks, tubes or pipes for holding anything, swords, umbrellas, embroidered slippers, turbans, diadems, whisks of the yak's tail, and long-fringed white robes.

The monk Gotama refrains from such means of adorning and beautifying the person.'

17. "Or he might say: 'Whereas some recluses or Brahmins while living on food provided by the philanthropic and generous, are addicted to such low talks as these:

talks about kings, robbers, and ministers of state;
armies, dangers, and war;
eating and drinking, clothes and dwellings, garlands, perfumes;
relations, chariots, villages, markets, towns, and districts;
women and heroes;
street talks, talks by the well;
talks about those departed in days gone by;
tittle-tattle;
talks about land and sea and gain and loss.

The monk Gotama refrains from such low talk.'

18. "Or he might say: 'Whereas some recluses and Brahmins while living on food provided by the philanthropic and generous, enter into wrangling conversations, such as:

You don't understand this Dhamma and Vinaya, I do.

How should you know about this Dhamma and Vinaya?
You are practicing wrong views. It is I who practice the right one.
I am talking about relevant facts, whereas you are not.
You speak last what ought to be spoken first and first what ought to be spoken last.
All that you have practiced is upset.
I have pointed out the fault in your views.
I have reproved you.
Set to work to rebut my statements.
Do so yourself if you can.

The monk Gotama refrains from such wrangling conversations.'

19. "Or he might say: 'Whereas some recluses and Brahmins while living on food provided by the philanthropic and generous, work as mediators and messengers, such as:

Acting as mediators and messengers of kings, ministers of state, royal families, Brahmins, or youths, saying:
Go there, come here, take this with you, bring that from that place.

The monk Gotama refrains from such servile duties.'

20. "Or he might say: 'Whereas some recluses and Brahmins while living on food provided by the philanthropic and generous, are tricksters, chanters of holy words for gain, interpreters of signs and omens, exorcists and endeavor to obtain a lot of money from others after spending a little of their own.

The monk Gotama refrains from such trickeries and deceptions.'"

Here ends the Majjhima Sīla (The Medium Morality).

MAHĀ SĪLA (The Major Morality)

21. "Or he might say: 'Whereas some recluses and Brahmins while living on food provided by the philanthropic and generous, earn their living by wrong means of livelihood, by low arts, such as:

prophesying long life, prosperity, etc., or the reverse, from marks on limbs, hands and feet of a person;
divining by means of omens and signs;
auguries drawn from thunderbolts;
prophesying by interpreting dreams;
palmistry or chiromancy;
auguries from the marks gnawed by mice;
fire-oblation;
offering oblations from a ladle;
making offerings to gods of husks, of broken rice, of rice, of ghee, and of oil;
offering oblations from the mouth,
sacrifice or human blood to gods;
fortune telling concerning the loss of properties and sickness;
determining whether the site for a proposed house or garden is lucky or not;
public administration;
knowledge of appeasing charms;
laying ghosts;
knowledge of charms to be pronounced by one living in an earth-house;
snake charming;
the poison craft;
the scorpion craft;
the art of curing rat bites;
the bird craft;
the crow craft;
foretelling the number of years that a man has to live;
charms to ward off arrows;
charms to understand the languages of animals.

The monk Gotama refrains from such low arts.'

22. "Or he might say: 'Whereas some recluses and Brahmins while living on food provided by the philanthropic and generous, earn their living by wrong means, of livelihood, by low arts, such as:

Knowledge of the signs of good and bad qualities and the marks denoting the health or luck of their owners in:

Gems, apparel, staves, swords and spears, two-edged swords, arrows, bows, other weapons, women, men, boys, girls, slaves, slave girls, elephants, horses, buffaloes, bulls, oxen, goats, sheep, fowls, quails, iguanas, bucks and deer.

The monk Gotama refrains from such low arts.'

23. "Or he might say: 'Whereas some recluses and Brahmins while living on food provided by the philanthropic and generous, earn their living by wrong means of livelihood, by low arts, such as:

Predictions to the effect that—The chieftains will march out; the chieftains will march back; our chiefs will attack, and the enemy will retreat; the enemy will attack and ours will retreat; our chief will win the battle, and the foreign chiefs will suffer defeat; the foreign chiefs will win the battle and ours will suffer defeat;

Thus this chief will succeed and that chief not.

The monk Gotama refrains from such low arts.'

24. "Or he might say: 'Whereas some recluses and Brahmins while living on food provided by the philanthropic and generous, earn their living by wrong means of livelihood, by low arts, such as foretelling that there will be an eclipse of the moon, of the sun, of a constellation; that the sun or the moon will go on its usual course, there will be an aberration of the sun or the moon, or that the constellations will go on their usual course, that there will be aberrations of the constellations; that there will be a fall of meteors, *disā ḍāha* ("sky-glow"), an unusual redness of the horizon, that there will be an earthquake, that there will be a wild *Deva-dundubhi* (a supernatural rumble), that there will be rising and setting, clearness and dimness, of the sun or the moon or the constellations.

The monk Gotama refrains from such low arts.'

25. "Or he might say: 'Whereas some recluses and Brahmins while living on food provided by the philanthropic and generous, earn their livelihood by such wrong means, by such low arts as - foretelling an abundant rainfall, a deficient rainfall, a good harvest, a bad harvest or scarcity of food, tranquillity, disturbances, pestilence, a healthy season, counting on the fingers, by means of arithmetic; by means of formulae, prosody, *lokāyataṃ* (popular lore and custom).

The monk Gotama refrains from such low arts.'

26. "Or he might say: 'Whereas some recluses and Brahmins while living on food provided by the philanthropic and generous, earn their living by wrongful means of livelihood, by low arts, such as - effecting marriages in which the bride or bridegroom is brought home, or sent forth, effecting betrothals, or divorces, saving money, expending money, *subhagakaraṇaṃ* (using charms to make people happy), *dubbhagakaraṇaṃ* (using charms to make people unhappy), giving medicine to preserve the foetus in cases of abortive women, incantations to make the tongue stiff, to make the jaws of a person stiff, to make a man throw up his hands, to bring on deafness, making use of a mirror to obtain answers to questions put to it, obtaining oracular answers through a girl possessed, from a god, the worship of the sun, of the Brahmā, bringing forth flames from one's mouth, invoking the goddess of Luck.

The monk Gotama refrains from such low arts.'

27. "Or he might say: 'Whereas some recluses and Brahmins while living on food provided by the philanthropic and generous, earn their living by, wrongful means, by low arts, such as - vowing gifts to a god if a certain benefit be obtained, observing such vows, practicing ghost craft, practicing arts and crafts while lodging in an earth house, causing virility, causing femininity, preparing sites for buildings and consecrating them, causing a person to vomit, causing a person to take a bath, offering sacrificial fires, administering emetics, purgatives, expectorants and phlegmagogues, causing blood and other impurities to come out of the head and thus relieving it, preparing oil for people's ears, preparing oil to be used as eye-drops, administering drugs through the nose, preparing powerful eye-drops, preparing eye-drops that produce a cooling effect, curing cataracts, practicing surgery, practicing as a children's doctor, administering original drugs and medicines, and preparing new drugs and medicines.

The monk Gotama refrains from such low arts.'

"These, monks, are the trifling matters, the minor details, of mere morality, of which the worldling, when praising the Tathāgata, might speak."

Here ends the Mahā Sīla (The Major Morality).

WRONG VIEWS

28. "There are, monks, other Teachings, profound, difficult to realize, hard to understand, tranquillizing, exalted, not to be deduced by mere logic, subtle, comprehensible only by the wise. These dhammas—the Tathāgata, having himself realized them and seen them face to face, has set forth, and it is of them—that they, who would rightly praise the Tathāgata in accordance with the truth, should speak.[1]

"And what are they?"

Pubbantakappika (18 Views)

29. "There are some recluses and Brahmins, monks, who speculate on the past existences, whose speculations are concerned with the ultimate past, and who on eighteen grounds advance their arguments regarding the past existences. And about what, with reference to what, do these recluses and Brahmins do so?

30. "There are, monks, some recluses and Brahmins who are addicted to Eternity-belief, and who on four grounds, proclaim that both the *attā* (soul) and the world are eternal. And about what, with reference to what, do these recluses and Brahmins do so?

31. "In the first place, monks, some recluse or Brahmin by means of zeal, earnestness, constant application, vigilance, careful pondering, reaches up to such tranquillity of mind that, being clean and pure in mind, being free from impurities, and having overcome the defilements of the mind, he is able to remember what had happened in the past existences. In which way?

---

1. He enters on the discussion of Wrong Views to show how *Sabbaññuta-ñāṇa* can be comprehended, and to develop the doctrine of *Suññata* (Soullessness)

As the Venerable Nyanatiloka has pointed out in his *Buddhist Dictionary*, "... neither within these bodily and mental phenomena of existence nor outside of them, can be found anything that in the ultimate sense could be regarded as self-reliant real ego-entity or personality. This is the central doctrine of Buddhism, without an understanding of which a real knowledge of Buddhism is altogether impossible. It is the only specific Buddhist doctrine, with which the entire Buddhist structure stands and falls. All the remaining Buddhist doctrines may, more or less, be found in other philosophic systems and religions, but the Anattā-Doctrine has been clearly and unreservedly taught only by the Buddha, wherefore also the Buddha is known as the *anattā-vādī* or 'Teacher of lmpersonality'."

Sabbaññutañāṇassa mahantabhāvadassatthaṃ desanāya ca suññatā pakāsana vibhāvanatthaṃ samayantaraṃ anupavisanto dhammarājā, etc.

"In one existence, or two, or three, or four, or five, or ten, or twenty, or thirty, or forty, or fifty, or a hundred, or a thousand, or in several hundreds or thousands, or hundreds of thousands of existences in the past, to the effect that 'There I had such and such a name, was of such and such a lineage and caste, lived on such and such food, experienced such and such pains and pleasures, had such and such a span of years. And when I fell from thence, I was reborn here.' Thus, does he remember, in full detail saying: 'In that existence, I had such and such a name, was of such and such a caste, was of such and such complexion, lived on such and such food, experienced both pains and pleasures and having fallen from thence, was reborn here.' And he says to himself: 'The soul, as well as the world, is eternal, unproductive, is steadfast as a mountain peak, as a gate-post firmly fixed and though these living creatures run through and fare-on from this existence to that, fall from this existence and arise in another, yet there is the *attā*[2] and the world that may be compared to things eternal. And why must that be so? Because, I, by means of zeal, earnestness, constant application, vigilance, careful pondering, reach up to such tranquillity of mind that, being very clean and pure in mind, being free from impurities, and having overcome the defilements of the mind I am able to remember what had happened in past existences. In which way?

"'In one existence, or two, or three, or four, or five, or ten, or twenty, or thirty, or forty, or fifty, or a hundred, or a thousand, or several hundreds or thousands of existences in the past, to the effect that here I have such and such a name, am of such and such a lineage and caste, live on such and such food, experience such and such pains and pleasures, have such and such a span of years. And when I fell from thence was reborn here. There also I had such and such a name, was of such and such a lineage and caste, lived on such and such food, experienced such and such pains and pleasures; had such and such a span of years. For these reasons also I know this: The soul, as well as the world, is eternal, unproductive, is steadfast as a mountain peak, as a gate-post firmly fixed and though these living creatures run through and fare-on from this existence to that, fall from this existence and arise in another, yet there is the *attā* and the world that may be compared to things eternal.'

"This, monks, is the first state of things on account of which, objectifying which, some recluses and Brahmins are Eternalists and maintain that both the soul and the world are eternal."

2. In the sense of a permanent unchanging entity.

ETERNITY-BELIEF (Second and Third cases)

32–33. (*The Second and the Third cases set forth are in all respects the same except that the previous existences thus remembered by a person extend in the second case over a still longer period of up to ten world cycles and in the third case up to forty world cycles.*)

34. "And in the fourth case, monks, on what ground is it, objectifying on what, that those recluses and Brahmins are Eternalists and maintain that the *attā* and the world are eternal?

"In this world, monks, some recluse or Brahmin is addicted to logic and investigating things. He, through his logical reasoning and from his own investigation, says as follows: 'The soul, as well as the world, is eternal, unproductive, is steadfast as a mountain peak, as a gate-post firmly fixed and though those living creatures run through and fare-on from this existence to that, fall from this existence and arise in another, yet there is the *attā* and the world that are similar to things eternal.'

35. "These, monks, are those recluses and Brahmins who are Eternalists and in four ways maintain that both the soul and the world are eternal. Monks, all those recluses and Brahmins who maintain that both the *attā* and the world are eternal, do so in these four ways, or in one or other of the same and apart from these four, there is no other outside way.

36. 'The Tathāgata knows that such are the wrong views, such are the causes thereof and such is the manner in which they are held and persisted in, such will be the future existences of those who hold these wrong views and such will be the consequences after death of holding them.

'The Tathāgata knows all these. He knows also other things which are much higher.[3] But He does not regard such knowledge with *taṇhā* (craving), *māna* (conceit), and *diṭṭhi* (wrong views); so, He realizes that He has attained Nibbāna.

'The Tathāgata has achieved Freedom through detachment as He has realized, as they really are, the Origin, Cessation, Pleasantness and Unsatisfactoriness of *Vedanā* (Sensations), and emancipation therefrom.'"

37. "Monks, there are other Teachings, profound, difficult to realize, hard to understand, tranquillizing, exalted, not to be deduced by mere logic, subtle,

3. These are *sīla* (morality), *samādhi* (concentration) and *sabbaññutā-ñāṇa* (omniscience).

comprehensible only to the wise. These Teachings—the Tathāgata having himself realized them and seen them face to face, has set forth, and it is of them—that they who would rightly praise the Tathāgata in accordance with the truth, should speak."

Here ends the First Portion for Recitation.

EKACCA SASSATA VĀDA (Eternity-belief with regard to some and in regard to others Non-eternity-belief)

38. "There are, monks, some recluses and Brahmins who are Eternalists with regard to some and in regard to others Non-Eternalists; who on four grounds maintain that the *attā* and the world are partly eternal and partly not.

"Depending upon what and objectifying what do these recluses and Brahmins take it that the *attā* and the world are partly eternal and partly not?"

Ekacca Sassata Vāda (First View)

39. "Monks, at one time or another, after the lapse of many ages, this world system comes to an end. This kind of time exists. When the world system is destroyed, beings have mostly been reborn in the Ābhassara plane (plane of radiant Brahmā), and there they live made of mind, feeding on *pīti* (rapture), radiating light from their bodies, dwelling in the air, occupying glorious positions. Thus, they remain for many ages.

40. "Monks, at one time or another, after the lapse of many ages, this world system begins to spring up. This kind of time exists. When this happens a plane of Brahmā appears, but it is empty. At that time some being, either because his span of life comes to an end or his merit is exhausted, falls from that Ābhassara Brahmā plane and is reborn in the Brahmā plane which is empty. And there he lives made of mind, feeding on *pīti*, radiating light from his body, dwelling in the air, enjoying a glorious position. Thus, does he remain for many ages.

41. "Now there arises in him, from his dwelling there for a great length of time alone, an unsatisfactoriness and a longing: 'O! would that other beings might come to this plane.' And then, because their span of life has expired or their merit become exhausted, other beings fall from the Ābhassara Brahmā plane and arise in the Brahmā plane as companions to him. They live made of mind, feeding on *pīti*, radiating light from their bodies, dwelling in the air, occupying glorious positions and remain for many ages.

42. "Then, monks, the one who was first reborn thinks to himself: 'I am Brahmā, the Great Brahmā, the Conqueror, the One who cannot be conquered by others, surely All-seeing, All-powerful, the Ruler, the Creator, the Excellent, the Almighty, the One who has already practiced Calm, the Father of all that are and are to be. I have created these other beings; because a while ago I thought 'Would that they might come.' Thus, on my mental aspiration, these beings arise in this Brahmā plane.

"And these beings themselves, too, think: 'This must be Brahmā, the Great Brahmā, the Conqueror, the One who cannot be conquered by others, surely All-seeing, All-powerful, the Ruler, the Creator, the Excellent, the Almighty, the One who has already practiced Calm, the Father of all that are and are to be. And he has created us; because, as we see, this Great Brahmā arose in this plane first, and we came after him.'

43. "Then, monks, among them the one who first arose there is of a very long life, very beautiful and powerful. Those beings who appeared after him have shorter spans of life, not so beautiful and not so powerful.

44. "Monks, there is indeed a reason that a certain being after falling from that state should be reborn in this world of men and having done so might go forth from the household life into that of a recluse. And having thus become a recluse, by means of zeal, earnestness, constant application, vigilance, careful pondering, he reaches up to such tranquillity of mind that, having such a concentration of mind, he remembers his last dwelling place in the Brahmā plane and not more than that. He says to himself: 'Indeed, this being is the Brahmā, the Great Brahmā, the Conqueror, the One who cannot be conquered by others, surely All-seeing, All-powerful, the Ruler, the Creator, the Excellent, the Almighty, the One who has already practiced Calm, the Father of all that are and are to be. And he has created us. He is permanent, immutable, eternal, not subject to change, and shall remain as things eternal. But we who were created by him have arisen here as being impermanent, mutable, and limited in duration of life.'[4]

---

4. This view is held by many Western mystics and has been strikingly set forth by Wordsworth:

"Our birth is but a sleep and a forgetting;
The Soul that rises with us, our life's
Star, Hath had elsewhere its setting,
And cometh from afar;

Not in entire forgetfulness,
And not in utter nakedness,
But railing clouds of glory do we come,
From God, who is our home"

—Wordsworth, *Intimations of Immortality.*

"This, monks, is the first state of things based on which and taking which as their object some recluses and Brahmins, being Eternalists as to some and Non-eternalists as to others, maintain that the *attā* and the world are partly eternal and partly not."

Ekacca Sassata Vāda (Second View)

45. "In the second view also, depending on what and directing toward what object do these recluses and Brahmins profess the Eternity-belief with regard to some and Non-eternity-belief in regard to others? Why do they take it that the *attā* and the world are partly eternal and partly not?

"There are, monks, Devas by the name of Khiḍḍāpadosikā (debauched by pleasure).[5] For a very long period they pass their time in pursuit of merry-making and pleasure and having lost their self-possession, through such loss they fall from that state.

46. "Monks, there is indeed a reason that a certain being after falling from that state, should be reborn in this world of men and having done so might go forth from the household life into that of a recluse. And having thus become a recluse, by means of zeal, earnestness, of constant application, of vigilance, of careful pondering, reaches up to such tranquillity of mind that having such a concentration of mind, he remembers his last dwelling place in the Deva plane and not more than that.

"He says to himself: 'Those Devas are not Khiḍḍāpadosikā (Devas debauched by pleasure). They live for ages without being debauched by pleasure and having not corrupted their self-possession and not being such as we, they do not fall from that state. They are permanent, immutable, eternal, not subject to change, and shall remain as things eternal. But we who are Khiḍḍāpadosikā having lost our self-control by being debauched by pleasure, are impermanent, mutable, and limited in duration of life. Being subject to the law of passing away we are reborn in this world of men.'"

Ekacca Sassata Vāda (Third View)

47. "In the third view also, depending on what and directing toward what object do these recluses and Brahmins profess the Eternity-belief with regard to some things, and Non-eternity-belief in regard to others? Why do they take it that the *attā* and the world are partly eternal and partly not?

5. *Keci kabalīkārāhārūpa-jivino devā.*
Some of the Devas who live on material food.

"There are, monks, Devas by the name of Manopadosikā[6] (debauched in mind). For a very long time these Devas, having compared themselves enviously with others, their bodies become feeble and their minds tired. And they fall from that state.[7]

48. "Monks, there is indeed a reason that a certain being after falling from that state should be reborn in this world of men and having done so might go forth from the household life into that of a recluse. And having thus become a recluse, by means of zeal, of earnestness, of constant application, of vigilance, of careful pondering reaches up to such tranquillity of mind that, having such a concentration of mind, he remembers his last dwelling place in the Deva plane and not more than that.

"And he says to himself: 'These Devas are not Manopadosikā Devas (Devas debauched in mind). They do not compare themselves with others for a long time. As they are not tired in body as well as in mind, they do not fall from that state They are permanent, immutable, eternal, not subject to change, and shall remain as things eternal. But we who are Manopadosikā fell from that state as we compared ourselves enviously with others for a long time, our bodies became feeble and our minds tired. We are impermanent, mutable, and limited in duration of life. Being subject to the law of passing away we are reborn in this world of men.'

"Monks, depending on what and directing toward what object do these recluses and Brahmins profess the Eternity-belief with regard to some and in regard to others Non-eternity-belief. They take it that the *attā* and the world are partly eternal and partly not."

Ekacca Sassata Vāda (Fourth View)

49. "In the case of the fourth view also, depending on what and directing toward what object do these recluses and Brahmins profess the Eternity-belief with regard to some and Non-eternity-belief in regard to others? Why do they take it that the *attā* and the world are partly eternal and partly not?

"In this world, monks, some recluse or Brahmin is addicted to logic and investigating things. He, from his logical reasoning and his own investigation says:

---

6. *Eke cātumahārājika* - Some Devas from Cātumahārājika Deva abode.
7. cf. The fall of Satan and his cohorts in Semitic legend, through envy and ambition. This is possibly how that legend arose.

'This which is called eye and ear and nose and tongue and body is the *attā* which is impermanent, mutable, and subject to change. But this which is called a state of consciousness, or mind, or consciousness is the *attā* which is permanent, immutable, eternal, not subject to change, and shall remain as things eternal.'

"Monks, this is the fourth case. Depending on this and directing toward this object, some recluses and Brahmins profess the Eternity-belief with regard to some and Non-eternity-belief with regard to others. They maintain that the *attā* and the world are partly eternal and partly not.

50. "Monks, these are the recluses and Brahmins who profess the Eternity-belief with regard to some and Non-eternity-belief with regard to others, and with these four kinds of reasons they maintain that they are Eternalists with regard to some and with regard to others Non-eternalists. They maintain that the *attā* and the world are partly eternal and partly not.

"Monks, in these four ways they all maintain that they are Eternalists with regard to some and with regard to others Non-eternalists and apart from these four there is no other way.

51. "The Tathāgata knows that such are the wrong views, such are the causes thereof, and such is the manner in which they are held and persisted in, such will be the future existences of those who hold these wrong views, and such will be the consequences after death of holding them.

"The Tathāgata knows all these. He also knows other things which are much higher. But he does not regard such knowledge with *taṇhā* (craving), *māna* (conceit), and *diṭṭhi* (wrong views); so, He realizes that He has attained Nibbāna.

"The Tathāgata has achieved Freedom through detachment as He has realized, as they really are, the Origin, Cessation, Pleasantness and Unsatisfactoriness of *vedanā* (sensations), and emancipation therefrom."

ANTĀNANTA VĀDA (Belief that there is an end as well as no end of the world)

53. "Monks, there are some recluses and Brahmins who take it that there is an end and at the same time no end of the world. They set forth the finiteness and infinity of the world in four ways. Depending on what and directing toward what object do these recluses and Brahmins take it that there is an end as well, as no end of the world? How do they present their case with regard to these four ways?"

Antānanta Vāda (First View)

54. "In this world, monks, some recluse or Brahmin, by means of zeal, earnestness, constant application, vigilance, careful pondering reaches up to such tranquillity of mind that, having possessed such concentration of mind he thinks that there is finitude of the world. And he says to himself: 'This world has an end; there is a boundary to it. Because, I, by means of zeal, earnestness, constant application, vigilance, careful pondering, reach up to such tranquillity of mind that, having possessed such concentration of mind, I know that this world has an end and that there is a boundary to it.'"

Antānanta Vāda (Second View)

55. "In the second case also, depending on what and objectifying what do the recluses and Brahmins maintain the belief that there is an end and at the same time no end of the world? How do they present their case?

"In this world, monks, some recluse or Brahmin, by means of zeal, earnestness, constant application, vigilance, careful pondering, reaches up to such tranquillity of mind that, having possessed such concentration of mind he thinks that the world is without a limit and for that reason believes that the world is infinite and without a limit.

"Monks, this is the second case. Depending on this and objectifying this some recluses and Brahmins maintain the belief that the world is infinite and without a limit and that there is an end and at the same time no end of the world."

Antānanta Vāda (Third View)

56. "In the third case also, depending on what and objectifying what do the recluses and Brahmins maintain the belief that there is an end and at the same time no end of the world? How do they present their case?

"In this world, monks, some recluse or Brahmin, by means of zeal, earnestness, constant application, vigilance, careful pondering, reaches up to such tranquillity of mind that, having possessed such concentration of mind he imagines that the world is limited in the upward and downward directions, but infinite across.

"Monks, this is the third case. Depending on this and objectifying this some recluses and Brahmins maintain the belief that there is an end and at the same time no end of the world and that the world is both finite and infinite."

Antānanta Vāda (Fourth View)

57. "In the fourth case, depending on what and objectifying what do some recluses and Brahmins maintain the belief that there is an end and at the same time no end of the world? How do they present their case?

"In this world, monks, some recluse or Brahmin is addicted to logic and investigating things. He, from his logical reasoning and his own investigation, says: 'This world is neither finite nor infinite. Those recluses and Brahmins who maintain the first, or the second, or the third view are wrong. Neither is the world finite nor is it infinite.'

"Monks, this is the fourth case. Depending on this and objectifying this some recluses and Brahmins maintain the belief that there is an end and at the same time no end of the world.

58. "Monks, these are the recluses and Brahmins who maintain the belief that there is an end and at the same time no end of the world, and that the world is both finite and infinite, by means of these four ways.

"Monks, in these four ways they all maintain this, and they do so in these four ways or in one or other of the same; apart from these four ways, there is no other outside way.

59. "The Tathāgata knows that such are the wrong views, such are the causes thereof and such is the manner in which they are held and persisted in, such will be the future existences of those who hold these wrong views and such will be the consequence after death of holding them.

"The Tathāgata knows all these. He knows also other things which are much higher. But He does not regard such knowledge with *taṇhā* (craving), *māna* (conceit), and *diṭṭhi* (wrong views); so, He realizes that He has attained Nibbāna.

"The Tathāgata has achieved Freedom through detachment as He has realized, as they really are, the Origin, Cessation, Pleasantness and Unsatisfactoriness of *vedanā* (sensations), and emancipation therefrom.

60. "Monks, there are other Teachings, profound, difficult to realize, hard to understand, tranquillizing, exalted, not to be deduced by mere logic, subtle, comprehensible only by the wise. These Teachings—the Tathāgata having himself realized them and seen them face to face, has set forth, and it is of them—that they, who would rightly praise the Tathāgata in accordance with the truth, should speak."

AMARĀVIKKHEPA VĀDA (Eel-wriggling)

61. "There are, monks, some recluses and Brahmins who wriggle like eels. When a question is put to them on this and that, they wriggle like eels and ambiguously, equivocally, and evasively reply in the following four ways:

Amarāvikkhepa Vāda (First View)

62. "Monks, some recluse or Brahmin does not understand wholesome volitional action in its real sense, nor unwholesome volitional action. He thinks:

> 'I do not understand wholesome volitional action in its real sense, nor unwholesome volitional action. That being so, were I to affirm this to be wholesome volitional action or that to be unwholesome volitional action, my answer may be wrong. This mistake of mine may cause vexation to my mind, and that vexation may be a danger to me.'

"Thus, fearing and abhorring the speaking of falsehood, he will not answer whether this is wholesome volitional action or that is unwholesome volitional action.

"But on a question being put to him on this or that, he wriggles like an eel and will give the following equivocal and ambiguous reply: 'I don't take it this way. I don't take it the other way; I also don't take that in this way or that, and I don't take it that it is neither this way nor that.'

"Monks, this is the first case depending on this and objectifying this some recluses and Brahmins wriggle like eels and answer equivocally and evasively."

Amarāvikkiiepa Vāda (Second View)

63. "In the second view also, depending on what and objectifying what do the recluses and Brahmins wriggle like eels? When a question is put to them, why do they ambiguously answer and wriggle like eels?

"There is, in this world, some recluse or Brahmin who does not understand wholesome volitional action in its real sense, nor unwholesome volitional action. He thinks:

> 'I do not understand wholesome volitional action in its real sense, nor unwholesome volitional action. That being so, were I to affirm this to be wholesome volitional action or that to be unwholesome volitional action, my answer might cause the rising in me of *chanda* (intention), *rāga* (greed),

> *dosa* (hatred), *paṭigha* (grudge). Such *chanda*, *rāga*, *dosa*, and *paṭigha* might cause the rising in me of *upadāna* (grasping), and this grasping may cause vexation to my mind, and this vexation might be a danger to me.'

"Thus, fearing and abhorring the speaking of falsehood, he will not answer whether this is wholesome volitional action or that is unwholesome volitional action. But on a question being put to him on this or that, he wriggles like an eel and will give the following equivocal and ambiguous reply: 'I don't take it this way. I don't take it the other way; I also don't take it in this way or that, and I don't take it that it is neither this way nor that.'

"Monks, this is the second case. Depending on this and objectifying this some recluses and Brahmins wriggle like eels and answer equivocally and evasively."

Amarāvikkhepa Vāda (Third View)

64. "In the third view also, depending on what and objectifying what do the recluses and Brahmins wriggle like eels? When a question is put to them, why do they ambiguously answer and wriggle like eels?

"There is, in this world, some recluse or Brahmin who does not understand wholesome volitional action in its real sense nor unwholesome volitional action. He thinks:

> 'There are recluses and Brahmins who are learned, subtle, experienced in the views maintained by others, who are active arguers, and who are as skillful as hair-splitters. They go about smashing to pieces by their ability the speculations of others. l do not understand wholesome volitional action in its real sense, nor unwholesome volitional action. That being so, were I to answer this to be wholesome volitional action or that to be unwholesome volitional action, those recluses and Brahmins might ask for my view, ask for my reasons and point out my errors. And on their doing so, I might not be able to give them in full. That might again cause vexation to my mind, and that vexation might be a danger to me.'

"Thus, fearing and abhorring the speaking of falsehood, he will not answer whether this is wholesome, volitional action or that is unwholesome volitional action. But on a question being put to him on this or that, he wriggles like an eel and will give the following equivocal and ambiguous reply: 'I don't take it this way. I don't take it the other way; I also don't take it in this way or that, and I don't take it that it is neither this way nor that.'

"Monks, this is the third case. Depending on this and objectifying this some recluses and Brahmins wriggle like eels and answer equivocally and evasively."

Amarāvikkhepa Vāda (Fourth View)

65. "In the fourth view, depending on what and objectifying what do the recluses and Brahmins wriggle like an eel?

"In this world, monks, there is some recluse or Brahmin who is dull and full of delusion. Owing to his dullness and delusion, when any question is put to him on this or that, he wriggles like an eel and answers ambiguously and evasively:

> 'If I am asked whether there is another world, well, if I thought there were, I would say so. But I don't take it so. And I also don't take the other way. I don't take it to be otherwise nor the contrary. And I don't take it that there neither is nor is not, another world.'

"Thus, does he answer ambiguously and evasively and wriggle like an eel and in like manner, about each of such propositions as the following:

'There is not another world; there both is and is not another world; there neither is, nor is not, another world; there are "Spontaneously manifesting" beings - beings that are born without the instrumentality of parents; there are no such beings; there both are and are not, such beings; there neither are, nor are not, such beings; there is fruit, resultant effect of wholesome and unwholesome volitional actions; there is not; there both is and is not; there neither is, nor is not; a Tathāgata (being) continues to exist after death; he does not; he both does and does not; he neither does, nor does not.'

"Monks, this is the fourth case. Depending on this and objectifying this some recluses and Brahmins maintain beliefs in which they wriggle like eels. When a question is put to them on this or that, they wriggle like eels and answer ambiguously and evasively.

"Monks, when any question is put on this or that to those recluses and Brahmins who maintain the beliefs in which they wriggle like eels, they answer ambiguously and evasively in these four ways, just as the wriggling of eels.

66. "Monks, these are those recluses and Brahmins who wriggle like eels, and when a question is put to them on this or that, they wriggle like eels and reply ambiguously and evasively in these four ways or one or other of the same; apart from these four ways, there is no other outside way.

"The Tathāgata knows that such are the wrong views, such are the causes thereof, and such is the manner in which they are held and persisted in, such will be the future existences of those who hold these wrong views, and such will be the consequences after death of holding them.

"The Tathāgata knows all these. He knows also other things which are much higher. But He does not regard such knowledge with *taṇhā* (craving), *māna* (conceit), and *diṭṭhi* (wrong views); so, He realizes that He has attained Nibbāna.

"The Tathāgata has achieved Freedom through detachment as He has realized, as they really are, the Origin, Cessation, Pleasantness and Unsatisfactoriness of *vedanā* (sensations), and emancipation therefrom.

"Monks, there are other Teachings profound, difficult to realize, hard to understand, tranquillizing, exalted, not to be deduced by mere logic, subtle, and comprehensible only by the wise. These Teachings—the Tathāgata, having Himself realized them and seen them face to face, has set forth, and it is of them—that they, who would rightly praise the Tathāgata in accordance with the truth, should speak."

ADIDCCA SAMUPPANNA VĀDA
(Beliefs that things arise without a cause)

67. "There are, monks, some recluses and Brahmins who believe that things arise without a cause, and they in two ways maintain that the *attā* and the world arise without a cause.

"Depending on what and objectifying what do those recluses and Brahmins maintain the belief that things arise without a cause? And how do they maintain in these two ways that either the *attā* or the world arises without a cause?'

Adhicca Samuppanna Vāda (First View)

68. "There are, monks, certain Brahmās called "Unconscious Beings". When Perception arises in them, they pass from that state. Monks, there is this reason:

> A certain being passes from that plane and is reborn in this world of men, and in this world, he goes forth from the household life into that of a recluse. And having thus become a recluse he, by means of zeal, earnestness, constant application, vigilance, careful pondering reaches up to such tranquillity of mind that he is able to remember that he had received Perception, and not more than that. And he says: 'The *attā* or

the world arises without a cause. And why so? Because I had never been formerly. Even so I exist now.'

"Monks, this is the first case. Depending on this and objectifying this some recluses and Brahmins maintain the belief that things arise without a cause. They maintain that the *attā* or the world arises without a cause."

Adhicca Samuppanna Vāda (Second View)

69. "In this second view also, depending on what and objectifying what do these recluses and Brahmins maintain the belief that things arise without a cause? How do they show that either the *attā* or the world arises without a cause?

"Monks, in this world there is some recluse or Brahmin who is addicted to logic and investigating things. As the result of his reasoning and investigation, he says:

'The *attā* or the world arises without a cause.'

"Monks, this is the second case. Depending on this and objectifying this some recluses and Brahmins hold that things arise without a cause. They hold that the *attā* or the world arises without a cause.

70. "Monks, those recluses and Brahmins who hold that things arise without a cause, hold this belief in these two ways, or one or the other of the same; apart from these two ways there is no other outside way.

"The Tathāgata knows that such are the wrong views, such are the causes thereof, and such is the manner in which they are held and persisted in, such will be the future existences of those who hold these wrong views, and such will be the consequences after death of holding them.

"The Tathāgata knows all these. He knows also other things which are much higher. But He does not regard such knowledge with *taṇhā* (craving), *māna* (conceit), and *diṭṭhi* (wrong views); so, He realizes that He has attained Nibbāna.

"The Tathāgata has achieved Freedom through detachment as He has realized, as they really are, the Origin, Cessation, Pleasantness and Unsatisfactoriness of *vedanā* (sensations), and emancipation therefrom.

"Monks, there are other Teachings, profound, difficult to realize, hard to understand, tranquillizing, exalted, not to be deduced by mere logic, and comprehensible only by the wise. These Teachings—the Tathāgata having Himself realized them and seen them face to face, has set forth, and it is of them—that they, who would rightly praise the Tathāgata in accordance with the truth, should speak.

71. "Monks, those recluses and Brahmins who speculate on the past 'world cycles', whose speculations are concerned with the past, advance their arguments on various wrong views on eighteen grounds.

"Monks, they all present their case in these eighteen ways, or one or the other of the same. Apart from these, there is no other outside way.

72–73. "The Tathāgata knows that such are the wrong views, such are the causes thereof, and such is the manner in which they are held and persisted in, such will be the future existences of those who hold these wrong views, and such will be the consequences after death of holding them.

"The Tathāgata knows all these. He knows also other things which are much higher. But He does not regard such knowledge with *taṇhā* (craving), *māna* (conceit), and *diṭṭhi* (wrong views); so, He realizes that He has attained Nibbāna.

"The Tathāgata has achieved Freedom through detachment as He has realized, as they really are, the Origin, Cessation, Pleasantness and Unsatisfactoriness of *vedanā* (sensations), and emancipation therefrom.

"Monks, there are other Teachings, profound, difficult to realize, hard to understand, tranquillizing, exalted, not to be deduced by mere logic, and comprehensible only by the wise. These Teachings—the Tathāgata having Himself realized them and seen them face to face, has set forth, and it is of them—that they, who would rightly praise the Tathāgata in accordance with the truth, should speak."

APARANTAKAPPIKA (Speculators on the Future)

74. "Monks, there are some recluses and Brahmins who speculate on the future 'world cycles', whose speculations are concerned with the future; they advance their arguments regarding the wrong views in forty-four ways. Depending on what and objectifying what do they speculate as such, hold as such, and speak as such?"

SAÑÑI-VĀDA (Belief that there is Perception after death)

75. "Monks, there are some recluses and Brahmins who hold that there exists the *attā* and the saññā (Perception) after death. They maintain their views on this in sixteen ways. Depending on what and objectifying what do these recluses and Brahmins hold that there exists the *attā* and Perception after death? How do they present their case in these sixteen ways?

76. "They say of *attā*: 'The *attā*, after death is not subject to decay and is percipient,

(1) has form;
(2) is formless;
(3) has and has not, form;
(4) neither has nor is without form;
(5) is finite;
(6) is infinite;
(7) is both;
(8) is neither;
(9) has one mode of perception;
(10) has various modes of perception;
(11) has limited perception;
(12) has unlimited perception;
(13) is absolutely agreeable;
(14) is absolutely disagreeable;
(15) is both;
(16) is neither.'

77. "Monks, these recluses and Brahmins who say that there exists the *attā* and Perception after death present their case in these sixteen ways that there exists Perception and the *attā* after death.

"Monks, those recluses and Brahmins, who hold that there exists the *attā* and the Perception after death, hold this belief in these sixteen ways, or in one or the other of the same; apart from these sixteen ways, there is no other outside way.

"The Tathāgata knows that such are the wrong views, such are the causes thereof, and such is the manner in which they are held and persisted in, such will be the future existences of those who hold these wrong views, and such will be the consequences after death of holding them.

"The Tathāgata knows all these. He also knows other things which are much higher. But He does not regard such knowledge with *taṇhā* (craving), *māna* (conceit), and *diṭṭhi* (wrong views); so, He realizes that He has attained Nibbāna.

"The Tathāgata has achieved Freedom through detachment as He has realized, as they really are, the Origin, Cessation, Pleasantness and Unsatisfactoriness of *vedanā* (sensations), and emancipation therefrom.

"Monks, there are other Teachings, profound, difficult to realize, hard to understand, tranquillizing, exalted, not to be deduced by mere logic, and comprehensible only by the wise. These Teachings—the Tathāgata having Himself realized them and seen them face to face, has set forth, and it is of them—that they, who would rightly praise the Tathāgata in accordance with the truth, should speak."

Here ends the Second Portion for Recitation.

ASAÑÑI VĀDA (Belief that there exists no Perception after death)

78. "Monks, there are some recluses and Brahmins who hold that there exists the *attā* but not Perception after death. They present their case in eight ways.

"Depending on what and objectifying what do these recluses and Brahmins say that after death there exists the *attā* but not Perception? How do they present their case in these eight ways?

79. "They say of the *attā*: 'The *attā* after death is not subject to decay, is impercipient, has form; is formless; has and has not, form; neither has nor is without form; is finite; is infinite; is both; is neither.'

80. "Monks, these recluses and Brahmins who say that there exists the *attā* but not Perception after death, present their case in these eight ways.

"Monks, those recluses and Brahmins who hold that there exists the *attā* but not Perception after death, hold this belief in these eight ways, or one or the other of the same; apart from these eight ways, there is no other outside way.

"The Tathāgata knows that such are the wrong views, such are the causes thereof, and such is the manner in which they are held and persisted in, such will be the future existences of those who hold these wrong views, and such will be the consequences after death of holding them.

"The Tathāgata knows all these. He also knows other things which are much higher. But He does not regard such knowledge with *taṇhā* (craving), *māna* (conceit), and *diṭṭhi* (wrong views); so, He realizes that He has attained Nibbāna.

"The Tathāgata has achieved Freedom through detachment as He has realized, as they really are, the Origin, Cessation, Pleasantness and Unsatisfactoriness of *vedanā* (sensations), and emancipation therefrom.

"Monks, there are other Teachings, profound, difficult to realize, hard to understand, tranquillizing, exalted, not to be deduced by mere logic, and comprehensible only by the wise. These Teachings—the Tathāgata having Himself realized them and seen them face to face, has set forth, and it is of them—that they, who would rightly praise the Tathāgata in accordance with the truth, should speak."

NEVASAÑÑI NASAÑÑI VĀDA (Belief that there exists neither Perception nor Non-perception after death)

81. "Monks, there are some recluses and Brahmins who hold that there exists the *attā* after death, but neither Perception nor Non-perception. They present their case in eight ways.

"Depending on what and objectifying what do these recluses and Brahmins say that after death there exists the *attā*, but neither Perception nor Non-perception? How do they present their case in these eight ways?

82. "They say of the *attā*: 'The *attā* after death, is not subject to decay and is neither percipient nor impercipient, has form; is formless; has and has not, form; neither has nor is without form; is finite; is infinite; is both; is neither.'

83. "Monks, there are some recluses and Brahmins who hold that there exists the *attā* after death, but neither Perception nor Non-perception and who present their case in these eight ways.

"Monks, those recluses and Brahmins who hold that there exists the *attā* after death, but neither Perception nor Non-perception, hold this belief in these eight ways, or one or the other of the same; apart from these eight ways, there is no other outside way.

"The Tathāgata knows that such are the wrong views, such are the causes thereof and such is the manner in which they are held and persisted in, such will be the future existences of those who hold these wrong views and such will be the consequences after death of holding them.

"The Tathāgata knows all these. He also knows other things which are much higher. But He does not regard such knowledge with *taṇhā* (craving), *māna* (conceit), and *diṭṭhi* (wrong views); so, He realizes that He has attained Nibbāna.

"The Tathāgata has achieved Freedom through detachment as He has realized, as they really are, the Origin, Cessation, Pleasantness and Unsatisfactoriness of *vedanā* (sensations), and emancipation therefrom.

"Monks, there are other Teachings, profound, difficult to realize, hard to understand, tranquillizing, exalted, not to be deduced by mere logic, and comprehensible only by the wise. These Teachings—the Tathāgata having Himself realized them and seen them face to face, has set forth, and it is of them—that they, who would rightly praise the Tathāgata in accordance with the truth, should speak."

UCCHEDA VĀDA (Annihilation-Belief)

84. "Monks, there are some recluses and Brahmins who are Annihilationists, who in seven ways maintain the breaking up, the destruction, and the annihilation of a living being.

"Depending on what and objectifying what do these recluses and Brahmins present their case in these seven ways?

85. "Monks, in this world there is some recluse or Brahmin who sets forth the following view and holds the same view:

'Friend, since this *attā* has form, is made of the Four Great Essentials, is caused by the instrumentality of the father and the mother, it breaks off and is destroyed on the dissolution of the body and does not continue after death. Friend, in these ways the *attā* is completely annihilated.'

"Thus, some maintain the breaking up, the destruction, and the annihilation of a living being.

86. "To him another says: 'Friend, there is such a soul as you say. That I do not deny. But the whole soul, friend, is not then completely annihilated. For there is another *attā* that exists in the form that arises in the Deva country of the sensuous plane and which feeds on solid food. That you neither know of nor perceive. But I know and perceive. And since that *attā*, on the dissolution of the body, breaks off and is destroyed, does not continue after death, then is it, friend that the *attā* is completely annihilated.'

"Thus, some maintain the breaking up, the destruction, and the annihilation of a living being.

87. "To him another says: 'There is, friend, such a soul as you say. That I do not deny. But the whole soul, friend, is not then completely annihilated. For there is another *attā* that exists in the form that arises in the Rūpa-Brahmā plane, made of mind, with all its major and minor parts complete, not deficient in any organ. This you neither know of nor perceive. But I know and perceive.

'And since this *attā,* on the dissolution of the body, breaks off and is destroyed, does not continue after death, then is it, friend, that the *attā* is completely annihilated.'

88. "To him another says: 'Friend, there is such a soul as you say. I admit it. But the whole soul, friend, is not then completely annihilated. For there is another *attā* that arises in the Ākāsānañcāyatana Brahmā plane—the Sphere of Unbounded Space-through the total overcoming of the corporeality-perceptions, through the vanishing of the reflex-perceptions, and the non-attention to the multiformity-perceptions, at the idea, "Unbounded is space". This you neither know of nor perceive. But I do. And since this *attā,* on the dissolution of the body, breaks off and is destroyed, does not continue after death; then is it, friend, that the *attā* is completely annihilated.'

89. "To him another says: 'Friend, there is such a soul as you say. That I do not deny. But the whole soul, friend, is not then completely annihilated. For there is another *attā* that arises in the Viññāṇañcāyatana Brahmā plane (the Sphere of Unbounded Consciousness), through the total overcoming of the sphere of unbounded space and at the idea: "Unbounded is consciousness". This you neither know of nor perceive. But I do. And since this *attā,* on the dissolution of this body, breaks off and is destroyed, does not continue after death, then is it, friend, that the *attā* is completely annihilated.'

90. "To him another says: 'Friend, there is such a soul as you say. I admit that. But the whole soul, friend, is not then completely annihilated. For there is another *attā* that arises in the Ākiñcaññāyatana Brahma plane (the Sphere of Nothingness), through the total overcoming of the sphere of unbounded consciousness and at the idea: "Nothing is there". This you neither know of nor perceive. But I do. And since this *attā,* on the dissolution of the body, breaks off and is destroyed, does not continue after death, then is it, friend, that the *attā* is completely annihilated.'

91. "To him another says: 'Friend, there is such a soul as you say. I admit that. But the whole soul, friend is not then completely annihilated. For there is another *attā* that arises in the Nevasañña-nāsaññāyatana Brahmā plane (the Sphere of Neither-Perception-Nor-Non-Perception), through the total overcoming of the

sphere of nothingness. This you neither know of nor perceive. But I do. And since this *attā,* on the dissolution of the body, breaks off and is destroyed, does not continue after death, then is it, friend, that the *attā* is completely annihilated.'

92. "These, monks, are the recluses and Brahmins who are Annihilationists and in seven ways maintain the breaking off, the destruction, and the annihilation of a living being. Whosoever does so, they, all of them, do so in one or the other of these seven ways: apart from these there is no other outside way.

"The Tathāgata knows that such are the wrong views, such are the causes thereof and such is the manner in which they are held and persisted in, such will be the future existences of those who hold these wrong views and such will be the consequences after death of holding them.

"The Tathāgata knows all these. He also knows other things which are much higher. But He does not regard such knowledge with *taṇhā* (craving), *māna* (conceit), and *diṭṭhi* (wrong views); so, He realizes that He has attained Nibbāna.

"The Tathāgata has achieved Freedom through detachment as He has realized, as they really are, the Origin, Cessation, Pleasantness and Unsatisfactoriness of *vedanā* (sensations), and emancipation therefrom.

"Monks, there are other Teachings, profound, difficult to understand, tranquillizing, exalted, not to be deduced by mere logic, subtle, and comprehensible only by the wise. These Teachings—the Tathāgata having Himself realized them and seen them face to face, has set forth, and it is of them—that they, who would rightly praise the Tathāgata in accordance with the truth, should speak."

DIṬṬHADHAMMA NIBBĀNA VĀDA (The belief that there is the biggest bliss in this very life)

93. "Monks, there are some recluses and Brahmins who hold that there is earthly Nibbāna in this life. They, in five ways, maintain that there is the highest bliss in this very life. Depending on what and objectifying what do they present their case in these five ways?

94. "Monks, in this world there is some recluse or Brahmin who sets forth the following views and holds the same:

'Friend, this *attā* possessing the five sensuous pleasures fully enjoys them. In this way, friend, the *attā* has attained the highest bliss in this life—the earthly Nibbāna.' Thus, some recluses and Brahmins maintain that there is earthly Nibbāna in this life.

95. "To him another says: 'Friend, there is such an *attā* as you say. That I do not deny. But the *attā* does not by that alone attain the highest earthly Nibbāna. And why not? Because, friend, the sensuous pleasures are impermanent, full of miseries, and subject to change. And out of the instability and change of these sensuous pleasures arise sorrow, lamentation, pain, grief, and despair. Detached from the sensual objects, detached from unwholesome states of mind, the *attā* passes into and abides in the first Jhāna, which is accompanied by Thought Conception and Discursive Thinking, is born of Detachment, and is filled with Rapture and Joy. Friend, in this way only the *attā* has attained the earthly Nibbāna.'

"Thus, some recluses and Brahmins maintain that there is earthly Nibbāna in this life.

96. "To him another says: 'There is, friend, such an *attā* as you say. That I do not deny. But the *attā* by that alone does not attain the highest earthly Nibbāna. And why not? Because in as much as that state involves Thought conception and Discursive Thinking it is proclaimed as being coarse. But whensoever, friend, the *attā* suppressing both Thought Conception and Discursive Thinking enters into and abides in the Second Jhāna, which is born of Concentration and filled with Rapture and Joy, then, friend, has the *attā* attained, in this visible world, to the highest earthly Nibbāna.'

"Thus do some recluses and Brahmins maintain the highest earthly Nibbāna, in this visible world, of a living being.

97. "To him another says: 'There is, friend, such an *attā* as you say. That I do not deny. But the *attā* by that alone does not attain the highest earthly Nibbāna. And why not? Because in as much as that state involves Rapture, gladdening of heart, it is proclaimed as being coarse. But whensoever, friend, the *attā* having no longing for Joy dwells in equanimity, attentive, clearly conscious he experiences in his person that feeling of which the Noble Ones say, "Happy lives the man of equanimity and attentive mind."' Thus, he enters into and abides in the Third Jhāna.

"Thus do some recluses and Brahmins maintain the highest earthly Nibbāna, in this visible world, of a living being.

98. "To him another says: 'There is, friend, such an *attā* as you say. That I do not deny. But the *attā* by that alone does not attain the highest earthly Nibbāna. And why not? Because in as much as that state involves a constant dwelling of mind on the happiness it has enjoyed, it is proclaimed as being coarse. But whensoever, friend, by giving up pleasure and pain, and through

the disappearance of previous joy and grief, he enters into a state beyond pleasure, he enters into and abides in the Fourth Jhāna, which is purified by equanimity and attentiveness.'

"Thus do some recluses and Brahmins maintain the highest earthly Nibbāna, in this visible world, of a living being.

99. "Monks, these are recluses and Brahmins who hold the belief that there is earthly Nibbāna in this present life, who in these five ways maintain the highest earthly Nibbāna, in this visible world, of a living being. And those who do so, all of them, do so in one or the other of these five ways; apart from these five ways, there is no other outside way.

"The Tathāgata knows that such are the wrong views, such are the causes thereof and such is the manner in which they are held and persisted in, such will be the future existences of those who hold these wrong views and such will be the consequences after death of holding them.

"The Tathāgata knows all these. He also knows other things which are much higher. But He does not regard such knowledge with *taṇhā* (craving), *māna* (conceit), and *diṭṭhi* (wrong views); so, He realizes that He has attained Nibbāna.

"The Tathāgata has achieved Freedom through detachment as He has realized, as they really are, the Origin, Cessation, Pleasantness and Unsatisfactoriness of *vedanā* (sensations), and emancipation therefrom.

"Monks, there are other Teachings, profound, difficult to realize, hard to understand, tranquillizing, exalted, not to be deduced by mere logic, subtle, and comprehensible only by the wise. These Teachings—the Tathāgata having Himself realized them and seen them face to face, has set forth, and it is of them—that they, who would rightly praise the Tathāgata in accordance with the truth, should speak.

"These then, monks, are the recluses and Brahmins who speculate on the future 'world cycles', whose speculations are concerned with the future, and who on forty-four grounds advance their arguments regarding the future 'world cycles'. And of those who do so, all of them, do so in one or the other of these forty-four ways; apart from these forty-four ways, there is no other outside way.

"The Tathāgata knows that such are the wrong views, such are the causes thereof and such is the manner in which they are held and persisted in, such will be the future existences of those who hold these wrong views and such will be the consequences after death of holding them.

"The Tathāgata knows all these. He also knows other things which are much higher. But He does not regard such knowledge with *taṇhā* (craving), *māna* (conceit), and *diṭṭhi* (wrong views); so, He realizes that He has attained Nibbāna.

"The Tathāgata has achieved Freedom through detachment as He has realized, as they really are, the Origin, Cessation, Pleasantness and Unsatisfactoriness of *vedanā* (sensations), and emancipation therefrom.

"Monks, there are other Teachings, profound, difficult to realize, hard to understand, tranquillizing, exalted, not to be deduced by mere logic, subtle, and comprehensible only by the wise. These Teachings—the Tathāgata having Himself realized them and seen them face to face, has set forth, and it is of them—that they, who would rightly praise the Tathāgata in accordance with the truth, should speak.

"And these then, monks, are the recluses and Brahmins who speculate on the past and future 'world cycles', or who do both, whose speculations are concerned with both and who in sixty-two ways advance their arguments with regard to the past, and to the future and those who do so, all of them, do so in one or other of these sixty-two ways. There is none beside.

"The Tathāgata knows that such are the wrong views, such are the causes thereof and such is the manner in which they are held and persisted in, such will be the future existences of those who hold these wrong views and such will be the consequences after death of holding them.

"The Tathāgata knows all these. He also knows other things which are much higher. But He does not regard such knowledge with *taṇhā* (craving), *māna* (conceit), and *diṭṭhi* (wrong views); so, He realizes that He has attained Nibbāna.

"The Tathāgata has achieved Freedom through detachment as He has realized, as The Tathāgata has achieved Freedom through detachment as He has realized, as they really are, the Origin, Cessation, Pleasantness and Unsatisfactoriness of *vedanā* (sensations), and emancipation therefrom.

"Monks, there are other Teachings, profound, difficult to realize, hard to understand, tranquillizing, exalted, not to be deduced by mere logic, subtle, and comprehensible only by the wise. These Teachings—the Tathāgata having Himself realized them and seen them face to face, has set forth, and it is of them—that they, who would rightly praise the Tathāgata in accordance with the truth, should speak."

PARITASSITAVIPPHANDITA (The Wrong Views which are conditioned or influenced by *Taṇhā* (Craving) and *Diṭṭhi* (Bias))

"Of these, monks, those recluses and Brahmins who are Eternalists maintain in four ways that the *attā* and the world are eternal. These recluses and Brahmins neither know nor perceive the truth and are subject to Craving and Bias (*taṇhā* and *diṭṭhi*). So, their opinion which is based on their personal experiences is conditioned or influenced by Craving and Bias.

"Of these, monks, these recluses and Brahmins who are Semi-eternalists maintain in four ways that the *attā* and the world are partly eternal and partly not.

"These recluses and Brahmins neither know nor perceive the truth and are subject to Craving and Bias (*taṇhā* and *diṭṭhi*).

"So ....Bias.

"Of these, monks, those recluses and Brahmins who believe that there is an end and at the same time no end of the world maintain the finitude and infinitude of the world.

"These recluses and Brahmins ....Bias.

"Of these, monks, those recluses and Brahmins who wriggle like eels equivocally give evasive replies in four ways when a question is put to them on this or that.

"These recluses and Brahmins...Bias.

"Of these, monks, those recluses and Brahmins who believe that things arise without a cause maintain in two ways that the *attā* and the world arose without a cause.

"These recluses and Brahmins...Bias.

"Of these, monks, those recluses and Brahmins in these eighteen ways speculate on the past 'world cycles'.

"These recluses and Brahmins...Bias.

"Of these, monks, those recluses and Brahmins who believe that there is Perception after death maintain in sixteen ways that the *attā* after death is percipient.

"These recluses and Brahmins...Bias.

"Of these, monks, those recluses and Brahmins who believe that there exists no Perception after death maintain in eight ways that there exists the *attā* but not Perception after death.

"These recluses and Brahmins...Bias.

"Of these, monks, those recluses and Brahmins who believe that the *attā* after death is neither percipient nor impercipient, maintain such in eight ways.

"These recluses and Brahmins..Bias.

"Of these, monks, those recluses and Brahmins who are Annihilationists maintain in seven ways the breaking up, the destruction, and the annihilation of a living being.

"These recluses and Brahmins..Bias.

"Of these, monks, those recluses and Brahmins who believe in the existence of the earthly Nibbāna maintain in five ways that there is the highest earthly Nibbāna, in this visible world, of a living being.

"These recluses and Brahmins..Bias.

"Of these, monks, those recluses and Brahmins who speculate on the future 'world cycles' and whose speculations are concerned with the future 'world cycles' advance their arguments with regard to the future 'world cycles' in forty-four ways.

"These recluses and Brahmins..Bias.

"Of these, monks, those recluses and Brahmins who speculate on the past as well as the future 'world cycles' and whose speculations are concerned with the past as well as the future 'world cycles' in sixty-two ways advance their arguments with regard to the past and the future 'world cycles'.

"These recluses and Brahmins neither know nor perceive the truth and are subject to Craving and Bias (*taṇhā* and *diṭṭhi*). So, their opinion which is based on their personal experiences is always conditioned or influenced by Craving and Bias.'

PHASSA-PACCAYA (With the aid of Contact)

"Of these, monks, those who are Eternalists maintain in four ways that the *attā* and the world are eternal. Their opinions are based on personal experience which itself is the result of *phassa* (contact).

"There really is no possibility for them to experience anything without *phassa* (contact).

"Of these, monks, those recluses and Brahmins who are Semi-eternalists maintain in four ways that the *attā* and the world are partly eternal and partly not. Their opinions are based on *phassa*.

"There really is no possibility for them to experience anything without *phassa*.

"Of these, monks, those recluses and Brahmins who believe that there is an end as well as no end of the world maintain in four ways the finitude and infinitude of the world. Their opinions also are based on *phassa.*

"There really is no possibility for them to experience anything without *phassa.*

"Of these, monks, those recluses and Brahmins who wriggle like eels and ambiguously give evasive replies in four ways when a question is put to them on this or that, their opinions are also based on *phassa.*

"There really is no possibility for them to experience anything without *phassa.*

"Of these, monks, those recluses and Brahmins who believe that things arise without a cause maintain that the *attā* and the world arose without a cause. Their opinions also are based on *phassa.*

"There really is no possibility for them to experience anything without *phassa.*

"Of these, monks, those recluses and Brahmins speculate on the past "World cycles" in these eighteen ways and their speculations are concerned with the past. Their opinions also are based on *phassa.*

"Of these, monks, those recluses and Brahmins who believe that there is Perception after death maintain in sixteen ways that the *attā* after death is percipient. Their opinions also are based on *phassa.*

"There really is no possibility for them to experience anything without *phassa.*

"Of these, monks, those recluses and Brahmins who believe that there is no Perception after death maintain in eight ways that the *attā* after death is neither percipient nor impercipient, maintain such in eight ways. Their opinions also are based on *phassa.*

"There really is no possibility for them to experience anything without *phassa.*

"Of these, monks, those recluses and Brahmins who are Annihilationists maintain in seven ways the breaking up, the destruction, and the annihilation of a living being. Their opinions also are based on *phassa.*

"There really is no possibility for them to experience anything without *phassa.*

"Of these, monks, those recluses and Brahmins who believe in the existence of the earthly Nibbāna maintain in five ways that there is the highest earthly Nibbāna, in this visible world, of a living being. Their opinions also are based on *phassa.*

"There really is no possibility for them to experience anything without *phassa.*

"Of these, monks, those recluses and Brahmins who speculate on the future 'world cycles' and whose speculations are concerned with the future, advance their arguments with regard to the future in forty-four ways. Their opinions also are based on phassa.

"There really is no possibility for them to experience anything without *phassa.*

"Of these, monks, those recluses and Brahmins who speculate on the past as well as on the future 'world cycles' and whose speculations are concerned with the past as well as the future, advance their arguments in sixty-two ways. Their opinions also are based on *phassa.*

"There really is no possibility for them to experience anything without *phassa.*

"They, all of them, experience *vedanā* (Sensation) by Contact through one of the Six Bases of Contact.[8] To them on account of Sensation arises Craving, on account of Craving arises Clinging, on account of Clinging arises the Process of Becoming, through the Process of Becoming arises Rebirth, and from Rebirth comes Old Age and Death, Sorrow, Lamentation, Pain, Grief, and Despair."[9]

(Now, the Buddha proceeds to show the difference between those who hold the Wrong Views and are therefore subject to the Laws of Paṭiccasamuppāda (Dependent Origination) and a disciple of the Buddha who holds the Right View and can therefore attain Nibbāna.)

"When a Bhikkhu realizes the Origin, Cessation, Pleasantness, and Unsatisfactoriness of the Six Bases of Contact, and emancipation from them, he realizes what is much higher than all these.[10]

---

8. Six Bases of Contact are: *Cakkhāyatana*-Eye Base; *Sotāyatana*-Ear Base; *Ghānāyatana*-Nose Base; *Jivhāyatana*-Tongue Bases; *Kāyāyatana*-Body Base; *Manāyatana*-Mind Base.

9. "*Vedanā mūlakaṃ paṭiccasamuppādaṃ.*" Here, the Buddha discusses the Doctrine of Dependent Origination beginning with *vedanā* to show that those who hold the Wrong Views cannot attain Nibbana.

10. Refers to the Paṭiloma-paṭicca-samuppāda (Dependent Origination in the reverse order which is as follows: "When Contact ceases, Sensation ceases; when Sensation ceases, Craving ceases; when Craving ceases, Clinging ceases; when Clinging ceases, the Process of Becoming ceases; when the Process of Becoming ceases, Old Age, Death, Sorrow, Lamentation, Pain, Grief, and Despair cease. Thus ceases this whole mass of Suffering."

"Monks, indeed, whoever, whether recluse or Brahmin, are speculators on the past or the future 'world cycles' or are speculators on both, advance their views in these sixty-two ways only. So, they all fall within the net of this Discourse and they sink or swim in it only."

(Now, the Buddha proceeds to show that this Discourse comprehends all possible Wrong Views.)

"Just, monks, as when a skillful fisherman or his disciple spreads a fine-meshed net over a tiny pool of water, he might think: 'All sizeable beings in this pool are under this net. They sink or swim under it only.'

"Monks, indeed, whoever, whether recluse or Brahmin, are speculators on the past or the future 'world cycles' or are speculators on both, advance their views in these sixty-two ways. So, they all fall within the net of this Discourse and they sink or swim in it only."

(Now, the Buddha proceeds to show that He Himself is not caught in any net.)

"The Tathāgata's *kāya* (life-continuum) stands without any Craving that can lead to future existence. Devas and men will see Him only so long as that *kāya* stands.

"Just, monks, as when the stalk of a bunch of mangoes has been cut, all the mangoes that were hanging on that stalk go with it; just so, monks, the Tathāgata's *kāya* (life-continuum) is deprived of Craving for rebirth. So long as His *kāya* shall last, so long will Devas and men behold Him. On the dissolution of the *kāya*, beyond the end of His life, neither Devas nor men will behold Him.'[11]

"When He had spoken thus, the Venerable Ānanda addressed the Bhagavā: 'Strange, Lord, is this and wonderful! And what is the name of this exposition of the Dhamma?'

"Ānanda, you may bear in mind this exposition as the Net of *attha* (Advantage), as the Net of Dhamma, as the Supreme Net,[12] as the Net of Views, and as the Incomparable Victory of a battle!"

---

11. The implication is that the Tathāgata would pass into Apannaṭṭhika-bhāva (Nibbāna).

12. "*Yasmā ca ettha seṭṭhaṭhena brahmaṃ sabbaññutañāṇaṃ vibhattaṃ, tasmā brahmajālanti pinaṃ dhārehi.*"

—Aṭṭhakathā

[This Discourse is to be known as Brahmajāla because the Sabbaññutañaṇa (Omniscience) which is "Brahmin" in the sense of being supreme has been expounded (by implication) therein.]

The monks were glad to hear the Discourse delivered by the Bhagavā, and glad at heart, they exalted His word. And on the delivery of this Discourse, the ten thousand world systems shook.

Here ends the Discourse on the Supreme Net.

APPENDIX I

Brahmajala Sutta

Ditthi (Views)

Sammā-diṭṭhi (Right Understanding)	Micchā-diṭṭhi* (Wrong Views)	
	Pubbantakappika-diṭṭhi (18 views)	Aparantakappika-diṭṭhi (44 views)
1. Kammassakata-Sammā-diṭṭhi (6 kinds) 2. Dasavatthuka-Sammā-diṭṭhi (10 kinds) 3. Catusacca-Sammā-diṭṭhi (4 kinds)	Sassata-vāda (4 views) Ekacca-sassatavāda (4 views) Antānantavāda (4 views) Amarāvikkhepavāda (4 views) Adhicca-samuppanna-vāda (2 views)	Saññi-vāda (16 views) Asaññi-vāda (8 views) Nevasaññā-nāsañña-vāda (8 views) Uccheda-vāda (7 views) Diṭṭhadhamma-nibbāna-vāda (5 views)
Total 20 kinds	Total 18 views	Total 44 views

* (i) "*Visesato pubbenivāsa-ñāṇa-lābhino pubbantakappika honti, dibba-cakkhuka aparantakappikā*"

—Aṭṭhakathā, page 101

(Those who have attained *Pubbenivāsa-ñāṇa*, i.e. those who have acquired the worldly *abhiññā* of remembering previous existences especially become speculators on the past, and those who have attained *dibbacakkhu*, i.e. those who acquired the worldly *abhiññā* of *dibbacakkhu* and are able to see like Devas, especially become speculators on the future as their knowledge is limited. The former cannot remember existences beyond forty world cycles; the latter cannot see life after death in the respective planes of existence. Their knowledge is further limited as they have only practiced *samatha* (mental concentration) and they have no *vipassanā-paññā* (direct knowledge gained through Insight), *magga-paññā* (knowledge pertaining to the Holy Paths) nor *phala-paññā* (knowledge pertaining to the Fruitions).

(ii) The 62 Wrong Views include 7 *uccheda-diṭṭhi* (annihilation-belief) and 55 *sassata-diṭṭhi* (eternity belief).

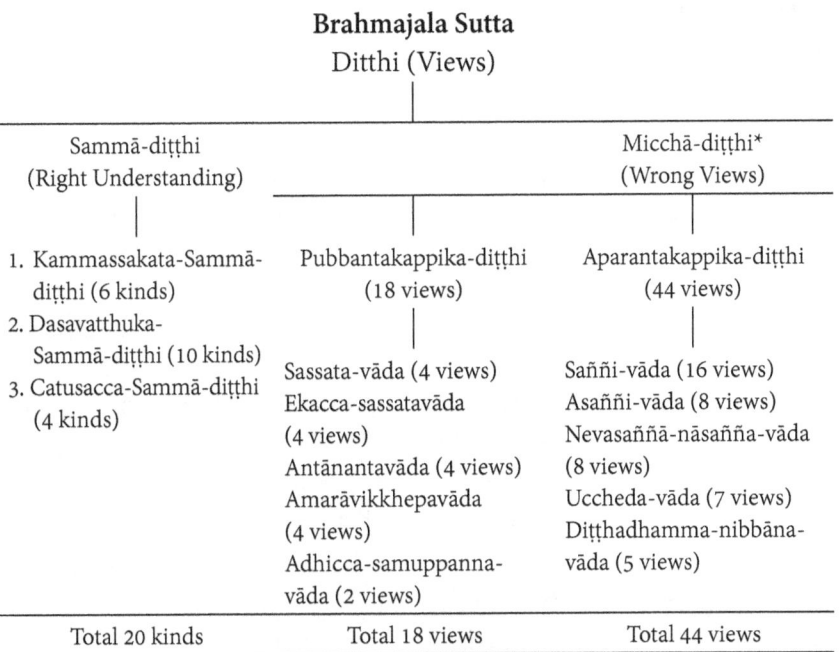

APPENDIX II

Three kinds of *Sammā-diṭṭhi*:

1. *Kammassakatā Sammā-diṭṭhi.*
2. *Dasavatthuka Sammā-diṭṭhi.*
3. *Catu-sacca Sammā-diṭṭhi.*

   1. *Kammassakatā-Sammā-diṭṭhi* - Right understanding or penetration of the truth about the fact that in the case of beings, only the two things, namely, the wholesome and unwholesome actions done by them, are their own properties that always accompany their life-continua, wherever they may wander in many a becoming or *kappa* (world cycle).
   2. *Dasavatthuka Sammā-diṭṭhi* - Right understanding of the ten kinds of objects relating to penetrating Insight.
   3. *Catu-sacca Sammā-diṭṭhi* - Right understanding of the actual existence of the Four Realities or Four Great Truths.

Kammassakatā Sammā-diṭṭhi—Sabbe sattā kammassakā, kammadāyādā, kammayoni, kammabandhū, kammappaṭisaraṇā, yaṃ kammaṃ karissanti kalayānaṃ vā pāpakaṃ vā tassa dāyādā bhavissanti.

1. *Sabbe sattā Kammasakā*—Only the wholesome and unwholesome actions done by all sentient beings are their own properties that always accompany their life-continua, wherever they may wander in many a becoming or *kappa* (world cycle).
2. *Kamma dāyādā*—All beings are the heirs of their own *kamma* (wholesome and unwholesome actions).
3. *Kamma yoni*—All beings are the descendants of their own *kamma.*
4. *Kamma bandhū*—*Kamma* alone is the real relative of all beings.
5. *Kammappaṭisaraṇā*—*Kamma* alone is the real Refuge of all beings. Whatever wholesome or unwholesome actions are done by beings bodily, verbally or mentally, they become the heirs of their *kamma.*

Dassavatthuka Samma-diṭṭhi—Atthi dinnaṃ, atthi yiṭṭhaṃ, atthi hutaṃ, atthi sukata dukkhaṭānaṃ kammānaṃ phalaṃ vipāko, atthi mātā, atthi pitā, atthi sattā opapātikā, atthi ayaṃ loko, atthi paro loko, atthi loke samaṇā-brāhmaṇā samaggatā sammā paṭipannā, ye imañca lokaṃ parañca lokaṃ sayaṃ abhiñña sacchikatvā pavedenti.

1) *Atthi dinnaṃ*—There really exist almsgiving (*dāna*) as cause (*kamma*) and its result as *vipāka*.
2) *Atthi yiṭṭhaṃ*—There really exist offering on a big scale as cause (*kamma*) and its result as *vipāka*.
3) *Atthi hutaṃ*—There really exist offering on a small scale as cause (*kamma*) and its result as *vipāka*.
4) *Atthi sukata-dukkhatānaṃ kammānaṃ phalaṃ vipāko*—There really exist wholesome and unwholesome volitional actions as causes (*kamma*) and their results as *vipāka*.
5) *Atthi mātā*—There really exist the good and the evil deeds done to one's mother as causes (*kamma*) and their results as *vipāka*.
6) *Atthi pitā*—There really exist the good and the evil deeds done to one's father as their causes (*kamma*) and their results as *vipāka*.
7) *Atthi sattā opapātikā*—There really exist spontaneously-manifesting beings, such as infernal beings, devas, and Brahmās, who cannot ordinarily be seen by men.
8) *Atthi ayaṃ loko*—There really exists this world which is under our very eyes.
9) *Atthi paro loko*—There really exist the other worlds or planes where one is destined to arise after "Death". (Here, *paro loko* means the 4 Lower Worlds, 6 Deva planes, and 20 Brahmā planes.)
10) *Atthi loke samaṇā-brāhmaṇā samaggatā sammāpatipannā, ye imañca lokaṃ parañca lokaṃ ayaṃ abhiññā, sacchikatvā pavedenti* There really exist in this world those persons like Supreme Buddhas, monks, and brahmins, who have followed the Dhamma-path and possess tranquillity of mind and having themselves seen, through "Higher Spiritual Powers", this very world and the other worlds, expound their knowledge to others.

Catu-sacca Sammā-diṭṭhi—Dukkhe ñāṇaṃ, dukkha samudaye ñāṇaṃ, dukkha nirodhe ñāṇaṃ, dukkha nirodhagāmini paṭipadāya ñāṇaṃ.

1. *Dukkhe ñāṇaṃ*—Penetrative insight into the truth of Suffering;
2. *Dukkha samudaye ñāṇaṃ*—Penetrative insight into the truth of the Origin of Suffering;
3. *Dukkha nirodhe ñāṇaṃ*—Penetrative insight into the truth of the Extinction of Suffering;
4. *Dukkha nirodhagāmini patipadā nāṇaṃ*—Penetrative insight into the truth of the path leading to the Extinction of Suffering.

APPENDIX III

EXPOSITION OF MICCHĀ-DIṬṬHI (Wrong Views)

Sassata-Vāda (Eternity-Belief)

1. *Sassata-vāda,* First View

   This view is held by *Pubbenivāsānussati-ñāṇalābhi-manda-paññā, i.e.* those who can remember only up to the last one hundred thousand existences.[13]

2. *Sassata-vāda,* Second View

   This view is held by *Pubbenivāsānussati-ñāṇalābhi-majjhima-paññā, i.e.* those who can remember only up to the last 10 world cycles. *

3. *Sassata-vāda,* Third View

   This view is held by *Pubbenivāsānussati-ñānalābhi-tikkha-paññā, i.e.* those who can remember only up to the last 40 world cycles. *

4. *Sassata-vāda,* Fourth View

   This view is held by *Takkī vimansī, i.e.* those who are mere speculators or investigators.

Ekaccasassata-vāda (Eternity-belief with regard to some and Non-eternity belief in regard to others)

5. *Ekacca-sassata-vāda,* First View

   This view is held by one who has fallen from Ābhassara Brahmā plane and is able to remember his last existence only.

6. *Ekacca-sassata-vāda,* Second View

   This view is held by those who were Khiḍḍapadosika Devas (debauched by pleasure) in their last existence and who can remember only that existence.

7. *Ekacca-sassata-vāda,* Third View

   This view is held by those who were Manopadosika Devas (Devas debauched in mind) in their previous existence and who can remember only that existence.

---

13. They hold the respective views as the *attā* and the world appears to be permanent so far as they can remember.

8. *Ekacca-sassata-vāda,* Fourth View
   This view is held by Takkī vimansī, i.*e.* those who are mere speculators and investigators.

Antānanta-vada (Belief that there is an end as well as no end of the world)

9. *Antānanta-vāda,* First View
   The belief that the world has an end and there is a boundary to it.
10. *Antānanta-vāda,* Second View
    The belief that the world is infinite and without a limit.
11. *Antānanta-vāda,* Third View
    The belief that the world is limited in the upward and downward directions, but infinite across.
12. *Antānanta-vāda,* Fourth View
    The belief that this world is neither finite nor infinite. It is held by Takkī vimansī, *i.e.* those who are mere speculators and investigators.

Amarāvikkhepa-vāda (Eel-wriggling)

13. *Amarāvikkhepa-vāda,* First View
    This belief is held by *Musāvāda-parijeguccha* (One who has an intense dislike of speaking falsehood.) On any question being put to him on this or that, he will equivocally and evasively answer as follows: "I don't take it this way. I don't take it the other way; I also don't take that in this way or that, and I don't take it that it is neither this way nor that."
14. *Amarāvikkhepa-vāda,* Second View
    This view is held by *Upādāna-parijegucchā* (One who is disgusted with the four *upādānas* (graspings)). On a question being put to him on this or that, he will wriggle like an eel and give the same equivocal and ambiguous reply: "I don't take it in this way; I don't take it the other way; I also don't take that in this way or that, and I don't take it that it is neither this way nor that."
15. *Amarāvikkhepa-vāda,* Third View
    This view is held by *Anuyoga-parijegucchā* (One who is disgusted with *anuyoga*) *i.e.* "with being challenged by others".
16. *Amarāvikkhepa-vāda,* Fourth View
    This view is held by some recluse or Brahmin who is dull and deluded. Owing to his dullness and delusion, he answers ambiguously and evasively and wriggles like an eel.

Adhicca-Samuppanna-vāda (Belief that the world arises without a cause)

17. *Adhicca-samuppanna-vāda,* First View

    This view is held by a certain being who was, in the previous existence, an Asaññi Brahmā and who says: "The *attā* or the world arises without a cause. And why so? Because I had never been formerly. Even so, I am now."

18. *Adhicca-samuppanna-vāda,* Second View

    This view is held by Takkī vimansī, *i.e.* those who are mere speculators and investigators.

Aparantakappika (Belonging to the Future) Saññi-vāda (Belief that there is Perception after death)

Those who hold this view maintain this in the following sixteen ways:

The *attā* (soul) after death is, not subject to decay and percipient,

19. has form;
20. is formless;
21. has and has not, form;
22. neither has nor is without form;
23. is finite;
24. is infinite;
25. is both;
26. is neither;
27. has one mode of perception;
28. has various modes of perception;
29. has limited perception;
30. has unlimited perception;
31. is absolutely agreeable;[14]
32. is absolutely disagreeable;[15]

---

14. *Ekantasukhi* (The *attā* after death is not subject to decay, and is percipient, is absolutely agreeable). This view is held by those who by *dibba-cakkhu* (supernormal eyes) can see Brahmaloka.

15. *Ekantadukkhi* (The *attā* after death is not subject to decay, an 12d is percipient, is absolutely is agreeable.) This view is held by those who by *dibba-cakkhu* can see the Niraya (hell).

** *Sukhadukkhi* (The *attā* after death is not subject to decay, and is percipient, is both agreeable and disagreeable.) This view is held by those who by *dibba-cakkhu* can

33. is both; **
34. is neither. ***

Asaññi-vāda (Belief that there exists no Perception after death)

Those who hold this view maintain this in the following eight ways:

The *attā* after death, is not subject to decay and is impercipient,

35. has form;
36. is formless;
37. has and has not, form;
38. neither has nor is without form;
39. is finite;
40. is infinite;
41. is both;
42. is neither.

Nevasaññi Nāsaññi Vāda (Belief that there exists neither Perception nor Non-Perception after death)

Those who hold this view maintain this in the following eight ways:

The *attā* after death, is not subject to decay and is neither percipient nor impercipient,

43. has form;
44. is formless;
45. has and has not, form;
46. neither has nor is without form;
47. is finite;
48. is infinite;
49. is both;
50. is neither.

Uccheda-vāda (Annihilation-Belief)

This view is held by Annihilationists and they maintain this in the following seven ways:

---

see the human world.

*** *Adukkhamasukhi* (The *attā* after death is not subject to decay, and is percipient, is neither agreeable nor disagreeable.) This view is held by those who by *dibba-cakkhu* can see the Vehapphala Brahmā plane.

51. That the *attā* is destroyed on the dissolution of the body (in this world).
52. That the *attā* is destroyed on the dissolution of the body in the Deva plane.
53. That the *attā* is destroyed on the dissolution of the body in the Rūpa Brahmā plane.
54. That the *attā* is destroyed on the dissolution of the body in the Ākāsāñancāyatana Brahmā plane (the Sphere of Unbounded Space).
55. That the *attā* is destroyed on the dissolution of the body in the Viññāṇañcāyatana Brahmā plane (the Sphere of Unbounded Consciousness).
56. That the *attā* is destroyed on the dissolution of the body in the Ākiñcaññāyatana Brahmā plane (the Sphere of Nothingness).
57. That the *attā* is destroyed after the dissolution of the body in the Nevasaññā nāsaññāyatana Brahmā plane (the Sphere of Neither-Perception-Nor-Non-Perception).

Diṭṭhadhamma-Nibbāna-Vāda (The belief that there is the highest bliss in this very life)

Those who hold this view maintain this in the following five ways:

58. Full enjoyment of the five sensuous pleasures is the Highest Bliss in this very life.
59. The First Jhāna is the Highest Bliss in this very life.
60. The Second Jhāna is the Highest Bliss in this very life.
61. The Third Jhāna is the Highest Bliss in this very life.
62. The Fourth Jhāna is the Highest Bliss in this very life.

SĀMAÑÑAPHALA SUTTA

Discourse on the Advantages of a Samaṇa's Life

Thus, I have heard. At one time the Bhagavā was staying at Rājagaha in the Mango Grove of Jīvaka, the adopted son of Abhaya, the king's son, with a great company of the brethren, with twelve hundred and fifty of the brethren.

At that time, on the night of the full moon day of the month of Kattika, the end of the four months in which the white water-lily blossoms, King Ajātasattu of Magadha, the son of Queen Videha, was seated on the upper terrace of his palace surrounded by his ministers.

Then the king, on that Fast Day, uttered the following inspired oration:

"How pleasant, friends, is this moon light night!
How beautiful, friends, is this moon light night!
How lovely, friends, is this moon light night!
How soothing, friends, is this moon light night!
How remarkable, friends, is this moonlight night!

"Who is the samaṇa or brahmin we may visit tonight, who, when we call upon him, will be able to purify our minds?"

When he had thus spoken, a certain minister said to the king: "Your Majesty! There is Pūraṇa Kassapa, who is the head of an Order, has followers, is a teacher of a school of thought, is well known, and of repute as a man clever in argument, is declared by the people as a virtuous man, is a man of ripe experience, is one who has long been a samaṇa, knows events that took place in olden days, and well advanced in years. Let your Majesty pay a visit to him. It may well be that, on calling upon him, your Majesty's mind will be purified."

But when he had thus spoken, King Ajātasattu kept silent.

The second minister said to the king: "Your Majesty! There is Makkhali of the cow-pen, ..."

The third minister said to the king: "Your Majesty! There is Ajita of the garment of hair, ..."

The fourth minister said to the king: "Your Majesty! There is Pakudha Kaccāyana, ..."

The fifth minister said to the king: "Your Majesty.' There is Sañjaya Belaṭṭhaputta, ..."

The sixth minister said to the king: "Your Majesty! There is Nigaṇṭha Nāṭaputta, ..."

But when they had thus spoken, King Ajātasattu kept silent.

At that time, Jīvaka the doctor, was seated in silence, not far from King Ajātasattu, and the king said to him: "But you, friend, Jīvaka, why do you keep silent?"

"Your Majesty! One Worthy of Offerings, the Supremely Enlightened Buddha is now dwelling in our Mango Grove, with a great company of the brethren, with twelve hundred and fifty of the brethren. And this is the good news that has been widely spread as to the Supreme Buddha: 'That Enlightened One is accomplished and worthy of offerings, fully enlightened, possessed of clear vision and virtuous conduct, happily attained, the knower of worlds, the incomparable leader of men to be tamed, the teacher of Devas and men, enlightened and sublime.' Let your Majesty pay a visit to him. It may well be that, on calling upon Him, your Majesty's mind will be purified."

"Then, friend, Jīvaka, have the riding elephants made ready."

"Very well, your Majesty!" replied Jīvaka.

Then Jīvaka the doctor had five hundred she-elephants made ready and the state elephant the king used to ride, and addressed the king: "Your Majesty! The elephants have been richly dressed. Your Majesty now knows the best time to proceed."

Then the king had five hundred of his women mounted on she-elephants, one on each, and himself mounted on the state elephant, and he went forth, the attendants bearing torches, in royal pomp from Rājagaha to Jīvaka's Mango Grove.

And the king, on arriving near the Mango Grove, was suddenly stricken with fear and alarm, and the hairs on his body stood erect. In anxiety and excitement, he said to Jīvaka: "Jīvaka, is it sure that you are not playing tricks? Is it sure that you are not deceiving me? Is it sure that you are not betraying me to my enemies? How could it be possible that there should be no sound at all, not a sneeze nor a cough, in so large a company of the brethren, among twelve hundred and fifty of the brethren?"

"Do not fear, o king. I play no trick, neither deceive you; nor would I betray you to the enemy. Go on, your Majesty, go straight on! There, in the pavilion hall, the lamps are burning brightly."

Then the king went on, on his elephant as far as the path was passable for elephants and then on foot to the door of the pavilion, and then said to Jīvaka the doctor: "But Jīvaka, where is the Enlightened One?"

"Your Majesty! The One sitting against the middle pillar and facing the East, with the brethren around Him is the Enlightened One."

Then King Ajātasattu approached the Buddha and stood at one side. As he stood there and looked at the assembly, seated in perfect silence, calm as a clear lake, he exclaimed: "Would that my son, Udaya Bhadda, might have such calm as this assembly of brethren now has."

"So, your thoughts go where love guides them?" asked the Buddha.

"Lord, I love the boy and wish that he, Udaya Bhadda, might enjoy such calm as this assembly has," answered the king.

The king then paid his respects to the Enlightened One and stretching forth his hands as a token of respect to the Order took his seat and said to the Buddha: "I would like to question the Enlightened One on a certain matter, if He will allow me to do so."

The Buddha replied: "O king, ask what you wish."

"Lord, there are a number of ordinary crafts: mahouts, horsemen, charioteers, archers, standard bearers, adjutants, commandos, high military officers of royal birth, shock troops, men brave as elephants, extraordinarily brave men, mail-clad warriors, home-born slaves, cooks, barbers, bath attendants, confectioners, garland-makers, washermen, weavers, bamboo mat makers, potters, arithmeticians, accountants, and many other crafts of like nature. All these enjoy, in this very life, the visible advantages of their craft. They maintain themselves and their parents and children and friends, in happiness and comfort. They offer gifts, the object of which is to be reborn in the higher planes and the planes of Devas, to samaṇas and brahmins,—gifts that lead to rebirth in the higher planes, in the planes of Devas, that bring food and supreme results. Can you, Lord, declare to me any such immediate advantage, visible in this very life, of the life of a samaṇa?

"Do you remember, O king, that you have ever put the same question to other samaṇas or brahmins?" asked the Buddha.

"Yes, I do, Lord," replied the king.

"How did they answer it? If it is not a burden to you, please tell us how they answered it," said the Buddha.

"In the place where the Enlightened One sits, or others like Him, it is not a burden to me, Lord," replied the king.

"If that be the case, kindly speak, o king," said the Buddha.

Pūraṇa Kassapa's View

"Once I went to Pūraṇa Kassapa and after exchanging with him greetings and compliments of friendship and courtesy, I sat at one side and asked the following question:

"'O Pūraṇa Kassapa, there are many kinds of ordinary crafts. What are they? They are mahouts, horsemen, charioteers, ... visible in this very life, of the life of a samaṇa.'

"Then Pūraṇa Kassapa said to me: 'O king, to him who acts or causes another to act, to him who cuts or causes another to cut, to him who torments or causes another to torment, to him who harasses another or causes one to harass another, to him who frightens another or causes one to frighten another, to him who kills a living creature, who takes what is not given, who breaks into houses, who commits dacoity, or robbery, highway robbery, or adultery, or who tells lies, to him there is no evil action. If with a wheel fitted with razor blades he should make all living creatures on the earth one heap, one pile of flesh, there would be no evil action thence resulting, no increase of evil action. Were he to go along the south bank of the Ganges killing and causing to kill men, cutting and causing to cut men into pieces, oppressing and causing to oppress men, there would be no evil action thence resulting, no increase of unwholesome deed would ensue. Were he to go along the north bank of the Ganges giving alms, causing to give alms, offering sacrifices and causing to offer sacrifices, there would be no merit thence resulting, no increase of merit. In liberality, in control of the senses, in abstinence from evil deeds, in speaking the truth there is neither merit nor increase of it.'

"Thus, Lord, did Pūraṇa Kassapa, when asked what was the advantage of a samaṇa's life in this very life, expound his View of the Inefficacy of action. Just, Lord, as if a man, when asked what a mango was, should explain what a bread-fruit is. Just so did Pūraṇa Kassapa, when asked what was the advantage of a samaṇa's life in this very life, expound his View of the Inefficacy of action.

"Then Lord, it occurred to me: How should such a one as I think of blaming any samaṇa or brahmin residing in my kingdom?

"Lord, I neither applauded nor rejected what he said and though not agreeable to me, through neither applauding nor rejecting what he said, I did not say anything about my disagreement, and without accepting or paying attention to that answer of his, I rose from my seat and departed thence."

Makkhali-Gosāla's View

"On one occasion I went to Makkhali-Gosāla (Makkhali of the cow-pen). After exchanging with him greetings and compliments of friendship and courtesy, I sat at one side and put this question to him:

"'O Makkhali-Gosāla, there are many kinds of ordinary crafts. What are they? They are: mahouts, horsemen ... visible in this very life, of a samaṇa's life?'

"Then Makkhali-Gosāla said to me: 'O king, there is no cause or condition for beings to get defiled; without any cause or condition beings get defiled; there is no cause or condition for beings to be ethically pure; without any cause or condition they are ethically pure; there is no action done by oneself: there is no action done by another, there is no action done by a man; there is no Power; there is no Energy; there is no strength of a man; there is no exertion of a man. All sentient beings, everything that breathes, all living beings whatsoever, and all things that have the life principle, are without force and power and energy of their own. They happen to be according to their fate, the necessary conditions of the class to which they belong, and their individual nature, and it is according to their position in one or other of the six special castes that they experience pleasure or pain.

'There are one million four hundred and six thousand six hundred types of beings. There are five hundred kinds of Kamma and again five and again three and there is a whole Kamma and a half Kamma.

'There are sixty-two methods of practice, sixty-two world cycles, six kinds of special castes, the eight stages of a man, forty-nine hundred kinds of modes of living, forty-nine hundred kinds of wandering mendicants, forty-nine hundred abodes of Nāgas, two thousand faculties, three thousand hells, thirty-six places where atoms of dust accumulate, seven kinds of rebirth with perception and seven kinds of rebirth without perception, and seven kinds of rebirths from grafting, seven kinds of Devas, seven kinds of men, seven kinds of sprites, seven kinds of lakes, seven great protuberances, seven hundred small protuberances, seven great chasms, seven hundred small chasms, seven major dreams, and seven hundred minor dreams.

'There are eighty-four hundred thousand eons during which both fools and wise alike, wandering from one existence to another, shall at last, make an end of suffering. There is no such possibility as: By this virtue or this practice, or this austerity, or this righteousness will I make ripe the Kamma that is not ripe yet and I will get rid of the Kamma that has already ripened, as I come across it. The pleasure and pain have been measured as if with a measuring basket. The round of rebirths has its limit. There is no increase or decrease. Just as when a ball of string is thrown forward it will spread out just as far and no farther, than it can unwind, just so both fools and wise alike shall wander from one existence to another and enjoy pleasure and pain.'

"Thus, Lord, did Makkhali-Gosāla, when asked what was the advantage of a samaṇa's life in this very life, expound his View of the Uncausedness of existence. Just, Lord, as if a man, when asked what a mango was, should explain what a bread-fruit is. Just so did Makkhali-Gosāla, when asked what was the advantage of a samaṇa's life in this very life, expound his View of Uncausedness of existence.

"Then, Lord, it occurred to me: How should such a one as I think of blaming any samaṇa or brāhmaṇā residing in my kingdom?

"Lord, I neither applauded nor rejected what he said and though not agreeable to me through neither applauding nor rejecting what he said, I did not say anything about my disagreement and without accepting or paying attention to that answer of his, I rose from my seat and departed thence."

Ajita Kesakambala's View

"On one occasion I went to Ajita Kesakambala (Ajita of the garment of hair). After exchanging with him greetings and compliments of friendship and courtesy, I sat at one side and put the question to him:

"'O Ajita Kesakambala, there are many kinds of ordinary crafts: ...'

"Then Ajita Kesakambala said to me: 'O king! There does not really exist almsgiving. There really does not exist offering on a big scale. There really does not exist offering on a small scale. There really do not exist wholesome and unwholesome volitional actions as cause and their fruits as result. There really does not exist this world. There really do not exist the other worlds or planes. There is neither mother nor father, nor beings born without the instrumentality of parents. There really do not exist in this world samaṇas and brahmins who have followed the Dhamma-path and possess tranquillity of mind and having themselves seen, through "Higher Spiritual Powers", this very world and the other worlds, expound their knowledge to others. This being is nothing but the combination of the Four Great Essentials. On the dissolution of the body after death, the Element of Extension will go to the earth-group; the Element of Cohesion will go to the water-group; the Element of Kinetic Energy will go to the fire group; the Element of Motion will go to the wind-group, and the faculties move up to the sky. Four carriers (with the bier as the fifth) carry the corpse; the remains are seen up to the cemetery; the bones become pigeon-coloured and his offerings end in ashes. Almsgiving has been prescribed by fools. Their words are empty, false and idle. Both the foolish and the wise, on the dissolution of the body after death are annihilated and destroyed and nothing comes again into being.'

"Thus, Lord, did Ajita Kesakambala, when asked what was the advantage of a samaṇa's life in this very life, expound his view of Annihilation. Just, Lord, as if a man, when asked what a mango was, should explain what a bread-fruit is. Just so did Ajita Kesakambala, when asked what was the advantage of a samaṇa's life in this very life, expound his view of Annihilation.

"Then Lord, it occurred to me: How should such a one as I think of blaming any samaṇa or brāhmaṇā residing in my kingdom?

"Lord, I neither applauded nor rejected what he said and though not agreeable to me, neither applauding nor rejecting what he said, I did not say anything about my disagreement and without accepting or paying attention to that answer of his, I rose from my seat and departed thence."

Pakudha Kaccāyana's View

"On one occasion I went to Pakudha Kaccāyana. After exchanging with him greetings and compliments of friendship and courtesy, I sat at one side, and put the question to him:

"'O Pakudha Kaccāyana, there are many kinds of ordinary crafts: ....'

"Then Pakudha Kaccāyana said to me: 'O king, the following seven are neither made nor caused to be made,[16] neither created nor caused to be created, they are unproductive, immoveable as a mountain peak, as a pillar firmly planted. They do not waver, neither do they change, they do not interfere with one another, nor cause pleasure nor pain nor pleasure and pain. What are the seven?

'The four elements—earth, water, fire, and air—and pleasure, and suffering, and the life-principle. These seven are neither made nor caused to be made, neither created nor caused to be created; they are unproductive, immoveable as a mountain peak, as a pillar firmly planted. They do not waver, neither do they change; they do not interfere with one another, nor cause pleasure nor pain, nor pleasure and pain. Among those things there is neither killer nor the causer of killing, hearer or speaker, knower

16. Neither by any proximate cause nor caused by Kamma.

or maker-to-know. Even when one with a sharp weapon, cuts another's head into two, it does not mean that one kills another; only the weapon has penetrated in between these seven.'

"Thus, Lord, did Pakudha Kaccāyana, when asked what was the advantage of a samaṇa's life in this very life, expound the matter by means of some irrelevant things. Just, Lord, as if a man, when asked what a mango was, should explain what a bread-fruit is. Just so did Pakudha Kaccāyana, when asked what was the advantage of a samaṇa's life in this very life, expound the matter by means of some irrelevant things.

"Then Lord, it occurred to me: How should such a one as I think of blaming any samaṇa or brāhmaṇā residing in my kingdom?

"Lord, I neither applauded nor rejected what he said, and though not agreeable to me, neither applauding nor rejecting what he said, I did not say anything about my disagreement, and without accepting or paying attention to that answer of his, I rose from my seat, and departed thence."

Nigaṇṭha Nāṭaputta's View

"On one occasion I went to Nigaṇṭha Nāṭaputta. After exchanging with him greetings and compliments of friendship and courtesy, I sat at one side, and put this question to him:

"'O Aggivessana[17] there are many kinds of ordinary crafts ....'

"Then Nigaṇṭha Nāṭaputta said to me: 'O king, in this world a Nigaṇṭha is disciplined with four kinds of self-discipline. How? In this world, a Nigaṇṭha lives disciplined in respect to water; lives disciplined thus in respect to evil; has thrown all evil by thus controlling evil; and has been infused with the discipline in respect to all evil. O king, a Nigaṇṭha who lives disciplined in respect to these four kinds of self-discipline is said to be one who is self-perfected, self-controlled, steadfast.'[18]

"Thus, Lord, did Nigaṇṭha Nāṭaputta, when asked what was the advantage of a samaṇa's life in this very life, expound his view of the fourfold self-discipline. Just, Lord, as if a man, when asked what a mango was, should explain what a bread-fruit is. Just so did Nigaṇṭha Nāṭaputta, when asked what was the advantage of a samaṇa's life in this very life, expound his view of the fourfold self-discipline.

---

17. Aggivessana, the family name of Nigaṇṭha Nāṭaputta. The Nigaṇṭhas are also known as Jains.
18. The Jain ideal is control of evil: The Buddhist ideal is eradication of evil.

"Then Lord, it occurred to me: How should such a one as I think of blaming any samaṇa or brāhmaṇā residing in my kingdom?

"Lord, I neither applauded nor rejected what he said, and though not agreeable to me, neither applauding nor rejecting what he said, I did not say anything about my disagreement, and without accepting or paying attention to that answer of his, I rose from my seat, and departed thence."

Sañjaya Belaṭṭhaputta's View

"On one occasion I went to Sañjaya Belaṭṭhaputta. After exchanging with him greetings and compliments of friendship and courtesy, I sat at one side, and asked him this question:

"'O Sañjaya there are many kinds of ordinary crafts ....'

"Then Sañjaya Belaṭṭhaputta said to me: 'O king, if I am asked whether there is another world, if I thought there were, I should say so: But I don't take it this way. And also, I don't take it that way. I don't take it to be otherwise nor the contrary. And I don't take it that there neither is nor is not another world.

'If I be asked whether ...

'there is not another world; (peyyāla)[19]

'there both is, and is not, another world;

'there are 'spontaneously-manifesting' beings;

'there are no such beings;

'there both are, and are not, such beings;

'there is fruit, resultant effect of wholesome and unwholesome volitional actions;

'there is not;

'there both is, and is not;

'there neither is, nor is not;

'a being continues to exist after death; he does not;

'he both does and does not;

'he neither does, nor does not.'

"Thus, Lord, did Sañjaya Belaṭṭhaputta, when asked what was the advantage of a samaṇa's life in this very life, expound his evasive view. Just, Lord, as if a man, when asked what a mango was, should explain what a bread-fruit is. Just so did Sañjaya Belaṭṭhaputta, when asked what was the advantage of a samaṇa's life in this very life, expound his evasive view.

---

19. *Peyyāla*: "And so on and so on". The phrase occurs after each proposition below.

"Then, Lord, it occurred to me: Of all samaṇas and brāhmaṇas, this man is the most foolish and confused. When asked what was the advantage of a samaṇa's life in this very life, this man merely gave an evasive answer. Then, Lord, it occurred to me: How should such a one as I think of blaming any samaṇa or brāhmaṇa residing in my kingdom?

"Lord, I neither applauded nor rejected what he said, and though not agreeable to me, neither applauding nor rejecting what he said, I did not say anything about my disagreement, and without accepting or paying attention to that answer of his, I rose from my seat, and departed thence."

Advantage of a Samaṇa's Life Visible Here and Now

"And now, Lord, I put the question to the Bhagavā;

"There are many kinds of ordinary crafts. What are they? They are: mahouts, horsemen, charioteers, archers, standard bearers, adjutants, commandos, high military officers of royal birth, shock troops, men brave as elephants, extraordinarily brave men, mail-clad warriors, home-born slaves, cooks, barbers, bath attendants, confectioners, garland-makers, washermen, weavers, bamboo mat makers, potters, arithmeticians, accountants, and many other crafts of like nature. All these enjoy, in this very life, the visible advantages of their craft. They maintain themselves, and their parents and children and friends, in happiness and comfort. They offer gifts, the object of which is to be reborn in the higher planes and the planes of Devas, to samaṇas and brāhmaṇas,—gifts that lead to rebirth in the higher planes, in the planes of Devas, that bring food and supreme results. Can you, Lord, declare to me any such immediate advantage, visible in this very life, of the life of a Samaṇa?"

"Yes, I can, O king. And in order to do so I should like to put a counter-question to you, and you may answer it as you please. What opinion have you of the following?"

Example of a Slave

"Suppose among the people of your household there be a slave who works for you, gets up in the morning earlier than you, and goes to bed later than you, who is zealous to do your pleasure, anxious to please you in what he does and says, a man who watches your every look. Suppose he should consider: 'Friends! Wonderful is it and extraordinary, this rebirth due to meritorious deeds, and this resultant effect of meritorious deeds. Here is Ajātasattu, King of Magadha, son of Queen Videha. He is a man, as I am; but the king lives in full enjoyment of the five sensuous pleasures just like a Deva. Here am I a slave, working for him, getting up before him and going to bed later than he, zealous to do his pleasure, anxious to please him in what I do and say, watching his every look. If I were to perform meritorious deeds, I should be like him. Why should not I have my hair and beard shaved off, and wear the yellow robes, go out from the household state and renounce the world?' And suppose afterwards, he should go out from the household state and renounce the world, be admitted into an Order, and, live controlled in bodily, verbal and mental actions, content with but the requisite food and shelter, delighting in seclusion. And suppose your men should report to you: 'May it please your Majesty! Do you know that so and so, formerly your slave, who worked for you, got up in the morning earlier than you and went to bed later than you, who was zealous to do your pleasure, anxious to please you in what he did and said, a man who watched your every look, has now worn the yellow robes and has been admitted into an Order, and lives controlled in bodily, verbal and mental actions, content with but the requisite food and shelter, delighting in seclusion.'

"If they report to you so, will you then say: 'Friends let the man come back to me; let the man who worked for me, got up in the morning earlier than I, and went to bed later than I, who was zealous to do my pleasure, anxious to please me in what he did and said, a man who watched my every look, become a slave again?'"

"No, Lord, indeed, we should pay our respects to him, respectfully rise and welcome him and beg him to be seated. Also, we should invite him to accept our offer of the four requisites—robe, food, lodging, and medicine. And we should provide security measures for him according to the law."

"But what will you say, O king: that being so, is there, or is there not, the advantage of a samaṇa's life, visible in this very life?"

"Certainly, Lord, there is the advantage of a samaṇa's life, visible here and now."

'This then, O king, is the advantage of a samaṇa's life visible in this very life which I make known to you at the first instance."

The Second Advantage of a Samaṇa's Life, Visible in this Very Life

"Can you, Lord, declare to me any other such immediate advantage, visible in this very life, of the life of a samaṇa?"

"Yes, I can, O king. And in order to do so I should like to put a counter-question to you, and you may answer it as you please. What opinion have you of the following?"

Example of a Farmer

"Suppose there is in your kingdom a free man who cultivates his own land, a householder, who pays taxes to swell the king's coffers. Suppose he should think: 'Friends. Wonderful is it and extraordinary, this rebirth due to meritorious deeds, and this resultant effect of meritorious deeds. Here is Ajātasattu, King of Magadha, son of Queen Videha. He is a man, as I am; but the king lives in full enjoyment of the five sensuous pleasures just like a Deva. Here am l a free man who cultivates his own land, a householder, who pays taxes to swell the king's coffers. If I were to perform meritorious deeds, I should be like him. Why should not I have my hair and beard shaved off and wear the yellow robes, go out from the household state, and renounce the world?' And suppose afterwards, he should go out from the household state and renounce the world, be admitted into an Order, and live controlled in bodily, verbal and mental actions, content with but the requisite food and shelter, delighting in seclusion. And suppose your men should report to you: 'May it please your Majesty! Do you know that so and so, formerly a free man in your kingdom, who cultivated his own land, a householder, who paid taxes to swell the king's coffers, has now worn the yellow robes and has been admitted into an Order, and lives controlled in bodily, verbal and mental actions, content with but the requisite food and shelter, delighting in seclusion.'

"If they report to you so, will you then say: 'Friends, let the man come back to me; let the man who resided in my kingdom, who cultivated his own land, who paid taxes to swell the king's coffers, become my subject again?'"

"No, Lord, indeed, we should pay our respects to him, respectfully rise and welcome him and beg him to be seated. Also, we should invite him to accept our offer of the four requisites—rob, food, lodging, and medicine. And we should provide security measures for him according to the law."

"But what will you say, O king: that being so, is there, or is there not, the advantage of a samaṇa's life, visible in this very life?"

"Certainly, Lord, there is the advantage of a samaṇa's life, visible here and now."

"This then, O king, is the advantage of a samaṇa's life, visible in this very life, which I make known to you as a second."

Higher and Better Advantages of a Samaṇa's Life

"Can you, Lord, show me any other advantage of a samaṇa's life, visible in this very life an advantage higher and better than these?"

"Yes, I can, O king. Listen and pay attention and I will speak.

"O king! There arises in the world a Tathāgata who is a Perfect One, supremely enlightened, possessed of clear wisdom and action, happily attained, knower of worlds, the incomparable leader of men to be tamed, the Teacher of gods and men, the Enlightened One, the Exalted One. He, by His Omniscience, knows face to face this universe, including the worlds of Devas, the Brahmās and the Māras, and the world of men with its samaṇas and brāhmaṇas, its kings and men; and knowing it, proclaims the Dhamma to men—the Dhamma which is good at the beginning, good in the middle and good at the end, and which has the fullness of meaning in spirit and letter. He shows the pure life of a samaṇa, in all its fullness, and all its purity.

"A householder or one of his children, or a man of inferior caste listens to that Dhamma; and on hearing it he has confidence in the Tathāgata; and when he is possessed of that faith, he thinks to himself: 'Full of bondage is the household life, a path for the dirt of passion. Cool as the welcome shade of a cloud is a samaṇa's life. How difficult is it for a man who is a layman to live a chaste and pure life in all its fullness, in all its purity, in all its perfection. It would be better for me to cut my hair and beard, wear the yellow robes, and go out of the household life into the homeless state.'

"Then, before long, giving up his wealth, be it great or small, leaving his relatives, be they many or be they few, he cuts off his hair and beard, he wears the yellow robes, and goes out of the household life into the homeless state.

"When he has thus become a samaṇa he lives restrained by the samaṇa's Disciplinary Code. He is possessed of good conduct, and has a suitable subject for constant meditation, and perceiving danger even in the least offences, he disciplines himself in the rules. He has to his credit good deeds in act and word, and his livelihood is absolutely pure. He is perfect in conduct, and has guarded the doors of his senses. He attains Mindfulness and Clearness of Comprehension, and is altogether contented."

CŪḶA SĪLA (The Minor Morality)

"How, O king, is his conduct good?

"In this, O king, that the Bhikkhu having abstained from taking the life of any living being, refrains from the destruction of life. He has laid the stick and the weapon aside; he has moral shame and dread; shows kindness toward all beings, and is full of solicitude for the welfare of all sentient beings. This is that Bhikkhu's morality.

"Having abstained from taking what is not given, the Bhikkhu refrains from taking what is not given to him. He takes only what is given to him; appreciates the giving by others; and lives in honesty and purity of heart.

"Having abstained from unchastity, the Bhikkhu practices chastity. He refrains from the vulgar practice and also from the sexual act which is the practice of the country folk.

"Getting rid of lying words, the Bhikkhu refrains from falsehood. He speaks truth, and nothing but the truth; faithful and trustworthy, he does not break his word to the world.

"Getting rid of slander, the Bhikkhu refrains from calumny. What he hears here, he does not repeat elsewhere to raise a quarrel against the people here; what he hears elsewhere, he does not repeat here to raise a quarrel against the people there. Thus, he binds together those who are divided, encourages those who are friends, makes peace, loves peace, is impassioned for peace, a speaker of words leading to peace.

"Getting rid of rudeness of speech, the Bhikkhu refrains from using harsh language. He speaks only those words that are blameless, pleasant to the ear, lovely, reaching to the heart, polite, pleasing to the people, and beloved of the people.

"Getting rid of frivolous talk, the Bhikkhu refrains from vain conversation. At appropriate times he speaks, in accordance with the facts, words full of meaning, on the Doctrine, on the Vinaya. And at the right time, he speaks words worthy to be noted in one's mind, fitly illustrated, and divided according to relevancy of facts.

"The Bhikkhu refrains from causing injury to seeds and plants.

"He takes only one meal a day, not eating at night, and refrains from taking food after midday.

"He refrains from dancing, singing, playing music and witnessing shows with dances singing and music.

"He refrains from wearing, adorning or ornamenting himself with garlands, scents, and ointments.

"He refrains from the use of lofty and spacious resting places.

"He refrains from accepting. gold and silver.

"He refrains from accepting uncooked grain.

"He refrains from accepting raw meat. 'He refrains from accepting women or young girls.

"He refrains from accepting slave-servants of either sex.

"He refrains from accepting sheep or goats.

"He refrains from accepting fowls and pigs.

"He refrains from accepting elephants, cattle, horses, and mares.

"He refrains from accepting agricultural, or waste lands.

"He refrains from acting as an ambassador or messenger.

"He refrains from buying and selling.

'"He refrains from cheating with scales or coins or measures.

"He refrains from the cunning ways of bribery, cheating and fraud.

"He refrains from causing physical injury to anyone, murder, putting in bonds, highway robbery, dacoity and plunder. These are that Bhikkhu's morality."

Here ends the Cūḷa Sīla (the Minor Morality)

MAJJHIMA SĪLA (The Medium Morality)

"Whereas some samaṇas and brāhmaṇas while living on food provided by the philanthropic and generous, cause injury to seedlings and growing plants whether propagated from roots or stems or joints or buddings or seeds, the Bhikkhu refrains from causing such injury to seedlings and growing plants.

"Whereas some samaṇas and brāhmaṇas while living on food provided by the philanthropic and generous, use hoarded things, foods, drinks, clothing, conveyances, bedding, scents, and any eatables, the Bhikkhu refrains from storing such things up.

"Whereas some samaṇas and brāhmaṇas while living on food provided by the philanthropic and generous, visit shows; which are these shows? They are:

niccaṃ (dances);

gītaṃ (singing of songs);

vāditaṃ (playing instrumental music);

pekkaṃ (theatrical shows);

akkhānaṃ (telling stories with a mingling of doggerel and rhymes);

pānissaraṃ (music attended by clapping);

vetālaṃ (playing music by means of cymbals);
kumbhathūnaṃ (playing drums);
sobhanakaṃ (art exhibitions);
caṇḍāla-vaṃsa-dhovanaṃ (acrobatic feats on the top of a hoisted bamboo pole);
Combats of elephants, horses, buffaloes, bulls, goats, sheep, cocks, and quails; Exercising self-defence with quarterstaff, boxing, wrestling;
Sham-fight roll-calls, manoeuvres, troop-inspection.

The Bhikkhu refrains from visiting the above-mentioned shows.

"Whereas some samaṇas and brāhmaṇas while living on food provided by the philanthropic and generous, indulge in the following games and recreations:

aṭṭhapādaṃ (games on chess boards or boards with eight rows of squares);
dasapādaṃ (games on chess boards or boards with ten rows of squares);
akāsam parihāra-pathaṃ (Such games played by imagining such hoards in the air);
santikaṃ (games somewhat akin to hopscotch; or drawing diagrams on the ground, in which one steps only where one is allowed to);
khalikaṃ (throwing dice);
ghaṭikaṃ (hitting a short stick with a long one; games akin to tip-cat);
salākahatthaṃ (a play where the hand is dipped in dye and used as a brush); akkhaṃ (games with balls of all sizes);
paṅgacīraṃ (blowing through toy pipes made of leaves or papers);
vaṅkakaṃ (ploughing with miniature ploughs);
mokkhacikaṃ (turning somersaults);
ciṅgulikaṃ (playing with paper windmills);
pattāḷakaṃ (playing with toy measures);
rathakaṃ (playing with toy chariots);
dhanukaṃ (playing with toy bow);
akkharikaṃ (a game where one has to find out the missing letter or letters);
manesikaṃ (guessing others' thoughts);
yathāvajjaṃ (games involving mimicry of deformities).

The Bhikkhu refrains from such games and recreations. These are that monk's morality.

"Whereas some samaṇas and brāhmaṇas while living on food provided by the philanthropic and generous, use high and luxurious resting places such as:

an extra-long chair or spacious couch;
thrones with animal figures carved on the supports;
carpets or coverlets with very long fleece;
patchwork counterpanes of many colours;
white blankets;
woollen coverlets richly embroidered;
quilts stuffed with cotton wool;
coverlets embroidered with figures of lions, tigers, etc.;
rugs with fur on both sides or with fur on one side;
coverlets embroidered with gold threads, or silk coverlets;
carpets woven with furs;
elephant, horse, or chariot rugs;
rugs of antelope skins sewn together;
carpets with awnings overhead;
sofas with red pillows for the head and feet.

The Bhikkhu refrains from using such high and luxurious resting places. Such is that Bhikkhu's morality.

"Whereas some samaṇas and brāhmaṇas while living on food provided by the philanthropic and generous, use means for adorning and beautifying themselves, such as:

rubbing scented powder on one's body, massaging with oil and bathing with scents;

massaging or patting the limbs so as to develop muscles.

The use of mirrors, eye-ointments, garlands, rouge, cosmetics, face powders, make-up, bracelets, top-knot, walking sticks, tubes or pipes for holding anything, swords, umbrellas, embroidered slippers, turbans, diadems, whisks of the yak's tail and long-fringed white robes.

The Bhikkhu refrains from such means of adorning and beautifying the person.

"Whereas some samaṇas and brāhmaṇas while living on food provided by the philanthropic and generous, are addicted to such low talks as these:

talks about kings, robbers, and ministers of state;
armies, dangers and war;
eating and drinking, clothes and dwellings, garlands, perfumes;

relations, chariots, villages, markets, towns and districts;
women and heroes;
street talks, talks by the well;
talks about those departed in days gone by;
tittle-tattle;
talks about land and sea; and gain and loss.

The Bhikkhu refrains from such low talk.

"Whereas some samaṇas and brāhmaṇas while living on food provided by the philanthropic and generous, enter in wrangling conversations, such as:

'You don't understand this Dhamma and Vinaya, I do.'
'How should you know about this Dhamma and Vinaya?'
'You are practicing wrong views. It is I who practice the right one.'
'I am talking about relevant facts, whereas you are not.'
'You speak last what ought to be spoken first, and first what ought to be spoken last.'
'All that you have practiced is upset.'
'I have pointed out the fault in your views;
'I have reproved you.'
'Set to work to rebut my statements.'
'Do so yourself if you can'.

The Bhikkhu refrains from such wrangling conversations.

"Whereas some samaṇas and brāhmaṇas while living on food provided by the philanthropic and generous, work as mediators and messengers, such as:

acting as mediators and messengers of kings, ministers of state, royal families, brahmins, or youths, saying:
'Go there, come here, take this with you, bring that from that place.'

The Bhikkhu refrains from such servile duties.

"Whereas some samaṇas and brāhmaṇas while living on food provided by the philanthropic and generous, are tricksters, chanters of holy words for gain, interpreters of signs and omens, exorcists, and endeavour to obtain a lot of money from others after spending a little of their own. The Bhikkhu refrains from such trickeries and deceptions. Such is that Bhikkhu's morality."

Here ends the Majjhima Sīla (The Medium Morality).

MAHĀ SĪLA (The Major Morality)

"Whereas some samaṇas and brāhmaṇas while living on food provided by the philanthropic and generous, earn their living by wrong means of livelihood, by low arts, such as:

prophesying long life, prosperity, etc., or the reverse, from marks on limbs, hands and feet of a person;
divining by means of omens and signs;
auguries drawn from thunderbolts;
prophesying by interpreting dreams;
palmistry or Chiromancy;
auguries from the marks gnawed by mice;
fire-oblation;
offering oblations from a ladle;
making offerings to gods of husks, of broken rice, of rice, of ghee and of oil;
offering oblations from the mouth;
sacrifice of human blood to gods;
fortune telling concerning the loss of properties and sickness;
determining whether the site for a proposed house or garden is lucky or not;
public administration;
knowledge of appeasing charms;
laying ghosts;
knowledge of charms to be pronounced by one living in an earth-house;
snake charming;
the poison craft;
the scorpion craft;
the art of curing rat-bites;
the bird craft;
the crow craft;
foretelling the number of years that a man has to live;
charms to ward off arrows;
charms to understand the language of animals.

The Bhikkhu refrains from such low arts.

"Whereas some samaṇas and brāhmaṇas while living on food provided by the philanthropic and generous, earn their living by wrong means of livelihood, by low arts, such as:

knowledge of the signs of good and bad qualities and of the marks denoting the health or luck of their owners in:

> gems, apparel, staves, swords and spears, two-edged swords, arrows, bows, other weapons, women, men, boys, girls, slaves, slave-girls, elephants, horse, buffaloes, bulls, oxen, goats, sheep, fowls, quails, iguanas, bucks and deer.

The Bhikkhu refrains from such low arts.

"Whereas some samaṇas and brāhmaṇas while living on food provided by the philanthropic and generous, earn their living by wrong means of livelihood, by low arts, such as:

> predictions to the effect that the chieftains will march out; the chieftains will march back; our chiefs will attack, and the enemy will retreat; the enemy will attack and ours will retreat; our chief will win the battle and the foreign chiefs will suffer defeat; the foreign chiefs will win the battle and ours will suffer defeat; thus this chief will succeed and that chief not.

The Bhikkhu refrains from such low arts.

"Whereas some samaṇas and brāhmaṇas while living on food provided by the philanthropic and generous, earn their living by wrong means of livelihood, by low arts, such as foretelling that there will be an eclipse of the moon, of the sun, of a constellation; that the sun or the moon will go on its usual course, there will be an aberration of the sun or the moon, or that the constellations will go on their usual course, that there will be aberrations of the constellations; that there will be a fall of meteors, *disā-dāha* ("sky-glow"), an unusual redness of the horizon, that there will be an earthquake, that there will be a wild *Deva-dundubhi* (a supernatural rumble), that there will be rising and setting, clearness and dimness, of the sun or the moon or the constellations. The Bhikkhu refrains from such low arts.

"Whereas some samaṇas and brāhmaṇas while living on food provided by the philanthropic and generous, earn their livelihood by such wrong means, by such low arts as: foretelling an abundant rainfall, a deficient rainfall, a good harvest, a bad harvest or scarcity of food, tranquillity, disturbances, pestilence, a healthy season, counting on the fingers, by means of arithmetic; by means of formulae, prosody, *lokāyataṃ* (popular lore and custom). The Bhikkhu refrains from such low arts.

"Whereas some samaṇas and brāhmaṇas while living on food provided by the philanthropic and generous, earn their living by wrongful means of livelihood, by low arts, such as—effecting marriages in which the bride or bridegroom is brought home, or sent forth, effecting betrothals, or divorces, saving money, expending money, *subhagakaraṇaṃ* (using charms to make people happy), *dubbhagakaraṇaṃ* (using charms to make people unhappy), giving medicine to preserve the foetus in cases of abortive women, incantations to make the tongue stiff, to make the jaws of a person stiff, to make a man throw up his hands, to bring on deafness, making use of a mirror to obtain answers to questions put to it, obtaining oracular answers through a girl possessed, from a god, the worship of the sun, of the Brahmā, bringing forth flames from one's mouth, invoking the goddess of Luck. The Bhikkhu refrains from such low arts.

"Whereas some samaṇas and brāhmaṇas while living on food provided by the philanthropic and generous, earn their living by wrongful means, by low arts, such as—vowing gifts to a god if a certain benefit be obtained, observing such vows, practicing ghost craft, practicing arts and crafts while lodging in an earth house, causing virility, causing femininity preparing sites for buildings and consecrating them, causing a person to vomit, causing a person to take a bath, offering sacrificial fires, administering emetics, purgatives, expectorants and phlegmagogues, causing blood and other impurities to come out of the head and thus relieving it, preparing oil for people's ears, preparing oil to be used as eye-drops, administering drugs through the nose, preparing powerful eye-drops, preparing eye-drops that produce a cooling effect, curing cataracts, practicing surgery, practicing as a children's doctor, administering original drugs and medicines, and preparing new drugs and medicines. The Bhikkhus refrains from such low arts.

"Such is the morality of this Bhikkhu."

Here ends the Mahā Sīla (The Major Morality).

"O king, that Bhikkhu who has established himself in morality sees no danger from any side, so far as his restraint of conduct is concerned. Just, O king, as a sovereign, duly crowned, whose enemies have been defeated, sees no danger from any side, so far as his enemies are concerned, that Bhikkhu who has established himself in morality, sees no danger whatsoever, in regard to his restraint of conduct. And possessed of this group of excellent moralities, he experiences within himself a sense of unalloyed happiness. Thus, O King, that Bhikkhu has established himself in morality."

Guarding the Senses

"How, O king, is the Bhikkhu guarded as to the sense doors? Whenever the Bhikkhu perceives a form with the eye, he is neither led away by the general outward appearance nor its details and he strives to guard his sense of sight to ward off such mean and evil things as covetousness and grief, which would flow in over him, if he were to remain with unguarded sense of sight. He enters upon this course in regard to the faculty of sight; he guards his sense of sight, and he restrains his sense of sight.

"Whenever he hears a sound with the ear, ...

"Whenever he smells an odour with the nose, ...

"Whenever he tastes a flavour with the tongue, ...

"Whenever he feels a contact with the body, ...

"Whenever he cognises a mental object with his mind, he is neither entranced with the general outward appearance nor its details, and he strives to guard his sense of sight to ward off such mean and evil things, a s covetousness and grief which would flow in over him, if he were to remain with unguarded senses. He enters upon this course in regard to the faculty of mind; he guards his sense of mind, and he restrains his sense of mind.

"And possessed of this superior kind of self-restraint, he experiences within himself, a sense of unalloyed happiness. Thus, is it, O king, that the Bhikkhu becomes guarded as to the sense doors."

Mindfulness and Clearness of Comprehension

"How, O king, does the Bhikkhu possess Mindfulness and Clearness of Comprehension?

"O king, in this Sāsana the Bhikkhu practices only clear comprehension in going and coming back. So also, in looking forward, or in looking round; in bending his arm, or in stretching it again; in wearing his robes and carrying his bowl; in eating, drinking, chewing and savoring; in defecating and urinating; in walking, in standing; in sitting, in falling asleep, in waking, in speaking or in keeping quiet.

"Thus, O king, the Bhikkhu becomes replete with mindfulness and clearness of Comprehension.

"How, O king, is the Bhikkhu contented?

"O king, in this Sāsana, the Bhikkhu is contented with robes just sufficient to protect his body, and with food just sufficient to sustain his belly. Wherever he goes, he goes freely, taking his requisites only. Just, O king, as a bird flies anywhere freely, having only its wings as its burden, that Bhikkhu is contented with the requisite robes and food. Thus, is it, O king, that the Bhikkhu becomes contented.

"Then that Bhikkhu, having established himself in this group of moralities, possessed of this noble restraint of the senses, having attained this noble mindfulness and clearness of comprehension, filled with this noble contentedness, chooses some lonely spot in the woods, at the foot of a tree, on a hillside, in a cave, a mountain cleft, a cemetery, or a forest thicket, or the open air, or on a heap of straw. After his meal and on his return from the alms round, he repairs thence, sits down, when his meal is done, cross-legged, keeping his body erect, and concentrates his attention on the subject of meditation.

"That Bhikkhu banishes sensual desire; he dwells with a mind free from sensual desire; from sensual desire, he cleanses his mind.

"He banishes ill will; he dwells with a mind free from ill will; with goodwill and compassion towards all living beings, he cleanses his mind from ill will.

"He banishes torpor and languor; he dwells free from torpor and languor; with clear perception, with watchful mind, with clear comprehension, he cleanses his mind from torpor and languor.

"He banishes restlessness and worry; dwelling with mind undisturbed, with a mind full of peace, he cleanses his mind from restlessness and worry.

"He banishes skeptical doubt; dwelling free from doubt, full of confidence in the good, he cleanses his mind from doubt."

Example of Freedom from Sensual Desire

"Then just, O king, as when a man, after taking a loan should start a business, and his business should succeed, and he should not only be able to repay the loan there should be a surplus over to maintain his wife; then would he consider thus: 'I had formerly to carry on my business by taking a loan from others, but my business prospers and I have not only cleared up my debts but also have a surplus over to maintain my wife.' He would be glad at that, would be joyous at that."

Example of Freedom from Ill Will

"Then just, O king, as if a man were a victim to disease, in pain, and very ill, and had no appetite for food, and had lost his strength; after a time, he were to recover from that disease, his appetite return, and he gains in strength, then would he consider thus: 'Formerly I was a victim to disease, in pain, and very ill. I had no appetite for food and no strength. But now, I recover from that disease, my appetite returned, and I am gaining in strength.' He would be glad at that, and would be joyous at that."

Example of Freedom from Torpor and Languor

"Then just, O king, as if a man were confined in a prison, and after a time he should be released from the prison safe and sound, and without any confiscation of his property. Then would he consider thus: 'Formerly I was confined in prison, but now I have been released, safe and sound, and none of my property has been confiscated.' He would be glad at that, and would be joyous at that."

Example of Freedom from Restlessness and Worry

"Then just, O king, as if a man were a slave, not his own master, subject to another, unable to go where he wished, and after a time he should be freed from that slavery, become his own master, not subject to another, a free man, able to go where he wished. Then would he consider thus: 'Formerly I was a slave, not my own master, subject to another, unable to go where I wished, but now I am freed from that slavery, I have become my own master, not subject to another, a free man, able to go where I wish.' He would be glad at that, and would be joyous at that."

Example of Freedom from Sceptical Doubt

"Then just, O king, as if a man, carrying his riches and goods, were to find himself on a long road, in a desert, where food was scarce, danger a bounding, and after a time he were to find himself out of that long, dangerous road and arrived at a village where there was security and peace. Then would he consider thus: 'Formerly I, carrying riches and goods was on a long road, in the desert, where food was scarce but danger abounding. But now I am out of that dangerous road, safe and sound, in a village where there is security and peace.' He would be glad at that, and would be joyous at that.

"Just so, O king, he, as long as these five Hindrances are not banished from him, looks upon himself as in debt, diseased, in prison, in slavery, or a long and dangerous road. But when these five Hindrances have been banished, he looks upon himself as freed from debt, recovered from disease, released from prison, freed from slavery, and out of the long and dangerous road.

"When he realizes that these five Hindrances have been banished from his mind, gladness springs up within him, and joy arises to him in this glad state, and thus rejoicing, all his body becomes calm, and being thus calm he enjoys happiness, and being thus happy, his mind becomes tranquil."

The First Jhāna

"Then that Bhikkhu will be devoid of sensuous pleasures and evil thoughts and abide in the first Jhāna, which is accompanied by Thought Conception and Discursive Thinking, is born of Detachment, and filled with Rapture and Joy.

"His whole being does he so pervade, drench, permeate, and suffuse with Rapture and Joy born of Detachment, that there is no spot in his whole body not suffused with it.

"Just, O king, as when a skillful bath attendant or his apprentice strews scented powder in a metal dish, and. then sprinkles it with water and kneads it together to form a soft lump, the water gradually soaks the powder and forms an amorphous mass, the water permeates through the whole of the scented powder and pervades it within and without, and there is no possible exudation.

"In the same way, O king, the Bhikkhu causes his body to be soaked with Rapture and Joy born of Detachment; causes the whole body to be pervaded with Rapture and Joy; and filled with them. Rapture and Joy permeate his whole body within and without, and not a single space whatsoever is left unpermeated.

"This, O king, is the advantage of a samaṇa's life, visible in this very life, higher than the advantages previously mentioned."

The Second Jhāna

"Then, the Bhikkhu, after calming down putting away, Thought conception and Discursive Thinking, which is Noble and gives one-pointedness of mind, abides in the second Jhāna, which is free from Thought conception and Discursive Thinking, born of Concentration, and accompanied by Rapture and Joy.

"And his body does he so pervade, drench, permeate, and suffuse with Rapture and Joy born of Concentration, that there is no spot in his whole body not suffused therewith.

"Just, O king, as if there were a deep pool, with water welling up from a spring below. There is no inlet from the east or the south, from the west or north, and it does not rain heavily and regularly. Even then the cool water welling up from that spring would pervade, fill, permeate, and suffuse the pool with cool water, and there would be no place whatsoever in that pool not suffused therewith.

"In the same way, O king, the Bhikkhu soaks his body with Rapture and Joy born of Concentration, and is filled with them. Rapture and Joy permeate through his whole body within and without, and not a single space whatsoever is left unpermeated.

"This, O king, is the advantage of a samaṇa's life, visible in this very life, higher than the advantages previously mentioned."

The Third Jhāna

"Then the Bhikkhu after the fading away of Rapture dwells in equanimity, is mindful and of clear comprehension and experiences in his person that sense of pleasure which the Noble Ones talk of when they say: 'Happy lives the man of equanimity and attentive mind'; thus, the Bhikkhu abides in the third Jhāna.

"And his body does he so pervade, drench, permeate, and suffuse with that sense of pleasure, rapture being absent, that there is no place in his whole body not suffused therewith.

"Just, O king, as when in a pond of blue, red, and white lotus, some blue or red or white lotus flowers, produced in the water, growing in the water, nourished by the depths of the water, are so pervaded, drenched, permeated and suffused from their tips down to their roots with the cool moisture thereof, that there is no spot in the whole plant, whether of the blue lotus, or the red, or the white, not suffused therewith.

"In the same way, O king, the Bhikkhu makes himself to be soaked with rapture free pleasure, filled with it, and suffused with it. There is no part of that Bhikkhu's body not suffused therewith.

"This, O king, is the advantage of a samaṇa's life, visible in this very life, higher than the advantages of a samaṇa's life previously mentioned."

The Fourth Jhāna

"Then, the Bhikkhu, after giving up pleasure and pain, and through the disappearance of the previous happiness and sadness which he had, enters into a state beyond pleasure and pain, into the fourth Jhāna, a state of pure mindfulness brought about by equanimity.

"And he sits there so suffusing his whole body with that sense of purification of mind, of clearness of mind that there is no spot in his body not suffused therewith.

"Just, O king, as if a man were sitting so rapt from head to foot in a clean white robe that there was no spot on his whole body not in clean white robe—just so, O king, does that Bhikkhu sits there, so suffusing his body with that sense of purification of mind, of clearness of mind that there is no spot of his whole body not suffused therewith.

"This, O king, is the advantage of a samaṇa's life, visible in this very life, higher than the advantages of a samaṇa's life previously mentioned."

Insight Knowledge

"Again, O king, with his mind thus tranquil, purified, cleansed, flawless, free from defilements, supple, ready to act, firm and imperturbable, he applies and bends his mind to insight knowledge. The Bhikkhu thus understands: 'This body of mine is made up of Four Great Root Elements,[20] it springs from father and mother, it thrives on account of nutriment, it has the nature of impermanence, must be cleansed and massaged, is fragile and certain of destruction; and so also is this consciousness of mine which is connected with it, which depends on it.'

"Just, O king, as if there were a Veḷuriya gem, brilliant, genuine, with eight facets, excellently cut, of the purest quality, clear, translucent, flawless and satisfying all conditions. If a man, who is not blind; were to thread it on a

---

20. *Mahā-bhūta*, Four Great Root Elements. They are: (1) Element of Extension (2) Element of cohesion or Liquidity; (3) Element of Kinetic Energy; and (4) Element of Motion. Pāḷi is (1) *pathavī*; (2) *āpo*; (3) *tejo*; (4) *vāyo*.

string of brown, orange, red, white, or yellow colour, and having taken the gem in his hand, would reflect thus: 'This gem is brilliant, genuine, with eight facets, excellently cut, of the purest quality, clear, translucent, flawless and satisfying all conditions. It is now fixed to a brown string; an orange string; a red string; a white string; or a yellow string.'

"In the same way, O king, when his mind is thus tranquil, purified, cleansed flawless, free from defilements, supple, ready to act, firm, and imperturbable, he applies and bends his mind to that insight knowledge. Then he understands thus: 'This body of mine is made up of Four Great Root Elements, it springs from father and mother, it thrives on account of nutriment, it has the nature of impermanence, must be cleansed and massaged, is fragile and certain of destruction; and so also is this consciousness of mine which is connected with it, which depends on it.'[21]

"This, O king, is the advantage of a samaṇa's life, visible in this very life, better and higher than the advantages of a samaṇa's life previously mentioned."

Mental Creative Powers

"Again, O king, with his mind thus tranquil, purified, cleansed, flawless, free from defilements, supple, ready to act, firm, and imperturbable, he applies and bends his mind to the creation of mentally produced bodies. The Bhikkhu lets proceed from his body, another mentally produced body, having all limbs and parts, not destitute of any organ.

"Just, O king, as if a man were to pull out a reed from. its sheath. He would reflect: 'This is the reed, this the sheath. The reed is one thing, the sheath another. It is from the sheath that the reed has been drawn forth.' Or, O king, take this example. If a man were to take out a sword from its scabbard. He would reflect: 'This is the sword, this the scabbard. The sword is one thing, the scabbard another. It is from the scabbard that the sword has been drawn out.'

"O king, take another example. If a man were to take out a snake from its slough. He would reflect: 'This is the snake, this the slough. The snake is one thing, the slough another. It is from the slough that the snake has been taken out.'

"O king, when his mind is thus tranquil, purified, cleansed, flawless, free from defilements, supple, ready and to act, bends firm, and imperturbable, he applies and bends his mind to the creation of mentally produced bodies. Then the Bhikkhu lets proceed from his body, another mentally produced body, having all limbs and parts, not destitute of any organ.

---

21. *Viññāṇa*: Consciousness. This passage refutes any idea of the existence of a "soul".

"This, O king, is the advantage of a samaṇa's life, visible in this very life, better and higher than the advantages of a samaṇa's life previously mentioned."

Supernormal Knowledge

"Again, O king, with his mind thus tranquil, purified, cleansed, flawless, free from defilements, supple, ready to act, firm and imperturbable, he applies and bends his mind to the knowledge pertaining to supernormal powers. The Bhikkhu then enjoys the various supernormal powers—being one he becomes many, and having become many he again becomes one; he becomes visible or invisible; without being obstructed he passes through walls and mountains, just as if through the air; he walks on water without sinking, just as if on the earth; in the earth he dives, and rises again, just as if in the water; cross-legged he floats through the air, just as a winged bird; with his hand, he touches sun and moon, these so mighty ones, so powerful ones; even up to the Brahmā plane has he mastery over his body.

"Just, O king, as a clever potter or his apprentice could make, could succeed in getting out of well-prepared clay, any shape of vessel he wanted to have.

"Or as, O king, an ivory carver or his apprentice could make, could succeed in getting out of properly prepared ivory, any design he wanted to have.

"Or as, O king, a goldsmith or his apprentice could make, could succeed in getting out of the properly worked gold, any kind of article he wanted to have.'

"O king, when his mind is thus tranquil, purified, cleansed, flawless, free from defilements, supple, ready to act, firm, and imperturbable, he applies and bends his mind to the knowledge pertaining to supernormal powers. The Bhikkhu then enjoys the various supernormal powers—being one he becomes many, and having become many he again becomes one; he becomes visible or invisible; without being obstructed he passes through walls and mountains, just as if through the air; he walks on water without sinking, just as if on the earth; in the earth, he dives, and rises again, just as if in the water; cross-legged he floats through the air just as a winged bird; with his hand, he touches sun and moon, these so mighty ones, so powerful ones; even up to the Brahmā plane has he mastery over his body.

"This, O king, is the advantage of a samaṇa's life, visible in this very life, better and higher than the advantages of a samaṇa's life previously mentioned."

The Celestial Ear

"Again, O king, with his mind thus tranquil, purified, cleansed, flawless, free from defilements, supple ready to act, firm, and imperturbable, he applies and bends his mind to the knowledge pertaining to the celestial ear. With the celestial ear he hears sounds, heavenly and human, far and near.

"Just, O king, as if a man going on a long journey were to hear the sound of a big drum, a cylindrical drum, a conch, a small drum, and a small kettle drum, he thus understands: 'This is the sound of the big drum, this is the sound of the cylindrical drum, this of the conch, this of the small drum, and this of the small kettle drum.'

"Thus, O king, the Bhikkhu hears sounds, heavenly and human, far and near.

"This, O king, is the advantage of a samaṇa's life, visible in this very life, better and higher than the advantages of a samaṇa's life previously mentioned."

Knowledge of the Minds of Others

"Again, O king, with his mind thus tranquil, purified, cleansed, flawless, free from defilements, supple, ready to act, firm, and imperturbable he applies and bends his mind to the knowledge pertaining to penetration of others' minds. He knows the minds of other beings, of other persons, by penetrating them with his own mind. He knows the lustful mind as lustful and the passionless one as passionless; knows the hostile mind as hostile and the friendly mind as friendly; knows the dull mind as dull and the alert mind as alert; knows the contracted mind as contracted and the scattered mind as scattered; knows the developed mind as developed and the undeveloped mind as undeveloped; knows the inferior mind as inferior and the superior mind as superior; knows the concentrated mind as concentrated and the wavering mind as wavering; and knows the freed mind as freed and the unfree mind as unfree.

"Just, O king, as a young woman, a man or a lad who is wont to beautify himself, on considering carefully the image of his face in a bright and clear mirror or a vessel of clear water would, if it had a mole on it, know that it had, and if not, would know it had not.

"Thus, O king, with his mind tranquil, purified, cleansed, flawless; and imperturbable, he applies and bends his mind to the knowledge pertaining to penetration of others' minds. He knows the lustful mind as lustful and the passionless one as passionless; knows the hostile mind as hostile and the friendly mind as friendly; knows the dull mind as dull and the alert mind as alert; knows the contracted mind as contracted and the scattered mind as scattered; knows the developed mind as developed and the undeveloped mind as undeveloped; knows the inferior mind as inferior and the superior mind as superior; knows the concentrated mind as concentrated and the wavering mind as wavering; and knows the freed mind as freed and the unfree mind as unfree.

"This; O king, is the advantage of a samaṇa's life, visible in this very life, better and higher than the advantages of a samaṇa's life previously mentioned."

Knowledge of Former Existences

"Again, O king, with his mind thus tranquil, purified, cleansed, flawless, free from defilements, supple, ready to act, firm, and imperturbable, he applies and bends his mind to the knowledge pertaining to remembrance of former existences. He remembers various former births, such as one birth, two, three, four, five, ten, twenty, thirty, forty, fifty, one hundred, one thousand, one hundred thousand, births, remembers many formations and dissolutions of world cycles: 'These I was, such a name I had, such a clan I belonged to, such complexion I had, such food I ate, such pleasures I enjoyed and such a life span I had; and vanishing from there I entered in a certain existence. There such a name I had, ... and vanishing from there I again reappeared here.' Thus, he remembers, together with the marks and peculiarities, many a former existence.

"Just, O king, as if a man were to go to another village, and from that one to another, and thence should return home. Then he would know: 'From my own village I came to that other one. There I stood in such and such a way, sat thus, spoke thus, and remained silent thus. Thence I came to another village; there I stood in such and such a way, sat thus, spoke thus, and remained silent thus. And now from that certain village,' I have returned home again.

"Thus, O king, with his mind tranquil, purified, cleansed, flawless, free from defilements, supple, ready to act, firm, and imperturbable, he applies and bends his mind to the knowledge pertaining to remembrance of former existences. He remembers various former births, such as one birth, two, three, four, five, ten, twenty, thirty, forty, fifty, one hundred, one thousand, one hundred thousand, births, remembers many formations and dissolutions of world cycles: 'There I was, such a name I had, such a clan I belonged to, such complexion I had, such food I ate, such pleasures he enjoyed and such a life span I had and vanishing from there I entered in a certain existence. There such a name I had, ... and vanishing from there I again reappeared here.' Thus, he remembers, together with the marks and peculiarities, many a former existence.

"This, O king, is the advantage of a samaṇa's life visible in this very life, better and higher than the advantages of a samaṇa's life previously mentioned."

The Celestial Eye

"Again, O King, with his mind thus tranquil, purified, cleansed, flawless, free from defilements, supple, ready to act, firm, and imperturbable, he applies and bends his mind to the knowledge pertaining to vanishing and reappearing of beings, with his supernormal knowledge, surpassing that of men, he sees beings vanishing and reappearing, low and noble ones, beautiful and ugly ones, happy and unhappy ones, sees how beings are reappearing according to their deeds. These beings, indeed, followed evil ways in bodily actions, words, and thoughts, insulted the Noble Ones, held wrong views, and according to their wrong views, they acted. At the dissolution of their bodies after death, they appeared in the lower worlds, in painful states of existence, in the world of perdition, in hell. Certain other beings have good actions, bodily, verbal, and mental, did not insult the Noble Ones, held Right Views, and according to their Right Views, they acted. At the dissolution of their bodies after death, they appeared in a happy state of existence, in a heaven state.

"Thus, with his supernormal knowledge, surpassing that of men, he sees beings vanishing, and reappearing, low and noble ones, beautiful and ugly ones, happy and unhappy ones, sees how beings are reappearing according to their deeds.

"Just, O king, as if there were a mansion with an upper terrace on it at a crossroads, and a man standing thereon, and with observation, should watch men entering a house, and coming out of it, and walking up and down the street, and sitting at the junction of the four roads. Then that man knows: 'These men are entering a house, and those are leaving it, and those are walking up and down the street, and these are sitting at the junction of the four roads.'

"Thus, O king, with his mind thus tranquil, purified, cleansed, flawless, free from defilements, supple, ready to act, firm, and imperturbable, he applies and bends his mind to the knowledge pertaining to vanishing and reappearing of beings. With his supernormal knowledge, surpassing that of men, he sees beings vanishing and reappearing, low and noble ones, beautiful and ugly ones, happy and unhappy ones, sees how beings are reappearing according to their deeds. These beings, indeed, followed evil ways in bodily actions, words, and thoughts, insulted the Noble Ones, held wrong views, and according to their wrong views, they acted. At the dissolution of their bodies after death, they appeared in the lower worlds, in painful states of existence, in the world of perdition, in hell. Certain other beings, have good actions, bodily, verbal, and mental, did not insult the Noble Ones, held Right Views, and according to their Right Views, they acted. At the dissolution of their bodies after death, they appeared in a happy state of existence, in a heaven state.

"Thus, with his supernormal knowledge, surpassing that of men, he sees beings vanishing and reappearing, low and noble ones, beautiful and ugly ones, happy and unhappy ones, sees how beings are reappearing according to their deeds.

"This, O king, is the advantage of a samaṇa's life, visible in this very life, better and higher than the advantages of a samaṇa's life previously mentioned."

Extinction of the Āsavas

"Again, O king, with his mind thus tranquil, purified, cleansed, flawless, free from defilements, supple, ready to act, firm; and imperturbable, he applies and bends his mind to the knowledge pertaining to extinction of all āsavas. He knows as it really is: 'This is suffering'. He knows as it really is: 'This is the origin of suffering'. He knows as it really is: 'This is the extinction of suffering'. He knows as it really is: 'This is the Path leading to the extinction of suffering'. He knows as they really are: 'These are āsavas'. He knows as it really is: 'This is the origin of āsavas'.[22] He knows as it really is: 'This is the extinction of āsavas'. He knows as it really is: 'This is the Path leading to the extinction of āsavas'. To him, thus realizing, thus seeing, his mind is set free from Sensuous Āsava, is set free from Āsava of existence, is set free from Āsava of ignorance. In him, thus set free, there arises the knowledge of his Freedom, and he realizes: 'Rebirth is no more; I have lived

---

22. *Āsava*: This word has been translated as "poisons", "banes", "biases", "inflows". cankers", "intoxicants", "fluxes" and, fluxions". The latter are perhaps academically correct translations but "canker" (Childers) seems to give the more correct concept to the average Westerner. It is used figuratively in the sense of surrounding or flowing up to much as in Western writings one finds the expression" a wave of sentiment" or" "an upwelling of ...." The Āsavas are: *Kāmāsava*. Sensuous Canker; *Bhavāsava*, Canker of existence; *Diṭṭhāsava*, Canker of views; *Avijjāsava*, Canker of ignorance; and they are of course corrupting biases or cankers and the manner in which they may be overcome or eradicated or cured is taught in the Bhavāsava Sutta of the Majjhima Nikāya.

the pure life, I have done what ought to be done; I have nothing more to do for the realisation of Arahatship'.

"Just, O king, as if in a mountain glen there were a pool of water, crystal clear and transparent; and a man standing on the bank sees all the shells, gravel bars, and shoals of fishes, either moving about or lying still. He then knows: 'This pool of water is crystal clear and transparent. In this pool of water, there exist gravel bars and shells and shoals of fishes either moving about or lying still.'

"In the same way, O king, the Bhikkhu with his mind thus tranquil, purified, cleansed, flawless, free from defilements, supple, ready to act, firm, and imperturbable, applies and bends his mind to the knowledge pertaining to extinction of all Āsavas. He knows as it really is: 'This is suffering'. He knows as it really is: 'This is the origin of suffering'. He knows as it really is: 'This is the extinction of suffering'. He knows as it really is: 'This is the Path leading to the extinction of suffering'. He knows as they really are: 'These are āsavas'. He knows as it really is: 'This is the origin of āsavas'. He knows as it really is: 'This is the extinction of āsavas'. He knows as it really is: 'This is the Path leading to the extinction of āsavas'. To him, thus realizing, thus seeing, his mind is set free from Sensuous Āsava, is set free from Āsava of existence, is set free from Āsava of ignorance. In him, thus set free, there arises the knowledge of his freedom, and he realizes: 'Rebirth is no more; I have lived the pure life; I have done what ought to be done; I have nothing more to do for the realization of Arahatship.'

"This, O king, is the advantage of a samaṇa's life, visible in this very life, better, and higher than the advantages of a samaṇa's life previously mentioned.

"O king, there is no other advantage of a samaṇa's life, visible in this very life better and higher than this."

Ajātasattu's Conversion

And when the Bhagavā had thus spoken, King Ajātasattu addressed the Buddha:

"Lord! It is wonderful! It is indeed wonderful! Just as, Lord, one should turn up that which is upside down or lay bare that which is concealed or tell the way to one who is lost or hold a lamp in the dark so that those who have eyes might see; even so have you revealed the Dhamma to me in many ways. I take, refuge in the Buddha, in the Dhamma, and in the Order of Bhikkhus; may the Buddha accept me as a lay disciple who has taken refuge from today onward as long as my life lasts. Sin overcame me, Lord, weak and foolish and wrong that I was, in that, for the sake of sovereignty, I put to death my father, that virtuous man, that virtuous king! May the Enlightened One accept my confession of this act as a sin to the end that in future I may restrain myself.

"Surely, O king, it was sin that overcame you in acting thus through weakness, foolishness and ignorance, in that you killed your father, a righteous king. But in as much as you understand it to be a sin and make amends by confessing it as such, according to what is right, your confession thereof is accepted as to that. For, O king, whosoever looks upon his wrong doing as a wrong doing, makes amends by confessing it as such, and abstains from it in future will progress according to the Rules."

After the Buddha had spoken, King Ajātasattu said:

"Now, Lord, we may be allowed to go. We are busy, and there is much work to do."

"Do, O king, whatever you may deem fit and proper."

Then King Ajātasattu, pleased and delighted with the words of the Enlightened One, arose from his seat, and after expressing veneration to the Buddha, keeping him on the right hand as he passed, departed from that place.

After King Ajātasattu had left, the Buddha said: "O Bhikkhus, this king has been ruined, completely ruined. If he had not put to death his father, that virtuous man, that righteous king, the Dhamma-Eye[23] would have arisen in him, even as he sat down here."

Thus spoke the Bhagavā, and the brethren were gladdened and rejoiced thereat.

Here ends the Discourse on the Advantages of a Samaṇa's Life.

---

23. A synonym for Sotāpatti-phala, the knowledge of the Stream-winner, the first stage of Holiness. B.S.C.P.-No.3 t. 19-19-58-1,000.

AMBAṬṬHA SUTTA
—Pages 82–102, 6th Synod Edition

Buddha's visit to Brāhmana Pokkharasāti's Territory

Thus, I have heard. On one occasion while the Exalted One was touring through the kingdom of Kosala with a great company of brethren—with about five hundred brethren,—He arrived at a Brahmin village in Kosala named Icchānaṅgala, and He stayed in the Icchānaṅgala Wood nearby.

At that time, the Brahmin Pokkharasāti ruled over Okkaṭṭha, a royal domain which was densely populated, abounded in cattle, with plenty supply of grass, firewood, water and corn, and which was granted to him by King Pasenadi of Kosala as a royal legacy (Rājadāyaṃ), and as a gift in the highest form (Brāhmadeyyaṃ).[24]

The Brahmin Pokkharasāti heard thus: "Friends! It is said that the Samaṇa Gotama of the Sākyan Clan, who went forth from a Sākya family into a homeless life, while touring through the Kingdom of Kosala with a great company of brethren—with about five hundred brethren—has now arrived at the village of Icchānaṅgala and is staying at the Icchānaṅgala Wood nearby. And this is the good news that has been widely spread as to the Samaṇa Gotama: 'That Enlightened One is accomplished and worthy of offerings, Supremely Enlightened, Possessed of Clear Wisdom and Conduct, Happily Attained, Knower of Worlds, the Incomparable Leader of men to be tamed, the Teacher of Devas and men, the Enlightened One, the Exalted One. He, by His Omniscience, knows face to face this universe, including the worlds of Devas, the Brahmās, and the Māras, and the world of men with its *samaṇas* and *brāhmaṇas*, its kings and men, and knowing it, proclaims the Dhamma to men which is good at the beginning, good in the middle and good at the end, and which has the fulness of meaning in spirit and letter. He shows the course of noble practice (*Brahmacariya*), in all its fulness and in all its purity.' To pay one's veneration to such an Arahat is well and good."

24. I.e. as an irrecoverable gift (Commentary).

Ambaṭṭha being sent by Pokkharasāti to find out if Gotama really was a Buddha

Now at that time, there was a youth named Ambaṭṭha, a disciple of Pokkharasāti, the Brahmin. He was able to recite the Vedic verses, and also carried the Vedas by heart. He had mastered the Three Vedas[25] with *Nighaṇḍu, Ketubhānaṃ* and *Akkharappabheda*, and mastered the five Vedas with *Itihāsa* as the fifth,[26] and could explain the Vedas word by word.

He was also well conversant with *Lokāyata* (sophistry), and the reading of the bodily marks of great men. In regard to his master's explanations of the Three Vedas himself, his master had admitted "You know what I know", and he had professed "I know what you know".

Then the Brahmin Pokkharasāti said to Ambaṭṭha the youth: "Dear Ambaṭṭha, it is said that the Samaṇa Gotama, of the Sākyan clan, who went forth from a Sākya family into a homeless life, while touring through the kingdom of Kosala with a great company of brethren—with about five hundred brethren,—has now arrived at the village of Icchānaṅgala and is staying at the Icchānaṅgala Wood nearby. And this is the good news that has been widely spread as to the Samaṇa Gotama: 'That Enlightened One is accomplished and worthy of offerings, Supremely Enlightened, Possessed of Clear Wisdom and Conduct, Happily Attained, Knower of Worlds, the Incomparable Leader of men to be tamed, the Teacher of Devas and men, the Enlightened One, the Exalted One. He, by His Omniscience, knows face to face this universe, including the worlds of Devas, the Brahmās, and the Māras, and the world of men with its *samaṇas* and *brāhmaṇas*, its kings and men; and knowing it, proclaims the Dhamma to men—which is good at the beginning, good in the middle, and good at the end, and which has the fulness of meaning in spirit and letter. He shows the course of noble practice (*Brahmacariya*), in all its fulness and in all its purity.' To pay one's veneration to such an Arahat is well and good.

"Come, dear Ambaṭṭha. Go to the Samaṇa Gotama and verify for our information whether the repute is based on facts or not—whether He is such or not."

"But how, Sir, shall I verify, whether the repute is based on facts or not—whether He is such or not?"

---

25. I.e. Iruveda, Yajuveda and Sāmaveda (Commentary).
26. I.e. the said Three Vedas plus Ātappana Veda and Itihāsa —Ibid.

"Dear Ambaṭṭha, in our Vedas mention has been made of the thirty-two bodily marks of a great man—bodily marks for the possessor of which, there are two alternatives only, and nothing else. If he leads a household life, he will be a Universal Monarch, a righteous monarch, a ruler to the four ends (of the world), a conqueror, a ruler of a peaceful state, a possessor of the seven precious things. And these are the seven precious things that he has the Wheel, the Elephant, the Horse, the Ruby, the Woman, the Banker, and the Eldest son as the seventh. Besides, he has more than a thousand brave and heroic sons of good physique, able to defeat the armies of the foe. And he peacefully reigns over this earth from ocean to ocean, ruling it in righteousness without the necessity of using a stick or a weapon. But if he goes forth from the household life into the homeless life, he will become one worthy of offerings—a Supremely Enlightened Buddha who knows all the Dhammas by Himself, and removes the veil (of mental and moral defilements) in the universe.

"Indeed, Ambaṭṭha I taught you the Vedic verses and you have learnt them."

"Very well, Sir," replied Ambaṭṭha and rising from his seat and paying his respects to Pokkharasāti, he mounted a chariot and proceeded with a retinue of young Brahmins to the Icchānaṅgala Wood. He then travelled in the chariot as far as the road was passable for vehicles, and after getting down, went on foot to the monastery.

Ambaṭṭha's Interview with Gotama Buddha

Now at that time a great number of Bhikkhus were walking up and down in the open air meditatively. Ambaṭṭha approached them and said: "Sirs, where will the Venerable Gotama be staying now? We have come to this place to pay our veneration to Him."

Then those Bhikkhus considered thus: "This young Brahmin Ambaṭṭha is of prominent family, and a pupil of the prominent Brahmin Pokkharasāti. It will not be a burden to the Exalted One to hold conversation with such a one."

Then they said to Ambaṭṭha; "There, Ambaṭṭha, is His *vihāra* (monastery), the door of which is shut. Go there quietly, enter the porch gently, give a cough and tap the door, then the Exalted One will open the door for you.'

When Ambaṭṭha the youth quietly approached the monastery, gently entered the porch, and gave a cough and tapped the door, the Exalted One opened the door, and Ambaṭṭha went in. The other young Brahmins also exchanged greetings and compliments of felicitation with the Exalted One, sat at one side.

Ambaṭṭha's Rudeness

As for the youth Ambaṭṭha, he greeted the Exalted One by passing some derogatory remarks walking while the Exalted One was seated and by passing some derogatory remarks standing while the Exalted One was seated.

Then the Exalted One said to the youth Ambaṭṭha: "Ambaṭṭha, is that the way you would speak to aged teachers, and teachers of your teachers well advanced in years, as you do now, walking about or standing up while I am sitting?"

Ambaṭṭha's First Reproach

"No indeed, Gotama. It is befitting to speak walking to a Brahmin who is walking, and to speak sitting to a Brahmin who is seated, and to speak lying to a Brahmin who lies down. But, indeed, Gotama: with shavelings, bogus samaṇas as of low caste,[27] black coloured, born of the Brahmā's heels, I would talk to them as I do to you."

"Ambaṭṭha, you came here on business. You should concentrate your mind on the business on which you have come. Friends, this Ambaṭṭha thinks that he has been well trained although he is not. What other reason than lack of good training can there be (for this rudeness)?"

When the Exalted One said he did not have good training, Ambaṭṭha was very angry and displeased. Then, having a desire to retaliate, reproach and accuse the Exalted One, and with the thought: Gotama will be put by me in his proper place (with reference to rudeness, etc.). Taunting, deriding and accusing, Ambaṭṭha said: "O Gotama, the Sākyas are wild, rude, light hearted and talkative. Although they are of comparatively low caste, they do not revere Brahmins; they do not pay regard to Brahmins; they do not make offerings to Brahmins; they do not pay respects to Brahmins. It is not fit and proper for Sākyas who are mere *ibbhās*, not to revere Brahmins, not to pay regard to them, nor esteem them, nor to give presents to them, nor to pay respects to them."

Thus, the youth Ambaṭṭha for the first time reproached the Sākyas with the word *ibbhā*.

"How have the Sākyas offended you, Ambaṭṭha?"

---

27. *Ibbhā*, i.e. *Gahapatikā* according to the Commentary (Editor: a householder, merchant, farmer below the Brahmin class).

Ambaṭṭha's Second Reproach

"O Gotama, on one occasion I had to go to Kapilavatthu on a certain business of Pokkharasāti's, and went into the Sākyas' Assembly Hall. At that moment, many Sākyas were seated on raised platforms in the ball, tickling one another with their fingers, laughing heartily; and laughing gently. In fact, it seems to me that they were laughing at me. Nobody in the hall offered me a seat. That, Gotama, is neither fit nor proper, that the Sākyas, who are *ibbhās*, should neither revere Brahmins, nor pay regard to them, nor esteem them, nor give presents to them, nor pay respects to them."

Thus did the youth Ambaṭṭha for the second time reproach the Sākyas with the word *ibbhā*

Ambaṭṭha's Third Reproach

"Ambaṭṭha, even a female skylark can make such noise as she pleases in her own nest. This Kapilavatthu is the Sākyas'. Ambaṭṭha, you should not bear grudge on the Sākyas for such a trifling thing."

"Gotama, there are four castes—the ruling class, the Brahmins, the traders, and the working class. Of these four, the ruling class, the traders and the working class are, in fact, the attendants on the Brahmins. So, Gotama, that is neither fit nor proper, that the Sākyas, who are of comparatively low caste as *ibbhās* should neither revere Brahmins, nor pay regard to them, nor esteem them, nor give presents to them, nor pay respects to them."

Thus did the youth Ambaṭṭha reproach the Sākyas with the word *ibbhā*.

Origin of Kaṇhāyanas (Ambaṭṭha being one of them) and Origin of Sākyas (Gotama Buddha being one of them)

Then the Exalted One thought thus: "This youth Ambaṭṭha intensely degrades the Sākyas as *ibbhās*. Should I not ask him his lineage?"

After that, the Exalted One asked Ambaṭṭha: "Ambaṭṭha, to what family do you belong?"

"I belong to Kaṇhāyana family."

"Ambaṭṭha, if the name and lineage of your parents be recollected, the Sākyas are descendants of a master, and you are a descendant of his slave girl."

"Ambaṭṭha, the Sākyas recognised King Okkāka as their foremost ancestor. What had happened in former days was this: King Okkāka being desirous of giving the throne in succession to the son of his favourite queen, exiled his elder sons—Okkāmukha, Karakaṇḍa, Hatthinika, and Sinisūra—from the country. Those elder sons who were thus exiled from the country took up their residence in a teak grove near a lake on the slopes of the Himalayas. Fearing that the purity of their lineage would be polluted, they intermarried with their sisters.

"Then, King Okkāka asked the ministers at his court: 'Ministers, where do the children live now?

'Your Majesty! The young princes are now living in a teak grove near a lake on the slopes of the Himalayas. Fearing that the purity of their lineage may be polluted, they have intermarried with their sisters.'

"Ambaṭṭha, King Okkāka then exclaimed: 'Ministers, skilful (*sakyā*) are my sons! Very skilful are my sons!' Ambaṭṭha, since that exclamation, Sākyas[28] have appeared, and he is their foremost ancestor.

"Ambaṭṭha, King Okkāka had a slave girl named Disā. She gave birth to a black child. As soon as he was born the newly born child said: 'Wash me, mother. Bathe me, mother. Clean the dirt from my body. I shall be of use to you.'

"Ambaṭṭha, just as nowadays when people see demons, they call them *pisāca* (demons), in those days too when the people saw demons, they called them *kaṇha* (blackies). They said: 'This youngster spoke as soon as he was born. A *kaṇha* was born. A demon was born.' Depending on this word *kaṇha*, the descendants of this black child became known as *Kaṇhāyana*. That *kaṇha* is the foremost ancestor of the *Kaṇha* lineage. Thus, Ambaṭṭha, if the name and lineage of your parents be remembered, the Sākyas are descendants of a master, and you are a descendant of his slave girl."

When He had thus spoken, the young Brahmins said to the Exalted One: "Venerable Gotama, do not degrade Ambaṭṭha too severely with this reproach of being a descendant of a slave girl. Venerable Gotama, Ambaṭṭha belongs to a good caste and a good family; he is well informed, good at speaking and learned. He is able to discuss this matter with the Venerable Gotama."

Then the Exalted One said to them: "If you consider that Ambaṭṭha does not belong to a good caste, or a good family, is not well informed, is not good at speaking, is not learned and is not able to discuss the matter with Venerable Gotama, let Ambaṭṭha stop. You better discuss the matter with me. But, if you consider that Ambaṭṭha belongs to a good caste and a good family, is well

---

28. *Sākya* means a skilled person.

informed, is good at speaking, is learned, and is able to discuss this matter with the Venerable Gotama, you better stop; and let Ambaṭṭha discuss this matter with me."

"Venerable Gotama, Ambaṭṭha belongs to a good caste and a good family, is well informed, is good at speaking, is learned and is able to discuss this matter with the Venerable Gotama. We shall remain silent. Let Ambaṭṭha discuss the matter with the Venerable Gotama."

Then the Exalted One said to the youth Ambaṭṭha: "Now, Ambaṭṭha, there arises a relevant question which you will have to answer although you may not want to do so. If you do not give a definite answer, or give an evasive answer, or remain silent, or go away without answering, your head will split into seven pieces here and now.

Ambaṭṭha, how do you consider this? What have you heard when Brahmins, old and well advanced in years, teachers of teachers of yours, were talking, as to whence the Kaṇhāyanas first appeared and who is their foremost ancestor?"

When He had thus questioned, Ambaṭṭha remained silent. For the second time the Exalted One asked Ambaṭṭha thus: "Ambaṭṭha, how do you consider this? What have you heard when Brahmins old and well advanced in years, teachers of teachers of yours, were talking, as to whence the Kaṇhāyanas first appeared and who is their foremost ancestor?"

For the second time too Ambaṭṭha remained silent.

Then the Exalted One said to Ambaṭṭha: "Ambaṭṭha, better make a reply. This is not the time for you to remain silent, for the head of whoever does not make a reply when the Tathāgata had put a relevant question to him up to three times, will split into seven pieces on the spot."

At that time the Vajirapānī Yakkha[29] stood above Ambaṭṭha in the sky with a mighty sledge hammer all fiery, dazzling, and aglow, with the intention, if he (Ambaṭṭha) did not answer, there and then to split his head into seven pieces. Only the Exalted One and Ambaṭṭha perceived the Vajirapānī Yakkha.

Then Ambaṭṭha who was terrified and startled, the hairs of whose body were standing on end, seeking safety, refuge and protection in the Exalted One alone, sat close to the Exalted One and said: "What was it the Exalted One said? Please say it again."

"What do you think, Ambaṭṭha? What have you heard when Brahmins old and well advanced in years, teachers of teachers of yours, were talking

---

29. The deva who has *Vajira* (Thunder-head) weapon in his hand i.e. Sakka, king of devas.

together, as to whence the Kaṇhāyanas first appeared and who is the foremost ancestor?"

"I too, Venerable Gotama, have heard just as the Venerable Gotama has said. The Kaṇhāyanas are the descendants of that Kaṇha, and he is their foremost ancestor of the Kaṇhāyanas."

And when he had thus spoken the Brahmin youths became rowdy and said tumultuously: "Comrades, they say, Ambaṭṭha the youth does not belong to a good caste; he is not a descendent of a good family, they say, he is a descendent of a slave girl of the Sākyans; and comrades, they say, the Sākyans are descendants of his master. We had wrongly thought that the Venerable Gotama who had spoken the truth should be censured."

Then a thought arose in the Buddha's mind: "These Brahmin youths are harassing Ambaṭṭha too hard as a descendent of a slave girl. Should I not save him?"

Then the Exalted One said to them: "O youths! Do not harass Ambaṭṭha too hard with the words 'descendant of a slave girl.' That Kaṇha was an eminent *isi* (hermit). He went to a suburb in the southern part of the Ganges, and after learning the supreme mantras there, he returned to King Okkāka and demanded his daughter, Maddarūpī, in marriage.

"King Okkāka saying 'Comrades, this Kaṇha being the son of my slave girl, why should he come and ask for my daughter Maddarūpī in marriage?', got enraged and being displeased, fitted an arrow to his bow.

"But neither could King Okkāka let the arrow fly, nor could he take it off the string again. O youths, then the ministers and courtiers approached the *isi* Kaṇha and said: 'Let the King be safe, Sir; let the king be safe.'

"'The King shall be safe. But should he shoot the arrow downwards, the earth in the whole of his realm would collapse.'

"'Let the king be safe, Sir, and the realm too.'

"'The king as well as his realm shall be safe. But should he shoot the arrow upwards, there would be no rain in his realm for seven years.'

"'Let the king be safe, Sir, and the realm too; and let it rain.'

"'The king as, well as the realm shall be safe, and it shall rain. But let the king aim his arrow at his eldest son. The prince shall suffer no harm and not a single hair of his body shall stand on its end.'

"O youths, the ministers then addressed King Okkāka: 'Let King Okkāka aim the arrow at his eldest son. The prince will suffer no harm and not a single hair of his body will stand on its end.'

"Then King Okkāka aimed the arrow at his eldest son and the prince suffered no harm and not a single hair of his body stood on its end. Then King Okkāka gave his daughter Maddarūpī in marriage to the *isi* Kaṇha as he was afraid and agitated and the hairs of his body stood on end through fright of supreme punishment (*Brāhmadaṇḍena*). O youths, you should not harass Ambaṭṭha too hard with the words 'descendant of a slave girl.' That Kaṇha was an eminent *isi*."

Superiority of Khattiyas

I. The Exalted One said to Ambaṭṭha: "Ambaṭṭha, what do you think of this. If, in this world, a young Khattiya marries a Brāhmaṇī maiden, and from their union a son is born, would the son thus born of the Brāhmaṇī maiden through the Khattiya youth get a seat and water among Brahmins?"

"Yes, he would, Venerable Gotama."

"And would the Brahmins allow him to partake of meals offered for the benefit of the dead, or of meals given in ceremonies, or of offerings to gods, or of meals offered to guests?"

"Yes, they would, Gotama."

"And would Brahmins teach him the mantras or not?"

"They would, Venerable Gotama."

"And would he be eligible, or not, for their women?"

"He would not be ineligible, Venerable Gotama."

"But, would the Khattiyas consecrate him as a Khattiya?"

"Certainly not, Venerable Gotama, because he is not of royal descent on the mother's side."

II. "Then what do you think, Ambaṭṭha? If a Brahmin youth marries a Khattiya maiden, and from their union a son is born, would the son thus born to the Khattiya maiden through the Brahmin youth get a seat and water among Brahmins?"

"Yes, he would, Venerable Gotama."

"And would the Brahmins allow him to partake of meals offered for the benefit of the dead, or of meals given in ceremonies, or of offerings to gods, or of meals offered to guests?"

"Yes, they would, Gotama."

"And would Brahmins teach him the mantras or not?"

"They would, Venerable Gotama."

"And would he be eligible, or not, for their women?"

"He would not be ineligible, Venerable Gotama."

"But, would the Khattiyas consecrate him as a Khattiya?"

"Certainly not, Venerable Gotama, because he is not of royal descent on the father's side."

"Then, Ambaṭṭha, comparing woman with woman, and man with man, Khattiyas are superior and Brahmins inferior."

III. "What do you think of this, Ambaṭṭha? Suppose, in this world, for one offence or another, Brahmins shave the head of a Brahmin, sprinkle ashes over his head and banish him from the realm or town. Would he get a seat or water among Brahmins?"

"No, he would not, Venerable Gotama."

"And would Brahmins allow him to partake of meals offered for the benefit of the dead, or of meals given in ceremonies, or of offerings to gods, or of meals offered to guests?"

"No, they would not, Gotama."

"And would Brahmins teach him the mantras or not?"

"No, they would not, Venerable Gotama."

"And would he be eligible, or not, for their women?"

"He would be ineligible, Venerable Gotama."

IV. "Ambaṭṭha, if for one offence or another, Khattiyas banish a Khattiya from the realm or town shaving his head and sprinkling ashes over his head, would he get a seat and water among Brahmins?"

"Yes, he would, Venerable Gotama."

"And would the Brahmins allow him to partake of meals offered for the benefit of the dead, or of meals given in ceremonies, or of offerings to gods, or of meals offered to guests?"

"Yes, they would, Gotama."

"And would Brahmins teach him the mantras or not?"

"Yes, they would, Venerable Gotama."

"And would he be eligible, or not, for their women?"

"Yes, he would be eligible, Venerable Gotama."

"The Khattiya who has been banished from the realm or town by Khattiyas after shaving his head is degraded to the lowest position.

"Thus Ambaṭṭha, a Khattiya is superior and Brahmins are inferior even when he has been degraded to the lowest position. Those who have Knowledge and Conduct are the most eminent:

"Ambaṭṭha, the Brahmā Sanañkumāra also uttered the following verses:

"'Among the people who are particular about lineage, Khattiyas are the most eminent. Among the *devas* and men one who is replete with *vijjā-caraṇa* (Knowledge and Conduct) is the most eminent.'

"Now this verse, Ambaṭṭha, was well sung and not ill sung by Brahmā Sanañkumāra. It was well recited and not ill recited. It is beneficial and not unbeneficial. I endorse it; and Ambaṭṭha, I also say:

"Among the people who are particular about lineage, Khattiyas are the most eminent. Among the *devas* and men one who is replete with *vijjā-caraṇa* (Knowledge and Conduct) is the most eminent."

Vijjā (Knowledge) and Caraṇa (Conduct)

"But what, Venerable Gotama, is *caraṇa* (Conduct), and *vijjā* (Knowledge)?"

"To be replete with incomparable Knowledge and Conduct, one should not talk of birth or lineage, nor use the words of pride: 'Are you worthy of me?, Are you not worthy of me?' When there is giving a daughter in marriage or taking a daughter in marriage or both giving and taking a daughter in marriage there is talk of birth, lineage and proud talk: 'Are you worthy of me?, Are you not worthy of me?'

"Ambaṭṭha, those who are addicted to talking about birth and lineage, to proud talk or to giving and asking daughters in marriage, are far from being replete with *vijjā-caraṇa* (Knowledge and Conduct). It is only by getting rid of such addiction that repletion with Knowledge and Conduct can be attained."

"But what, Venerable Gotama is that *caraṇa* (Conduct) and what *vijjā* (Knowledge)?"

"Ambaṭṭha, there arises in the world a Tathāgata Enlightened, who is a Perfect One, Supremely Enlightened, Possessed of Clear Wisdom and Conduct, Happily attained, Knower of worlds, the Incomparable leader of men to be tamed the Teacher of gods and the Enlightened One, the Exalted One. He by His Omniscience, knows face to face this universe, including the worlds of Devas, the Brahmās and the Māras, and the world of men with its *samaṇas* and *brāhmaṇas*, its kings and men; and knowing it, proclaims the Dhamma to men—the Dhamma which is good at the beginning, good in the middle and good at the end, and which has the fullness of meaning in spirit and letter. He shows the pure life of a *samaṇa*, in all its fullness and in all its purity.

"A householder or one of his children, or a man of inferior caste listens to that Dhamma and on hearing it he has confidence in the Tathāgata; and when he is possessed of that faith, he thinks to himself: Restricted with bonds is the household life and a source of passions. Unbounded like the sky is a samaṇa's life. How difficult is it for a man who is a layman to live a chaste and pure life in all its fulness, in all its purity, in all its perfection. It would be better for me to cut my hair and beard wear the yellow robes, and go out of the household life into the homeless state.

"Then before long, giving up his wealth, be it great or small, leaving his relatives, be they many or be very few, he cuts off his hair and beard, he wears the yellow robes and goes out of the household life into the homeless state.

"When he has thus become a *samaṇa* he lives restrained by the *samaṇa's* disciplinary code. He is possessed of good conduct, and has a suitable subject for constant meditation; and perceiving danger even in the least offences, he observes strictly the rules of training. He has to his credit good deeds in act and word and his livelihood is absolutely pure. He is perfect in conduct, and guards his sense doors. He attains Mindfulness and Clearness of Comprehension, and is altogether contented."

CARAṆA (CONDUCT)
CŪḶA-SĪLA (The Minor Morality)

"How, O Ambaṭṭha, is his conduct good?

"In this, O Ambaṭṭha, that the Bhikkhu having abstained from taking the life of any living being, refrains from the destruction of life. He has laid the stick and the weapon aside; he has moral shame and dread; shows kindness towards all beings; and is full of solicitude for the welfare of all sentient beings.

"Having abstained from the taking of what is not given, the Bhikkhu refrains from taking what is not given to him. He takes only what is given to him; appreciates the giving by others; and lives in honesty and purity of heart.'

"Having abstained from unchastity, the Bhikkhu practices chastity. He refrains from the vulgar practice and also from the sexual act which is the practice of the country folk.'

"Getting rid of lying words, the Bhikkhu refrains from falsehood. He speaks truth, and nothing but the truth; faithful and trustworthy, he does not break his word to the world.

"Getting rid of slander, the Bhikkhu refrains from calumny. What he hears here he does not repeat elsewhere to raise a quarrel against the people here; what he hears elsewhere he does not repeat here to raise a quarrel against the people there. Thus, he binds together those who are divided, encourages those who are friends, makes peace, loves peace, is impassioned for peace, a speaker of words leading to peace.

"Getting rid of rudeness of speech, the Bhikkhu refrains from using harsh language. He speaks only those words that are blameless, pleasant to the ear, lovely, reaching to the heart, polite, pleasing to the people and beloved of the people.

"Getting rid of frivolous talk, the Bhikkhu refrains from vain conversation. At appropriate times he speaks, in accordance with the facts, words full of meaning, on the Doctrine, on the Vinaya. And at right time he speaks words worthy to be noted in one's mind, fitly illustrated and divided according to relevancy of facts.

"The Bhikkhu refrains from causing injury to seeds and plants.

"He takes only one meal a day, not eating at night, and refrains from taking food after midday.

"He refrains from dancing, singing, playing music and witnessing shows with dances, singing and music.

"He refrains from wearing, adorning or ornamenting himself with garlands, scents, and ointments.

"He refrains from the use of lofty and spacious resting places.

"He refrains from accepting gold and silver.

"He refrains from accepting uncooked grain.

"He refrains from accepting raw meat.

"He refrains from accepting women or young girls.

"He refrains from accepting slave-servants of either sex.

"He refrains from accepting sheep or goats.

"He refrains from accepting fowls and pigs.

"He refrains from accepting elephants, cattle, horses, and mares.

"He refrains front accepting agricultural, or waste lands.

"He refrains from acting as an ambassador or messenger.

"He refrains from buying and selling.

"He refrains from cheating with scales or coins or measures.

"He refrains from the cunning ways of bribery, cheating and fraud.

"He refrains from causing physical injury to anyone, murder, putting in bonds, highway robbery, dacoity and plunder. These are that Bhikkhu's morality."

Here ends the Cūḷa Sīla (The Minor Morality).

MAJJHIMA SĪLA (The Medium Morality)

"Whereas some samaṇas and brāhmaṇas, while living on food provided by the philanthropic and generous, cause injury to seedlings and growing plants whether propagated from roots or stems or joints or buddings or seeds, the Bhikkhu refrains from causing such injury to seedlings and growing plants.

"Whereas some samaṇas and brāhmaṇas, while living on food provided by the philanthropic and generous, use hoarded things—foods, drinks, clothing, conveyances, bedding, scents and any eatables, the Bhikkhu refrains from storing such things up.

"Whereas some samaṇas and brāhmaṇas, while living on food provided by the philanthropic and generous, visit shows; which are these shows? They are:

niccaṃ (dances);
gītaṃ (singing of songs);
vāditaṃ (playing instrumental music);
pekkaṃ (theatrical shows);
akkhānaṃ (telling stories with a mingling of doggerel and rhymes);
pānissaraṃ (music attended by clapping);
vetālaṃ (playing music by means of cymbals);
kumbhathūnaṃ (playing drums);
sobhanakaṃ (art exhibitions);
caṇḍāla-vaṃsa-dhovanaṃ (acrobatic feats on the top of a hoisted bamboo pole);
combats of elephants, horses, buffaloes, bulls, goats, sheep, cocks, and quails;
exercising self-defence with quarterstaff, boxing, wrestling;
sham-fight, roll-calls, manoeuvres, troop-inspection.

The Bhikkhu refrains from visiting 'the above-mentioned shows.

"Whereas some samaṇas and brāhmaṇas while living on food provided by the philanthropic and generous, indulge in the following games and recreations:

aṭṭha padaṃ (games on chess boards or boards with eight rows of squares);

dasa padaṃ (games on chess boards or boards with ten rows or squares);
akāsam parihāra-pathaṃ (such games played by imagining such hoards in the air);
santikaṃ (games somewhat akin to hopscotch; or drawing diagrams on the ground, in which one steps only where one is allowed to);
khalikaṃ (throwing dice);
ghaṭikaṃ (hitting a short stick with a long one; games akin to tip-cat);
salākahatthaṃ (a play where the hand is dipped in dye and used as a brush); akkhaṃ (games with balls of all sizes);
paṅgacīraṃ (blowing through toy pipes made of leaves or papers);
vaṅkakaṃ (ploughing with miniature ploughs);
mokkhacikaṃ (turning somersaults);
ciṅgulikaṃ (playing with paper windmills);
pattāḷakaṃ (playing with toy measures);
rathakaṃ (playing with toy chariots);
dhanukaṃ (playing with toy bow);
akkharikaṃ (a game where one has to find out the missing letter or letters);
manesikaṃ (guessing others' thoughts);
yathāvajjaṃ (games involving mimicry of deformities).

The Bhikkhu refrains from such games and recreations. These are that monk's morality.

"Whereas some samaṇas and brāhmaṇas, while living on food provided by the philanthropic and generous, use high and luxurious resting places such as:

an extra-long chair or spacious couch;
thrones with animal figures carved on the supports;
carpets or coverlets with very long fleece;
patchwork counterpanes of many colours;
white blankets;
woollen coverlets richly embroidered;
quilts stuffed with cotton wool;
coverlets embroidered with figures of lions, tigers, etc.;
rugs with fur on both sides or with fur on one side;
coverlets embroidered with gold threads, or silk coverlets;
carpets woven with furs;

elephant, horse, or chariot rugs;
rugs of antelope skins sewn together;
carpets with awnings overhead;
sofas with red pillows for the head and feet.

The Bhikkhu refrains from using such high and luxurious resting places. Such is that Bhikkhu's morality.

"Whereas some samaṇas and brāhmaṇas, while living on food provided by the philanthropic and generous, use means for adorning and beautifying themselves, such as:

rubbing scented powder on one's body, massaging with oil and bathing with scents;
massaging or patting the limbs so as to develop muscles.
The use of mirrors, eye-ointments, garlands, rouge, cosmetics, face powders, make-up, bracelets, top-knot, walking sticks, tubes or pipes for holding anything, swords, umbrellas, embroidered slippers, turbans, diadems, whisks of the yak's tail and long-fringed white robes.

The Bhikkhu refrains from such means of adorning and beautifying the person.

"Whereas some samaṇas and brāhmaṇas, while living on food provided by the philanthropic and generous, are addicted to such low talks as these:

talks about kings, robbers, and ministers of state;
armies, dangers and war;
eating and drinking, clothes and dwellings, garlands, perfumes;
relations, chariots, villages, markets, towns and districts;
women and heroes;
street talks, talks by the well;
talks about those departed in days gone by;
tittle-tattle;
talks about land and sea; and gain and loss.

The Bhikkhu refrains from such low talk.

"Whereas some samaṇas and brāhmaṇas, while living on food provided by the philanthropic and generous, enter in wrangling conversations, such as:

'You don't understand this Dhamma and Vinaya, I do.'
'How should you know about this Dhamma and Vinaya?'

'You are practicing wrong views. It is I who practice the right one.'

'I am talking about relevant facts, whereas you are not.'

'You speak last what ought to be spoken first, and first what ought to be spoken last.'

'All that you have practiced is upset.'

'I have pointed out the fault in your views;

'I have reproved you.'

'Set to work to rebut my statements.'

'Do so yourself if you can'.

The Bhikkhu refrains from such wrangling conversations.

"Whereas some samaṇas and brāhmaṇas, while living on food provided by the philanthropic and generous, work as mediators and messengers, such as:

acting as mediators and messengers of kings, ministers of state, royal families, brahmins, or youths, saying:

'Go there, come here, take this with you, bring that from that place.'

The Bhikkhu refrains from such servile duties.

"Whereas some samaṇas and brāhmaṇas, while living on food provided by the philanthropic and generous, are tricksters, chanters of holy words for gain, interpreters of signs and omens, exorcists, and endeavour to obtain a lot of money from others after spending a little of their own. The Bhikkhu refrains from such trickeries and deceptions.

"Such is that Bhikkhu's morality."

Here ends the Majjhima Sīla (The Medium Morality)

MAHĀ SĪLA (The Major Morality)

"Whereas some samaṇas and brāhmaṇas, while living on food provided by the philanthropic and generous, earn their living by wrong means of livelihood, by low arts, such as:

prophesying long life, prosperity, etc., or the reverse, from marks on limbs, hands and feet of a person;

divining by means of omens and signs;

auguries drawn from thunderbolts;

prophesying by interpreting dreams;

palmistry or Chiromancy;

auguries from the marks gnawed by mice;

- fire-oblation;
- offering oblations from a ladle;
- making offerings to gods of husks, of broken rice, of rice, of ghee and of oil;
- offering oblations from the mouth;
- sacrifice of human blood to gods;
- fortune telling concerning the loss of properties and sickness;
- determining whether the site for a proposed house or garden is lucky or not;
- public administration;
- knowledge of appeasing charms;
- laying ghosts;
- knowledge of charms to be pronounced by one living in an earth-house;
- snake charming;
- the poison craft;
- the scorpion craft;
- the art of curing rat-bites;
- the bird craft;
- the crow craft;
- foretelling the number of years that a man has to live;
- charms to ward off arrows;
- charms to understand the language of animals.

The Bhikkhu refrains from such low arts.

"Whereas some samaṇas and brāhmaṇas, while living on food provided by the philanthropic and generous, earn their living by wrong means of livelihood, by low arts, such as:

knowledge of the signs of good and bad qualities and of the marks denoting the health or luck of their owners in:

> gems, apparel, staves, swords and spears, two-edged swords, arrows, bows, other weapons, women, men, boys, girls, slaves, slave-girls, elephants, horse, buffaloes, bulls, oxen, goats, sheep, fowls, quails, iguanas, bucks and deer.

The Bhikkhu refrains from such low arts.

"Whereas some samaṇas and brāhmaṇas while living on food provided by the philanthropic and generous, earn their living by wrong means of livelihood, by low arts, such as:

> predictions to the effect that the chieftains will march out; the chieftains will march back; our chiefs will attack, and the enemy will retreat; the enemy will attack and ours will retreat; our chief will win the battle and the foreign chiefs will suffer defeat; the foreign chiefs will win the battle and ours will suffer defeat; thus this chief will succeed and that chief not.

The Bhikkhu refrains from such low arts.

"Whereas some samaṇas and brāhmaṇas, while living on food provided by the philanthropic and generous, earn their living by wrong means of livelihood, by low arts, such as foretelling that there will be an eclipse of the moon, of the sun, of a constellation; that the sun or the moon will go on its usual course, there will be aberration of the sun or the moon, or that the constellations will go on their usual course, that there will be aberrations of the constellations; that there will be a fall of meteors, *disā-dāha* ('sky-glow'), an unusual redness of the horizon, that there will be an earthquake, that there will be a wild *Deva-dundubhi* (a supernatural rumble), that there will be rising and setting, clearness and dimness, of the sun or the moon or the constellations. The Bhikkhu refrains from such low arts.

"Whereas some samaṇas and brāhmaṇas, while living on food provided by the philanthropic and generous, earn their livelihood by such wrong means, by such low arts as: foretelling an abundant rainfall, a deficient rainfall, a good harvest, a bad harvest or scarcity of food, tranquillity, disturbances, pestilence, a healthy season, counting on the fingers, by means of arithmetic; by means of formulae, prosody, *lokāyataṃ* (popular lore and custom). The Bhikkhu refrains from such low arts.

"Whereas some samaṇas and brāhmaṇas, while living on food provided by the philanthropic and generous, earn their living by wrongful means of livelihood, by low arts, such as—effecting marriages in which the bride or bridegroom is brought home, or sent forth, effecting betrothals, or divorces, saving money, expending money, *subhagakaraṇaṃ* (using charms to make people happy), *dubbhagakaraṇaṃ* (using charms to make people unhappy), giving medicine to preserve the foetus in cases of abortive women, incantations to make the tongue stiff, to make the jaws of a person stiff, to make a man throw up his hands, to bring on deafness, making use of a mirror to obtain answers to questions put to it, obtaining oracular answers through a girl possessed, from a god, the worship of the sun, of the Brahmā, bringing forth flames from one's mouth, invoking the goddess of Luck. The Bhikkhu refrains from such low arts.

"Whereas some samaṇas and brāhmaṇas; while living on food provided by the philanthropic and generous, earn their living by wrongful means, by low arts, such as—vowing gifts to a god if a certain benefit be obtained, observing such vows, practicing ghost craft, practicing arts and crafts while lodging in an earth house, causing virility, causing femininity preparing sites for buildings and consecrating them, causing a person to vomit, causing a person to take a bath, offering sacrificial fires, administering emetics, purgatives, expectorants and phlegmagogues, causing blood and other impurities to come out of the head and thus relieving it, preparing oil for people's ears, preparing oil to be used as eye-drops, administering drugs through the nose, preparing powerful eye-drops, preparing eye-drops that produce a cooling effect, curing cataracts, practicing surgery, practicing as a children's doctor, administering original drugs and medicines, and preparing new drugs and medicines. The Bhikkhus refrains from such low arts.

"Such is the morality of this Bhikkhu."

Here ends the Mahā Sīla (The Major Morality).

Guarding the Senses

"How, O Ambaṭṭha, is the Bhikkhu guarded as to the sense doors? Whenever the Bhikkhu perceives a form with the eye, he is neither led away by the general outward appearance nor its details and he strives to guard his sense of sight to ward off such mean and evil things as covetousness and grief, which would flow in over him, if he were to remain with unguarded sense of sight. He enters upon this course in regard to the faculty of sight; he guards his sense of sight; and he restrains his sense of sight.

"Whenever he hears a sound with the ear, ...

"Whenever he smells an odour with the nose, ...

"Whenever he tastes a flavour with the tongue, ...

"Whenever he feels a contact with the body, ...

"Whenever he cognises a mental object with his mind, he is neither entranced with the general outward appearance nor its details, and he strives to guard his sense of sight to ward off such mean and evil things, as covetousness and grief which would flow in over him, if he were to remain with unguarded senses. He enters upon this course in regard to the faculty of mind; he guards his sense of mind; and he restrains his sense of mind.

"And possessed of this superior kind of self-restraint, he experiences within himself, a sense of unalloyed happiness. Thus, is it, O king, that the Bhikkhu becomes guarded as to the sense doors. Thus, is it, O Ambaṭṭha, that the Bhikkhu becomes guarded as to the sense doors."

Mindfulness and Clearness of Comprehension

"How, O Ambaṭṭha, does the Bhikkhu possess Mindfulness and Clearness of Comprehension?

"O Ambaṭṭha, in this Sāsana the Bhikkhu practices only clear comprehension in going and coming back. So also, in looking forward, or in looking round; in bending his arm, or in stretching it again; in wearing his robes and carrying his bowl; in eating, drinking, chewing and savouring; in defecating and urinating; in walking, in standing; in sitting, in falling asleep, in waking, in speaking or in keeping quiet.

"Thus, O Ambaṭṭha, the Bhikkhu becomes replete with mindfulness and clearness of Comprehension.

"How, O Ambaṭṭha, is the Bhikkhu contented?

"O king, in this Sāsana, the Bhikkhu is contented with robes just sufficient to protect his body, and with food just sufficient to sustain his belly. Wherever he goes, he goes freely, taking his requisites only. Just, O king, as a bird flies anywhere freely, having only its wings as its burden, that Bhikkhu is contented with the requisite robes and food. Thus is it, O Ambaṭṭha, that the Bhikkhu becomes contented.

"Then that Bhikkhu, having established himself in this group of moralities, possessed of this noble restraint of the senses, having attained this noble mindfulness and clearness of comprehension, filled with this noble contentedness, chooses some lonely spot in the woods, at the foot of a tree, on a hill side, in a cave, in a mountain cleft, in a cemetery, or in a forest thicket, or in the open air, or on a heap of straw. After his meal and on his return from the alms round, he repairs thence, sits down, when his meal is done, cross-legged, keeping his body erect and concentrates his attention on the subject of meditation.

"That Bhikkhu banishes sensual desire; he dwells with a mind free from sensual desire; from sensual desire he cleanses his mind.

"He banishes ill will; he dwells with a mind free from ill will; with goodwill and compassion towards all living beings, he cleanses his mind from ill will.

"He banishes torpor and languor; he dwells free from torpor and languor; with clear perception, with watchful mind, with clear comprehension, he cleanses his mind from torpor and languor.

"He banishes restlessness and worry; dwelling with mind undisturbed, with mind full of peace, he cleanses his mind from restlessness and worry.

"He banishes sceptical doubt; dwelling free from doubt, full of confidence in the good, he cleanses his mind from doubt."

Example of Freedom from Sensual Desire

"Then just, O Ambaṭṭha, as when a man, after taking a loan should start a business, and his business should succeed, and he should not only be able to repay the loan there should be a surplus over to maintain his wife; then would he consider thus: 'I had formerly to carry on my business by taking a loan from others, but my business prospers and I have not only cleared up my debts, but also have a surplus over to maintain my wife.' He would be glad at that, would be joyous at that."

Example of Freedom from Ill Will

"Then just, O Ambaṭṭha, as if a man were a victim to disease, in pain, and very ill, and had no appetite for food, and had lost his strength; after a time, he were to recover from that disease, his appetite return, and he gain in strength, then would he consider thus: 'Formerly I was a victim to disease, in pain, and very ill. I had no appetite for food and had no strength. But now, I recover from that disease, my appetite returns, and I am gaining in strength.' He would be glad at that, and would be joyous at that."

Example of Freedom from Torpor and Languor

"Then just, O Ambaṭṭha, as if a man were confined in a prison, and after a time he should be released from the prison safe and sound, and without any confiscation of his property. Then would he consider thus: 'Formerly I was confined in prison, but now I have been released, safe and sound, and none of my property has been confiscated.' He would be glad at that, and would be joyous at that."

Example of Freedom from Restlessness and Worry

"Then just, O Ambaṭṭha, as if a man were a slave, not his own master, subject to another, unable to go where he wished, and after a time he should be freed from that slavery, become his own master, not subject to another, a free man, able to go where he wished. Then would he consider thus: 'Formerly I was a slave, not my own master, subject to another, unable to go where I wished, but now I am freed from that slavery, I have become my own master, not subject to another, a free man, able to go where I wish.' He would be glad at that, and would be joyous at that."

Example of Freedom from Sceptical Doubt

"Then just, O Ambaṭṭha, as if a man, carrying his riches and goods, were to find himself on a long road, in a desert, where food was scarce danger a bounding, and after a time he were to find himself out of that long, dangerous road and arrived at a village where there was security and peace. Then would he consider thus: 'Formerly I, carrying riches and goods was on a long road, in the desert, where food was scarce but danger abounding. But now I am out of that dangerous road, safe and sound, in a village where there is security and peace.' He would be glad at that, and would be joyous at that.

"Just so, O Ambaṭṭha, he, as long as these five Hindrances are not banished from him, looks upon himself as in debt, diseased, in prison, in slavery, or a long and dangerous road. But when these five Hindrances have been banished, he looks upon himself as freed from debt, recovered from disease, released from prison, freed from slavery and out of the long and dangerous road.

"When he realizes that these five Hindrances have been banished from his mind, gladness springs up within him, and joy arises to him in this glad state, and thus rejoicing, all his body becomes calm, and being thus calm he enjoys happiness, and being thus happy, his mind becomes tranquil."

The First Jhāna

"Then that Bhikkhu will be devoid of sensuous pleasures and evil thoughts and abide in the first Jhāna, which is accompanied by Thought Conception and Discursive Thinking, is born of Detachment, and filled with Rapture and Joy.

"His whole being does he so pervade, drench, permeate, and suffuse with Rapture and Joy born of Detachment, that there is no spot in his whole body not suffused with it.

"Just, O Ambaṭṭha, as when a skilful bath attendant or his apprentice strews scented powder in a metal dish, and. then sprinkles it with water and kneads it together to form a soft lump, the water gradually soaks the powder and forms an amorphous mass, the water permeates through the whole of the scented powder and pervades it within and without, and there is no possible exudation.

"In the same way, O Ambaṭṭha, the Bhikkhu causes his body to be soaked with Rapture and Joy born of Detachment; causes the whole body to be pervaded with Rapture and Joy; and filled with them. Rapture and Joy permeate his whole body within and without, and not a single space whatsoever is left unpermeated.

"This is that Bhikkhu's *caraṇa* (Conduct)."

The Second Jhāna

"Then, the Bhikkhu, after calming down putting away, Thought conception and Discursive Thinking, which is Noble and gives one-pointedness of mind, abides in the second Jhāna, which is free from Thought conception and Discursive Thinking, born of Concentration, and accompanied by Rapture and Joy.

"And his body does he so pervade, drench, permeate, and suffuse with Rapture and Joy born of Concentration, that there is no spot in his whole body not suffused therewith.

"Just, O Ambaṭṭha, as if there were a deep pool, with water welling up from a spring below. There is no inlet from the east or the south, from the west or north, and it does not rain heavily and regularly. Even then the cool water welling up from that spring would pervade, fill, permeate, and suffuse the pool with cool water, and there would be no place whatsoever in that pool not suffused therewith.

"In the same way, O Ambaṭṭha, the Bhikkhu soaks his body with Rapture and Joy born of Concentration, and is filled with them. Rapture and Joy permeate through his whole body within and without, and not a single space whatsoever is left unpermeated.

"This is that Bhikkhu's *caraṇa* (Conduct)."

The Third Jhāna

"Then the Bhikkhu after the fading away of Rapture dwells in equanimity, is mindful and of clear comprehension and experiences in his person that sense of pleasure which the Noble Ones talk of when they say: "'Happy lives the man of equanimity and attentive mind'; thus, the Bhikkhu abides in the third Jhāna.

"And his body does he so pervade, drench, permeate, and suffuse with that sense of pleasure, rapture being absent, that there is no place in his whole body not suffused therewith.

"Just, O Ambaṭṭha, as when in a pond of blue, red, and white lotus, some blue or red or white lotus flowers, produced in the water, growing in the water, nourished by the depths of the water, are so pervaded, drenched, permeated and suffused from their tips down to their roots with the cool moisture thereof, that there is no spot in the whole plant, whether of the blue lotus, or of the red, or of the white, not suffused therewith.

"In the same way, O Ambaṭṭha, the Bhikkhu makes himself to be soaked with rapture free pleasure, filled with it, and suffused with it. There is no part of that Bhikkhu's body not suffused therewith.

"This is that Bhikkhu's *caraṇa* (Conduct)."

The Fourth Jhāna

"Then, the Bhikkhu, after giving up pleasure and pain, and through the disappearance of the previous happiness and sadness which he had, enters into a state beyond pleasure and pain, into the fourth Jhāna, a state of pure mindfulness brought about by equanimity.

"And he sits there so suffusing his whole body with that sense of purification of mind, of clearness of mind that there is no spot in his body not suffused therewith.

"Just, O Ambaṭṭha, as if a man were sitting so rapt from head to foot in a clean white robe that there were no spot on his whole body not in contact with the clean white robe—just so, O king, does that Bhikkhu sit there, so suffusing his body with that sense of purification of mind, of clearness of mind that there is no spot of his whole body not suffused therewith.

"This is that Bhikkhu's *caraṇa* (Conduct).

"O Ambaṭṭha, indeed, these four Jhānas are *caraṇa* (Conduct)."

VIJJĀ (KNOWLEDGE)
1) Insight Knowledge

"Again, O Ambaṭṭha, with his mind thus tranquil, purified, cleansed, flawless, free from defilements, supple, ready to act, firm and imperturbable, he applies and bends his mind to insight knowledge. The Bhikkhu thus understands: This body of mine is made up of Four Great Root Elements,[30] it springs from father and mother, it thrives on account of nutriment, it has the nature of impermanence, must be cleansed and massaged, is fragile and certain of destruction; and so also is this consciousness of mine which is connected with it, which depends on it.

"Just, O Ambaṭṭha, as if there were a Veḷuriya gem, brilliant, genuine, with eight facets, excellently cut, of the purest quality, clear, translucent, flawless and satisfying all conditions. If a man, who is not blind; were to thread it on a string of brown, orange, red, white, or yellow colour, and having taken the gem in his hand, would reflect thus: This gem is brilliant, genuine, with eight facets, excellently cut, of the purest quality, clear, translucent, flawless and satisfying all conditions. It is now fixed to a brown string; an orange string; a red string; a white string; or a yellow string.

"In the same way, O Ambaṭṭha, when his mind is thus tranquil, purified, cleansed flawless, free from defilements, supple, ready to act, firm, and imperturbable, he applies and bends his mind to that insight knowledge. Then he understands thus: This body of mine is made up of Four Great Root Elements, it springs from father and mother, it thrives on account of nutriment, it has the nature of impermanence, must be cleansed and massaged, is fragile and certain of destruction; and so also is this consciousness of mine which is connected with it, which depends on it.[31]

"This is that Bhikkhu's *vijjā* (Knowledge)."

Mental Creative Powers

"Again, O Ambaṭṭha, with his mind thus tranquil, purified, cleansed, flawless, free from defilements, supple, ready to act, firm, and imperturbable, he applies and bends his mind to the creation of mentally produced bodies.

---

30. *Mahā-bhūta*, Four Great Root Elements. They are: (1) Element of Extension (2) Element of cohesion or Liquidity; (3) Element of Kinetic Energy; and (4) Element of Motion. Pāḷi is (1) *Pathavī*; (2) *Āpo*; (3) *Tejo*; (4) *Vāyo*.

31. *Viññāṇa*: Consciousness. This passage refutes any idea of the existence of a "soul".

The Bhikkhu lets proceed from his body another mentally produced body, having all limbs and parts, not destitute of any organ.

"Just, O Ambaṭṭha, as if a man were to pull out a reed from. its sheath. He would reflect: This is the reed, this the sheath. The reed is one thing, the sheath another. It is from the sheath that the reed has been drawn forth.

"Or, O Ambaṭṭha, take this example. If a man were to take out a sword from its scabbard. He would reflect: This is the sword, this the scabbard. The sword is one thing, the scabbard another. It is from the scabbard that the sword has been drawn out.

"O Ambaṭṭha, take another example. If a man were to take out a snake from its slough. He would reflect: This is the snake, this the slough. The snake is one thing, the slough another. It is from the slough that the snake has been taken out.

"O Ambaṭṭha, when his mind is thus tranquil, purified, cleansed, flawless, free from defilements, supple, ready and to act, bends firm, and imperturbable, he applies and bends his mind to the creation of mentally produced bodies. Then the Bhikkhu lets proceed from his body another mentally produced body, having all limbs and parts, not destitute of any organ.

"This is that Bhikkhu's *vijjā* (Knowledge)."

Supernormal Knowledge

"Again, O Ambaṭṭha, with his mind thus tranquil, purified, cleansed, flawless, free from defilements, supple, ready to act, firm and imperturbable, he applies and bends his mind to the knowledge pertaining to supernormal powers. The Bhikkhu then enjoys the various supernormal powers—being one he becomes many, and having become many he again becomes one; he becomes visible or invisible; without being obstructed he passes through walls and mountains, just as if through the air; he walks on water without sinking, just as if on the earth; in the earth he dives and rises up again, just as if in the water; cross-legged he floats through the air, just as a winged bird; with his hand he touches sun and moon, these so mighty ones, so powerful ones; even up to the Brahmā plane has he mastery over his body.

"Just, O Ambaṭṭha, as a clever potter or his apprentice could make, could succeed in getting out of well-prepared clay, any shape of vessel he wanted to have.

"Or as, O Ambaṭṭha, an ivory carver or his apprentice could make, could succeed in getting out of properly prepared ivory, any design he wanted to have.

"Or as, O Ambaṭṭha, a goldsmith or his apprentice could make, could succeed in getting out of the properly worked gold, any kind of article he wanted to have.'

"O Ambaṭṭha, when his mind is thus tranquil, purified, cleansed, flawless, free from defilements, supple, ready to act, firm, and imperturbable, he applies and bends his mind to the knowledge pertaining to supernormal powers. The Bhikkhu then enjoys the various supernormal powers—being one he becomes many, and having become many he again becomes one; he becomes visible or invisible; without being obstructed he passes through walls and mountains, just as if through the air; he walks on water without sinking, just as if on the earth; in the earth he dives and rises up again, just as if in the water; cross-legged he floats through the air just as a winged bird; with his hand he touches sun and moon, these so mighty ones, so powerful ones; even up to the Brahmā plane has he mastery over his body.

"This is that Bhikkhu's *vijjā* (Knowledge)."

The Celestial Ear

"Again, O Ambaṭṭha, with his mind thus tranquil, purified, cleansed, flawless, free from defilements, supple ready to act, firm, and imperturbable, he applies and bends his mind to the knowledge pertaining to the celestial ear. With the celestial ear he hears sounds, heavenly and human, far and near.

"Just, O Ambaṭṭha, as if a man going on a long journey were to hear the sound of a big drum, a cylindrical drum, a conch, a small drum and a small kettle drum, he thus understands:

"This is the sound of the big drum, this is the sound of the cylindrical drum, this of the conch, this of the small drum, and this of the small kettle drum."

"Thus, O Ambaṭṭha, the Bhikkhu hears sounds, heavenly and human, far and near.

"This is that Bhikkhu's *vijjā* (Knowledge)."

Knowledge of the Minds of Others

"Again, O Ambaṭṭha, with his mind thus tranquil, purified, cleansed, flawless, free from defilements, supple, ready to act, firm, and imperturbable he applies and bends his mind to the knowledge pertaining to penetration of others' minds. He knows the minds of other beings, of other persons, by penetrating them with his own mind. He knows the lustful mind as lustful and the passionless one as passionless; knows the hostile mind as hostile and the friendly mind as friendly; knows the dull mind as dull and the alert mind as alert; knows the contracted mind as contracted and the scattered mind as scattered; knows the developed mind as developed and the undeveloped mind as undeveloped; knows the inferior mind as inferior and the superior mind as superior; knows the concentrated mind as concentrated and the wavering mind as wavering; and knows the freed mind as freed and the unfree mind as unfree.

"Just, O Ambaṭṭha, as a young woman, a man or a lad who is wont to beautify himself, on considering carefully the image of his face in a bright and clear mirror or in a vessel of clear water would, if it had a mole on it, know that it had, and if not, would know it had not.

"Thus, O Ambaṭṭha, with his mind tranquil, purified, cleansed, flawless; and imperturbable, he applies and bends his mind to the knowledge pertaining to penetration of others' minds. He knows the lustful mind as lustful and the passionless one as passionless; knows the hostile mind as hostile and the friendly mind as friendly; knows the dull mind as dull and the alert mind as alert; knows the contracted mind as contracted and the scattered mind as scattered; knows the developed mind as developed and the undeveloped mind as undeveloped; knows the inferior mind as inferior and the superior mind as superior; knows the concentrated mind as concentrated and the wavering mind as wavering; and knows the freed mind as freed and the unfree mind as unfree.

"This is that Bhikkhu's *vijjā* (Knowledge)."

Knowledge of Former Existences

"Again, O Ambaṭṭha, with his mind thus tranquil, purified, cleansed, flawless, free from defilements, supple, ready to act, firm, and imperturbable, he applies and bends his mind to the knowledge pertaining to remembrance of former existences. He remembers various former births, such as one birth, two, three, four, five, ten, twenty, thirty, forty, fifty, one hundred, one thousand, one hundred thousand, births, remembers many formations and dissolutions of world cycles: 'These I was, such a name I had, such a clan I belonged to, such complexion I had, such food I ate, such pleasures I enjoyed and such a life span I had; and vanishing from there I entered in a certain existence. There such a name I had, ... and vanishing from there I again reappeared here.' Thus, he remembers, together with the marks and peculiarities, many a former existence.

"Just, O Ambaṭṭha, as if a man were to go to another village, and from that one to another, and thence should return home. Then he would know: 'From my own village I came to that other one. There I stood in such and such a way, sat thus, spoke thus, and remained silent thus. Thence I came to a certain other village; there I stood in such and such a way, sat thus, spoke thus, and remained silent thus. And now from that certain village,' I have returned home again.

"Thus, O Ambaṭṭha, with his mind tranquil, purified, cleansed, flawless, free from defilements, supple, ready to act, firm, and imperturbable, he applies and bends his mind to the knowledge pertaining to remembrance of former existences. He remembers various former births, such as one birth, two, three, four, five, ten, twenty, thirty, forty, fifty, one hundred, one thousand, one hundred thousand, births, remembers many formations and dissolutions of world cycles: 'There I was, such a name I had, such a clan I belonged to, such complexion I had, such food I ate, such pleasures he enjoyed and such a life span I had and vanishing from there I entered in a certain existence. There such a name I had, ... and vanishing from there I again reappeared here.' Thus, he remembers, together with the marks and peculiarities, many a former existence.

"This is that Bhikkhu's *vijjā* (Knowledge)."

The Celestial Eye

"Again, O Ambaṭṭha, with his mind thus tranquil, purified, cleansed, flawless, free from defilements, supple, ready to act, firm, and imperturbable, he applies and bends his mind to the knowledge pertaining to vanishing and reappearing of beings, with his supernormal knowledge, surpassing that of men, he sees beings vanishing and reappearing, low and noble ones, beautiful and ugly ones, happy and unhappy ones, sees how beings are reappearing according to their deeds.

"These beings, indeed, followed evil ways in bodily actions, words and thoughts, insulted the Noble Ones, held wrong views, and according to their wrong views they acted. At the dissolution of their bodies after death, they have appeared in the lower worlds, in painful states of existence, in the world of perdition, in hell.

"Certain other beings have good actions, bodily, verbal and mental, did not insult the Noble Ones, held Right Views, and according to their Right Views they acted. At the dissolution of their bodies after death, they have appeared in a happy state of existence, in a heaven state.

"Thus, with his supernormal knowledge, surpassing that of men, he sees beings vanishing, and reappearing, low and noble ones, beautiful and ugly ones, happy and unhappy ones, sees how beings are reappearing according to their deeds.

"Just, O Ambaṭṭha, as if there were a mansion with an upper terrace on it at a crossroads, and a man standing thereon, and with observation, should watch men entering a house, and coming out of it, and walking up and down the street, and sitting at the junction of the four roads. Then that man knows: 'These men are entering a house, and those are leaving it, and those are walking up and down the street, and these are sitting at the junction of the four roads.'

"Thus, O Ambaṭṭha, with his mind thus tranquil, purified, cleansed, flawless, free from defilements, supple, ready to act, firm, and imperturbable, he applies and bends his mind to the knowledge pertaining to vanishing and reappearing of beings. With his supernormal knowledge, surpassing that of men, he sees beings vanishing and reappearing, low and noble ones, beautiful and ugly ones, happy and unhappy ones, sees how beings are reappearing according to their deeds. 'These beings, indeed, followed evil ways in bodily actions, words and thoughts, insulted the Noble Ones, held wrong views, and according to their wrong views they acted. At the dissolution of their bodies after death, they have appeared in the lower worlds, in painful states of existence, in the world of perdition, in hell. Certain other beings, have good actions, bodily, verbal and mental, did not insult the Noble Ones, held Right Views, and according to their Right Views they acted. At the dissolution of their bodies after death, they have appeared in a happy state of existence, in a heaven state.'

"Thus, with his supernormal knowledge, surpassing that of men, he sees beings vanishing and reappearing, low and noble ones, beautiful and ugly ones, happy and unhappy ones, sees how beings are reappearing according to their deeds.

"This is that Bhikkhu's *vijjā* (Knowledge)."

Extinction of the Āsavas[32]

"Again, O Ambaṭṭha, with his mind thus tranquil, purified, cleansed, flawless, free from defilements, supple, ready to act, firm; and imperturbable, he applies and bends his mind to the knowledge pertaining to extinction of all āsavas. He knows as it really is: 'This is suffering'. He knows as it really is: 'This is the origin of suffering'. He knows as it really is: 'This is the extinction of suffering'. He knows as it really is: 'This is the Path leading to the extinction of suffering'. He knows as they really are: 'These are āsavas'. He knows as it really is: 'This is the origin of āsavas'. He knows as it really is: 'This is the extinction of āsavas'. He knows as it really is: 'This is the Path leading to the extinction of āsavas'. To him, thus realising, thus seeing, his mind is set free from Sensuous Āsava, is set free from Āsava of existence, is set free from Āsava of ignorance. In him, thus set free, there arises the knowledge of his Freedom, and he realizes: 'Rebirth is no more; I have lived the pure life, I have done what ought to be done; I have nothing more to do for the realisation of Arahatship'.

"Just, O Ambaṭṭha, as if in a mountain glen there were a pool of water, crystal clear and transparent; and a man standing on the bank sees all the shells, gravel bars and shoals of fishes, either moving about or lying still. He then knows: 'This pool of water is crystal clear and transparent. In this pool of water there exist gravel bars and shells and shoals of fishes either moving about or lying still.'

"In the same way, O Ambaṭṭha, the Bhikkhu with his mind thus tranquil, purified, cleansed, flawless, free from defilements, supple, ready to act, firm, and imperturbable, applies and bends his mind to the knowledge pertaining to extinction of all Āsavas. He knows as it really is: 'This is suffering'. He knows as it really is: 'This is the origin of suffering'. He knows as it really is: 'This is the extinction of suffering'. He knows as it really is: 'This is the Path leading to the extinction of suffering'. He knows as they really are: 'These are āsavas'. He knows as it really is: 'This is the origin of āsavas'. He knows as it really is: 'This is the extinction of āsavas'. He knows as it really is: 'This is the Path leading to the extinction of āsavas'. To him, thus realising, thus seeing, his mind is set free from Sensuous Āsava, is set free from Āsava of existence, is set free from Āsava of ignorance. In him, thus set free, there arises the knowledge of his freedom, and he realizes: 'Rebirth is no more; I have lived the pure life; I have

32. *Āsava* means "mental impurity". Please see the Light of Dhamma, Vol. V-No.1, p. 42.

done what ought to be done; I have nothing more to do for the realisation of Arahatship.'

"This is that Bhikkhu's *vijjā* (Knowledge).

"O Ambaṭṭha, indeed, these eight are *vijjā* (Knowledge).

"O Ambaṭṭha, this Bhikkhu is said to be perfect in *vijjā* (Knowledge), perfect in *caraṇa* (Conduct), perfect in Knowledge and Conduct. And there is no other perfection in Knowledge and Conduct higher and better than this."[33]

Four Causes of Failure

"Now, Ambaṭṭha, there are four Causes of Failure to achieve perfection in this incomparable *vijjā*[34] (Knowledge) and *caraṇa*[35] (Conduct). And what are the four?

(1) "In this world, Ambaṭṭha, some *samaṇa* or *brāhmaṇa*, not being, able to achieve perfection in this incomparable *vijjā* and *caraṇa,* enters a forest carrying the outfit s of an *isi* (hermit) with a yoke on his shoulder, with the intention 'I will be one who lives only on fruits that have fallen of themselves'. He, in fact, becomes only an attendant on one who has attained perfection in Knowledge and Conduct. This, Ambaṭṭha, is the first Cause of Failure to achieve perfection in this incomparable Knowledge and Conduct.

(2) "And again, Ambaṭṭha, in this world some *samaṇa* or *brāhmaṇa*, not being able to achieve perfection in this incomparable Knowledge and Conduct, and also not being able to become one who lives only on fruits that have fallen of themselves, enters a forest, carrying a hoe and a basket with him with the intention 'I will be one who lives only on bulbs, roots and fruits.' He, in fact, becomes only an attendant on one who has attained perfection in Knowledge and Conduct. This Ambaṭṭha, is the second Cause of Failure to achieve perfection in this incomparable Knowledge and Conduct.

33. *Caraṇa* (Conduct) is of fifteen kinds, namely:

(1) Morality, (2) Guarding of senses, (3) Moderation in eating, (4) Wakefulness, (5) Faith, (6) Mindfulness, (7) Moral Shame, (8) Moral Deed, (9) Great Learning, (10) Energy, (11) Wisdom, (12-15) Four Jhānas.

—Majjhima Paṇṇāsa, Sekha Sutta, p. 20, 6th Syn. Edn.

34. There are eight kinds of *vijjā* (knowledge). They are: 1. Insight-Knowledge; 2. Knowledge pertaining to Mental Creative Powers; 3. Knowledge pertaining to Supernormal Powers; 4. The Celestial Ear; 5. Knowledge of the Minds of others; 6. Knowledge of Former Existences; 7. The Celestial Eye; and 8. Knowledge pertaining to the Extinction of Āsavas.

35. Majjhima Nikāya, Majjhima Paṇṇāsa, Sekha Sutta, p. 20, 6th Syn. Edn.

(3) "And again, Ambaṭṭha, in this world, some *samaṇa* or *brāhmaṇa*, not being able to attain perfection in this incomparable Knowledge and Conduct, not being able to become one who lives only on fruits that have fallen of themselves, not being able to become one who lives only on bulbs, roots and fruits, builds a fire-house near a village or a suburb, and stays there attending to the fire. He, in fact, becomes only an attendant on one who has attained perfection in Knowledge and Conduct. This, Ambaṭṭha, is the third Cause of Failure to achieve perfection in this incomparable Knowledge and Conduct.

(4) "And again, Ambaṭṭha, in this world, some *samaṇa* or *brāhmaṇa*, not being able to attain perfection in this incomparable Knowledge and Conduct, not being able to become one who lives only on fruits that have fallen of themselves, not being able to become one who lives only on bulbs, roots and fruits, and also not being able to become one who attends to the fire, builds a four-doored house at a junction of four roads and stays there with the intention 'I will make offerings to the best of my ability to those *samaṇas* and *brāhmaṇas* who come from the four directions.' He, in fact, becomes only an attendant on one who has attained perfection in Knowledge and Conduct. This, Ambaṭṭha, is the fourth Cause of Failure to achieve perfection in this incomparable Knowledge and Conduct.

"Ambaṭṭha, these are the four Causes of Failure to achieve perfection in this incomparable Knowledge and Conduct."

Inquiry about Ambaṭṭha and his teacher

"What do you think, Ambaṭṭha? Have you and your teacher attained perfection in the incomparable Knowledge and Conduct?"

"No! Venerable Gotama. Who are my teacher and myself? What are the incomparable Knowledge and Conduct? My teacher and I are far from perfection in the incomparable Knowledge and Conduct."

(1) "Ambaṭṭha, what do you think? Not being able to achieve perfection in the incomparable Knowledge and Conduct, have you and your teacher, ever entered a forest carrying the outfits of an *isi* with yokes on your shoulder with the intention 'We will live only on fruits that have fallen of themselves?'"

"Not even that, Venerable Gotama."

(2) "Ambaṭṭha, what do you think? Not being able to achieve perfection in the incomparable Knowledge and Conduct and also not being able to become those who live only on fruits that have fallen of themselves, have you and your

teacher ever entered the forest carrying hoes and baskets, with the intention 'We will live only on bulbs, roots and fruits?'"

"Not even that, Venerable Gotama."

(3) "Ambaṭṭha, what do you think? Not being able to achieve perfection in the incomparable Knowledge and Conduct, not being able to become those who live only on fruits that have fallen of themselves, not being able to become those who live only on bulbs, roots and fruits, have you and your teacher ever built a fire-house near a village or a suburb and stayed there, attending to the fire?"

"Not even that, Venerable Gotama."

(4) "Ambaṭṭha, what do you think? Not being able to achieve perfection in the incomparable Knowledge and Conduct, not being able to become those who live only on fruits that have fallen of themselves, not being able to become those who live only on bulbs, roots and fruits, not being able to become those who build a fire-house near a village or a suburb and stay there attending to the fire, have you and your teacher ever built a four-doored house at a junction off our roads and stayed there with the intention 'We will make offerings to the best of our ability to those samaṇas and brāhmaṇas who come from the four directions?'"

"Not even that, Venerable Gotama."

"Thus, Ambaṭṭha, you together with your teacher have failed to achieve perfection in the incomparable Knowledge and Conduct and even to practice the four Causes of Failure to achieve it."

"Ambaṭṭha, Pokkharasāti Brahmin has uttered the words 'Who are these shavelings, bogus samaṇas, of low caste, black coloured, born of the Brahmā's heels. And what is the discussion of those who, are conversant with the three Vedas!', although he himself has not practiced even the said Causes of Failure. See, Ambaṭṭha, how great is this fault of your teacher Pokkharasāti Brahmin.

"Ambaṭṭha, Pokkharasāti is enjoying what has been given to him by Pasenadi, the king of Kosala. But the king does not allow him to see him face to face.[36] When he consults with him, he speaks to him only from behind a curtain. Why should not Pasenadi, the king of Kosala allow one, who takes only what he gets lawfully, to see him face to face! See Ambaṭṭha, how great is this fault of your teacher Pokkharasāti Brahmin."

---

36. The king did not allow him to see him face to face as he had by exercise of his Avaṭṭanīmāya (art of hypnotism or mesmerism) obtained some valuable ornaments which he (the king) never meant to give him. Dīgha Nikāya, Sīlakkhandhavaggaṭṭhakathā, Pg. 243, 6th 9Synd. Ed.

Making Ambaṭṭha realize that he and his teacher are not *isis*

"What do you think of this, Ambaṭṭha? Suppose a king either sitting on the neck of his elephant or on the back of his horse, or standing on the foot rug of his chariot, should discuss certain affairs with his ministers or princes. And suppose as he left the place and stepped on one side, a commoner or the slave of a commoner should come up and, standing there, discusses the matter saying; 'King Pasenadi said in this manner. King Pasenadi said in this manner.' Even though he says what the king has said or discusses what the king has discussed, would he thereby become the king, or even one of his ministers?"

"Certainly not, Venerable Gotama."

"In the same way, Ambaṭṭha, there were *isis* (hermits) who were predecessors of *brahmins* and who were authors and teachers of the Vedas. The ancient Vedas which were chanted, recited and compiled by them are being chanted, recited, explained and taught by the present day brahmins following their example. They were: Aṭṭhaka, Vāmaka, Vāmadeva, Vessāmitta, Yamadaggi, Aṅgīrassa, Bhāradvāja, vāseṭṭha Kassapa, and Bhagu. You may say, 'I recite those Vedas together with my teacher', but there is no reason why you would by that much become an *isi* or one who is trying to become an *isi*.

"Now what do you think of this, Ambaṭṭha? What have you heard when *brahmins*, old and well advanced in years, teachers of yours or their teachers, were talking together? There were *isis* (hermits) who were predecessors of *brahmins* and who were authors and teachers of the Vedas. The ancient Vedas which were chanted, recited and compiled by them are being chanted, recited, explained and taught by the present day *brahmins* following their example. They were: Aṭṭhaka, Vāmaka, Vāmadeva, Vessāmitta, Yamadaggi, Aṅgīrassa, Bhāradvāja, vāseṭṭha Kassapa, and Bhagu.

"Have you ever heard that they went about in the midst of sensual pleasures—well washed, well perfumed, well groomed, with hair and beard well trimmed wearing ruby ornaments and clad in white—like you and your teacher now?"

"No! I have never heard so, Venerable Gotama."

"Have you ever heard that those *isis* lived on boiled rice of the pure strain, from which all the black specks had been sought out and removed, with many soups and curries like you and your teacher now?"

"No! I have never heard so, Venerable Gotama."

"Have you ever heard that they went about in the company of women with fringes and flounces round their loins, just as you and your teacher do now?"

"No! I have never heard so, Venerable Gotama."

"Have you ever heard that they went about driving chariots, drawn by asses with hairs on their bodies properly brushed, poking them with long whips, like you and your teacher now?"

"No! I have never heard so, Venerable Gotama."

"Have you ever heard that they had themselves guarded in fortified towns, with moats dug round them and cross-bars at the gates, by men armed with long swords, like you and your teacher now?"

"No! I have never heard so, Venerable Gotama."

"So, Ambaṭṭha, neither you nor your teacher is an *isi* nor one who is trying to become an *isi*. However, anyone who is in doubt and perplexity about me, may ask me and I shall make it clear with my answer."

Showing Two Bodily Marks

Then the Exalted One went to the *caṅkama*,[37] and began to walk up and down. Ambaṭṭha followed suit. And as he thus walked up and down, following the Exalted One, he examined whether the thirty-two bodily marks of a real superman appeared on the body of the Exalted One or not. He perceived all the bodily marks except the two—the male organ concealed under a sheath and the extensive tongue. With respect to these two bodily marks of a real superman, he was in doubt and perplexity, could not make a decision and could not believe.

Then the Exalted One thought: This youth Ambaṭṭha has perceived all my thirty-two bodily marks of a real superman except the two—the male organ concealed under a sheath and the extensive tongue. As regards these two bodily marks he is in doubt and perplexity, cannot make a decision, and cannot believe. It will be well and good if I were to let him perceive these two bodily marks of a real superman by means of my supernormal power.

Then, the Exalted One exercised His Psychic Power in such a way that Ambaṭṭha could perceive the male organ concealed under a sheath. He then bent His tongue round in such a way that it touched and stroke both of His ears and both of His nostrils, and covered the whole surface of His forehead.

And Ambaṭṭha the youth thought: The Samaṇa Gotama is fully—and not partially—endowed with the thirty-two bodily marks of a real superman.

37. Caṅkama: Passage; walk;

And he said to the Exalted One: "Now, Lord, we must go. We are busy, and there is much work to do."

"Ambaṭṭha, do what you think it is the time for," replied the Exalted One.

Ambaṭṭha returned to Pokkharasāti

At that time the Brahmin Pokkharasāti went from Ukkaṭṭha with a great retinue of brahmins, and stayed at his garden waiting for Ambaṭṭha. Then, Ambaṭṭha went to that garden. He went in his chariot as far as the path was passable for chariots, then he got down from his chariot, went on foot to where Pokkharasāti was, saluted him respectfully and sat on one side. And when he was so seated, Pokkharasāti said to him: "Dear Ambaṭṭha, did you see the Exalted One?"

"Yes, Sir, we saw Him."

"Dear Ambaṭṭha! Is the general repute about the Venerable Gotama in accordance with what He really is and not otherwise? Is He such a one and not otherwise?"

"He is, Sir, as His reputation is widely spread, and not otherwise. He is such, not otherwise. And He is endowed fully—and not partially—with the thirty-two bodily marks of a real superman."

"Did you have any talk with the Venerable Gotama, Ambaṭṭha?"

"Yes, Sir, I had."

"What was your talk with the Venerable Gotama like?"

Then the youth Ambaṭṭha told Pokkharasāti all the conversation that had taken place between him and the Exalted One.

When he was informed thus, the Brahmin Pokkharasāti said to the youth Ambaṭṭha, "Really admirable is our wise young man! Really admirable is our well-informed young man! Really admirable is our young master of three Vedas! It has been said that on account of such a spy, one might, on the dissolution of the body, after death, be reborn in the lower regions, bad abodes, woeful states and hell.

"Ambaṭṭha, as you spoke rebuking and rebuking the Venerable Gotama in that manner, the Venerable Gotama spoke revealing and revealing our faults in that manner. Really admirable is our wise young man! Really admirable is our well-informed young man! Really admirable is our young master of three Vedas! It has been said that on account of such a spy, one might, on the dissolution of the body, after death, be reborn in the lower regions, bad abodes, woeful states and hell."

Thus saying, being angry and displeased, he kicked and rolled Ambaṭṭha with his foot; and he had a desire to go and see the Exalted One then and there.

Pokkharasāti's Approach to the Exalted One

The brahmins there spoke to Pokkharasāti: "Sir, it is now too late today to go and see the Venerable Gotama. You will go and see the Venerable Gotama tomorrow."

Then the Brahmin Pokkharasāti ordered delicious eatables to be made at his house put them on chariots, and went out to Ukkaṭṭha to the Icchānaṅgala Wood with blazing torches. He went in his chariot as far as the path was passable for chariots, and then on foot to where the Exalted One was, and, after exchanging greetings and compliments of felicitation and courtesy with the Exalted One, sat on one side.

Having been seated thus, Pokkharasāti addressed the Buddha as follows:

"Venerable Gotama, has our pupil Ambaṭṭha the brahmin youth been here?"

"Yes, brahmin, he has."

"And did you have any conversation with him, Venerable Gotama?"

"Yes, brahmin, I had."

"What was your conversation with him like, Venerable Gotama?"

Then the Exalted One related to the Brahmin Pokkharasāti all the conversation that had taken place between Him and the brahmin youth Ambaṭṭha.

When he had thus spoken, Pokkharasāti said to the Buddha: "Venerable Gotama, that brahmin youth Ambaṭṭha is young and foolish. Please forgive him, Venerable Gotama."

The Exalted one replied: "Brahmin, let the brahmin youth Ambaṭṭha be happy."

And the Brahmin Pokkharasāti examined whether the thirty-two bodily marks of a real superman appeared on the person of the Exalted One or not. He was able to perceive all the thirty-two bodily marks of a real superman except the two—the male organ concealed under a sheath and the extensive tongue. With respect to these two bodily marks of a real superman, Pokkharasāti was in doubt and perplexity, could not make a decision and could not believe.

Then the Exalted One thought thus: This Brahmin Pokkharasāti has perceived all the thirty-two bodily marks on my person except the two—the male organ concealed under a sheath and the extensive tongue. As regards these two things which he cannot perceive, he is in doubt and perplexity, cannot make a decision and cannot believe. It will be well and good if I were to let him perceive these two.

Thus thinking, the Exalted One exercised His Psychic Power in such a way that Pokkharasāti could perceive the male organ concealed under a sheath. He then bent round His tongue in such a way that it touched and stroke both of His ears and both of His nostrils, and covered the whole surface of His forehead.

And Pokkharasāti thought: The Samaṇa Gotama is endowed with the thirty-two bodily marks of a real superman. It is not that He is not endowed with all the thirty-two bodily marks of a real superman.

Thus thinking, Pokkharasāti said to the Exalted One: "May the Venerable Gotama be pleased to take His morning meal tomorrow at my house along with the members of the Order." And the Exalted One accepted his request by remaining silent.

Then the Brahmin Pokkharasāti, knowing that the Exalted One had accepted his request by remaining silent, announced the time to the Exalted One thus: "It is time, Venerable Gotama, the meal is ready."

Then in the early morning the Exalted One, dressed Himself up, took His bowl and yellow robe and went, with a group of brethren, to Pokkharasāti's house, and sat on the seat specially prepared for Him.

And Pokkharasāti the Brahmin personally offered the delicious food to the Exalted One to His satisfaction, until He refused to take any more, and the young brahmins served the brethren. After the Exalted One had finished His meal and withdrawn His hands from His bowl, Pokkharasāti took a low seat and sat on one side.

Then to Pokkharasāti thus seated, the Exalted One delivered the following discourses in serial order:

(1) *dāna-kathaṃ* (Discourse on Liberality); (2) *sīla-katham* (Discourse on Morality); (3) *sagga-kathaṃ* (Discourse on the Heavenly Abodes); (4) *kammānaṃ ādinavaṃ, okāraṃ saṃkilesaṃ* (Discourse on the blemishes; meanness and vulgarity of sensuous pleasures); (5) *nekkhamme ānisaṃsaṃ* (Discourse on the Advantages of Renunciation).

When the Exalted One knew that Pokkharasāti had a mind capable (of realizing the four Noble Truths), meek, free (from hindrances) exalted and clear, He proclaimed the Dhamma which the Buddhas only have discovered—Suffering, the Origin of Suffering, the Cessation of Suffering, and Path leading to the Cessation of Suffering. Just as a clean stainless cloth readily takes the dye, Pokkharasāti the Brahmin on that very seat, obtained the pure "Eye of Wisdom"[38] And he realized that whatever has an origin must have an end.

38. Pokkharasāti became a Sotāpanna (Stream-winner).

And then the Brahmin Pokkharasāti, as one who had realized the Truth, mastered it, penetrated into it, overcome Sceptical Doubt and dispels uncertainty, had courage of conviction and who had not to rely on others as regards the Buddha Sāsana, addressed the Exalted One as follows:

"Wonderful, Venerable Gotama! Wonderful, Venerable Gotama! Just as one should turn up that which is upside down or lay bare that which is concealed, or tell the way to the one who has lost his way or hold a lamp in the dark so that those who have eyes might see things; the Dhamma has been revealed to me in more ways than one by the Venerable Gotama. So, I, with my sons, my wife, my people and my ministers take refuge in the Buddha, in the Dhamma and in the Order of monks; may the Venerable Gotama accept us as lay disciples from today onwards as long as our lives last.

"Now as the Venerable Gotama visits the families of His lay disciples at Ukkaṭṭha, even so let Him visit the family of Pokkharasāti. Then all the youths and maidens there will greet the Venerable Gotama respectfully, welcome Him, give Him a seat and also water, and that will be for their benefit and blessing for a long time."

"You have spoken well," replied the Buddha.

Here ends the Ambaṭṭha Sutta.

MAJJHIMA NIKĀYA

MAHĀGOPĀLAKA SUTTA

Great Discourse About Cowherds

—Suttanta Piṭaka, Mūlapaṇṇāsa, p. 281, 6th Synod Edition

Thus, I have heard: On one occasion, the Exalted One was staying at Sāvatthi at the Jetavana monastery of Anāthapiṇḍika. There the Exalted One addressed the Bhikkhus: "O Bhikkhus!" "Yes, Lord", answered those Bhikkhus to the Exalted One. The Exalted One delivered this discourse:

I

"Bhikkhus, a cowherd who has eleven defects is not qualified to look after a herd of cattle and make it prosperous. What are the eleven? In this world, a cowherd (1) is not conversant with *rūpa* (forms); (2) is not skilful in distinguishing the *lakkhaṇa* (characteristics); (3) does not get rid of flies' eggs; (4) does not dress the sore; (5) does not make a smoke; (6) does not know the ford; (7) does not know whether water has been drunk or not; (8) does not know the path; (9) is not clever about grazing grounds; (10) milks dry; and (11) does not do special honour to those bulls who are the fathers and leaders of the herd. Bhikkhus, a cowherd who has these eleven defects is unable to look after the herd and make it prosperous.

"Bhikkhus, similarly, a Bhikkhu[1] who has eleven defects is not qualified to achieve growth, progress and full development in this *dhamma-vinaya* (Teaching of the Buddha). What are the eleven? Bhikkhus, in this *Sāsana*, a Bhikkhu (1) is not conversant with *rūpa* (material qualities); (2) is not skilful in distinguishing the *lakkhaṇa* (characteristics); (3) does not get rid of flies' eggs; (4) does not dress the sore; (5) does not make a smoke; (6) does not know the ford; (7) does not know whether water has been drunk or not; (8) does not know the path; (9) is not clever about grazing grounds; (10) milks dry; and (11) does not pay special honours to those Bhikkhus who are of long standing, who have become Bhikkhus long ago, and who are the fathers and leaders of the order.

---

1. This term also includes a lay devotee who follows the Teaching of the Buddha and practices the dhamma.

(1) "And how, Bhikkhus, is a Bhikkhu not conversant with *rūpa* (material qualities)?

"In this *Sāsana*, Bhikkhus, a Bhikkhu does not understand as they really are, that all *rūpas* are the Four Great Primaries[2] and the material qualities derived from these four.

"Thus, Bhikkhus, a Bhikkhu is not conversant with *rūpa*.

(2) "And how, Bhikkhus, is a Bhikkhu not skilful in distinguishing the characteristics? In this Sāsana, Bhikkhus, a Bhikkhu does not understand, as it really is, that "A fool is characterised by his evil deeds only, and a wise man by his good deeds only." Thus, Bhikkhus, a Bhikkhu is not skilful in distinguishing the characteristics.

(3) "And how, Bhikkhus, does a Bhikkhu not get rid of flies' eggs? In this Sāsana, a Bhikkhu entertains a thought of sensuous pleasure (*kāma vitakka*) that has arisen; he does not abandon it, does not dispel it; does not get rid of it, does not make it disappear. He entertains a malevolent thought (*byāpāda vitakka*) that has arisen; he does not abandon it, does not dispel it, does not get rid of it, does not make it disappear. He entertains a cruel though (*vihiṃsā vitakka*) that has arisen; he does not abandon it, does not dispel it, does not get rid of it, does not make it disappear. He entertains whatever evil has arisen (in him); he does

---

2. There are twenty-eight kinds of material qualities. They are:
   - (i) Four Great Primaries, namely, (1) the element of extension, (2) the element of cohesion or liquidity, (3) the element of kinetic energy. (4) the element of motion or support.
   - (ii) The six bases, namely, (5) the eye basis, (6) the ear basis, (7) the nose basis, (8) the tongue basis, (9) the body basis, (10) the heart basis:
   - (iii) The two sexes, namely, (11) the male sex (12) the female sex.
   - (iv) Material quality of life, namely, (13) the vital force.
   - (v) (14) Material quality of nutrition.
   - (vi) The four sense fields, namely, (15) visible form, (16) sound, (17) odour, (18) savour.
   - (vii) Material quality of limitation, namely, (19) space.
   - (viii) The two communications, namely, (20) intimation through the body, (21) intimation through speech,
   - (ix) The three plasticities, namely, (22) lightness, (23) pliancy, (24) adaptability.
   - (x) The four salient factors, namely, (25) integration (26) continuance, (27) decay, (28) impermanence or death.

   The Four Great Primaries are called *underived material qualities*.

   The remaining twenty-four species are called *derived material qualities*.

not abandon them, does not dispel them, does not get rid of them, does not make them disappear. Thus, Bhikkhus, a Bhikkhu does not get rid of flies' eggs.

(4) "And how Bhikkhus, does a Bhikkhu not dress a sore? In this Sāsana, Bhikkhus, whenever a Bhikkhu perceives a form with the eye, he is led away by the general outward appearance or its details and he does not strive to guard his sense of sight to ward off such mean and evil things as covetousness and grief, which would flow him over him, if he were to remain with unguarded sense of sight. He does not enter upon this course in regard to faculty of sight; he does not guard his sense of sight; and he does not restrain his sense of sight.

"Whenever he hears a sound with the ear, ...

"Whenever he smells an odour with the nose, ...

"Whenever he tastes a flavour with the tongue, ...

"Whenever he feels a contact with the body, ...

"Whenever he cognises a mental object with his mind, he is entranced with the general outward appearance or its details, and he does not strive to guard his mind and ward off such mean and evil things as covetousness and grief, which would flow in over him, if he were to remain with unguarded senses. He does not enter upon this course in regard to the faculty of mind; he does not guard his mind; and he does not restrain his mind Thus, Bhikkhus, a Bhikkhu does not dress the sore.

(5) "And how, Bhikkhus, does a Bhikkhu not make a smoke? In this Sāsana, a Bhikkhu does not teach dhamma in detail to others as he has heard or as he has learnt by heart. Thus, Bhikkhus, a Bhikkhu does not make a smoke.

(6) "And how, Bhikkhus, a Bhikkhu does not know the ford? In this Sāsana, a Bhikkhu occasionally visits those monks who are well informed and who have learnt *dhamma-vinaya* and *pātimokkha* by heart, yet he does not ask: "What is the etymology of this word, Sirs? What is the meaning of this word, Sirs?" Then those venerable monks do not disclose to him what is to be disclosed, do not make clear what is to be made clear, and on various doubtful points of doctrine they do not set his doubts at rest. Thus Bhikkhus, a Bhikkhu does not know the ford.

(7) "And how Bhikkhus, does a Bhikkhu not know whether water has been drunk or not? In this Sāsana, Bhikkhus, when the *dhamma-vinaya* (Teaching of the Buddha) is being expounded, a Bhikkhu does not get the knowledge of the meaning, does not get the knowledge of the Text, does not get that delight which is associated with realization of the dhamma. Thus, Bhikkhus, a Bhikkhu does not know whether water has been drunk or not.

(8) "And how, Bhikkhus does a Bhikkhu not understand the path? In this Sāsana, a Bhikkhu does not understand as they really are, the Noble Eightfold Path.[3] Thus, Bhikkhus, a Bhikkhu does not understand the path.

(9) "And how, Bhikkhus, is a Bhikkhu not clever about grazing grounds? In this Sāsana, a Bhikkhu does not understand as they really are, the Four Applications of Mindfulness.[4] Thus, Bhikkhus, a Bhikkhu is not clever about grazing grounds.

(10) "And how, Bhikkhus, does a Bhikkhu milk dry? In this Sāsana, when devout householders offer him robes, alms, lodgings, and medicines for the sick, he does not know moderation in accepting them. Thus, a Bhikkhu milks dry.

(11) "And how, Bhikkhus, does a Bhikkhu not pay special honour to those Bhikkhus who are of long-standing, who have become Bhikkhus long ago, and who are the fathers and leaders of the Order. In this Sāsana, a Bhikkhu does not treat such Bhikkhus with kind deeds, words and thoughts both in the public and in private. Thus, Bhikkhus, a Bhikkhu does not pay special honour to those Bhikkhus who are of long-standing, who have become Bhikkhus long ago, and who are the fathers and leaders of the Order.

"Bhikkhus, a Bhikkhu who has these eleven *defects* is not qualified to achieve growth, progress and full development in this Sāsana."

II

"Bhikkhus, a cowherd who has the eleven qualities is qualified to look after a herd of cattle and make it prosperous. What are the eleven? In this world, a cowherd (1) is conversant with *rūpa* (forms); (2) is skilful in distinguishing the *lakkhaṇa* (characteristics); (3) gets rid of flies' eggs; (4) dresses the sore; (5) makes a smoke; (6) knows the ford; (8) knows whether water has been drunk or not; (9) is clever about grazing grounds; (10) does not milk dry; and (11) does special honour to those bulls who are the fathers and leaders of the herd. Bhikkhus, if a cowherd has these eleven qualities, he is qualified to look after the herd of cattle and make it prosperous.

---

3. 1. Right View, 2. Right Thinking, 3. Right Speech, 4. Right Action, 5. Right Livelihood, 6. Right Effort, 7. Right Mindfulness, 8. Right Concentration.

4. 1. Contemplation on the body, 2. Contemplation on sensations, 3. Contemplation on consciousness, 4. Contemplation on mental objects.

"Bhikkhus, similarly, if a Bhikkhu has eleven qualities, he is qualified to achieve growth, progress and full development in this *dhamma-vinaya* (Sāsana). What are the eleven? In this Sāsana, Bhikkhus, a Bhikkhu (1) is conversant with *rūpa* (material qualities); (2) is skilful in distinguishing the *lakkhaṇa* (characteristics); (3) gets rid of flies' eggs; (4) dresses the sore; (5) makes a smoke; (6) knows the ford; (7) knows whether water has been drunk or not; (8) knows the path; (9) is clever about grazing grounds; (10) does not milk dry; and (11) pays special honour to those Bhikkhus who are of long-standing, who have become Bhikkhus long ago, and who are the fathers and leaders of the Order.

(1) "And how, Bhikkhus, is a Bhikkhu conversant with *rūpa*? In this Sāsana, Bhikkhus, a Bhikkhu understands as they really are, that all *rūpas* are the Four Great Primaries and the material qualities derived from these four. Thus, Bhikkhus, a Bhikkhu is conversant with *rūpa*.

(2) "And how, Bhikkhus, is a Bhikkhu skilful in distinguishing the characteristics? In this Sāsana, Bhikkhus, a Bhikkhu understands, as it really is, that: "A fool is characterised by this evil deeds only, and a wise man by his good deeds only. "Thus, Bhikkhus, a Bhikkhu is skilful in distinguishing the characteristics.

(3) "And how, Bhikkhus, does a Bhikkhu get rid of flies' eggs? In this Sāsana, Bhikkhus, a Bhikkhu does not entertain a thought of sensuous pleasure. Whenever it arises, he abandons it, dispels it, gets rid of it and makes it disappear. He does not entertain a malevolent thought. Whenever it arises, he abandons it, dispels it, gets rid of it and makes it disappear. He does not entertain a cruel thought. Whenever it arises, he abandons it, dispels it, gets rid of it and makes it disappear. He does not entertain any evil thought. Whenever it arises, he abandons it, dispels it, gets rid of it and makes it disappear. Thus, Bhikkhus, a Bhikkhu gets rid of flies' eggs.

(4) "And how, Bhikkhus, does a Bhikkhu dress the sore? In this Sāsana, Bhikkhus, whenever a Bhikkhu perceives a form with the eye, he is not led away by the general outward appearance nor its details, and he strives to guard his sense of sight to ward off such mean and evil things as covetousness and grief, which would flow in over him, if he were to remain with unguarded sense of sight. He enters upon the course in regard to the faculty of sight, he guards his sense of sight; and he restrains his sense of sight.

"Whenever he hears a sound with the ear ....

"Whenever he smells an odour with the nose, ...

"Whenever he tastes a flavour with the tongue, ...

"Whenever he feels a contact with the body, ...

"Whenever he cognises a mental object with his mind, he is neither entranced with the general outward appearance nor its details, and he strives to guard his mind and ward off such mean and evil things as covetousness and grief, which would flow in over him, if he were to remain with unguarded senses. He enters upon this course in regard to the faculty of mind; he guards his mind; and he restrains his mind. Thus, Bhikkhus, a Bhikkhu dresses the sore.

(5) "And how, Bhikkhus, does a Bhikkhu make a smoke? In this Sāsana, a Bhikkhu teaches dhamma in detail to others as he has heard or as he has learnt by heart. Thus, Bhikkhus, a Bhikkhu makes a smoke.

(6) "And how, Bhikkhus, does a Bhikkhu know the ford? In this Sāsana, a Bhikkhu who occasionally visits those monks who are well informed and who have learnt *dhamma-vinaya* and *pātimokkha* by heart, asks: "What is the etymology of this word, Sirs? What is the meaning of this word Sirs?" Then those venerable monks disclose to him what is to be disclosed, make clear what is to be made clear, and on various point of the doctrine they set his doubts at rest. Thus Bhikkhus, a Bhikkhu knows the ford.

(7) "And how, Bhikkhus, does a Bhikkhu know whether water has been drunk or not? In this Sāsana, Bhikkhus, when the *dhamma-vinaya* is being expounded, a Bhikkhu gets the knowledge of the meaning, gets the knowledge of the dhamma, gets that delight which is associated with the realization of the dhamma. Thus, Bhikkhus, a Bhikkhu knows whether water has been drunk or not.

(8) "And how, Bhikkhus, does a Bhikkhu understand the path? In this Sāsana, a Bhikkhu understands, as they really are, the Noble Eightfold Path. Thus, Bhikkhus, a Bhikkhu understands the path.

(9) "And how, Bhikkhus, is a Bhikkhu clever about grazing grounds? In this Sāsana, a Bhikkhu understands as they really are, the Four Applications of Mindfulness. Thus, Bhikkhus, a Bhikkhu is clever about grazing grounds.

(10) "And how, Bhikkhu, does not a Bhikkhu milk dry? In this Sāsana, when devout householders offer him robes, alms, lodgings, and medicines for the sick, he knows the moderation in accepting them. Thus, Bhikkhus, a Bhikkhu does not milk the cow dry.

(11) "And how, Bhikkhus, does a Bhikkhu pay special honour to those Bhikkhus who are of long-standing, who have become Bhikkhus long ago, and who are the fathers and leaders of the Cider? In this Sāsana, a Bhikkhu treats

such Bhikkhus with kind deeds, words and thoughts both in the public and private. Thus, Bhikkhus, a Bhikkhu pays special honour to those Bhikkhus who are of long-standing, who have become Bhikkhus long ago, and who are the fathers and leaders of the Order.

"Bhikkhus, a Bhikkhu who has these eleven qualities is qualified to achieve growth, progress and full development in this Sāsana."

MAHĀGOPĀLAKA SUTTA VAṆṆANĀ[5]
Commentary on Mahāgopālaka Sutta

In the case of the unskilful cowherd

I. *Na rūpaññū hoti*: "Is not conversant with *rūpa* (form)". The cowherd does not know his cows by way of enumeration or by outward appearance. (1) *By enumeration*—He does not know how many heads of cattle he is tending, whether they are a hundred or a thousand. Even if some of his cows have been killed, or if they have gone astray, he does not count the number of his cows, saying to himself: "Today so many of my cows are missing." He does not endeavour to fetch the missing cows in the neighbouring forest nor in the spaces between two or three neighbouring forests nor in the spaces between two or three neighbouring villages. Even if other people's cows have come and mingled with his own, he does not endeavour to count the number of his cows and drive away the extra ones with his stave. When other people find that their cows have been in his herd, they frighten him saying: "This man has kept our cows in his herd so long." So saying, they take away their own cows. Thus, the number of his cows becomes diminished, and he is precluded from enjoyment of five milk products.[6] (2) *By outward appearance*—Again, the cowherd does not know: So many of my cows are of white colour, so many of red colour, so many of black colour, so many have specks on their bodies, and so many are of brown colour. Even if some of his cows have been killed or if they have gone astray, he does not count the number of his cows, saying to himself: "Today so many of my cows are missing", and look for the cows which have strayed into the neighbouring forests or into the spaces between villages. Even if other people's cows have come and mingled with his own, he does not endeavour to count the number of his cows and drive away the extra ones with his stave. When other people find that their cows have been in

5. Mūlapaṇṇāsaṭṭhakathā, Vol. II, p. 159, 6th Syn. Edn.
6. Milk, cream, buttermilk, butter, ghee.

his herd, they frighten him saying: "This man has kept our cows so long." So saying, they take away their own cows. Thus, the number of his cows becomes diminished, and he is precluded from enjoyment of five milk products.

II. *Na lakkhaṇakusalo hoti*: "Is not skilful in distinguishing the *lakkhaṇas* (signs or characteristics)" It means: The cowherd does not know about the marks such as arrows, spears and spikes made on the bodies of his cows. Even if some of his cows have been killed, or if they have gone astray, he does not count the number of his cows, saying to himself: "Today my cows with such and such marks are missing." ... Thus, the number of his cows becomes diminished, and he is precluded from enjoyment of five milk products.

III. *Na āsātikaṁ hāreta*: "Does not get rid of flies' eggs. It means thus: when cows are pricked with thorns or struck against tree stumps, they sustain wounds and eventually flies lay their eggs in them. These eggs should be removed from the wounds with a stick and the wounds dressed up. The unskilful cowherd does not do so. Thus, it is said: "Does not get rid of flies' eggs". The cows' wounds get worse and worse and deeper and deeper, and the worms enter the internal organs of the cows. The cows are thus oppressed by those wounds. They are unable to eat grass or drink water to their satisfaction. Milk dries up in the breasts of those cows and they are reduced in strength. Both these endanger the cows. Thus, the number of his cows becomes diminished and he is precluded from enjoyment of five milk products.

IV. *Na vanaṁ paṭicchādetā hoti*: "Does not dress the sore." It means: Medicine should be applied to the aforesaid wounds and they should be dressed up and bandaged with fibres and cloth bandage. The unskilful cowherd does not do so. Impure blood and pus flow out from the cows' wounds. When their bodies rub against the bodies of other cows, the latter would sustain diseases through infection. Thus, the cows are oppressed by those wounds. They are unable to eat grass to their satisfaction .... Thus, the number of his cows becomes diminished, and he is precluded from enjoyment of five milk products.

V. *Na dhūmaṁ kattā hoti*: "Does not make a smoke." It means: When the cows enter the cattle-pen in the rainy season when gadflies and mosquitoes are plentiful, the pen should be fumigated. The unskilful cowherd does not do so. Thus, the cows are harassed by the gadflies, etc., the whole night without getting proper sleep. The next day they went to the forest and laid themselves down at the foot of the tree the whole day. They are unable to eat grass to their satisfaction .... Thus, the number of his cows becomes diminished, and he is precluded from enjoyment of five milk products.

VI. *Na titthaṃ jānāti*: "Does not know the ford." It means: The cowherd does not know whether the ford is smooth or rough, whether it is infested with aqueous beasts of prey. When the cows are taken to a place other than the ford, they may tread on gravels and thus hurt themselves or break their legs. If they happen to be taken to a place where there are aqueous beasts of prey, they may be seized by crocodiles, etc. Then the cowherd comes to a stage when he has to say: "Today so many cows of mine are ruined. Today so many cows of mine are ruined." Thus, his herd decreases and he himself is precluded from enjoyment of five milk products.

VII. *Na pītaṃ jānāti*: "Does not know whether water has been drunk or not." It means: The cowherd should know thus: "Such and such cows have taken water, and such and such have not: such and such cows have the opportunity to drink water at the ford and such and such cows have not." After tending his cows in the forest the whole day, that cowherd saying: "My cows shall take water," takes them to the river or a single-banked pond. Heifers, bulls and strong cows gore old and weak cows with their horns, or take the opportunity of pushing them aside with their bodies, and having entered the water thigh-deep drink water to their satisfaction. The remaining cows having no opportunity to drink clean water are obliged to stand at the bank and drink the turbid water polluted with mud, or to remain without taking any water. Then that cowherd strikes the backs of his cows and drives them back to the forest. Then those cows which have not taken water are unable to eat grass to their satisfaction .... Thus, the number of his cows becomes diminished, and he is precluded from enjoyment of five milk products.

VIII. *Na vīthiṁ jānāti:* "Does not know the path." It means: The cowherd does not know that such and such a path is even and free from danger and such and such a path is rough, risky and dangerous. Avoiding the safe path, he allows his cows to go by the other path. Thus, his cows are oppressed by the smell of lions, tigers, etc., and are also attacked by thieves and robbers. Then they stand stretching out their necks just as the trembling deer. They cannot eat grass to their satisfaction .... Thus, the number of his cows becomes diminished. and he is precluded from enjoyment of five milk products.

IX. *Na gocarakusalo hoti*: "Is not clever about grazing grounds." It means; Surely the cowherd should know the grazing grounds, i.e. whether they are grazing grounds to which cattle can be sent only once in five days or once in seven days. Having allowed his cows to eat grass at one grazing ground one day, he should not send them to the same place again on the next day. The grazing ground where several cows take grass is as clean as the surface of a drum. There is no grass in it. The water there also is muddy. So, the cowherd should send his cows to take grass at a grazing ground only once in five days or seven days. This statement is also true, because in this time fresh grass grows up and the water also becomes clean. The cowherd who does not know that the grazing ground is one to which he should send his cows only once in five or seven days, sends his cows to the same grazing ground every day. Then that cowherd's cows cannot get green grass and have to eat dry grass and take polluted water. In that cow-pen there is a shortage of milk. The cows cannot eat grass to their satisfaction .... Thus, the number of his cows becomes diminished, and he is precluded from enjoyment of five milk products.

X. *Anavasesadohī hoti*: "Milks dry." It means: A skilful cowherd should milk the cow leaving one or two nipples, i.e., as much as will sustain the flesh and blood of its calf. The unskilful cowherd milks dry without leaving any milk for the calf. Then the young calf which lives on the mother's milk gets parched through hunger for milk, and being unable to stand, it trembles, falls in front of its mother and dies. The cow, feeling "My child does not get even its mother's milk to drink," through grief for its child cannot take enough grass or water, and the milk ceases in her nipples. Thus, the number of his cows becomes diminished, and he is precluded from enjoyment of five milk products.

XI. *Na atirekapūjā-ya*: "Does not pay special honour." It means: A skilful cowherd does utmost honour to those bulls, who are the fathers and leaders of the herd. He gives them decent food. He dips five fingers in the scent and besmears it on the bodies of these bulls, and adorn them with flowers. He fits silver and gold ferrules to the horns of these bulls. At night he lights a lamp for them and allows them to sleep under a ceiling made of cloth. The unskilful cowherd does not do so. The bulls do not look after the remaining cows and avert dangers as they do not get the utmost honour. Thus, the number of his cows becomes diminished, and he is precluded from enjoyment of five milk products.

The case of the unskilful Bhikkhu may be explained as follows:

Here in the text,

Idha means "In this sāsana."

I. *Na rūpaññū hoti*: "Is not conversant with *rūpa*." The Bhikkhu does not understand the Four Great Primaries either by enumeration or by their origin (*samuṭṭhāna*). (1) Just as the unskilful cowherd does not know the *rūpa* (form) of the cows by enumeration, the unskilful Bhikkhu also does not know the following twenty-five parts of the body as mentioned in the Pāḷi

Texts: (1) the eye basis, (2) the ear basis, (3) the nose basis, (4) the tongue basis, (5) the body basis, (6) visible form, (7) sound, (8) odour, (9) taste, (10) touch, (11) the male sex, (12) the female sex, (13) the vital force, (14) bodily intimation, (15) verbal intimation, (16) material quality of limitation, namely, space, (17) the element of cohesion or liquidity, (18) lightness, (19) pliancy, (20) adaptability, (21) integration, (22) continuation, (23) decay, (24) impermanence or material quality, (25) nutrition.[7]

This Bhikkhu is like the cowherd who does not know his cattle by enumeration. Not knowing by enumeration, he is unable to make his *kammaṭṭhāna* (practice of meditations) reach the climax by (1) grasping *rūpa* (matter) and determining *arūpa* (what is not matter, i.e. mind and mental factors.)

(2) grasping *rūpa* and *arūpa* and noting their causes and

(3) meditating on their characteristics. Just as the herd of that cowherd does not thrive, he does not thrive in this sāsana with virtue, mental concentration, spiritual insight, path, fruition and nibbāna. Just as the cowherd is precluded from enjoyment of five milk products so he is precluded from the five kinds of Dhammakkhandhas, namely, (1) the morality of an Arahat, (2) the concentration of an Arahat, (3) wisdom of an Arahat, (4) emancipation of an Arahat, and (5) knowledge arising from such emancipation.

(4) "Does not know their origin" means does not know that such and such physical phenomena are born of one root cause; such and such, of two root causes; such and such of three root causes; such and such of four root causes; and such and such physical phenomena are not born of any root cause. This Bhikkhu not knowing *rūpa* by its origin (*samuṭṭhāna*) just as a cowherd does not know their outward appearance, is precluded from the five kinds of Dhammakkhandhas ... emancipation.

II. *Na lakkhaṇakusalo hoti*: The Bhikkhu does not know that good and evil deeds are the characteristics of the wise and the foolish as stated in the Text "A fool is characterised by his deed. A wise man is characterised by his deed." Thus, not knowing, this Bhikkhu does not shun the foolish nor associate with the wise; he does not know what he should do and what he should not do; what is good and what is evil; what is innocent and what is not innocent; what is a slight offence and what is a serious offence; what offence can be cured and what offence cannot be cured; what is reasonable and what is not reasonable. As he does not know all these, he cannot take a subject for meditation and

7. Although only 25 are specifically mentioned, No. 10 'touch' comprises the remaining three elements of extension, motion and kinetic energy.

develop his concentration thereon. Just as the herd of the cowherd does not thrive this Bhikkhu also does not thrive in this Sāsana with the above-mentioned *sīla*, etc. Just as the cowherd is precluded from enjoyment of five milk products so he is precluded from the five kinds of Dhammakkhandhas.

III. *Na āsāṭikaṃ hāretā hoti*: "Does not get rid of flies' eggs" means that the Bhikkhu does not get rid of the *kāma-vitakka* (thoughts of sensuous pleasure) which have arisen. As he does not get rid of evil thoughts, he becomes one who is under the influence of evil thoughts and as he goes about as such, he is unable to take a subject for meditation and develop his concentration thereon. Just as the herd of the cowherd does not thrive, this Bhikkhu also does not thrive in this *Sāsana* with the above mentioned *sīla*, etc. Just as the cowherd is precluded from enjoyment of five milk products so he is precluded from the five kinds of Dhammakkhandhas.

IV. *Na vanaṃ paticchādetā hoti*: "Does not dress the sore." Just as that cowherd does not dress the sore the Bhikkhu does not practice restraint as stated in the Texts like "Seeing a visible object with his eyes, he is swayed by its general outward appearance only." As he goes about with all his sense doors open, he is unable to take a subject for meditation and develop his concentration thereon. Just as the cowherd is precluded from enjoyment of five milk products so he is precluded from the five kinds of Dhammakkhandhas.

V. *Na dhūmaṃ kattā hoti*: "Does not make a smoke." Just as the cowherd does not make a smoke, this Bhikkhu does not make a smoke of the Teaching. He does not make a discourse of the Dhamma; he does not recite the Dhamma; he does not discuss the Dhamma while sitting together; nor does he utter any appreciation (e.g. on the occasion of almsgiving by others). So, people do not know whether that Bhikkhu is learned and has noble qualities. As they do not know this, they do not support him with the four requisites. As he experiences difficulty about the four requisites, he is unable to recite the Teaching of the Buddha to fulfil his duties and obligation and to take a subject of meditation and develop his concentration thereon. Just as the herd of the cowherd does not thrive, this Bhikkhu also does not thrive in this Sāsana with the above-mentioned *sīla*, etc. Just as the cowherd is precluded from enjoyment of five milk products so he is precluded from the five kinds of Dhammakkhandhas.

VI. *Na titthaṃ jānāti*: "Does not know the ford." It means that this Bhikkhu does not approach the well-informed Bhikkhus who resemble the ford. Even if he approaches them, he does not ask them: "What is the etymology of this word, Sirs? What is the meaning of this word, Sirs? What does the Text say in this connection? What does it make clear in this context?" As they are not asked thus, they do not explain to him what is to be been explained, do not teach him in detail, do not make easy to understand what is difficult, and do not make obvious what is obscure. Not having visited the well-informed Bhikkhus who resemble the ford, he is not free from sceptical doubt and is unable to take a subject of meditation and develop his concentration thereon. Just as that cowherd does not know the ford, this Bhikkhu does not know the Dhamma "Ford". Not knowing it he asks questions of wrong persons. Having approached one who is learned in Abhidhamma (philosophy) he asks questions as to what should be done and what should not be done according to the rules of Vinaya. Having approached one who is learned in Vinaya he asks him questions on delimitation of *nāma* and *rūpa* (mind and matter). As he asks questions of wrong persons, they cannot answer them; as he is not free from sceptical doubt, he is unable to take a subject of meditation and develop his concentration thereon. Just as the cowherd ... Dhammakkhandhas.

VII. *Na pītaṃ jānāti*: "Does not know whether water has been drunk." Just as that cowherd does not know whether water has been drunk or not, this Bhikkhu does not know that delight which is associated with the realization, of the Dhamma, does not get any benefit which arises from the wholesome volitional act of hearing the Dhamma. Having gone to a place where religious Discourses are delivered, he does not listen to them with veneration. He either sleeps, while seated, or speaks to other people, or thinks of other things. As he does not listen the Dhamma respectfully, he is unable to take a subject of meditation and develop his concentration thereon. Just as ... Dhammakkhandhas.

VIII. *Na vīthiṃ jānāti*: "Does not know the path." Just as the cowherd does not know which is the path and which is not the path, he does not know the Noble Eightfold Path as it really is, i.e. which is mundane and which is supramundane. Not knowing this, he concentrates on the mundane Eightfold Path and is unable to develop the supramundane Path. Just as ... Dhammakkhandhas.

IX. *Na gocarakusalo hoti*: "Is not clever about grazing grounds." Just as the cowherd does not know whether a grazing ground is one to which he could send his cows once only in five or seven days, he does not know the Four Applications of Mindfulness as they really are, i.e. which are mundane and which are supramundane. Not knowing this, he exercises his intellect on what are difficult to comprehend, concentrates on mundane Application of Mindfulness and is unable to develop supramundane Application of Mindfulness. Just as ... Dhammakkhandhas.

X. *Anavasesadohī ca hoti*: "Milks dry" here means "milks dry, not knowing how much only should be taken." Herein, offerings are of two kinds, namely, (1) invitation by word of mouth (2) invitation by production of things to offer. Verbal offering means thus: People go to a Bhikkhu and invites him thus, "Sir, tell us what you want." Invitation by production of things: People bring cloth, oil, treacle, etc. to a Bhikkhu and say to him: "Sir, please take as much as you want." That Bhikkhu does not know how much should be taken. Instead of taking only as much as is proper in accordance with Rathavinīta Sutta[8] wherein it is stated, "A Bhikkhu should know: (1) the donor's wish; (2) whether he offered thing is suitable for him; (3) his own capacity", he takes all things.

People, being displeased, do not invite him anymore and he, being in difficulty about the four requisites, is unable to take a subject or meditation and make progress with it. Just as ... Dhammakkhandhas.

XI. *Te na atirekapūjāya pūjetā hoti*: "Does not do most honour to them." Just as the cowherd does not do most honour to the bulls which are the fat hers and leaders of the herd, that Bhikkhu does not do most honours to the Elder Bhikkhus; deeds, words and thoughts of (loving-kindness) both publicly and privately. The elders, thinking "These young Bhikkhus do not treat us with respect," do not help them with two kinds of help. (1) They do not help them with *āmisa* (materials) i.e. robes, bowls, accessories to bowls or lodgings; and they do not look after them also when they are in difficulty or sorrow. (2) They do not teach them the Pāḷi Texts or the Commentaries, or ancient and difficult scriptures. Young Bhikkhus who do not get the two kinds of help at all from the elderly Bhikkhus are unable to remain in the *Sāsana*. Just as the herd of the cowherd does not prosper, so the young Bhikkhu's morality etc. do not improve. Just as ... Dhammakkhandhas.

The good part (i.e. comparison with a skilful cowherd) should be understood as the reverse of what has been said on the bad part.

Here ends the Great Discourse About Cowherds.

---

8. Majjhima Nikāya, Mūlapaṇṇāsa Pāḷi, 3. Opama-vagga, 4. Rathavinita Sutta, p. 199, 6th Syn. Edn.

SUTTANTA PIṬAKA, MAJJHIMA NIKĀYA, MŪLAPAṆṆĀSA—5. CŪḶAYAMAKA-VAGGA

4. CŪḶAVEDALLA SUTTA (Pages 373–9, 6th Synod Edition)

Questions and Answers on Sakkāya, Sakkāya-diṭṭhi, the Noble Eightfold Path and Latent Tendencies

Thus, I have heard. On one occasion the Exalted One was staying near Rājagaha in the Bamboo Grove at the squirrels' feeding place. Then, the male devotee Visākha[9] approached the nun Dhammadinnā; having approached her and having given his deep respects to her, he sat down at one side. As he was sitting down there, he spoke to her thus:

"Lady, it is said '*sakkāya*,' '*sakkāya*.'[10] Now, Lady, what is called *sakkāya* by the Exalted One?"

"Friend Visākha, these Five Constituent Groups of Existence which form the objects of Clinging are called *sakkāya* by the Exalted One, that is to say, (1) the Corporeality-group which forms the object of Clinging, (2) the Sensation-group which forms the object of Clinging, (3) the Perception-group which forms the object of Clinging, (4) the Mental-Formations-group which forms the object of Clinging, and (5) the Consciousness group which forms the object of clinging. These Five Constituent Groups of Existence, friend Visākha, are called *sakkāya* by the Exalted One.

"It is good, Lady." And the male devotee Visākha having rejoiced at the nun Dhammadinnā's words, having thanked her, asked her another question.

"Lady, it is said 'the Origin of *sakkāya*', 'the Origin of *sakkāya*'. Now, Lady, what is called 'the Origin of *sakkāya*' by the Exalted One?"

"Friend Visākha, this very Craving which gives rise to ever fresh rebirth, is bound up with pleasure and lust and finds ever fresh delight now here and now there—namely, *kāma-taṇhā* (Craving for Sensual pleasures), *bhava-taṇhā* (Craving for Existence) and *vibhava-taṇhā* (Craving for Self-annihilation)—is called 'the Origin of *sakkāya*' by the Exalted One."

---

9. Not to be confused with Visākha the millionaire Upāsika.
10. *Sakkāya* (*Santo kāyo sakkāyo*) "Group of Existence." This word is mostly translated as Personality but according to the commentaries it corresponds to *sat-kāya* 'existing-group'.

"Lady, it is said 'the Extinction of *sakkāya*', 'the Extinction of *sakkāya*.' Now, Lady, what is called 'the Extinction of *sakkāya*' by the Exalted One?"

"Friend Visākha, the complete fading away and Extinction of this very Craving, the forsaking and giving it up, and liberation and detachment from it—this, friend Visākha, is called 'the Extinction of *sakkāya*' by the Exalted One."

"Lady, it is said 'the Path leading to the Extinction of *sakkāya*,' 'the Path leading to the Extinction of *sakkāya*'. Now, Lady, what is called 'the Path leading to the Extinction of *sakkāya*' by the Exalted One?"

"Friend Visākha, this very Noble Eightfold Path,—namely, Right Understanding Right Thinking, Right Speech, Right Action, Right Livelihood, Right Effort, Right Mindfulness and Right Concentration—is called 'the Path leading to the Extinction of *sakkāya*' by the Exalted One."

"Is this Clinging the same as the Five Constituent Groups of Existence, or is it apart from the Five Constituent Groups of Existence?"

"No, friend Visākha, this Clinging is not the same as the Five Constituent Groups of Existence, and there is no Clinging apart from them. Whatever, friend Visākha, is the Greed and Desire for the Five Groups of Existence which form the objects of Clinging that is Clinging to them."

"But how, Lady, does there come to be *sakkāya-diṭṭhi* (Personality-belief)?"

"In this world, friend Visākha, a worldling who has no learning, who never visits the Holy Ones, who is not skilled in the Sublime Dhamma, who is untrained in the Sublime Dhamma who never visits the good and worthy men, not skilled in the true Dhamma, untrained in the True Dhamma, considers (1) that Corporeality is *attā* (soul-essence), (2) that *attā* has Corporeality, (3) that Corporeality is in *attā*, or (4) that *attā* is in Corporeality.

"He considers (5) that Sensation is *attā*, (6) that *attā* has Sensation; (7) that Sensation is in *attā*, or (8) that *attā* is in Sensation.

"He considers (9) that Perception is *attā*, (10) that *attā* has Perception, (11) that Perception is in *attā*, or (12) that *attā* is in Perception.

"He considers (13) that Mental-Formations are *attā*, (14) that *attā* has Mental Formations, (15) that Mental-Formations are in *attā*, or (16) that *attā* is in Mental Formations.

"He considers (17) that Consciousness is *attā*, (18) that *attā* has Consciousness, (19) that Consciousness is in *attā*, or (20) that *attā* is in Consciousness. Thus, friend Visākha, does there come to be *sakkāya-diṭṭhi*."

"How, Lady, does there come to be no *sakkāya-diṭṭhi* (Personality-belief)?"

"In this world, friend Visākha, a devotee who is the follower of the Buddha and who has attained the Paths and the Fruitions thereof, who, visits the Holy Ones, who is skilful in the Sublime Dhamma, who visits the good and worthy men, and who is skilful in the true Dhamma and is well trained therein does not, consider (1) that Corporeality is *attā*, (2) that *attā* has Corporeality, (3) that Corporeality is in *attā*, or (4) that *attā* is in Corporeality.

"He does not consider (5) that Sensation is *attā*, (6) that *attā* has Sensation, (7) that Sensation is in *attā*, or (8) that *attā* is in Sensation.

"He does not consider (9) that Perception is *attā*, (10) that *attā* has no Perception, (11) that Perception is in *attā*, or (12) that *attā* is in Perception.

"He does not consider (13) that Mental Formations are *attā*, (14) that *attā* has Mental Formations, (15) that Mental-Formations are in *attā*, or (16) that *attā* is in Mental-Formations.

"He does not consider (17) that Consciousness is *attā*, (18) that *attā* has Consciousness, (19) that Consciousness is in *attā*, or (20) that *attā* is in Consciousness. Thus, friend Visākha, does there come to be no *sakkāya-diṭṭhi*."

"But what, Lady, is the Noble Eightfold Path?"

"This, friend Visākha, is the Noble Eightfold Path, that is to say, Right Understanding, Right Thinking, Right Speech, Right Action, Right Livelihood, Right Effort, Right Mindfulness, Right Concentration."

"But, Lady, is the Noble Eightfold Path conditioned or unconditioned?"

"The Noble Eightfold Path is conditioned."

"Now, Lady, are the three Groups of Training contained in the Noble Eightfold Path or is the Noble Eightfold Path contained in the three Groups of Training?"

"Friend Visākha, the three Groups of Training are not contained in the Noble Eightfold Path, but the Noble Eightfold Path is contained in the three Groups of Training. Friend Visākha, Right Speech, Right Action and Right Livelihood—these things are contained in the Group of *Sīla* (Morality), Right Effort, Right Mindfulness and Right Concentration—these things are contained in the Group of *Samādhi* (Mental Concentration). Right Understanding and Right Thinking—these things are contained in the Group of *Paññā* (wisdom)."

"And what, Lady, is Mental Concentration, what are things which lead to supports of Mental Concentration, what are the requisites for Mental Concentration and what is development of Mental Concentration?"

"Friend Visākha, one-pointedness of mind, is Mental Concentration; the four Applications of Mindfulness are the things which lead to Mental Concentration; the four Right Efforts are the requisites for Mental Concentration, the practice, development and increase of these very things is development of Mental Concentration."

"And how many *saṅkhāras* (Kamma-formations) are there, Lady?"

"There are three *saṅkhāras*, friend Visākha. They are: Kamma-formations of body, Kamma-formations of speech and Kamma-formations of mind."

"And what, Lady, are Kamma-formations of body, speech and mind?"

"In-and Out-breathing, friend Visākha, is Kamma-formation of body; Thought conception and Discursive Thinking is Kamma-formation of speech; Perception and Sensation is Kamma-formation of mind."

"In-and Out-breathing, friend Visākha—these are bodily things dependent on the body; therefore In-and Out-breathing, is Kamma-formation of body."

"Having first had Thought conception and Discursive thinking, one subsequently utters a speech; therefore Thought conception and Discursive thinking is Kamma-formation of speech."

"Perception and Sensation—these are things dependent on mind; therefore, Perception and Sensation is Kamma-formation of mind."

"And how, Lady, does there come to be *Saññā-vedayita Nirodha-sammāpatti* (Attainment of Cessation of Perception and Sensation)?"

"Friend Visākha, it does not occur to a monk who is attaining the Cessation of Perception and Sensation: 'I will attain the Cessation of Perception and Sensation'; or 'I am attaining the Cessation of Perception and Sensation'; or 'I have attained the Cessation of Perception and Sensation'. However, his mind has been so previously developed that it leads him to the state of the Cessation of Perception and Sensation."

"But, Lady, when a monk is attaining the Cessation of Perception and Sensation, what things cease first; Kamma-formation of body, or Kamma-formation of speech, or Kamma-formation of mind?"

"Friend Visākha, when a monk is attaining the Cessation of Perception and Sensation, Kamma-formation of speech ceases first, then the Kamma-formation of body, and then Kamma-formation of mind."

"And how, Lady, does there come to be the rising from *Saññā-vedayita Nirodha-sammāpatti*?" Friend Visākha, it does not occur to a monk who is rising from the Attainment of Cessation: 'I will rise from the Attainment of Cessation', or 'I am rising from the Attainment of Cessation'; or 'I have risen from the Attainment of Cessation'. However, his mind has been so previously developed that it leads to rise from the state of 'Cessation of Perception and Sensation'."

"But, Lady, when a monk is rising from the Attainment of Cessation, what things arise first: Kamma-formation of body, or Kamma-formation of speech, or Kamma-formation of mind?"

"Friend Visākha, when a monk is rising from the Attainment of Cessation, Kamma-formation of mind arises first, then Kamma-formation of body, then Kamma-formation of speech."

"Lady, how many kinds of *phassa* (contact) impress a monk who has risen from the Attainment of Cessation?"

"Friend Visākha, when a monk has risen from the Attainment of Cessation of Perception and Sensation, three kinds of Contact impress him. They are:

1) *Suññata-phassa* (Contact with the Devoid, i.e. Nibbāna which is devoid of defilements, such as *rāga*, *dosa* and *moha*);
2) *Animmita-phassa* (Contact with the Unconditioned, i.e. Nibbāna which has no such indication as *rāga*, *dosa* and *moha*);
3) *Appaṇihita-phassa* (Contact with Freedom from Desire, i.e. Nibbāna where there is no desire arising from *rāga*, *dosa* and *moha*)."

"Lady, when a monk has risen from the Attainment of Cessation of Perception and Sensation, towards what does his mind bend, slide and gravitate?"

"Friend Visākha, the mind of a monk who has risen from the Attainment of Cessation of Perception and Sensation bends, slides and gravitates towards *viveka* (detachment, i.e. Nibbāna)."

"How many kinds of Sensations are there, Lady?"

"There are three kinds of Sensations. They are: Agreeable Sensation, Disagreeable Sensation and Indifferent Sensation."

"And what, Lady, is Agreeable Sensation, what Disagreeable Sensation and what is Indifferent Sensation?"

"That, friend Visākha, which is experienced whether by body or mind, and is pleasant and agreeable, that is an Agreeable Sensation. That, friend Visākha, which is experienced whether by body or mind, and is painful or disagreeable, that is a Disagreeable Sensation. That, friend Visākha, which is experienced whether by body or mind, and is neither agreeable nor disagreeable, this is an Indifferent Sensation."

"But, Lady, how is Agreeable Sensation agreeable, and how disagreeable? How is Disagreeable Sensation disagreeable, and how agreeable? How is Indifferent Sensation agreeable and how disagreeable?"

"Friend Visākha, Agreeable Sensation is agreeable while it lasts, but it becomes disagreeable when it changes; Disagreeable Sensation is disagreeable, while it lasts, but it becomes agreeable when it changes; Indifferent Sensation is agreeable if its real nature is known, disagreeable if its real nature is not known."

"But, Lady, what *anusaya* (Inherent tendency) lies latent in Agreeable Sensation, what *anusaya* in Disagreeable Sensation, and what *anusaya* in Indifferent Sensation?"

"Friend Visākha, *rāgānusaya* (Inherent tendency towards Sensuous Greed) lies latent in Agreeable Sensation; *paṭighānusaya* (Inherent tendency towards Friction) lies latent in Disagreeable Sensation; and *avijjānusaya* (Inherent tendency towards Ignorance) lies latent in Indifferent Sensation."

"But, Lady, does *rāgānusaya* lie latent in all Agreeable Sensations; does *paṭighānusaya* lie latent in all Disagreeable Sensation; and does *avijjānusaya* lie latent in all Indifferent Sensation?"

"Friend Visākha, *rāgānusaya* does not lie latent in all Agreeable Sensations, nor *paṭighānusaya* in all Disagreeable Sensations, nor *avijjānusaya* in all Indifferent Sensations."

"But, Lady, what is to be eradicated in Agreeable Sensation, what in Disagreeable Sensation, and what in Indifferent Sensation?"

"Friend Visākha, *rāgānusaya* is to be eradicated in Agreeable Sensation; *paṭighānusaya* is to be eradicated in Disagreeable Sensation; and *avijjānusaya* is to be eradicated in Indifferent Sensation."

"But, Lady, is *rāgānusaya* to be eradicated from every Agreeable Sensation? Is *paṭighānusaya* to be eradicated from every Disagreeable Sensation? Is *avijjānusaya* to be eradicated from every Indifferent Sensation?"

"No, friend Visākha, *rāgānusaya* is not be eradicated from every Agreeable Sensation; *paṭighānusaya* is not to be eradicated from every Disagreeable Sensation; and *avijjānusaya* is not to be eradicated from every Indifferent Sensation.

"In this *Sāsana*, friend Visākha, having detached oneself from sensuous pleasures and unwholesome volitional actions, one enters on and abides in the first Jhāna which is accompanied by Thought conception and Discursive Thinking, and rapture and agreeable sensation arising from the absence of

Hindrances. By that Jhāna one eradicates *rāga* (Greed), and no *rāgānusaya* lies latent there.

"In this Sāsānā, friend Visākha, a monk reflects thus: 'When shall I enter on and abide in that plane which the Holy Ones have entered on and are abiding in (i.e. Arahatship)'. Having set up a desire for Incomparable Freedom, i.e. Arahatship, *domanassaṃ* (Mentally Disagreeable Sensation) arises, as a result of that desire (i.e. when the desired Arahatship is not attained). *Paṭigha* is eradicated by it and no *paṭighānusaya* (Inherent tendency towards Friction) lies latent there.

"In this Sāsana, friend Visākha, a monk, by eradicating *sukha* (bodily agreeable sensation) and *dukkha* (bodily disagreeable sensation) and through previous disappearance of *somanassa* (mentally agreeable sensation) and *domanassa* (mentally disagreeable sensation), enters on and abides in the fourth Jhāna, which has only Indifferent Sensation and which is entirely purified by equanimity and mindfulness, and thereby eradicates Ignorance, and *avijjānusaya* (Inherent tendency towards Ignorance) does not lie latent there."

"But, Lady, what is the *paṭibhāga* (opposite) of Agreeable Sensation?"

"Friend Visākha, the opposite of Agreeable Sensation is Disagreeable Sensation."

"And what, Lady, is the opposite of Disagreeable Sensation?"

"Friend Visākha, Agreeable Sensation is the opposite of Disagreeable Sensation."

"And what, Lady, is the counterpart of Indifferent Sensation?"

"Friend Visākha, Ignorance is the counterpart of Indifferent Sensation."

"And what, Lady, is the opposite of Ignorance?"

"Friend Visākha, *vijjā* (Insight knowledge) is the opposite of *avijjā* (Ignorance)."

"And what, Lady, is the counterpart of Insight knowledge?"

"Friend Visākha, *vimmutti* (Freedom) is the counterpart of Insight knowledge."

"And what, Lady, is the counterpart of Freedom?"

"Friend Visākha, Nibbāna is the counterpart of Freedom."

"And what, Lady, is the counterpart of Nibbāna?"

"This question goes too far, friend Visākha; you are unable to observe the limit for questions,[11] Brahmacariya (practice of the Eightfold Path) culminates

---

11. Nibbāna has no equal or counterpart; and yet he asked what was its equal or counterpart.

in Nibbāna. It does not go beyond it. It has Nibbāna as its ultimate goal. Friend Visākha, if you like you can go to the Exalted One and ask Him about this and note as the Exalted One explains to you."

Then the male devotee Visākha, rejoiced in what Arahat Dhammadinnā had said, thanked her, rose from his seat, wished her farewell, keeping his right side towards her and approached the Exalted One. Having drawn near, and having paid his deep respects to the Exalted Onc, he sat down at one side. As he was sitting down there, Visākha told the Exalted One the whole of the conversation that had taken place between him and the nun Dhammadinnā. When He had been told the whole conversation, the Exalted One spoke thus to Visākha: "Wise, Visākha, is the nun Dhammadinnā, of great wisdom, Visākha, is the nun Dhammadinnā. If you had asked me, Visākha, about this matter, I too would have answered exactly as the nun Dhammadinnā; and this is indeed the meaning of that; thus should you note it."

Thus spoke the Exalted One. Delighted, the male devotee Visākha rejoiced in what the Exalted One had said.

* * *

"There are three advantages, friend Ānanda, on account of which it was so prescribed by the Exalted One, namely for restraining ill-natured persons, for the well-being of pious brethren (lest evil wishers, backed by a clique, should bring discord into the Order), and for the tender care of the families. It is these three advantages on account of which three only at a meal was prescribed by the Order."

—Saṃyutta Nikāya, XVl-11.

Here ends the Questions and Answers on Sakkāya, Sakkāya-diṭṭhi, ...

SUTTANTA-PĪṬAKA (MAJJHLMA NIKĀYA)
Majjhima -Paṇṇāsa, Gahapati-Vagga ... Jīvaka-Sutta
Discourse on Jīvaka the Doctor

Thus, I have heard. At one time the Bhagavā was staying at Rājagaha in the Mango Grove of Jīvaka Komārabhacca, the adopted son of Abhaya, the King's son. Then Jīvaka Komārabhacca approached the Blessed One. Having approached and made obeisance to Him, he sat down at one side and having sat down Jīvaka Komārabhacca asked the Blessed One:

"Lord, I have heard that animals are slaughtered on purpose for the recluse Gotama, and that the recluse Gotama knowingly eats the meat killed on purpose for him. Lord, do those who say animals are slaughtered on purpose for the recluse Gotama, and the recluse Gotama knowingly eats the meat killed on purpose for him speak the Word of the Buddha, or do they falsely accuse the Buddha? Do they speak the truth, according to the truth? Are your declarations and supplementary declarations not thus subject to be ridiculed by others in any manner?"

"Jīvaka, those who say 'Animals are slaughtered on purpose for the recluse Gotama, and the recluse Gotama knowingly eats the meat killed on purpose for him' do not say according to what I have declared, and they falsely accuse me. Jīvaka, I have declared that one should not make use of meat if it is seen, heard or suspected to have been killed on purpose for a monk. I allow the monks meat that is quite pure in three respects: if it is not seen, heard or suspected to have been killed on purpose for a monk.

"Jīvaka, in this Sāsana a monk resides in a certain village or suburb with a mind full of Loving-kindness pervading first one direction, then a second one, then a third one, then the fourth one, just so above, below and all around; and everywhere identifying himself with all, he pervades the whole world with mind full of Loving-kindness, with mind wide, developed, unbounded, free from hate and ill will.

"A certain householder or his son approaches that monk and invites him to the morning meal in his house the next day. Jīvaka, the monk, willingly accepts the invitation. Having passed that night, early the next morning that monk puts on his inner robe, dresses himself and having taken a bowl goes to the householder or his son's house. Having reached the house of the householder he sits down at a place specially meant for him. Then the householder or his son offers him a delicious meal. To that monk no such thought arises: 'How good it would be if this householder or his son were to offer me a delicious meal;' or 'How good it would be, were this householder to offer me such a delicious meal in future.' That monk has no craving for that meal, does not brood over the matter, and has no attachment for it; on the contrary, he contemplates the miseries in connection with material food, and having possessed himself of Wisdom pertaining to the finding of a way to Freedom, he eats the meal.

"Jīvaka, what do you think (about him in the matter)? Has he caused ill will towards himself or another or both?"

"No, Venerable Sir."

"Jīvaka, did not that monk eat a meal that was free from blemishes at that time?"

"Yes, Venerable Sir.

"Lord, I have heard that the Brahmā lives with Loving-kindness. Lord, I have now seen with my own eyes that the Bhagavā is that very Brahmā because He lives with Loving-kindness."

"Jīvaka, ill will is caused by *rāga* (greed), *dosa* (hatred) and *moha* (delusion); but the Bhagavā has already eradicated *rāga*, *dosa* and *moha*, and as they have been cut at the roots, they will never arise in future. Jīvaka, if you really speak in that light, I shall accept your words."

"Lord, I really spoke in that light."

"Again, Jīvaka, in this Sāsana a monk resides in a certain village or suburb with a mind full of Compassion, of Altruistic Joy and of Equanimity directed first in one direction, then a second one, then a third one, then the fourth, just so above, below and all around; and everywhere identifying himself with all, he pervades the whole world with mind full of Equanimity, with mind wide, developed, unbounded, free from hate, and ill will.

"A certain householder or his son approaches that monk and invites him to the morning meal in his house the next day. Jīvaka that monk willingly accepts the invitation. Having passed that night, early the next morning that monk puts on his inner robe, dresses himself, and having taken a bowl goes to the householder's house. Having reached the house he sits down at a place specially prepared for him. Then the householder or his son offers him a delicious meal. To that monk no such thought arises: 'How good it would be, were this householder to offer me a delicious meal;', or 'How good it would be were this householder to offer me such a delicious meal in future.' That monk has no craving for that meal, does not brood over the matter, and has no attachment for it; on the contrary, he contemplates the miseries in connection with material food, and having possessed himself of Wisdom pertaining to the finding of a way to Freedom, he eats the meal.

"Jīvaka, what do you think about him in the matter? Has he caused ill will against himself or another or both?"

"No, Venerable Sir."

"Jīvaka, did not that monk eat a meal that was free from blemishes at that time?"

"Yes, Venerable Sir.

"Lord, I have heard that the Brahmā lives with Equanimity. Lord, I have now seen with my own eyes that the Bhagavā is that very Brahmā because He lives with Equanimity."

"Jīvaka, ill will is caused by *rāga* (greed), *dosa* (hatred) and *moha* (delusion); but the Bhagavā has already eradicated *rāga*, *dosa* and *moha*, and as they have been cut at the roots, they will never arise again in future. Jīvaka, if you really speak in that light, I shall accept your words."

"Lord, I really spoke in that light."

"Indeed, Jīvaka, if the householder slaughters an animal on purpose for the Tathāgata or His disciples, he performs the following five kinds of unwholesome volitional actions:

(1) 'Go and bring such and such an animal here', orders the householder. Thus, he has firstly committed an unwholesome volitional action.

(2) Secondly, this householder has committed an unwholesome volitional action by causing the animal to be dragged by the neck thus making the animal suffer disagreeable mental sensations.

(3) Thirdly, he has committed an unwholesome volitional action by ordering his men to kill the animal.

(4) Fourthly, he has committed an unwholesome volitional action by having the animal killed, thus causing it disagreeable mental sensations.

(5) Fifthly, he has committed an unwholesome volitional action by offering the Tathāgata and His disciples meat slaughtered on purpose for a monk."

This being said, Jīvaka Komārabhacca, the adopted son of Abhaya, the king's son, said to the Bhagavā: "It is wonderful; O Gotama, it is wonderful. Just as, O Gotama, one should set upright that which is upside down or lay bare that which is concealed, or tell the way to a man who has lost his way, or hold a lamp in the dark so that those who have eyes might see things; even so, the Dhamma has been revealed to me in many ways by the Venerable Gotama. I take refuge in the Venerable Gotama, in the Dhamma and the Order of monks; may the Venerable Gotama accept me as a lay disciple who has taken refuge from today onward as long as my life lasts."

Here ends the Discourse on Jīvaka the Doctor.

MAJJHIIMA NIKĀYA, UPARIPAṆṆĀSA, ANUPADA-VAGGA, ĀNĀPĀNASSATI SUTTA

Thus, I have heard on one occasion the Bhagavā was staying with many of His distinguished disciples: Sāriputta, Moggallāna, Mahākassapa, Mahākaccāyana, Mahākoṭṭila, Mahākappina, Mahācunda, Anuruddha, Revata, Ānanda, and many other distinguished monks in Pubbārāma, the monastery offered by Visākha.

At that time the senior monks gave instructions on the Dhamma to the junior monks; some gave instructions to ten, some to twenty, some to thirty and some to forty junior monks. When the junior monks heard the instructions given to them by the senior monks, they understood the knowledge pertaining to Tranquillity and Insight, which arose in their minds after they had established themselves in morality.

Then, on the night of the termination of the Vassa, the full moon day, the fifteenth day of the month, the Bhagavā surrounded by many monks sat in the open air. Then the Bhagavā looked round at the monks, who kept silent, and said: "O monks, you are bent on this practice to the Dhamma, you have resolved to perform this practice. You should strive more energetically, so that you may reach the Fruition of Holiness which you have not yet attained, and realize the Fruition of Holiness which you have not yet realized. I shall remain at Sāvatthi till the full moon day of the month of Kattika, the end of the four months in which the water-lily blossoms."

The monks living in the neighbouring rural areas heard that the Bhagavā would remain at Sāvatthi till the full moon day of Kattika and came to Sāvatthi to pay their respects to the Bhagavā. The senior monks gave intensive training to the junior monks. Some gave training to ten, some to twenty, some to thirty, and some to forty junior monks. When the junior monks received training from their teachers, they understood the knowledge pertaining to Tranquillity and Insight which arose in their minds after they had established themselves in morality.

On the night of the full moon day of the month of Kattika, the end of the four months in which the white water-lily blossoms, the Bhagavā surrounded by the monks sat in the open air. Then, looking round at the monks, who kept silent the Bhagavā said: "O monks, this assembly is devoid of pithless stuff; this assembly being devoid of pithless stuff is purified and is full of essence. O monks, all these monks here are of such nature. Such monks are worthy of offerings, worthy of receiving hospitality, worthy of gifts, worthy of being honoured with raised hands, are unsurpassed fields for gaining merit. Presenting small gifts to such an assembly is advantageous; presenting greater gifts to such an assembly is more advantageous. O monks, it is very difficult for people to pay homage adequately to such an assembly.

"O monks, among those present here there are Arahats, who have eradicated all defilements; who have reached perfection; who have laid down their burdens; Who are no longer fettered by any tie to any form of existence; and who have been liberated by their wisdom.

"O monks, among those present here there are Anāgāmins who, having overcome the five lower fetters reappear as spontaneously manifesting beings in the Su'dhāvāsa. Brahma-plane (Abode of Purity) and without returning from that plane will reach Nibbāna.

"O monks, among those present here there are Sakadāgāmins who, having destroyed the three lower fetters, have overcome the fetters of Sensuous Craving and Ill will in their grosser form, and will return only once to this sensuous world.

"O monks, among those present here there are Sotāpannas who, after overcoming the three fetters of Personality-belief, Sceptical Doubt and Attachment to rites and ritual, have entered the stream to Nibbāna, are firmly established and destined to full enlightenment.

"O monks, among those present here there are those who practice the four Applications of Mindfulness;[12] those who practice the four Right Efforts;[13] those who practice the four Roads to Power;[14] those who practice the five Spiritual Faculties;[15] those who practice the five Mental Powers;[16] those who practice the seven Links of Enlightenment,[17]

---

12. Contemplation of Body, of Feeling, of Mind and of Mental Objects.

13. The efforts to avoid unwholesome states as yet unrisen as evil thoughts, etc; to overcome unwholesome states that have arisen; to develop wholesome states as yet unrisen such as the seven Factors of Enlightenment; and to maintain the wholesome states that have arisen.

14. Concentration of Determination, of Energy, of Consciousness and of Investigation.

15. Faith (Confidence in the Buddha and His Teaching), Energy, Mindfulness, Concentration and Wisdom.

16. Faith, Energy, Mindfulness, Concentration and Wisdom.

17. Mindfulness, Investigation of the Dhamma, Energy, Rapture, Tranquillity, Concentration and Equanimity.

and those who practice the Eightfold Noble Path.[18]

"O monks, among those present here there are those who practice *mettābhāvanā* (development of all-embracing loving kindness); those who practice *karuṇā-bhavaṇā* (development of compassion); those who practice *muditābhāvanā* (development of altruistic joy); those who practice *upekkhā bhāvanā* (development of equanimity); those who practice *asubhakammaṭṭhāna* (reflections on the loathsomeness of the body); and those who practice *anicca-saññā* (contemplation of impermanence).

"O monks, among those present here there are those who practice *ānāpānassati* (watching over in-and-out breathing).

"Contemplation of in-and-out breathing, O monks, developed and frequently practiced, brings high reward and advantages. And how so?

"There the monk retires to a forest, to the foot of a tree, or to a solitary place, seats himself cross-legged, body erect, attentiveness fixed before him. Attentively he breathes in, attentively he breathes out.

"While breathing in a long inhalation he knows: 'I breathe in a long inhalation;' while breathing out a long exhalation he knows: 'I breathe out a long exhalation.'

"While breathing in a short inhalation he knows: 'I breathe in a short inhalation;' while breathing out a short exhalation he knows: 'I breathe out a short exhalation.'

"'Being clearly sensible of the whole body[19] I breathe in': thus, he trains himself; 'Being clearly sensible of the whole body I breathe out': thus he trains himself.

"'Calming the bodily activities, I breathe in': thus he trains himself; 'Calming the bodily activities I breathe out': thus he trains himself.

"'Sensible of rapture I breathe in': thus he trains himself; 'Sensible of rapture I breathe out': thus he trains himself.

"'Sensible of joy I breathe in'; thus he trains himself; 'Sensible of joy I breathe out': thus he trains himself.

---

18. Right Understanding, Right Thoughts, Right Speech, Right Action, Right Livelihood, Right Effort, Right Mindfulness and Right Concentration.

These 37 things are the "Bodhipakkhiya-dhammā" (Things pertaining to Enlightenment.) It may be noted that Mindfulness considered in its different aspects, can be a spiritual faculty, a mental power and a link of Enlightenment, and others have both aspects of "Roads to Power" and "Spiritual Faculties".

19. *Sabbakāya* (according to Buddhaghosa's Commentary 'the whole body of the breath')(Editor: others experience 'the whole body' via *bhaṇga-ñāṇa* or dissolution.)

"'Sensible of the mental activities I breathe in': thus he trains himself, 'Sensible of the mental activities I breathe out': thus he trains himself.

"'Calming the mental activities, I breathe in': thus he trains himself; 'Calming the mental activities I breathe out'; thus he trains himself.

"'Being clearly sensible of the mind I breathe in': thus he trains himself; 'Being clearly sensible of the mind I breathe out': thus he trains himself.

"'Composing the mind, I breathe in': thus he trains himself; 'Composing the mind I breathe out': thus he trains himself.

"'Concentrating the mind, I breathe in': thus he trains himself; 'Concentrating the mind I breathe out': thus he trains himself.

"'Freeing the mind, I breathe in': thus he trains himself; 'Freeing the mind I breathe out': thus he trains himself,

"'Reflecting on Impermanence I breathe in': thus he trains himself, 'Reflecting on Impermanence I breathe out': thus he trains himself.

"'Reflecting on Detachment I breathe in': thus he trains himself; 'Reflecting on Detachment I breathe out': thus he trains himself."

ANĀPANASSATI

"'Reflecting on the Extinction of Biases[20] I breathe in': thus he trains himself; 'Reflecting on the extinction of biases I breathe out' thus he trains himself.

"'Reflecting on Renunciation I breathe in'; thus he trains himself; 'Reflecting on renunciation I breathe out': thus he trains himself.

"Thus, O monks, developed and frequently practiced, contemplation of in-and-out breathing brings high reward and great advantage.

"But how, O monks, does the contemplation of in-and-out breathing, developed and frequently practiced, bring the four Applications of Mindfulness to full perfection?

"Whenever the monk is mindful in taking a long breath or in taking a short breath, or is training himself to inhale or exhale whilst being sensible of the body, or is calming down the bodily activities, at such a time the monk is dwelling in 'Contemplation of the Body', full of energy, clearly conscious, attentive, subduing worldly greed and grief. Inhalation and exhalation, indeed, I declare as a phenomenon amongst the phenomena of the body.

"Whenever the monk is training himself to inhale and exhale whilst being sensible of rapture, or joy, or the mental activities, or whilst calming down the

20. The four kinds of Biases are: Sensuous Bias, Bias for Existence, Bias for Wrong Views, and Bias of Ignorance.

mental activities, at such a time he is dwelling in 'Contemplation of Sensation', full of energy, clearly conscious, attentive, after subduing worldly greed, and grief. The sensation experienced in respiration; indeed, I declare as one of the sensations (feelings) amongst the other[21] sensations (feelings) of the mind.

"Whenever the monk is training himself to inhale and exhale whilst being sensible of the mind, or whilst composing the mind, or whilst concentrating the mind, or whilst setting the mind free—at such a time he is dwelling in 'Contemplation of the Mind', full of energy, clearly conscious, attentive, after subduing worldly greed and grief. Without mindfulness and clear comprehension, indeed, there is no attention to in-and-out breathing, I say.

"Whenever the monk is training himself to inhale or exhale whilst Contemplating Impermanence or Detachment or Extinction or Renunciation—at such a time he is dwelling in 'Contemplation of the Mental Objects', full of energy, clearly conscious, attentive after subduing worldly greed and grief.

"Contemplation of in-and-out breathing, thus developed and frequently practiced, brings the four Applications of Mindfulness to full perfection.

"But how do the four Applications of Mindfulness, developed and frequently practiced, bring the seven Links of Enlightenment to full perfection?

"Whenever the monk is dwelling in contemplation of Body, Sensation, Mind and Mental Objects, full of energy, clearly conscious, attentive, after subduing worldly greed and grief, at such a time his mindfulness is undisturbed; and whenever his mindfulness is present and undisturbed, at such a time he has gained and is developing the Link of Enlightenment 'Mindfulness'; and thus, this link of enlightenment reaches full perfection.

"Whenever, whilst dwelling with attentive mind, he wisely investigates, examines and considers the dhamma, at such a time he has gained and is developing the Link of Enlightenment 'Investigation of the Dhamma', and thus this link of enlightenment reaches full perfection.

"Whenever, whilst investigating, examining and considering the dhamma, his energy is firm and unshaken, at such a time he has gained and is developing the Link of Enlightenment 'Energy', and thus, this link of enlightenment reaches full perfection.

"Whenever, in him, whilst firm in energy, arises rapture free from sensuous desires—at such a time he has gained and is developing the Link of Enlightenment 'Rapture', and thus, this link of enlightenment reaches full perfection.

---

21. *Vedanā.*

"Whenever, whilst enraptured in mind, his mind and body become tranquil, at such a time he has gained and is developing the Link of Enlightenment 'Tranquillity', and thus, this link of enlightenment reaches full perfection.

"Whenever, whilst tranquillised in mind and body and happy, his mind becomes concentrated, at such a time he has gained and is developing the Link of Enlightenment 'Concentration', and thus, this link of enlightenment reaches full perfection.

"Whenever he looks on his mind with complete indifference, thus concentrated, at such a time he has gained and is developing the Link of Enlightenment 'Equanimity' and thus this link of enlightenment reaches full perfection.

"The four Applications of Mindfulness thus developed and frequently practiced, bring the seven Links of Enlightenment to full perfection.

"But how do the seven Links of Enlightenment, developed and frequently practiced, bring Wisdom and deliverance to full perfection?

"There the monk develops the links of enlightenment, bent on seclusion, detachment, and extinction of biases, and leading to renunciation.

"The seven Links of Enlightenment, thus developed and frequently practiced, bring wisdom and deliverance to full perfection."

Thus spoke the Bhagavā: being glad those brethren rejoiced at the words of the Bhagavā.

"Just as, brethren, in the autumn season, when the sky is opened up and cleared of clouds, the sun, leaping up into the firmament, drives away all darkness from the heavens, and shines and burns and flashes forth; even so, brethren, the perceiving of impermanence, if practiced and enlarged, wears out all sensual lust, wears out all lust for body, all desire for rebirth, all ignorance, wears out, tears out all conceit of 'I am'.

"And in what way, brethren, does it wear them out?

"It is by seeing: Such is body; such is the arising of body; such is the ceasing of body. Such is feeling, perception, the activities, such is consciousness, its arising and its ceasing.

"Even thus practiced and enlarged, brethren, does the perceiving of impermanence wear out all sensual lust, all lust for body, all desire for rebirth, all ignorance, wears out, tears out all conceit of 'I am'."

—Saṃyutta Nikāya, XXII; Sec. 102

Here ends the Ānāpānassati Sutta.

SAṂYUTTA NIKĀYA

SAMYUTTA NIKĀYA, DUKKHA-VAGGA, NIDĀNA-SUTTA

Discourse on "Dependent Origination"

On one occasion the Bhagavā was staying among the Kurus[1] at Kammāsaddhamma, a township of the Kurus. And the Venerable Ānanda approached Him, paid homage to Him, and sat down at one side. So seated he addressed the Exalted One thus:

"Wonderful, Bhante, marvellous, Bhante, is the depth of this *Paṭiccasamuppāda* (Dependent Origination) and how deep it appears. And yet do I regard it as quite plain to understand."

The Buddha:

"Do not say so, Ānanda, do not say so! Deep indeed is this Dependent Origination and deep it appears to be. It is through not knowing, not understanding, not penetrating that Dhamma, that this world of men has become entangled like a ball of string, and covered with blight, resembles muñja[2] grass and rushes, and unable to escape the doom of *Apāya* (the 4 Lower worlds), *Duggatiṃ* (the 4 Woeful Courses of Existence), *Vinipātaṃ* (the World of Perdition) and *Saṃsāra* (the Round of Rebirths).

"In him, Ānanda, who contemplates the enjoyment of all things that make for Clinging, Craving arises; through Craving, Clinging is conditioned; through Clinging the Process of Becoming is conditioned; through the Process of Becoming, Rebirth is conditioned; through Rebirth are conditioned Old Age and Death, Sorrow, Lamentation, Pain, Grief and Despair. Thus arises the whole mass of suffering again in the future.

"Just as if there were a great tree whose roots go down and across and draw up the nutritive essence. Verily, Ānanda, so great a tree thus nourished, thus supplied with nutriment would stand for a long time.

"Just so, Ānanda, in one who contemplates the enjoyment of all things that make for Clinging, Craving arises; through Craving, Clinging is conditioned; through Clinging, the Process of Becoming is conditioned; through the Process of Becoming, Rebirth is conditioned; through Rebirth are conditioned

1. Kurus were the inhabitants of the country now identified with the neighbourhood of Delhi in India.
2. *Muñjā* is a kind of grass (*Saccharum munja Roxb.*).

Old Age and Death Sorrow, Lamentation, Pain, Grief and Despair. Thus arises the whole mass of suffering again in the future.

"But in him, Ānanda, who dwells contemplating the misery of all things that make for Clinging, Craving ceases; when Craving ceases, Clinging ceases; when Clinging ceases, the Process of Becoming ceases; when the Process of Becoming ceases, Rebirth ceases; when Rebirth ceases, Old Age and Death, Sorrow, Lamentation, Pain, Grief and Despair cease. Thus, the entire mass of Suffering ceases.

"Suppose Ānanda, there were a great tree and a man were to come with an axe and basket, and were to cut down that tree at the root. After cutting it by the root he were to dig a trench and were to pull out the roots even to the rootlets and fibres of them. Then he were to cut the tree into logs, and were then to split the logs, and were then to make the logs into chips. Then he were to dry the chips in wind and sun, then burn them with fire, collect them into a heap of ash, then winnow the ashes in a strong wind, or let them be carried away by the swift stream of a river.

"Surely that great tree thus cut down at the roots, would be made as a palm tree stump become unproductive, become unable to sprout again in the future.

"Just so, Ānanda, in him who dwells contemplating the misery of all things that make for Clinging, Craving ceases; when Craving ceases, Clinging ceases; when Clinging ceases, the Process of Becoming ceases; when the Process of Becoming ceases, Rebirth ceases; when Rebirth ceases, Old Age and Death, Sorrow, Lamentation, Pain, Grief and Despair cease. Thus, the entire mass of suffering ceases."

SAMYUTTA NIKĀYA, NIDHĀNA-VAGGA, ASSUTAVĀ-SUTTA

Sermon on the Untaught

Thus, I have heard. On one occasion the Bhagavā was staying at Jeta's grove in the monastery of Anāthapiṇḍika at Sāvatthi.

The Buddha:

"O monks, even the worldlings who have never heard the Holy Ones may feel disgust with this body which is composed of the Four Great Essentials, may have no craving for it, or may wish to be emancipated from it. Why so? Because they discern the growth and decay of this body which is composed of the Four Great Essentials, its arising and its dissolution. Hence the worldlings who have not heard the Holy Ones may feel disgust with this body which is composed of the Four Great Essentials, may have no craving for it, may wish to be emancipated from it.

"Yet this, O monks, that we call *citta* (state of consciousness), that we call *mano* (mind), that we call *viññāṇa* (consciousness), concerning this the worldlings who have not heard the Holy Ones, are not able to feel disgust, are not able to be detached from it, are not able to be emancipated from it. Why so? For a long time, monks, has it been, for the worldlings who have not heard the Holy Ones, that to which they cling, that which they call 'mine', that which they erroneously view, thinking: this is mine, this I am; this is my *attā* (soul). Hence the worldlings who have not heard the Holy Ones are not able to feel disgust with it, are not able to be detached from it, are not able to be emancipated from it.

"It is better monks; if the worldlings who have not heard the Holy Ones took this body, which is composed of the Four Great Essentials, as the soul rather than the mind. Why so? They discern, monks, how this body which is composed of the Four Great Essentials, persists for a year, persists for two years, persists for three, four, five, ten, twenty, thirty years, persists for forty, for fifty years, persists for a hundred years and even longer. But this, monks, that we call *citta*, that we call *mano* that we call *viññāṇa*, arises as one thing and dissolves as another by day or by night. Just as a monkey, wandering in the woods, through the great forest, catching hold of a bough, releases it seizing another, even that which we call *citta*, *mano*, *viññāṇa*, arises as one thing and dissolves as another.

"Herein, monks, the well-trained Noble disciple thoroughly gives wise consideration to Paṭiccasamuppāda (Dependent Origination): this being, that comes to be; from the arising of this, that arises. This not being, that does not come to be; from the cessation of this, that ceases. That is to say, dependent on ignorance arise formative activities; dependent on formative activities arises consciousness; dependent on consciousness arise mind and matter; dependent on mind and matter arise the six bases; dependent on the six bases arises contact; dependent on contact arises sensation; dependent on sensation arises craving; dependent on craving arises attachment; dependent on attachment arises process of becoming; dependent on process of becoming arises rebirth; dependent on rebirth arise old age and death, sorrow lamentation, pain, grief and despair. Thus, the entire mass of suffering arises. When ignorance completely fades away and ceases formative activities cease; when formative activities cease, consciousness ceases; when consciousness ceases, mind and matter cease; when mind and matter cease the six bases cease; when the six bases cease, contact ceases; when contact ceases, sensation ceases; when sensation ceases, craving ceases; when craving ceases, attachment ceases; when attachment ceases, process of becoming ceases; when process of becoming ceases, rebirth ceases; when rebirth ceases, old age and death, sorrow, lamentation, pain, grief and despair cease. Thus, the entire mass of suffering ceases.

"Thus realising, monks, the well-trained noble disciple becomes disgusted with the corporeality-group, the sensation-group, the perception-group, the group of mental formations and the consciousness-group. Being disgusted with them he has no craving for them, he is detached from them and the knowledge that he has attained freedom that arises in his mind-continuum. And he knows that rebirth is extinguished, the holy life accomplished, done that which was to be done, there is no more arising again to be subject to these conditions."

NIDĀNASAṂYUTTA, (7) MAHĀVAGGA, (10) SUSIMAPARIBBĀJAKA SUTTA

Discourse on the Wandering Ascetic Susima

Thus, I have heard. At one time the Buddha was residing at Rājagaha in the Bamboo grove in Kalaṇḍaka Nivāpa. Now at that time the Buddha was honoured, revered, esteemed, worshipped and respected by the multitude. He was the recipient of all requisites such as robes, food, lodging and medicine. But the wandering ascetics who belonged to other groups were neither honoured, revered, esteemed, worshipped nor respected by the people. They received no requisites of robes, food, lodging and medicine.

Now, Susima, a wandering ascetic, was living in Rājagaha together with his many companions, and his friends said to him: "Come friend, Susima. Live the holy life under the monk Gotama, learn the Teachings thoroughly and teach us. Having mastered those Teachings, we will recite them to the laymen. In this way, we also will be honoured, revered, esteemed, worshipped and respected by them. We will also plentifully receive requisites of robes, food, lodgings and medicines." "That is well, friends," replied Susima and approached to where the Venerable Ānanda was. Having approached he exchanged greetings and compliments of friendship and courtesy, sat at one side and said to the Venerable Ānanda: "O friend Ānanda, I wish to live the holy life in this Teaching and discipline."

Then the Venerable Ānanda brought Susima to the Buddha. Having approached, he paid homage to the Buddha, sat at one side and said: "Revered Sir, this wandering ascetic, Susima has said: 'O friend Ānanda, I wish to live the holy life in this teaching and Discipline.'" "Well then, Ānanda, you ordain him." Thus, the wandering ascetic Susima received the initiation and full ordination in the presence of the Buddha.

At that time many monks had declared their attainment of Arahatship in the presence of the Buddha in this way: "Rebirth is destroyed. We have lived the holy life and performed those duties that ought to be done. We realize that there is no more birth for us after this life."

The monk Susima heard about this, approached them and greeted them. Having exchanged greetings and compliments of friendship and courtesy, he sat at one side and asked: "Revered Sirs, is it true that you have declared the attainment of Arahatship in the presence of the Buddha in this way: 'Rebirth is destroyed. We have lived the holy life and performed those duties that ought to be done. We realize that there is no more birth for us after this birth.'?" "Yes friend," replied the monks.

"Revered Sirs, having seen and having realized thus, do you enjoy various supernormal powers? Do you become many from being one? Having become many, do you become one again? Do you become visible or invisible at will? Without being obstructed, do you pass through walls and mountains just as if through the air? Do you walk on water without sinking, just as if on the earth? Do you dive into the earth and rise up again, just as if in the water? Do you float cross-legged through the air, just as a winged bird? Do you touch with hands, the sun and the moon, though they are of great power? Are you able to transport your body even up to the Brahmā plane?"

"No, friend."

"Having realized and having seen thus, do you hear the sound of both men and devas, whether far or near, through the divine ear which is pure and surpassing that of human beings?"

"No, friend."

"Having realized and having seen thus, do you know the minds of other beings of other persons, penetrating them with your own mind? Do you know the lustful mind as lustful and the passionless one as passionless, the hostile mind as hostile and the friendly mind as friendly, the dull mind as dull and the alert mind as alert, the contracted mind as contracted and the scattered mind as scattered, the developed mind as developed and the undeveloped mind as undeveloped, the inferior mind as inferior and the superior mind as superior, the concentrated mind as concentrated and the wavering mind as wavering, the freed mind as freed and the unfreed mind as unfreed?"

"No, friend."

"Having realized and having seen thus, do you remember various former births, such as one birth, two, three, four, ten, twenty, thirty, forty, fifty, a hundred, a thousand, ten thousand, or a hundred-thousand births, many formations and dissolutions of world cycles? There, such a name l had, such food I ate, such pleasures I enjoyed, and such a life span I had; passing away from there, I was reborn in such a place. There, such a name I had, such a clan I belonged to, such a complexion I had, such food I ate, such pleasures I enjoyed, and such a life span I had; passing away from there, I reappeared here again. Thus, together with the marks and peculiarities, do you remember many a former existence?"

"No, friend."

"Sirs, having realized and having seen thus, do you, with supernormal knowledge, surpassing that of men, see beings vanishing and reappearing, low and noble ones, beautiful and ugly ones, happy and unhappy ones, see how beings are reappearing according to their deeds; these beings indeed followed evil ways in bodily actions, words and thoughts, insulted the noble ones, held wrong views and according to their wrong views they acted. At the dissolution of their bodies after death they appeared in lower worlds, in painful states of existence, in the world of perdition, in hell. Some other beings had performed good actions, bodily, verbal and mental, did not insult the noble ones, held right views, and according to their right views they acted. At the dissolution of their bodies after death they appeared in happy states of existence; thus, do you see, with supernormal knowledge surpassing that of men, beings vanishing and reappearing, low and noble ones, beautiful and ugly ones, happy and unhappy ones, do you see beings reappearing according to their deeds?"

"No, friend."

"Sirs, having realized and having seen thus, do you live enjoying the peaceful *Arūpa Jhānas*[3] which surpass those of the sphere of Form (*Rūpa*) and are free from defilements?"

"No, friend."

"Revered Sirs, now, in this case, this is your answer and your non-attainment in this doctrine. How shall I take this, friends?"

"O Susima, we gained freedom through insight wisdom (*paññāvimuttā*)."

"I cannot understand, in full the venerable one's brief statement. It would be well if the venerable ones would explain so that I may understand it in detail."

"O Susima, whether you understand it or not, we gained freedom through Insight wisdom."

Then the monk Susima got up from his seat, approached the Buddha, paid respects to him and sat at one side. Having sat down, he told all about the conversation with those monks. "Susima, Insight Knowledge (*Dhammaṭṭhiti ñāṇa*) comes first, after this comes the Path Knowledge (*Nibbāna ñāṇa*)," said the Buddha.

"Sir, I cannot understand the meaning in detail of the brief statement of the Buddha. It would be well, Sir, if the Buddha would explain the brief statement so that I may understand its meaning in detail."

3. Jhānas of immaterial states.

"Susima, whether you understand it or not, Insight Knowledge (*Dhammaṭṭhiti ñāṇa*) arises first and then comes the Path Knowledge (*Nibbāna ñāṇa*)."

"O Susima, what do you think of this? Is the form permanent or impermanent?" "Impermanent, Sir." "Is that which is impermanent, painful or pleasant?" "Painful, Sir."

"Is it proper to regard that which is impermanent, painful and subject to change, as 'This is mine; this is I; this belongs to myself.'?" "It is not proper, Sir."

"Is feeling (*vedanā*) permanent or impermanent?" "Impermanent, Sir." "Is that which is impermanent, painful or pleasant?" "Painful, Sir." "Is it proper to regard that which is impermanent, painful and subject to change, as 'This is mine; this is I; this belongs to myself.'?" "It is not proper, Sir."

"Is perception (*saññā*) permanent or impermanent?" "Impermanent, Sir." "Is that which is impermanent, painful or pleasant?" "Painful, sir." "Is it proper to regard that which is impermanent, painful and subject to change, as 'This is mine; this is I; this belongs to myself.'?" "It is not proper, Sir."

"Is mental formation (*saṅkhāra*) permanent or impermanent?" "Impermanent, Sir." "Is that which is impermanent, painful or pleasant?" "Painful Sir." "Is it proper to regard that which is impermanent, painful and subject to change, as 'This is mine; this is I; this belongs to myself.'?" "It is not proper, Sir."

"Is consciousness (*viññāṇa*) permanent or impermanent?" "Impermanent, Sir." "Is that which is impermanent, painful or pleasant?" "Painful, Sir." "Is it proper to regard that which is impermanent, painful and subject to change, as 'This is mine; this is I; this belongs to myself.'?" "It is not proper, Sir."

"Therefore, Susima, whatsoever form which has been, will be and is now, belonging to oneself, to others, or gross or subtle, inferior or superior, far or near, all forms should be considered by right knowledge in this way, 'This is not mine, this is not I, this does not belong to myself.'"

"Whatever feeling, which has been, will be and is now, belonging to oneself, to others or gross or subtle; inferior or superior, far or near, all forms should be considered by right knowledge, in this way, 'This is not mine, this is not I, this does not belong to myself.'"

"Whatever perception, which has been, will be and is now, belonging to oneself, to others, or gross or subtle, inferior or superior, far or near, all forms should be considered by right knowledge in this way, 'This is not mine; this is not I; this does not belong to myself.'"

"Whatever mental formations, which have been, will be and are now, belonging to oneself, to others, or gross or subtle, inferior or superior, far or near, all forms should be considered by right knowledge in this way, 'This is not mine, this is not l, this does not belong to myself.'"

"Whatever consciousness, which has been, will be and is now, belonging to oneself, to others, or gross or subtle, inferior or superior, far or near, all forms should be considered by right knowledge in this way, 'This is not mine, this is not I, this does not belong to myself.'"

"Having seen thus, Susima, learned, noble disciple becomes disgusted with the form, feeling, perception, mental formations and consciousness. Becoming disgusted, he discards the passions. Being free from passions, he becomes emancipated and insight arises in him, 'I am emancipated.' He realizes, 'Birth is destroyed, I have lived the holy life and fulfilled the duties that ought to be done. There is no more birth for me after this life.'"

"O Susima, do you realize that due to Rebirth (*Jāti*), Decay and Death (*Jarā maraṇa*) arise?" "Yes, Sir."

"Do you realize that due to the process of Becoming (*Bhava*), Rebirth arises?" "Yes, Sir."

"Do you realize that due to Grasping (*Upādāna*), the Process of Becoming arises?" "Yes, Sir."

"Do you realize that due to Craving (*Taṇhā*) Grasping arises?" "Yes, Sir."

"Do you realize that due to Feeling (*Vedanā*) Craving arises?" "Yes, Sir."

"Do you realize that due to Impression (*Phassa*), Feeling arises?" "Yes, Sir."

"Do you realize that due to the Six Sense Bases (*Saḷāyatana*), Impression arises?" "Yes, Sir."

"Do you realize that due to Name and Form (*Nāma rūpa*), the Six Sense Bases arise?" "Yes, Sir."

"Do you realize that due to Consciousness (*Viññāṇa*), Name and Form arise?" "Yes, Sir."

"Do realize that due to Mental Formations you (*Sankhāra*), Consciousness arises?" "Yes, Sir."

"Do you realize that due to Ignorance, (*Avijjā*), Mental Formations arise?" "Yes, Sir."

"O Susima, do you realize that when Rebirth ceases, Decay and Death cease?" "Yes, Sir."

"Do you realize that when the Process of Becoming ceases, Rebirth, ceases?" "Yes, Sir."

"Do you realize that when Grasping ceases, the Process of Becoming ceases?" "Yes, Sir."

"Do you realize that when Craving ceases, Grasping ceases?" "Yes, Sir."

"Do you realize that when Feeling ceases, Craving ceases?" "Yes, Sir."

"Do you realize that when lmpression ceases, Feeling ceases?" "Yes Sir."

"Do you realize that when the Six Sense Bases cease, Impression ceases?" "Yes, Sir."

"Do you realize that when Name and Form cease, the Six Sense Bases cease?" "Yes, Sir."

"Do you realize that when Consciousness ceases, Name and Form cease?" "Yes, Sir."

"Do you realize that when Mental Formations cease, Consciousness ceases?" "Yes, Sir."

"Do you realize that when Ignorance ceases, Mental Formations cease?" "Yes, Sir."

"O Susima, having realized thus and having seen thus, do you also enjoy various supernormal powers? Do you become many from being one? Having become many, do you become one again? Do you become visible or invisible at will? Without being obstructed do you pass through walls and mountains, just as if through the air? Do you walk on water without sinking, just as if on the earth? Do you dive into the earth and rise up again, just as if in the water? Do you float cross-legged through the air, just as a winged bird? Do you touch with hands the sun and the moon, though they are of great power? Do you have mastery over your body even up to the *Brahmā* plane?"

"No, Sir."

"Susima, having realized and having seen thus; do you hear the sound of both men and devas, whether far or near, through the divine ear which is pure and surpassing that of human beings?"

"No, Sir."

"Susima, having realized and having seen thus, do you know the minds of other beings, of other persons, by penetrating them with your own mind? Do you know the lustful mind as lustful and the passionless mind as passionless, the hostile mind as hostile and the friendly mind as friendly, the dull mind as dull and the alert mind as alert, the contracted mind as contracted and the scattered mind as scattered, the developed mind as developed and the undeveloped mind as undeveloped, the inferior mind as inferior and the superior mind as superior, the concentrated mind as concentrated and the wavering mind as wavering, the freed mind as freed and the unfreed mind as unfreed?"

"No, Sir."

"Susima, having realized and having seen thus, do you remember various former births, such as one birth, two, three, four, ten, twenty, thirty, forty, fifty, a hundred, a thousand, ten-thousand, or a hundred thousand births, many formations and dissolutions of world cycles? There such a name I had, such a clan I belonged to, such complexion I had, such food I ate, such pleasures I enjoyed, and such a life span I had; passing away from there, I was reborn in such a place. There such a name I had, such a clan I belonged to, such a complexion I had, such food I ate, such pleasures I enjoyed, and such a life span I had. Passing away from there, I reappeared here again. Thus, together with the marks and peculiarities do you remember many a former existence?"

"No, Sir."

"Susima, having realized and having seen thus, do you, with supernormal knowledge; surpassing that of men, see beings vanishing and reappearing, low and noble ones, beautiful and ugly ones, happy and unhappy ones; see how beings are reappearing according to their deeds; these beings indeed followed evil ways in bodily actions, words and thoughts, insulted the noble ones, held wrong views and according to their wrong views they acted. At the dissolution of their bodies after death they appeared in the lower worlds, in painful states of existence, in the world of perdition, in hell. Some other beings had performed good actions, bodily, verbal and mental, did not insult the noble ones, held right views and according to their right views they acted. At the dissolution of their bodies after death, they appeared in the happy states of existence; thus, do you see, with supernormal knowledge surpassing that of men, beings vanishing and reappearing, low and noble ones, beautiful and ugly ones, happy and unhappy ones. Do you see beings reappearing according ones to their deeds?"

"No, Sir."

"Susima, having realized and having seen thus, do you live enjoying the peaceful *Arūpa Jhānas*, which surpass those of the sphere of Form (*Rūpa*) and are free from defilements?"

"No, Sir."

"Now, Susima, in this case, this is your answer and your non-attainment in this doctrine. How shall I take that, Susima?"

Then the monk Susima fell with his head at the foot of the Buddha and said: "Revered Sir, as I am foolish, muddle-headed and ignorant, I have committed an offence. I have entered the Order under the well expounded Doctrine and Discipline (Dhamma Vinaya) as a thief. May the Revered One accept my confession of this act as a sin to the end that in future I may restrain myself."

"O Susima, you have committed an offense due to foolishness, muddle-headedness and ignorance. You entered the Order under the well expounded Doctrine and Discipline as a thief in this way. Susima, if one should catch a thief, a wicked one, and show him before the king saying, 'Lord, this is a wicked thief. May you impose punishment on him according to your wishes,' and the king should say, 'Go tie his hands at the back firmly with strong ropes, shave his head closely and playing the drum with a harsh sound, take him from carriage-road to carriage-road, from cross-road to cross-road; and going out by the southern gate cut off his head at the southern part outside the city.' The king's men would tie that man's hands at the back tightly with strong ropes, shave his head close, and playing the drum with a harsh sound take him from carriage-road to carriage-road, from cross-road to cross-road; and going out by the southern gate, cut off his head at the southern part outside the city. What do you think Susima, will that thief, in this case, suffer physical and mental painful feelings?" "Yes Sir, he will suffer."

"O Susima, that man, on account of his evil deed, will suffer such physical and mental painful feelings. Entering into the Order as a thief under the true Doctrine and Discipline bears more painful and more bitter resultant effects than that of stealing.

"But, O Susima, in as much as you understand it to be a sin and make amends, by confessing it as such, according to what is right, your confession thereof is accepted. For, O Susima, whosoever looks upon his wrong doing as a wrong doing makes amends by confessing it as such and abstains, from it in future will progress according to the Rules."

* * *

UPĀDĀNAPARIPAVATTANA SUTTA[4]

Discourse on What the Clinging Turns On

This Sutta was delivered at Sāvatthi.

(Then the Exalted One said:)

"Bhikkhus, there are five *upādānakkhandhas*[5] (constituent groups of existence which are the objects of Clinging). Which five? They are: (1) corporeality-group, (2) feeling-group. (3) perception-group, (4) mental-formations group, (5) consciousness-group.

"So long, Bhikkhus, as I did not understand fully, as they really are, these five groups of existence which are the objects of Clinging in four phases, so long I did not profess to have attained Incomparable Supreme Enlightenment in this world with the *devas*, the *Māras*, the *Brahmās*, amongst the hosts of *samaṇas* and *brāhmaṇas*, of *devas* and mankind.

"But, Bhikkhus, since I understood fully, as they really are, these five groups of existence which are the objects of Clinging in four phases,—then, Bhikkhus, I declared that I have attained Incomparable Supreme Enlightenment to the world, with the *devas*, the *Māras*, the *Brahmās*, amongst the hosts of *samaṇas* and *brāhmaṇas*, of *devas* and mankind.

"And how in these four phases?[6]

"I penetratingly understood corporeality; I penetratingly understood the origin of corporeality; I penetratingly understood the cessation of corporeality; I penetratingly understood the practice leading to the cessation of corporeality.

"I penetratingly understood feeling; I penetratingly understood the origin of feeling; I penetratingly understood the cessation of feeling; I penetratingly understood the practice leading to the cessation of feeling.

---

4. Saṃyutta Nikāya, Khandhavagga Saṃyutta Pāḷi, 1. Khandha Saṃyutta. (6) 1. Upayavagga, 4 Upādānaparipavattana Sutta, p. 48, 6th Syn. Edn.

5. The five constituent groups of existence, namely, corporeality-group, feeling-group, perception-group, mental-formations group and consciousness group, are called *khandhā*. As the mundane groups of existence are the objects of Clinging, they are called *Upādānakhandhā*.

6. This is called *Sacca-ñāṇa* (Knowledge of the Truth) of the Four Noble Truths.

"I penetratingly understood perception; I penetratingly understood the origin of perception; I penetratingly understood the cessation of perception; I penetratingly understood the practice leading to the cessation of perception.

"I penetratingly understood mental-formations; penetratingly understood the origin of mental-formations; I penetratingly under stood the cessation of mental-formations; | penetratingly understood the practice leading to the cessation of mental-formations.

"I penetratingly understood consciousness; I penetratingly understood the origin of consciousness; I penetratingly understood the cessation of consciousness; I penetratingly understood the practice leading to the cessation of consciousness.

I. "And what, Bhikkhus, is corporeality?

"It is the Four Great Primaries and those elements which are dependent on these Four Great Primaries. This, Bhikkhus, is called corporeality.

"Due to the arising of food accompanied by Craving therefore, corporeality arises; and when food ceases corporeality ceases. And the practice leading to the cessation of corporeality is this Noble Eightfold Path, namely, Right Understanding, Right Thinking, Right Speech, Right Action, Right Livelihood, Right Effort, Right Mindfulness, Right Concentration.

"Bhikkhus, those *samaṇas* and *brāhmaṇas*, by thus penetratingly understanding corporeality, the origin of corporeality, the cessation of corporeality, and the practice leading to the cessation of corporeality, practice for getting disgusted with corporeality, for detachment therefrom and the complete cessation thereof, are those who rightly practice; and those who rightly practice have a firm footing in this Dhamma Vinaya (Sāsana).

"Bhikkhus, those *samaṇas* and *brāhmaṇas* who, by their penetratingly understanding corporeality, the origin of corporeality, the cessation of corporeality and the practice leading to the cessation of corporeality, through disgust with corporeality, through detachment therefrom and the complete cessation thereof, are detached and liberated from defilements, are those who are well, liberated; and those who are well liberated are *kevalino* (those who have done all that ought to be done in this Sāsana). For them there is no more wandering in the round of rebirths.

II. "And what, Bhikkhus, is feeling?

"Bhikkhus, there are six kinds of feeling. They are:

(1) *Cakkhu-saṃphassajā-vedanā* (Feeling arising from eye-contact),

(2) *Sota-saṃphassajā-vedanā* (Feeling arising from ear-contact),

(3) *Ghāṇa-saṃphassajā-vedanā* (Feeling arising from nose-contact),

(4) *Jivhā-samphassajā-vedanā* (Feeling arising from tongue-contact),
(5) *Kāya-samphassaja-vedanā* (Feeling arising from body-contact),
(6) *Mano-samphassajā-vedanā* (Feeling arising from mind-contact).

These are called feelings.

"Bhikkhus, due to the arising of contact, feeling arises; and when contact ceases, feeling ceases. And the practice leading to the cessation of feeling is this Noble Eightfold Path, namely, Right Understanding, Right Thinking, Right Speech, Right Action, Right Livelihood, Right Effort, Right Mindfulness, Right Concentration.

"Bhikkhus, those *samaṇas* and *brāhmaṇas*, by thus penetratingly understanding, feeling, the origin of feeling, the cessation of feeling, and the practice leading to the cessation of feeling practice for getting disgusted with feeling, for detachment therefrom and the complete cessation thereof, are those who rightly practice; and those who rightly practice have a firm footing in this Dhamma Vinaya (Sāsana).

"Bhikkhus, those *samaṇas* and *brāhmaṇas* who, by their penetratingly understanding feeling, the origin of feeling, the cessation of feeling and the practice leading to the cessation of feeling, through disgust with feeling, through detachment therefrom and the complete cessation thereof, are detached and liberated from defilements, are those who are well liberated, and those who are well liberated are *kevalino* (those who have done all that ought to be done in this Sāsana). For them there is no more wandering in the round of rebirths.

III. "And what, Bhikkhus, is perception?

"Bhikkhus, there are six kinds of perception. They are:

(1) *Rūpa-saññā* (Perception having visible things as its objects),
(2) *Sadda-saññā* (Perception having sounds as its objects),
(3) *Gandha-saññā* (Perception having smells as its objects),
(4) *Rasa-saññā* (Perception having tastes as its objects),
(5) *Phoṭṭhabba-saññā* (Perception having physical contacts as its objects),
(6) *Dhamma-saññā* (Perception having mental as its objects).

These are called perception.

"Bhikkhus, owing to the arising of contact, perception arises, and when contact ceases, perception ceases. And the practice leading to the cessation of perception is this Noble Eightfold Path, namely, Right Understanding, Right Thinking, Right Speech, Right Action, Right Livelihood, Right Effort, Right Mindfulness, Right Concentration.

"Bhikkhus, those *samaṇas* and *brāhmaṇas*, by thus penetratingly understanding perception, the origin of perception, the cessation of perception, and the practice leading: to the cessation of perception, practice for getting disgusted with perception, for detachment therefrom and the complete cessation thereof, are those who rightly practice; and those who rightly practice have a firm footing in this Dhamma Vinaya (Sāsana).

"Bhikkhus, those *samaṇas* and *brāhmaṇas*, who, by their penetratingly understand perception, the origin of perception and the practice leading to the cessation of perception, through disgust' with perception, through detachment therefrom and the complete cessation thereof, are detached and liberated from defilements, are those who are well liberated; and those who are well liberated are *kevalino* (those who have done all that ought to be done in this Sāsana). For them there is no more wandering in the round of rebirths.

IV. "And what, Bhikkhus, are mental formations?

"Bhikkhus, there are six kinds of volitions. They are:

(1) *Rūpasañcetanā* (Volition having visible things as its objects),

(2) *Saddasañcetanā* (volition having sounds as its objects),

(3) *Gandhasañcetanā* (Volition having smells as its objects),

(4) *Rasasañcetanā* (Volition having tastes as its objects),

(5) *Phoṭṭhabbasañcetanā* (Volition having physical contacts as its objects),

(6) *Dhammasañcetanā* (Volition having mental states as its objects).

These are called *saṅkhārā* (mental-formation).*

"Bhikkhus, owing to the arising of contact, mental-formations arise; and when contact ceases, mental-formations cease. And the practice leading to the cessation of mental formations is this Noble Eightfold Path, namely, Right Understanding, Right Thinking, Right Speech, Right Action, Right Livelihood, Right Effort, Right Mindfulness, Right Concentration.

"Bhikkhus, those *samaṇas* and *brāhmaṇas*, by thus penetratingly understanding mental formations, the origin of mental-formations, the cessation of mental-formations and the practice leading to the cessation of mental formations, practice for getting disgusted with mental-formations, for detachment therefrom and the complete cessation thereof, are those who rightly practice; and those who rightly practice have a firm footing in this Dhamma Vinaya (Sāsana).

"Bhikkhus, those *samaṇas* and *brāhmaṇas* who, by their penetratingly understanding mental-formations, the origin of mental formations, the cessation of mental-formations, and the practice leading to the cessation of mental-formations, through disgust with mental-formations, through detachment therefrom and the complete cessation thereof, are detached and liberated from defilements, are those who are well liberated, and those who are well liberated are *kevalino* (those who have done all that ought to be done in this Sāsana). For them there is no more wandering in the round of rebirths.

V. "And what, Bhikkhus, is consciousness?

"Bhikkhus, there are six kinds of consciousness. They are:

(1) *Cakkhu-viññāṇaṃ* (Eye-consciousness),

(2) *Sota-viññāṇaṃ* (Ear-consciousness),

(3) *Ghāṇa-viññāṇaṃ* (Nose-consciousness),

(4) *Jivhā-viññāṇaṃ* (Tongue-consciousness),

(5) *Kāya-viññāṇaṃ* (Body-consciousness),

(6) *Mano-viññāṇaṃ* (Mind-consciousness).

These are called consciousness.

"Bhikkhus, owing to the arising of mind and body, consciousness arises; and when mind and body cease, consciousness ceases. And the practice leading to the cessation of consciousness is this Noble Eightfold Path, namely, Right Understanding, Right Thinking, Right Speech, Right Action, Right Livelihood, Right Effort, Right Mindfulness, Right Concentration.

"Bhikkhus, those *samaṇas* and *brāhmaṇas*, by thus penetratingly understanding consciousness, the origin of consciousness, the cessation of consciousness, and the practice leading to the cessation of consciousness, practice for getting disgusted with consciousness, for detachment therefrom and the complete cessation thereof, are those who rightly practice; and those who rightly practice have a firm footing in this Dhamma Vinaya (Sāsana).

"Bhikkhus, those *samaṇas* and *brāhmaṇas* who, by their penetratingly understanding consciousness, the origin of consciousness, the cessation of consciousness, and the practice leading to the cessation of consciousness, through disgust with consciousness, through detachment therefrom and the complete cessation thereof, are detached and liberated from defilements, are those who are well liberated; and those who are well liberated are *kevalino* (those who have done all that ought to be done in this Sāsana). For them there is no more wandering in the round of rebirths."

* * *

SATTAṬṬHĀNA SUTTA[7]

Discourse on the Seven Aspects

This Sutta was delivered at Sāvatthi.

Then the Exalted One said:

"Bhikkhus, a Bhikkhu who is skilful in the seven aspects, and who contemplates (phenomena) in three ways, is called *kevalino* (one who has done all that ought to be done in this Sāsana), *vusitavā* (one who has lived the Holy life), and *uttamapuriso* (one who is the noblest personage).

"And how, Bhikkhus, is a Bhikkhu skilful in the seven spheres?

"In this Sāsana, Bhikkhus, a Bhikkhu fully understands corporeality, the origin of corporeality, the cessation of corporeality, the practice leading to the cessation of corporeality, He fully understands the pleasantness that is in corporeality, the fault that is in corporeality, the deliverance from corporeality.

"In this world, Bhikkhus, a Bhikkhu fully understands feeling, the origin of feeling, the cessation of feeling and the practice leading to the cessation of feeling. He fully understands the pleasantness that is in feeling, the fault that is in feeling, the deliverance from feeling.

"In this world, Bhikkhus, a Bhikkhu fully understands perception, the origin of perception, the cessation of perception and the practice leading to the cessation of perception. He fully understands the pleasantness that is in perception, the fault that is in perception, the deliverance from perception.

"In this world, Bhikkhus, a Bhikkhu fully understands mental formations, the origin of mental formations, the cessation of mental formations and the practice leading to the cessation of mental formations. He fully understands the pleasantness that is in mental formations, the fault that is in mental formations, the deliverance from mental formations.

"In this world, Bhikkhus, a Bhikkhu fully understands consciousness, the origin of consciousness, the cessation of consciousness the practice leading to the cessation of consciousness. He fully understands the pleasantness that is in consciousness, the fault that is in consciousness, the deliverance from consciousness.

---

7. Saṃyutta Nikāya, Khandhavagga Saṃyutta Pāḷi, 1. Khandha Saṃyutta. (6) 1. Upayavagga, 5 Sattaṭṭhāna Sutta, p. 50, 6th Syn. Edn.

"And what, Bhikkhus, is corporeality?

"It is the Four Great Primaries and those elements which are dependent on these Four Great Primaries. This, Bhikkhus, is to be called corporeality.'

"Bhikkhus, due to the arising of food, corporeality arises; and when food ceases, corporeality ceases. And the practice leading to the cessation of corporeality is the Noble Eightfold Path, namely, Right Understanding, Right Thinking, Right Speech, Right Action, Right Livelihood, Right Effort, Right Mindfulness, Right Concentration. The comfort and pleasure which arise on account of corporeality is called the pleasantness that is in corporeality. In so far as corporeality is impermanent, is fraught with suffering, and changing, that is the fault that is in corporeality. The abolishing and giving up of the desire and lust (*chanda raga*) for corporeality is called the deliverance from corporeality.

"Bhikkhus, those *samaṇas* and *brāhmaṇas*, by thus penetratingly understanding corporeality, the origin of corporeality, the cessation of corporeality, the practice leading to the cessation of corporeality, the pleasantness, the fault and the way of deliverance from corporeality, practice for getting disgusted with corporeality, for detachment therefrom and the complete cessation thereof, are those who rightly practice; and those who rightly practice have a firm footing in this Dhamma Vinaya (Sāsana).

"Bhikkhus, those *samaṇas* and *brāhmaṇas*, by their penetratingly understanding corporeality, the origin of corporeality, the cessation of corporeality, the practice leading to the cessation of corporeality, the pleasantness, the fault and the way of deliverance from corporeality, through disgust with corporeality, through detachment therefrom and the complete cessation thereof are detached and liberated from defilements, are those who are well liberated; and those who are well liberated are *kevalino* (those who have done all that ought to be done in this Sāsana). For them there is no more wandering in the round of rebirths.

"And what, Bhikkhus, is feeling?

"Bhikkhus, there are six kinds of feeling. They are: (1) *Cakkhu-saṃphassajā-vedanā* (Feeling arising from eye-contact), (2) *Sota-saṃphassajā-vedanā* (Feeling arising from ear-contact), (3) *Ghāṇa-saṃphassajā-vedanā* (Feeling arising from nose-contact), (4) *Jivhā-saṃphassajā-vedanā* (Feeling arising from tongue-contact), (5) *Kāya-saṃphassaja-vedanā* (Feeling arising from body-contact), (6) *Mano-saṃphassajā-vedanā* (Feeling arising from mind-contact). These are called feelings. Owing to the arising of contact feeling arises; and when contact ceases, feeling ceases. And the practice leading to the cessation of feeling is the Noble Eightfold Path namely, Right Understanding, Right Thinking, Right Speech, Right Action, Right Livelihood, Right Effort, Right Mindfulness, Right Concentration.

"Bhikkhus, those *samaṇas* and *brāhmaṇas*, by thus penetratingly understanding feeling, the origin of feeling, the cessation of feeling, the practice leading to the cessation of feeling, the pleasantness, the fault and the way of deliverance from feeling, practice for getting disgusted with feeling, for detachment therefrom and the complete cessation thereof, are those who rightly practice; and those who rightly practice have a firm footing in this Dhamma Vinaya (Sāsana).

"Bhikkhus, those *samaṇas* and *brāhmaṇas*, by thus penetratingly understanding feeling, the origin of feeling, the cessation of feeling the practice leading to the cessation of feeling the pleasantness, the fault and the way of deliverance from feeling, through disgust with feeling, through detachment therefrom and the complete cessation thereof, are detached, and liberated from defilements, are those who are well liberated; and those who are well liberated are *kevalino* (those who have done all that ought to be done in this Sāsana). For them there is no more wandering in the round of rebirths.

"And what, Bhikkhus, is perception?

"Bhikkhus, there are six kinds of perception. They are: (1) *Rūpa-saññā* (Perception having visible things as its objects), (2) *Sadda-saññā* (Perception having sounds as its objects), (3) *Gandha-saññā* (Perception having smells as its objects), (4) *Rasa-saññā* (Perception having tastes as its objects), (5) *Phoṭṭhabba-saññā* (Perception having physical contacts as its objects). (6) *Dhamma-saññā* (Perception having mental as its objects). These are called perception.

"Bhikkhus, owing to the arising of contact, perception arises, and when contact ceases, perception ceases. And the practice leading to the cessation of perception is this Noble Eightfold Path, namely, Right Understanding, Right Thinking, Right Speech, Right Action, Right Livelihood, Right Effort, Right Mind fulness, Right Concentration.

"Bhikkhus, those *samaṇas* and *brāhmaṇas*, by thus penetratingly understanding perception, the origin of perception, the cessation of perception, the practice leading to the cessation of perception, the pleasantness, the fault and the way of deliverance from perception, practice for getting disgusted with perception, for detachment therefrom and the complete cessation thereof, are those who rightly practice; and those who rightly practice have a firm footing in this Dhamma Vinaya (Sāsana).

"Bhikkhus, those *samaṇas* and *brāhmaṇas*, by thus penetratingly understanding perception, the origin of perception, the cessation of perception, the practice leading to the cessation of perception, the pleasantness, the fault and the way of deliverance from perception, through disgust with perception, through detachment therefrom and the complete cessation thereof, are detached, and liberated from defilements, are those who are well liberated; and those who are well liberated are *kevalino* (those who have done all that ought to be done in this Sāsana). For them there is no more wandering in the round of rebirths.

"And what, Bhikkhus, are mental formations?

"Bhikkhus, there are six kinds of volition.[8] They are: (1) *Rūpasañcetanā* (Volition having visible things as its objects), (2) *Saddasañcetanā* (volition having sounds as its objects), (3) *Gandhasañcetanā* (Volition having smells as its objects), (4) *Rasasañcetanā* (Volition having tastes as its objects), (5) *Phoṭṭhabbasañcetanā* (Volition having physical contacts as its objects). (6) *Dhammasañcetanā* (Volition having mental states as its objects).

"Bhikkhus, owing to the arising of contact, mental-formations arise; and when contact ceases, mental-formations cease. And the practice leading to the cessation of mental formations is this Noble Eightfold Path, namely, Right Understanding, Right Thinking, Right Speech, Right Action, Right Livelihood, Right Effort, Right Mindfulness, Right Concentration.

"Bhikkhus, those *samaṇas* and *brāhmaṇas*, by thus penetratingly understanding mental formations, the origin of mental-formations, the cessation of mental-formations and the practice leading to the cessation of mental formations, practice for getting disgusted with mental-formations, for detachment therefrom and the complete cessation thereof, are those who rightly practice; and those who rightly practice have a firm footing in this Dhamma Vinaya (Sāsana).

"Bhikkhus, those *samaṇas* and *brāhmaṇas* who, by their penetratingly understanding mental-formations, the origin of mental formations, the cessation of mental-formations, and the practice leading to the cessation of mental-formations, through disgust with mental-formations, through detachment therefrom and the complete cessation thereof, are detached and liberated from defilements, are those who are well liberated, and those who are well liberated are *kevalino* (those who have done all that ought to be done in this Sāsana). For them there is no more wandering in the round of rebirths.

"And what, Bhikkhus, is consciousness?

---

8. The figure of speech used here is Synecdoche.

"Bhikkhus, there are six kinds of consciousness. They are: (1) *Cakkhu-viññāṇaṃ* (Eye-consciousness), (2) *Sota-viññāṇaṃ* (Ear-consciousness), (3) *Ghāṇa-viññāṇaṃ* (Nose-consciousness), (4) *Jivhā-viññāṇaṃ* (Tongue-consciousness), (5) *Kāya-viññāṇaṃ* (Body-consciousness), (6) *Mano-viññāṇaṃ* (Mind-consciousness). These are called consciousness.

"Bhikkhus, owing to the arising of mind and corporeality, consciousness arises; and when mind and corporeality cease, consciousness ceases. And the practice leading to the cessation of consciousness is this Noble Eightfold Path, namely, Right Understanding, Right Thinking, Right Speech, Right Action, Right Livelihood, Right Effort, Right Mindfulness, Right Concentration.

"Bhikkhus, those *samaṇas* and *brāhmaṇas*, by thus penetratingly understanding consciousness, the origin of consciousness, the cessation of consciousness, and the practice leading to the cessation of consciousness, the pleasantness, the fault and the way of deliverance from consciousness, practice for getting disgusted with consciousness, for detachment therefrom and the complete cessation thereof, are those who rightly practice; and those who rightly practice have a firm footing in this Dhamma Vinaya (Sāsana).

"Bhikkhus, those *samaṇas* and *brāhmaṇas* who, by their penetratingly understanding consciousness, the origin of consciousness, the cessation of consciousness, and the practice leading to the cessation of consciousness, the pleasantness, the fault and the way of deliverance from consciousness, through disgust with consciousness, through detachment therefrom and the complete cessation thereof, are detached and liberated from defilements, are those who are well liberated; and those who are well liberated are *kevalino* (those who have done all that ought to be done in this Sāsana). For them there is no more wandering in the round of rebirths.

"Thus, Bhikkhus, a Bhikkhu is skilful in seven aspects.

"And how, Bhikkhus, does a Bhikkhu become one who contemplates (phenomena) in three ways?

"As to that, Bhikkhus, a Bhikkhu contemplates phenomena by way of *dhātu* (elements) *āyatana* (bases) and *Paṭiccasamuppāda* (Dependent Origination).

"That is how a Bhikkhu contemplates phenomena in three ways.

"Bhikkhus, a Bhikkhu who is skilful in the seven aspects, and who contemplates (phenomena, in three ways, is called *kevalino* (one who has done all that ought to be done), *vusitavā* (one who has lived the Holy life), and *uttamapuriso* (one who is the noblest personage)."[9]

---

9. Note: this discourse is a eulogy of the qualities of Arahats which inspire those who are not yet Arahats.

ANATTĀ-LAKKHAṆA SUTTA[10]

Discourse on the Characteristic of Anattā[11]

Thus, I have heard. On one occasion the Exalted One was staying at Banaras, in the Deer Park at Isipattana.[12] There the Exalted One addressed the Bhikkhus: "O Bhikkhus!" "Yes, Lord," answered those Bhikkhus to the Exalted One. The Exalted One delivered this discourse.

"Bhikkhus, *rūpa* (corporeality) is *anattā* (not-self). If *rūpa* be self, then this *rūpa* would not be subject to disease, and one should be able to say, 'Let my *rūpa* be thus, let my *rūpa* be not thus'. And since *rūpa* is not-self, so it is subject to disease, and none can say, 'Let my *rūpa* be thus, let my *rūpa* be not thus'.

"Bhikkhus, *vedanā* (sensation) is not-self. If sensation be self, then this sensation would not be subject to disease, and one should be able to say, 'Let my sensation be thus, let my sensation be not thus'. And since sensation is not-self, so it is subject to disease, and none can say, 'Let my sensation be thus, let my sensation be not thus'.

"Bhikkhus, *saññā* (perception) is not-self. If perception be self, then this perception would not be subject to disease, and one should be able to say, 'Let my perception be thus, let my perception be not thus'. And since perception is not-self, so it is subject to disease, and none can say, 'Let my perception be thus, let my perception be not thus'.

"Bhikkhus, *saṅkhāra* (*kamma*-activities) are not-self. If *kamma*-activities be self, then these *kamma*-activities would not be subject to disease, and one should be able to say, 'Let my *saṅkhāra* be thus, let my *saṅkhāra* be not thus'. And since *saṅkhāra* are not self, so they are subject to disease, and none can say, 'Let my *saṅkhāra* be thus, let my *saṅkhāra* be not thus'.

"Bhikkhus, *viññāṇa* (consciousness) is not self. If consciousness be self,

---

10. Saṃyutta Nikāya, Khandha-vagga Pāḷi, 1. Khandha Saṃyutta, 1. Upaya-vagga, 7. Anattā-lakkhaṇa Sutta, p. 55, 6th Syn. Edn.

11. *Anattā*: Not-self; impersonality; soullessness; without soul-essence; without ego-entity.

12. Now identified with Sarnath, Banaras.

then this consciousness would not be subject to disease, and one should be able to say, 'Let my consciousness be thus, let my consciousness be not thus'. And since consciousness is not-self, so it is subject to disease, and none can say, 'Let my consciousness be thus, let my consciousness be not thus'.

"Bhikkhus, what do you think: is *rūpa* permanent or impermanent?" "Impermanent, venerable sir." "Now, is what is impermanent painful or pleasant?" "Painful, venerable sir." "Now, is what is impermanent, what is painful, what is subject to change, fit to be regarded thus: 'This is mine this is I, this is my self'?" "No, venerable sir."

"Bhikkhus, what do you think: is *vedanā* permanent or impermanent?" "Impermanent, venerable sir." "Now, is what is impermanent painful or pleasant?" "Painful, venerable sir." "Now is what is impermanent, what is painful, what is subject to change, fit to be regarded thus: 'This is mine, this is I, this is my self'?" "No, venerable sir."

"Bhikkhus, what do you think: is *saññā* permanent or impermanent?" "Impermanent, venerable sir. Now, is what is impermanent, painful, or pleasant?" "Painful, venerable sir." "Now, is what is impermanent, what is painful, what is subject to change, fit to be regarded thus: 'This is mine, this is I, this is my self'?" "No, venerable sir."

"Bhikkhus, what do you think: are *saṅkhāra* permanent or impermanent?" "Impermanent, venerable sir." "Now, are what are impermanent, painful or pleasant?" "Painful, venerable sir." "Now, are what are impermanent, what are painful, what are subject to change, fit to be regarded thus: 'This is mine, this is I, this is my self'?" "No, venerable sir."

"Bhikkhus, what do you think: is *viññāṇa* permanent or impermanent?" "Impermanent, venerable sir." "Now, is what is impermanent painful or pleasant?" "Painful, venerable sir." "Now, is what is impermanent, what is painful, what is subject to change, fit to be regarded thus: 'This is mine, this is I, this is my self'?" "No, venerable sir."

"So, Bhikkhus, any kind of *rūpa* whatever, whether past, future, or present, whether gross or subtle, whether internal or external, whether inferior or superior, whether far or near, must, with right understanding of things as they really are, be regarded thus: 'This is not mine, this is not I, this is not my self' ...."

"Bhikkhus, any kind of *vedanā* whatever, whether past, future, or present, whether gross or subtle, whether internal or external, whether inferior or superior, whether far or near, must, with right understanding of things as they really are, be regarded thus: 'This is not mine, this is not I, this is not my self'.

"Bhikkhus, any kind of *saññā* whatever, whether past, future, or present whether gross or subtle, whether internal or external, whether inferior or superior, whether far or near, must, with right understanding of things as they really are, be regarded thus: 'This is not mine, this is not I, this is not my self'.

"Bhikkhus, any kind of *saṅkhāra* whatever, whether past, future, or present, whether gross or subtle, whether internal or external, whether inferior or superior, whether far or near, must, with right understanding of things as they really are, be regarded thus: 'This is not mine, this is not I, this is not my self'.

"Bhikkhus, any kind of *viññāṇa* whatever, whether past, future, or present, whether gross or subtle, whether internal or external, whether inferior or superior, whether far or near, must, with right understanding of things as they really are, be regarded thus: 'This is not mine, this is not I, this is not my self'.

"Bhikkhus, seeing thus, the learned noble, disciple becomes wearied of *rūpa*, of *vedanā*, of *saññā*, of *saṅkhāra* and of *viññāṇa*. Becoming, wearied of all those he gets detached, and from detachment he attains to Deliverance.

"And he realizes: 'Rebirth is no more; I have lived the pure life; I have done what ought to be done; I have nothing more to do for the realization of Arahatship.'"

That is what the Exalted One said. The delighted Bhikkhus rejoiced at His words.

Now during this discourse, the minds of the Bhikkhus of the group of five were liberated from defilements through clinging no more.

* * *

SAMYUTTA NIKĀYA, KHANDAVAGGA SAṂYUTTA, THERAVAGGA, ANURĀDHA SUTTA

Discourse to Anurādha

Once the Buddha was residing at Kūṭāgāra monastery, in the great forest near Vesālī, and at that time Venerable Anurādha was staying in a hut in the forest not far from the Buddha.

Then many wandering ascetics approached the elder and exchanged greetings of pleasant courtesy. Having exchanged greetings, they sat at one side and said: "Friend Anurādha, the Tathāgata, the noble and Supreme One who has attained the highest goal must have pointed out and explained according to one of these four arguments:

A *Tathāgata*[13] exists after death.
A Tathāgata does not exist after death.
A Tathāgata exists and yet does not exist after death.
A Tathāgata neither exists nor does not exist after death."

The Venerable Anurādha replied: "Friends, that Tathāgata, the Noble and Supreme One who has attained the highest goal, has pointed out and explained apart from these four arguments:

A Tathāgata exists after death.
A Tathāgata does not exist after death.
A Tathāgata exists and yet does not exist after death.
A Tathāgata neither exists nor does not exist after death."[14]

On being told this, the wandering ascetics made the remark: "This monk must be a new one who has renounced the world recently. If he be an elder, he is a foolish and ignorant one." Then, being displeased with the elder they departed from that place abusing him with the terms 'novice and fool'.

Afterwards, not long after the wandering ascetics had departed, the Venerable Anurādha thought: "If these ascetics should put further questions to me, how should I reply so that I may be able to speak the

---

13. *Tathāgata* here means a being (*Satta*). It includes the Buddha, who is the Tathāgata. Saṃyutta Aṭṭhakathā (Commentary) 6th. Syn. Edn. Pp. 285-6.

14. 'He replied thus as he thought the Buddha would not have pointed out and explained as stated by the ascetics who were opponents of Buddhism.' op. cit. p. 287.

truth about the Buddha and not misrepresent Him? How shall I answer according to the Dhamma so that I may not be blamed by any follower of the Teaching of the Buddha?"

Then the Venerable Anurādha went to the Buddha and exchanged greetings of pleasant courtesy, paid respects and sat at one side. Having sat he reported to the Buddha: "Revered Sir, I am now staying in a forest hut not far away. A group of wandering ascetics came to me, exchanged greetings and said: 'The Tathāgata, the Noble and Supreme One must have pointed out and explained according to one of these four arguments:

A Tathāgata exists after death.
A Tathāgata does not exist after death.
A Tathāgata exists and yet does not exist after death.
A Tathāgata neither exists nor does not exist after death.'

To them I replied: "Friends, the Tathāgata, the Noble and Supreme One who has attained the highest goal, has pointed out and explained apart from these four arguments:

A Tathāgata exists after death.
A Tathāgata does not exist after death.
A Tathāgata exists and yet does not exist after death.
A Tathāgata neither exists nor does not exist after death.

"On being told this, those ascetics made the remark: 'This monk must be a newly ordained one. If he be an elder, he is a foolish and ignorant one.' Being displeased with me they went away abusing me with the terms 'novice and fool'.

"Not long after they had departed it occurred to me: 'If those wandering ascetics put further questions to me, how should I reply to them so that I may be able to speak the truth of the Buddha and not misrepresent Him? How shall I answer according to the Dhamma so that I may not be blamed by any follower of the Buddha?'"

"O Anurādha, what do you think is form (*rūpa*) permanent or impermanent?" "Impermanent, Sir." "Is that which is impermanent, painful or pleasant?" "Painful, Sir." "Is it proper to regard that which is impermanent, painful and subject to change as: 'This is mine; this is I, this is my *attā* (soul or permanent substance).'?" "It is not proper, Sir." "Is feeling (*vedanā*) permanent or impermanent?" "Impermanent Sir." "Is that which is impermanent, painful or pleasant?" "Painful, Sir."

"Is it proper to regard that which is impermanent, painful and subject to change as: 'This is mine; this is I; this is my *attā*.'?" "It is not proper, Sir." "Are perception (*saññā*) mental formations (*saṅkhāra*) and consciousness (*viññāṇa*) permanent or impermanent?" "Impermanent, Sir." "Is that which is impermanent, painful or pleasant?" "Painful, Sir." "Is it proper to regard that which is impermanent, painful and subject to change as: 'This is mine; this is I; this is my *attā*.'?" "It is not proper, Sir." "Therefore, whatever form, feeling, perception, mental formations, consciousness which has been, will be and is now connected with oneself, with others, or gross or subtle, inferior or superior, far or near; all forms, feelings, perceptions, mental formations and consciousness, should be considered by right knowledge in this way: 'This is not mine; this is not I; this is not my *attā*.' Having seen thus, a learned, noble disciple becomes disgusted with the form, feeling, perception, mental formations and consciousness. Becoming disgusted, he discards the passions. Being free from passions he becomes emancipated and insight arises in him: 'I am emancipated.'

"He realizes: 'Birth is destroyed, I have lived the holy life and fulfilled the duties that ought to be done. There is no more birth for me after this life.'

"What do you think, Anurādha, do you regard the form as a Tathāgata?" "No, Sir."

"O Anurādha, what is your view, do you see a Tathāgata in the form?" "No, sir." "Do, you see a Tathāgata apart from form?" "No Sir." "Do you see a Tathāgata in feeling, perception, mental formations or consciousness?" "No, Sir." "Do you see a Tathāgata apart from feeling, perception, mental formations or consciousness?" "No, Sir."

"O Anurādha, what do you think, do you regard that which is without form, feeling, perception, mental formations and consciousness as a Tathāgata?"

"No, Sir."

"Now, Anurādha, since a Tathāgata is not to be found in this very life, is it proper for you to say: 'The Noble and Supreme One, who has attained the highest goal, has pointed out and explained apart from these four arguments:[15]

A Tathāgata exists after death.

A Tathāgata does not exist after death.

---

15. Since there is no *Satta* or *Tathāgata* here and now, there can be no question of any *satta* or *Tathāgata* existing after death or not existing after death, etc. op. Cit p. 287.

A Tathāgata exists and yet does not exist after death.

A Tathāgata neither exists nor does not exist after death.'?"

"No, Sir."

"Well and good, O Anurādha. Formerly and now also I expound and point out only the truth of Suffering and the cessation of Suffering."[16]

* * *

16. 'The cause of Suffering and the way to the cessation of Suffering' are implied. op. cit. p. 287.

SUTTANTA PIṬAKA, SAṂYUTTA NIKĀYA, SAḶĀYATANA-VAGGA SAṂYUTTA, GAHAPATI-VAGGA, LOHICCA SUTTA[17]

Mahākaccāna's Discourse with Lohicca Brahmina on Guarded and Unguarded Sense Doors

On one occasion the Venerable Mahākaccāna was staying at a forest hermitage near the town of Makkarakaṭa in the kingdom of Avanti.

At that time many pupils of the Brahmin Lohicca, youths who were gathering firewood, approached the hermitage of the Venerable Mahākaccāna. On reaching there they walked up and down, here and there around the hermitage. Thus, walking and loitering in and around the hermitage, they made low as well as boisterous noises. Some of them played the game of leap-frog. And they said, "These tonsured Bhikkhus are well-to-do; they have evil conduct; they are the offspring of the Brahma's foot; the well-to-do people pay respects to them, revere, esteem, honour and support them."

Thereupon the Venerable Mahākaccāna came out of his hermitage and addressed the youths thus: "O youths! Please keep quiet. I shall give you a lecture on the Dhamma." Then the youths kept silent, and the Venerable Mahākaccāna addressed them as follows:

"Brahmins of olden days who remembered the ancient Brahma Dhamma, regarded morality (and not birth) as most important; and their sense doors were well guarded, as their anger had been suppressed.

"Brahmins of olden days, who remembered the ancient Brahma Dhamma, took delight in Dhamma (i.e. in performing the ten kinds of meritorious deeds) and *jhāna* (i.e. the eight stages of mental concentration).

"However, Brahmins of the present day, being proud of their descent (or lineage), saying. 'We shall have to recite' (i.e. imagining that one becomes a Brahmin by doing that much only), being overwhelmed by anger, being armed with various sticks, discard the said virtues and do misdeeds attacking those, who have no craving (*taṇhā*) although they themselves are full of craving.

"The practices of one, whose sense doors are unguarded, are useless and vain as wealth obtained in a dream.

---

17. Saḷāyatana-vagga Saṃyutta Pāḷi, p. 334, 6th Syn. Edition.

"Not taking food for one day, two days and so forth, lying on the ground strewn with grass, bathing early in the morning, learning the Three Vedas, wearing the black leopard's skin, wearing a matted hair, reciting mantras, performing rites and rituals, keeping filthy teeth, concealing this wrong doing, carrying a crooked staff, washing the rice with water—are 'virtues' which they practice for material benefit.

"Mind which is well and truly concentrated, pure, free from defilements and kind to all beings this is the means for attainment of the supreme state (*Brahmapattiyā*)."

Thereupon, the Brahmin youths got enraged and displeased, and went to the Brahmin Lohicca. On coming to him they said, "Venerable teacher! May we bring to your kind notice that the Venerable Mahākaccāna is attacking and abusing the sacred Vedas of the Brahmins."

At these words the Brahmin Lohicca became angry and displeased. Then a thought arose in him: "If I were to abuse the Venerable Mahākaccāna, or go at him, or scold him merely on the words of these youths, such kind of act would be improper. It would be better, if I were to approach him and ask him about it personally."

So, the Brahmin Lohicca went along with those youths to visit the Venerable Mahākaccāna. Having approached him, he greeted the Venerable Mahākaccāna cordially, and after the exchange of greetings and compliments, sat at one side. So seated he addressed Venerable Mahākaccāna: "Venerable Sir, is it a fact that our pupils, the youths who were gathering firewood reached this place?"

"It is true, Brahmin. They did come here."

"And did your venerable self have any conversation with them?"

"Yes, I had, O Brahmin!"

"May I know the topic of the conversation, venerable sir?"

"I spoke to them to this effect:

Brahmins of olden days who remembered the ancient Brahma Dhamma, regarded morality (and not birth) as most important; and their sense doors were well guarded as their anger had been suppressed.

Mind which is well and truly concentrated, pure; free from defilements and kind to all beings—this is the means for attainment of the supreme state (*Brahmapattiyā*)."

"Venerable Sir, you said, one who does not guard his sense doors. Now to what extent is one unguarded as regards one's own sense-doors?"

"In this world, Brahmin, one seeing an object with the eye, wants it (or is attracted by it) if it is pleasant (*lobha*) and is displeased with it if it be unpleasant (*dosa*). For want of well-established mindfulness, he remains narrow-minded; and he does not really know emancipation of mind (*cetovimutti*) and emancipation by knowledge (*paññāvimutti*) both of which arise from Fruition of Holiness and through which evils which have arisen in him wholly disappear (*moha*).

"Whenever he hears a sound with the ear ...

"Whenever he smells an odour with the nose ...

"Whenever he tastes a flavour with the tongue ...

"Whenever he feels a contact with the body ...

"Whenever he cognises a mental object with his mind ... wants it (or is attracted by it) if it is pleasant (*lobha*) and is displeased with it if it be unpleasant (*dosa*). For want of well-established mindfulness, he remains narrow-minded; and he does not really know emancipation of mind (*cetovimutti*) and emancipation by knowledge (*paññāvimutti*) both of which arise from Fruition of Holiness and through which evils which have arisen in him wholly disappear (*moha*). O Brahmin, thus I say, is one unguarded as regards one's own sense doors."

"Wonderful, Venerable Mahākaccāna! Marvellous, Venerable Mahākaccāna, is the way in which the Venerable Mahākaccāna has expounded the words 'one is unguarded as regards one's own sense doors.'"

"Venerable Sir, you said, 'one who guards his sense doors' ... Now to what extent is one guarded as regards one's own sense doors?"

"In this world, Brahmin, a bhikkhu, seeing an object with the eye, does not want it (or is not attracted by it) if it is pleasant (*alobha*) and is not displeased with it if it be unpleasant (*adosa*). By virtue of well-established mindfulness, he remains boundlessly broad minded; and he does really know emancipation of mind (*cetovimutti*) and emancipation by knowledge (*paññāvimutti*) both of which arise from Fruition of Holiness and through which evils which have arisen in him wholly disappear (*amoha*).

"Whenever the Bhikkhu hears a sound with the ear ...

"Whenever the Bhikkhu smells an odour with the nose ...

"Whenever the Bhikkhu tastes a flavour with the tongue ...

"Whenever the Bhikkhu feels a contact with the body ...

"Whenever the Bhikkhu cognises a mental object with his mind, does not want it (or is not attracted by it) if it is pleasant (*alobha*) and is not displeased with it if it be unpleasant (*adosa*). By virtue of well-established mindfulness, he remains boundlessly broad minded; and he does really know emancipation of mind (*cetovimutti*) and emancipation by knowledge (*paññāvimutti*) both of which arise from Fruition of Holiness and through which evils which have arisen in him do wholly disappear (*amoha*). O Brahmin, thus I say is one guarded as regards one's own sense doors."

"Wonderful, Venerable Mahākaccāna! Marvellous, is the way in which the Venerable Mahākaccāna has expounded the words 'one is guarded as regards one's own sense doors!'

"Just as, O Mahākaccāna, one should turn up that which is upside down or lay bare that which is concealed, or tell the way to the one who has lost his way or hold a lamp in the dark so that those who have eyes might see things; even so, the Dhamma has been revealed to me in many ways by the Venerable Mahākaccāna. So, I take refuge in the Buddha in the Dhamma and in the Order of monks; may the Venerable Mahākaccāna accept me as a lay disciple who has taken refuge from today onward as long as my life lasts.

"Now as the Venerable Mahākaccāna, visits the families of his supporters at Makkarakaṭa, even so let him visit the family of Lohicca. Then all the youths and maidens there, will revere and greet the Venerable Mahākaccāna, give him a seat and also water, and that will be a blessing and a benefit for them for a long time."

* * *

Not By Faith Alone

"The Arahat who has destroyed the fluxions, lived the life, done what was to be done, set down the burden, won self-weal, shattered life's fetter and is freed by Perfect Knowledge, has applied himself to six things: to dispassion, detachment, harmlessness, destroying craving, destroying grasping and to non-delusion.

"Perhaps some venerable person may think: 'Could it be that this venerable man has applied himself to dispassion relying on mere faith alone?' Let him not think so. The fluxion-freed who has lived the life, done what was to be done, who sees naught in himself to be done, naught to be added to what has been done, by the fact of being passionless, has applied himself to dispassion by destroying passion; by the fact of being without hatred, has applied himself to dispassion by destroying hatred; by the fact of being without delusion, has applied himself to dispassion by destroying delusion."

Aṅguttara Nikāya (*Book of the Sixes*)

"As to this what think you, brethren? Which is greater, this little sand lifted on my fingernail, or this great earth?"

"This lord, is greater, even this great earth. A trifle is the little sand lifted by the Exalted One on to his fingernail. It cannot form a fraction when compared with the great earth—this little sand lifted by the Exalted One on to his fingernail."

"Even so, brethren, are the beings that are reborn among humans few in number as against the greater number that are reborn in the four Lower Worlds."

Saṃyutta Nikāya, XX. 5

SAṂYUTTA NIKĀYA, SAḶĀYATANA SAṂYUTTA, ĀSĪVISAVAGGA, ĀSIVISOPAMA SUTTA[18]

Simile of the Virulent Serpents

"O bhikkhus. Suppose there are four fiery and virulent serpents and suppose there is a man who does not wish to die but desires to live, who loves pleasure and shrinks from suffering, and to him men should come and say: 'Friend, from time to time you are to rouse up, feed, bathe and put to sleep these four fiery and virulent serpents. Should one of these serpents become angry, then, good friend, you will come to dreadful pain or death. So, friend, do as you deem fit.'

"Suppose that person, being afraid of the four fiery and virulent serpents, runs here and there and to him men come and say: 'Friend, five murderous enemies are following after you saying: "We shall deprive him of life wherever we find him." So, friend, do as you deem fit.'

"Suppose, then that person fearing the fiery and virulent serpents and the five murderous enemies, should run here and there, and to him men should say: 'Friend, there is a sixth murderous insider with sword upraised coming close behind you with the thought: "I will deprive him of life wherever I find him." So, friend, do as you deem fit.'

"Now that person, being afraid of the four fiery and virulent serpents, the five murderous enemies and the sixth murderous insider with sword upraised, runs here and there. Seeing a deserted village, he enters it. Whichever house he enters, he finds it uninhabited and vacant and whichever bowl he touches he finds it empty, and to him men should say: 'Friend, there are plunderers of villages who frequent this uninhabited village. So, do as you deem fit.' Now that person fearing the four fiery and virulent serpents, the five murderous enemies and the sixth murderous insider with sword upraised, and the plunderers of villages, runs here and there. Then he sees a great river, the hither shore beset with fears and dangers but the other shore safe and secure. Suppose there is no boat to cross nor a bridge to go from shore to shore. A thought occurs to him: 'How would it be if I were to collect grass, wood, branches and leaves, construct a raft and depending on that and striving with arms and legs, cross to the other shore safely?'

18. 6th synod Edition.

"Then that person collects the grass, wood, branches and leaves, constructs a raft and, depending on that and striving with arms and legs, he reaches the further shore safely. Having crossed the river and reached the shore, the Noble man stands on land.

"Oh, bhikkhus! I have given a simile for your understanding. Here is the meaning.

"*The four fiery and virulent serpents*, bhikkhus, is a metaphor for the four great elements: the element of solidity, the element of cohesion, the element of heat and the element of motion.

"*The five murderous enemies*, bhikkhus is a metaphor for the five constituent groups of existence: form, feeling, perception, mental formations and consciousness.

"*The sixth murderous insider*, bhikkhus, is a metaphor for pleasure and lust (*nandi* and *rāga*).

"*The deserted village* is a metaphor for the six somatic bases: when a wise and learned man examines the body through the eye he finds it empty and void when he examines the body through the ear, he finds it empty and void; when he examines the body through the nose, he finds it empty and void; when he examines the body through the tongue, he finds it empty and void; when he examines the body through the body (by tactile sensation) he finds it empty and void; when he examines the body through the mental element, he finds it empty and void.

"O bhikkhus, *the plunderers of villages* is a metaphor for the six external bases. The eye is harassed by pleasant and unpleasant visible objects. The ear is harassed by pleasant and unpleasant sounds. The nose is harassed by pleasant and unpleasant smells. The tongue is harassed by pleasant and unpleasant tastes. The body is harassed by pleasant and unpleasant body impressions. The mental element is harassed by pleasant and unpleasant mental objects.

"*The great river*, bhikkhus, is a metaphor for the four floods: the flood of sensual pleasures; the flood of existence, the flood of views and the flood of ignorance.

"*The hither shore beset with dangers and fears* is a metaphor for the constituent Groups of Existence as objects of clinging.

"*The other shore which is safe and secure* is a metaphor for Nibbana.

"*The raft*, bhikkhus, is a metaphor for the Noble Eightfold Path: Right thought, Right speech, Right action, Right livelihood, Right effort, Right mindfulness Right concentration.

"*Striving with arms and legs* is a metaphor for putting forth energy.

'*Having reached the other shore, the Noble man stands on land* is a metaphor for an Arahat.

APPENDIX

From the Traditional Commentaries

The four serpents is a metaphor for the four great elements.

The element of solidity, of cohesion, of heat and of motion resemble the four kinds of serpents:

(1) *Kaṭṭhamukha* serpent having an injurious mouth.
(2) *Pūtimukha* serpent having a putrid mouth.
(3) *Aggimukha* serpent having a flaming mouth.
(4) *Satthamukha* serpent having a sharp mouth.

Just as the whole body becomes stiff and hardened when one is bitten by the *kaṭṭhamukha* serpent, so also when the element of solidity, is upset, the whole body becomes stiff and hardened.

When the *pūtimukha* serpent bites one, the whole body becomes rotten. In the same way when the element of cohesion is upset the whole body becomes putrid and foul.

Just as being bitten by the *aggimukha* serpent the whole body becomes heated, similarly when the element of heat is upset the whole body is overheated and feverish.

As if being bitten by the *satthamukha* serpent, the whole body is cut off and broken when the element of motion is upset.

Thus, like the four kinds of serpents the four great elements are much to be feared.

The five murderous enemies

The five murderous enemies is the metaphor for the five constituent groups of existence; form, feeling, perception, mental formations and consciousness. So long as the five Groups exist there result old age, death, sorrow, lamentation, pain, grief and despair. When any one of the Groups is destroyed the remaining Groups are also dissolved. Wherever the Groups appear there the burden of suffering is evident. Thus, the five Groups are like the murderous enemies.

The sixth murderous insider

The sixth murderous insider with sword upraised is the metaphor for lust. The metaphor is given here as lust resembles the murderer in two ways. It cuts the head of wisdom and it is the root cause for making one to be reborn in any of four kinds of rebirth.[19]

When the pleasant and agreeable object comes into contact with the eye, then on account of that object there arises greed or craving. The arising of this greed is the cutting of the head of wisdom and good qualities disappear. Due to the arising of greed, birth is caused. So, greed leads one to be reborn in any one of the four ways of rebirth.

The deserted village

The deserted village is the metaphor for the six somatic bases. In a deserted village there is no pleasurable and worthy property to be found. Similarly, when one examines the body with insight through the six somatic bases: the eye, ear, nose, tongue, body and mental element, there is no such thing as essence or substance which is to be regarded as 'it is I', 'it is mine', and 'it belongs to myself'.

The plunderers of villages

The plunderers of villages is the metaphor for the six external bases: the pleasant and unpleasant visible objects, sound, smell, taste, touch and mental objects. When these six, external bases come into contact with the six somatic bases, there arise the defilements. On account of these defilements, monks commit various offences and laymen perform evil acts: their own evil actions drag them to the lower states of existence. In this way the six external bases resemble the plunderers of villages.

The great river

The great river is the metaphor for the four floods. Just as it is very difficult for one to cross the great river where there is no bridge nor boat, he will be swept away by the swift and strong currents of the great river, so also, he is unable to find an escape from the round of rebirth as he is carried away by the floods of sensual pleasure, of existence, wrong views and of ignorance.

---

19. From the egg, from the mother, womb, from moisture and by apparitional or spontaneous birth.

The hither shore beset with dangers and fears and the other shore safe and secure.

The hither shore is the metaphor for the groups of existence as objects of clinging and the other shore is the metaphor for Nibbāna. So long as the groups of existence are not extinguished the burdens of suffering continually arise. Clinging and attachment to the groups of existence causes successive births and thus beings are greatly burdened by suffering. For this reason, the groups of existence are like the hither shore best with dangers and fears.

When the groups of existence are extinguished and when the fire of passion and pleasure is extinguished one attains *nibbana*. Nibbāna is beyond all kinds of suffering. So 'the other shore safe and secure' is the metaphor for Nibbāna.

The Raft

The raft is the metaphor for the Noble Eightfold Path. To reach the other shore one has to cross the river by means of a raft. The raft will carry one to the other shore safely. Similarly, the Noble Eightfold Path is the only vehicle by which one is able to cross the river of existence and reach the shore of Nibbāna.

Striving with arms and legs

Depending on the raft one strives with arms and legs is the metaphor for putting forth effort. Just as one has to construct a raft and with the help of hands and legs direct it to reach the other shore, so also one who wishes to attain Nibbāna has to practice the Noble Eightfold Path with effort and energy. He puts forth effort with mindfulness in the practice of the Noble Eightfold Path. There are four kinds of effort or exertion.

(*Sammapadhāna*)

Exertion for the restraint of one's senses;
Exertion for the abandonment of sinful thoughts;
Exertion for the practice of meditation;
Exertion for the guarding of one's character.

The noble man who reaches the other shore and stands on land is the metaphor for the Arahat, who has practiced diligently the Noble Eightfold Path, crossed over the river of Existence and attained the shore of Nibbāna.

PAṬHAMA-DĀRUKKHANDHOPAMA SUTTA[20]

Discourse on the Similitude of the Log of Wood

On one occasion the Exalted One was staying at Kosambi, on the bank of the river Ganges.

There the Exalted One saw a great log being carried down the Ganges, and on seeing it He called to His disciples, saying "Bhikkhus, do you see that great log being carried down the river?"

"Yes, Lord."

"Now, Bhikkhus, if this log does not (1) touch this bank, (2) or the other bank, (3) does not sink in midstream, (4) is not stranded upon land, (5) is not seized by men, (6) or by non-humans, (7) is not caught in a whirlpool, and (8) does not rot inwardly,—that log will float down to ocean, will slide down to ocean, will tend towards ocean.

"And why? Because, Bhikkhus, the stream of the Ganges floats down to ocean, slides down to ocean, tends towards ocean.

"Similarly, Bhikkhus, if you do not touch on this bank or the other bank, if you do not sink in midstream, if you are not stranded upon land, if you are not seized by men or non-humans, if you are not caught in a whirlpool, and if you do not rot inwardly,—then, Bhikkhus, your course will be directed towards Nibbāna. You will slide down to Nibbāna; you will tend towards Nibbāna. And why? Because, Bhikkhus, Right Understanding (*sammā-diṭṭhi*) floats down to Nibbāna, slides down to Nibbāna, and tends towards Nibbāna."

At these words a certain Bhikkhu said to the Exalted One:

"What, Lord, is *this bank*? What is *the other bank*? What is *sinking in midstream*? What is *stranded upon land*? What is *seized by men or non-humans*? What is *being caught in a whirlpool*? What is '*rotting inwardly*?"

"*This bank*, Bhikkhu, is a name for the six internal bases.[21] *The other bank*, Bhikkhu, is a name for the six external bases.[22] *Sinking in the midstream* is

---

20. Saṃyutta Nikāya, Khandha-vagga: Saḷāyatana Saṃyutta. 4. Āsīvisa-vagga, 4. Paṭhamadārukkhandh-opama Sutta, p. 316, 6th Synod Edition.

21. The six internal bases are: 1. Eye-base, 2. Ear-base, 3. Nose-base, 4. Tongue-base, 5. Body-base, 6. Mind base.

22. The six external bases are: 1. Visible object, 2. Sound, 3. Smell, 4. Taste, 5. Touch, 6. Mental-object.

a name for the lure of lust,[23] that is to say, addiction to the pleasures of the senses. *Being stranded upon land* means becoming a prey to the conceit of one's own personality.

"And what, Bhikkhu, is *being seized by men*?

"In this Sāsana, Bhikkhu, a monk lives in the company of laymen sharing their joys and sorrow, being happy when they are happy, being unhappy when they are unhappy, and helping them whenever there is anything to be done. This, Bhikkhu, is, *being seized by men*.

"And what, Bhikkhu, is *being seized by non-humans*?

"In this Sāsana, Bhikkhu, a monk lives the virtuous or religious life aspiring to be reborn in the company of a class of devas,[24] with the thought: 'May I, by observation of moral precepts and performance of certain duties or by living a religious life, become a deva or one of the devas.'

"*Being caught in a whirlpool*, Bhikkhus, is a name for the five kinds of sensual pleasures.

"And what, Bhikkhu, *is rotting inwardly*?

"In this Sāsana, Bhikkhu, a monk is immoral, vicious, impure, of dubious conduct, in the habit of acting stealthily. He pretends to be a samaṇa though he is really not. He pretends to lead a chaste life though he does not really do so. He is rotten within. He resembles a rubbish heap of lust. That, Bhikkhu, is *rotting in inwardly*."

At that time Nanda the cowherd was standing not far from the Exalted One. Then Nanda the cowherd addressed the Exalted One:

"Lord, I shall not touch this bank. I shall not touch the other bank. I shall not sink in midstream. I shall not be stranded upon land. I shall not let humans or non-humans seize me. No whirlpool shall catch me. I shall not rot inwardly. Lord, may I get ordination at the Exalted One's hands? May I get full ordination?"

"Then, Nanda, return the cattle to their owners."

"Lord, the cattle will go back. They are longing for their young ones."

"You had better return them to their owners, Nanda."

Thereupon Nanda the cowherd, having returned the cattle to their owners, came to the Exalted One and said: "Lord, the cattle have been returned to their owners. Lord, may I get ordination at the Exalted One's hands? May I get full ordination?"

23. *Nandi-rāga*: bound up with lust and greed.

24. Distinguished devas.

So, Nanda the cowherd first became a *sāmaṇera* and then a Bhikkhu under the preceptorship of the Exalted One.

The Venerable Nanda, dwelling solitary, detached, earnest, ardent and aspiring, in a short time attained that goal for which the sons of good families rightly leave home for the homeless life, even that unrivalled goal of righteous living, attained it[25] in that very life, and knowing it for himself lived in full realisation thereof: "Rebirth is no more; I have lived the pure life, I have done what ought to be done; I have nothing more to do for the realisation of Arahatship."

And Venerable Nanda was another of the Arahats.

25. The 'goal' means *Arahatta-phala* (Fruition of Holiness).

VEḶUDVĀREYYA SUTTA[26]

Discourse on the Dhamma-way to Compare Oneself with Another

Thus, I have heard. On one occasion while the Exalted One was touring in the kingdom of Kosala with a great company of brethren, He arrived at a *brahmin* village in Kosala named Veḷudvāra.

At that time the villagers of Veḷudvāra, both *brahmins* and householders alike had heard thus: "Friends! It is said that the Samaṇa Gotama of the Sākyan clan, who went forth from a Sākya family in to a homeless life, while touring through the kingdom of Kosala with a great company of brethren has now arrived at the village of Veḷudvāra. And this is the good news that has been widely spread as to the Samaṇa Gotama: 'That Enlightened One is accomplished and worthy of offerings. Supreme Enlightened, Possessed of Clear Wisdom and Conduct. Happily Attained, Knower of Worlds, the Incomparable Leader of men to be tamed, the Teacher of Devas and men, the Enlightened One, the Exalted one. He, by His Omniscience, knows this universe including the world of Devas and Brahmās and Māras and the world of men with its *samaṇas* and *brāhmaṇas*, its kings and men: and knowing it, proclaims the Dhamma—which is good at the beginning, good in the middle and good at the end, and which has the fulness of meaning in spirit and letter. He shows the course of noble practice (*Brahmacariya*) in all its fulness and in all its purity.' To pay our veneration to such an Arahat is well and good."

Then those *brahmin* and householders of Veḷudvāra village approached the Exalted One and having approached Him, some of them paid their obeisance to Him and sat at one side; some of them after exchanging greetings and compliments of felicitation and courtesy with the Exalted One sat at one side; some saluted Him by raising their palms to the head and sat at one side; some announced their names and lineage to the Exalted One and sat at one side; and some others did not say anything and sat at one side.

Having thus sat at one side, the *brahmins* and householders of Veḷudvāra addressed the Exalted One thus:

---

26. Saṃyutta Nikāya, Mahāvagga Pāḷi, Sotāpatti Saṃyutta, 1. Veḷudvāra-Vagga, 7, Veḷudvāreyya Sutta, p. 306, 6th Syn. Edn.

"Master Gotama, we are people of such wishes, such desires, and such senses as these: May we live in a crowded house packed with children! May we enjoy the use of Banaras Sandalwood! May we deck ourselves with garlands and unguents! May we handle gold and silver! When body breaks up after death, may we arise in the Heavenly Abodes where the virtuous are reborn! Let Master Gotama teach us who have such wishes, such desires, such senses, a *dhamma* by which we may live in a crowded house packed with children, enjoy the use of Banaras sandalwood, deck ourselves with garlands and unguents, handle gold and silver, and when body breaks up after death we may arise in the Heavenly Abodes where the virtuous are reborn!"

"Then, householders, I will teach you a Dhamma-way to compare oneself with another. Listen and pay attention to it. I will speak."

"Very well," answered the *brahmins* and householders. Then the Exalted One said:

"Now, householders, what is the Dhamma-way to compare oneself with another?

(1) "Herein, householders, the Noble disciple reflects thus: I want to live and do not die; I am fond of pleasure and averse from *dukkha*. Suppose someone would kill me who want to live and do not want to die, who am fond of pleasure and averse from *dukkha*, it would not be a thing pleasing and delightful to me. Also, if I would kill another who wants to live, who does not want to die, who is fond of pleasure and averse from *dukkha* it would not be a thing pleasing and delightful to him. For a dhamma that is not pleasing to me must be so to him also; and a dhamma that is not pleasing and delightful to me—how could I impose this on another?

"As a result of this reflection, he himself abstains from killing living beings; he encourages others so to abstain; and he speaks in praise of so abstaining. Thus, his bodily conduct is absolutely pure in three aspects.

(2) "Householders, as regards another dhamma, the Noble disciple reflects thus: If someone would, with the intent to steal, take what I have not given him, it would not be a thing pleasing and delightful to me. Also, if I would, with intent to steal, take from another what he has not given me, it would not be a thing pleasing and delightful to him also. A dhamma that is not pleasing and delightful to me must be so to him also; and a dhamma that is not pleasing and delightful to me—how could I impose this on another?

"As a result of this reflection, he himself abstains from taking what is not given him; he encourages others so to abstain; and he speaks in praise of so abstaining. Thus, his bodily conduct is absolutely pure in three aspects.

(3) "Householders, as regards another dhamma, the Noble disciple reflects thus: lf someone would commit adultery with my wives, it would not be a thing pleasing and delightful to me. Also, if I would commit adultery with another's wives, it will not be a thing pleasing and delightful to him also. A *dhamma* that is not pleasing and delightful to me must be so to him also; and a *dhamma* that is not pleasing and delightful to me—how could I impose this on another?

"As a result of this reflection, he himself abstains from committing adultery; he encourages others so to abstain; and he speaks in praise of so abstaining. Thus, his bodily conduct is absolutely pure in three aspects.

(4) "Householders, as regards another *dhamma*, the Noble disciple reflects thus: If someone would spoil my fortune by lying, it would not be a thing pleasing and delightful to me. Also, if I would spoil another's fortune by lying it would not be a thing pleasing and delightful to him. A *dhamma* that is not pleasing and delightful to me must be so to him also; and a *dhamma* that is not pleasing and delightful to me—how could I impose this on another?

"As a result of this reflection, he himself abstains from spoiling another's fortune by lying; he encourages others so to abstain; and he speaks in praise of so abstaining. Thus, his verbal conduct is absolutely pure in three aspects.

(5) "Householders, as regards another *dhamma*, the Noble disciple reflects thus: If someone would cause dissension between me and my friends by backbiting, it would not be a thing pleasing and delightful to me. Also, if I would cause dissension between another and his friends by backbiting, it would not be a thing pleasing and delightful to him. A *dhamma* that is not pleasing and delightful to me must be so to him also; and a *dhamma* that is not pleasing and delightful to me—how could I impose this on another?

"As a result of this reflection, he himself abstains from backbiting; he encourages others so to abstain; and he speaks in praise of so abstaining. Thus, his verbal conduct is absolutely pure in three aspects.

(6) "Householders, as regards another *dhamma*, the Noble disciple reflects thus: If someone would speak to me with rude words, it would not be a thing pleasing and delightful to me. Also, if I would speak to another with rude words, it would not be a thing pleasing and delightful to him also. A *dhamma* that is not pleasing and delightful to me must be so to him also; and a *dhamma* that is not pleasing and delightful to me—how could I impose this on another?

"As a result of this reflection, he himself abstains from speaking rude words; he encourages others so to abstain; and he speaks in praise of so abstaining. Thus, his verbal conduct is absolutely pure in three aspects.

(7) "Householders, as regards another *dhamma*, the Noble disciple reflects thus: If someone would speak to me things which are useless and foolish it would not be a thing pleasing and delightful to me. Also, if I would speak to another things which are useless and foolish, it would not be a thing pleasing and delightful to him. A *dhamma* that is not pleasing and delightful to me must be so to him also: and a *dhamma* that is not pleasing and delightful to me—how could I impose this on another?

"As a result of this reflection, he abstains from speaking things which are not conducive to the well-being of the beings; he encourages others so to abstain; and he speaks in praise of so abstaining. Thus, his verbal conduct is absolutely pure in three aspects.

"Then he has unshaken faith and confidence in the Buddha thus: 'That Enlightened One is accomplished and worthy of offerings, Supremely Enlightened, Possessed of Clear Wisdom and Conduct, Happily Attained, Knower of Worlds, the Incomparable Leader of men to be tamed, the Teacher of Devas and men, the Enlightened One, the Exalted One.'

"He has unshaken faith and confidence in the Dhamma thus: 'Well-expounded is the Dhamma by the Blessed One; to be self-realized; with immediate fruit; to be but approached to be seen; capable of being entered upon; to be attained by the wise, each for himself.'

"He has unshaken faith and confidence in the Saṅgha thus: 'Of good conduct is the Order of the Disciples of the Blessed One, of upright conduct is the Order of the Disciples of the Blessed One, of wise conduct is the Order of the Disciples of the Blessed One, of dutiful conduct is the Order of the Disciples of the Blessed One. This Order of the Disciples of the Blessed One namely, these four Pairs of Persons, the Eight Kinds of Individuals, is worthy of gifts, is worthy of hospitality, is worthy of offerings (for attainment of *magga phala* and Nibbāna), is worthy of reverential salutation, is an incomparable field of merit to the world.'

"He is possessed of virtues (*sīla*)[27] which are desired and cherished by and pleasant to *Ariyās*, virtues unbroken, whole, unspotted, untarnished, giving

27. Here, it means *ariyakanta-sīla*, i.e. the Five Precepts, which accompany the life-continuum of a Sotāpanna, till he attains Nibbāna.

freedom, praised by the wise; virtues untainted (by *taṇhā-diṭṭhiparāmāsa*),[28] which lead to the concentration of the mind.

"Householders, since the Noble disciple is possessed of these seven *dhammas* and these four desirable qualities,[29] if he so desired declare of himself: 'There is no more rebirth for me in hell; there is no more rebirth for me in the animal-world; there is no more rebirth for me in the peta-world; there is no more rebirth for me in Apāya region where evil doers are bound to be reborn. *Sotāpanna* (Stream-winner) am I, not to be ruined in the Lower Worlds, assured am I, bound for the next three higher Holy Paths.'"

At these words the *brahmins* and householders of Veḷudvāra addressed the Exalted One as follows:

> "Wonderful, Venerable Gotama! Wonderful, Venerable Gotama! Just as one should turn up that which is upside down or lay bare that which is concealed, or tell the way to the one who has lost his way or hold a lamp in the dark so that those who have eyes might see them; the Dhamma has been revealed to us in more ways than one by the Venerable Gotama. We take refuge in the Buddha, in the Dhamma and in the Order of monks; may the Venerable Gotama accept us as lay disciples from today onwards as long as our lives last."

---

28. Ego-belief, Craving, Ego-belief and Rites and rituals, *Taṇhā* (Craving).
29. The unshaken faith in Buddha, Dhamma and Saṅgha, and is possessed of *ariyakanta sīla* (the Five Precepts).

DHAMMACAKKAPPAVATTANA SUTTA[30]
THE FIRST SERMON
The Discourse on Setting the Wheel of the Doctrine in Motion

Thus, I have heard: On one occasion the Exalted One dwelt at Banaras, at Isipatana in the Deer Park. There the Exalted One addressed the five Bhikkhus:

"These two extremes, Bhikkhus, are not to be practiced by one who has gone forth from the world. What are the two? That conjoined with the passions and luxury low, vulgar, common, ignoble, and useless and that conjoined with self-torture, painful, ignoble and unprofitable.

"There is a Middle Way, O Bhikkhus, avoiding these two extremes, discovered by the Tathāgata—a path which opens the eyes and bestows understanding, which leads to peace of mind, to the higher wisdom, to full enlightenment, to Nibbāna.

"And what, Bhikkhus, is that Middle Path which opens the eyes and bestows understanding, which leads to peace of mind to the higher wisdom, to full enlightenment, to Nibbāna?

"Verily, it is this Noble Eightfold Path that is to say: Right Understanding, Right Thinking, Right Speech, Right Action, Right Livelihood, Right Effort, Right Mindfulness, Right Concentration.

---

30. There are two kinds of *dhammacakka*; namely, *paṭivedha-dhammacakka* and *desanā- dhammacakka*.

PAṬIVEDHA-DHAMMACAKKAṂ: While seated under the Bodhi Tree Bhagavā caused the *dhamma* comprising *Indriyas, Balas, Bojjhaṅgas, Maggaṅgas*, etc. to rise (in Himself). That *dhamma* itself is a *cakka* as it revolves like a crushing machine to destroy enemies in the form of *kilesas* (mental and moral defilements. So *Paṭivedha* (Penetration of the Truth) is a Dhamma-cakka.

DESANĀ-DHAMMACAKKAṂ: While seated at Isipatana and at the time of preaching the *dhamma*, Bhagavā turned the Desanā Cakka (the Wheel of Preaching) which is like a crushing machine as it revolves to destroy enemies in the form of *kilesas* in *Veneyyas* (those who understand the Dhamma) and also turned the *Dhamma Cakka* comprising *Indriyas, Balas, Bojjhaṅgas, Maggaṅgas*, etc. in *Veneyyas* (i.e. causes Indriyas, etc. to rise in them) destroying their enemies in the form of *kilesas* like a crushing machine. So Desanā (Preaching the Dhamma) is a Dhammacakka. Paṭisambhidāmaggaṭṭhakathā, page 221, 6th Syn. Edn.

For the Sutta, see Vinaya Piṭaka, Mahāvagga, Pañcavaggiyakathā, page 14, 6th Syn. Edn.

"This, Bhikkhus, is that Middle Path which opens the eyes and bestows understanding, which leads to peace of mind to the higher wisdom, to full enlightenment, to Nibbāna.

"Now this, Bhikkhus, is the Noble Truth of Suffering: Birth is Suffering; Decay is Suffering; Death is Suffering; association with those one does not love is Suffering; separation from those one loves is Suffering; not to get what one wants is Suffering; in short, the five constituent groups of existence which are the objects of Clinging are Suffering.

"Now this, Bhikkhus, is the Noble Truth of the Cause of Suffering: It is that Craving which gives rise to fresh rebirth, and bound up with lust and greed now here, now there, finds ever fresh delight. It is the Sensual Craving (*kāma-taṇhā*), the Craving for Existence (*bhava-taṇhā*) and the Craving for Self-Annihilation (*vibhava-taṇhā*).

"Now this, Bhikkhus, is the Noble Truth of the Cessation of Suffering: It is the complete fading away and extinction of this Craving, its forsaking and giving up liberation and detachment from it.

"Now this, Bhikkhus, is the Noble Truth of the Path leading to the Cessation of Suffering: It is this Noble Eightfold Path, namely, Right Understanding, Right Thinking, Right Speech, Right Action, Right Livelihood, Right Effort, Right Mindfulness, Right Concentration.

"Bhikkhus, there arose in me Vision, Insight, Wisdom, Knowledge, and Light that this is the Noble Truth of Suffering, with reference to the Dhammas[31] which have never been heard before.

"Bhikkhus, there arose in me Vision, Insight, Wisdom, Knowledge and Light that this Noble Truth of Suffering must be understood by me, with reference to the Dhammas which have never been heard before.

"Bhikkhus, there arose in me Vision, Insight, Wisdom, Knowledge and Light that this Noble Truth of Suffering has been understood by me, with reference to the Dhammas which have never been heard before.

"Bhikkhus, there arose in me Vision, Insight, Wisdom, Knowledge and Light that this is the Noble Truth of the Cause of Suffering, with reference to the Dhammas[32] which have never been heard before.

---

31. These Dhammas comprise *nāma* (mind) and *rūpa* (materiality), i.e. 81 kinds of mundane consciousness, 52 kinds of mental factors except the mental factor of *lobha*, and 28 kinds of material qualities.

32. These Dhammas are: 1. *Kāma-taṇhā* (Sensual Craving), 2. *Bhava-taṇhā* (Craving for Existence), and 3. *Vibhava-taṇhā* (Craving for Self-Annihilation).

"Bhikkhus, there arose in me Vision, Insight, Wisdom, Knowledge and Light that this Noble Truth of the Cause of Suffering must be got rid of, with reference to the Dhammas which have never been heard before.

"Bhikkhus, there arose in me Vision, Insight, Wisdom, Knowledge and Light that this Noble Truth of the Cause of Suffering has been got rid of by me, with reference to the Dhammas which have never been heard before.

"Bhikkhus, there arose in me Vision, Insight) Wisdom, Knowledge and Light that this is the Noble Truth of the Cessation of Suffering, with reference to the Dhammas[33] which have never been heard before.

"Bhikkhus, there arose in me Vision, Insight, Wisdom, Knowledge and Light that this Noble Truth of the Cessation of Suffering must be realized, with reference to the Dhammas which have never been heard before.

"Bhikkhus, there arose in me Vision, Insight, Wisdom, Knowledge, Light that this Noble Truth of the Cessation of Suffering has been realized by me, with reference to the Dhammas which have never been heard before.

"Bhikkhus, there arose in me Vision, Insight, Wisdom, Knowledge and Light that this is the Noble Truth of the Path leading to the Cessation of Suffering, with reference to the Dhammas[34] which have never been heard before.

"Bhikkhus, there arose in me Vision, Insight, Wisdom, Knowledge and Light that this Noble Truth of the Path leading to the Cessation of Suffering, must be developed, which have never been heard before.

"Bhikkhus, there arose in me Vision, Insight, Wisdom, Knowledge and Light that this Noble Truth of the Path leading to the Cessation of Suffering has been developed by me, with reference to the Dhammas which have never been heard before.

"Now so long, Bhikkhus, as my knowledge and insight into these Four Noble Truths in three phases and twelve ways,[35] were not fully purified—so

---

33. These Dhammas are: (1) *Sa-upā-di-sesa-nibbāna* (Nibbāna with the groups of existence still remaining and (2) *Anupādi-sesa-nibbāna* (Nibbāna without the groups of existence remaining).

34. Right Understanding, Right Thinking. Right Speech, Right Action, Right Livelihood, Right Effort, Right Mindfulness and Right Concentration.

35. Three phases are:

1. *Sacca-ñāṇa* (Knowledge of the nature of the Noble Truth)
2. *Kicca-ñāṇa* (Knowledge about what is to be done), and
3. *Kata-ñāṇa* (Knowledge of the fact that it has been done).

There are Four Noble Truths in each. Noble Truth having three phases there are altogether twelve ways.

long I did not profess to have attained Incomparable Supreme Enlightenment in this world together with the devas, the Māras, the brahmās among the hosts of *samaṇas* and *brāhmaṇas* of *devas* and mankind.

"But Bhikkhus, since my knowledge and insight into these Four Noble Truths in three phases and twelve ways, were fully purified,—then, Bhikkhus, I declared that I have attained Incomparable Supreme Enlightenment to the world, together with the devas, the Māras, the brahmās, among the hosts of *samaṇas* and *brāhmaṇas* of *devas* and mankind.

"Insight of retrospection[36] arose in me: 'My knowledge of the Fruition of Holiness cannot be destroyed by the opposite Dhammas; this is my last birth and there is no more becoming for me.'

Thus, the Exalted One spoke the words beginning with "*Dve me, bhikkhave*". The five Bhikkhus were delighted, and they rejoiced at the words of the Exalted One.

When the Exalted One set in motion the Wheel of Dhamma, the Bhummā *devās* proclaimed with one voice, "The Incomparable Wheel of Dhamma is turned by the Exalted One in the Deer Park at Isipatana near Banaras, and no *samaṇa*, *brāhmaṇa*, *deva*, Māra, brahmā, or other beings in the world can stop it."

The Cāturmahārājika devas having heard what the Bhummā *devās* said, proclaimed with one voice, "The Incomparable Wheel of Dhamma is turned by the Exalted One in the Deer Park at Isipatana near Banaras, and no *samaṇa*, *brāhmaṇa*, *deva*, Māra, brahmā, or other beings in the world can stop it."

This utterance was echoed and re-echoed in the upper realms and from Cātumahārājikā it was proclaimed in Tāvatiṃsa, Yāmā, Tusita, Nimmānarati and to Paranimmitavasavatti. The Brahmakāyika devas having heard what the Paranimmitavasavatti devas said, proclaimed with one voice, "The Incomparable Wheel of Dhamma is turned by the Exalted One in the Deer Park at Isipatana near Banaras, and no *samaṇa*, *brāhmaṇa*, *deva*, Māra, brahmā, or other beings in the world can stop it."

Thus, in a moment, an instant, a flash, the word about the turning the Wheel of Dhamma reached the Brahma-world; and the whole system of ten thousand universes pitched and tossed.

---

36. The moment of arising of the Magga and Phala Ñāṇa does not last even for a second. Then there arises reflection of the particular experiences of the "Magga, Phala and Nibbāna". This is *Paccava-kkhana-ñāṇa* (Insight of retrospection).

A boundless sublime radiance[37] surpassing the power of *devas* appeared on earth.

Then the Exalted One pronounced this solemn utterance: "Bhikkhus, truly Kodañña has realized the Four Noble Truths; truly Kodañña has realized the Four Noble Truths." On account of this solemn utterance, Venerable Kodañña received the name Aññāsikodañña (Kodañña who has realized the Four Noble Truths).

And Venerable Kodañña (who has now become a Sotāpanna) having realized the Four Noble Truths, having attained the Four Noble Truths, having fully understood the Four Noble Truths, having penetrated the Four Noble Truths, having overcome Doubt, having dispelled all uncertainties, having full confidence in the Teachings of the Buddha, having realized that there was none except the Buddha in whom to confide, spoke to the Exalted One: "Let me receive the full ordination from the Exalted One."

"Come, O Bhikkhu", said the Exalted One, "well taught is the doctrine; strive for the next three higher Holy Paths for the sake of the complete cessation of suffering." Thus, Venerable Kodañña received the full ordination as an *ehi bhikkhu* (Come, O Bhikkhu).

You yourselves must make the effort; Buddhas but point out the way. Those who meditate and follow it, will escape the bondage of Māra (*kilesas*).

Dhammapada, Verse 276

---

37. Radiance caused by the power of *Desanā-dhammacakka*.

AṄGUTTARA NIKĀYA

AṄGUTTARA NIKĀYA, EKAKANIPĀTA PĀḶI

(The Book of the Ones)

Homage to Him, the Most Exalted, the Purified,
the Supremely Enlightened Buddha.

1. RŪPĀDI-VAGGA[1] (Sight and the Rest)

The Sight of a Woman

I. Thus, have I heard: On one occasion, the Buddha was residing at the Jetavana Monastery of Anāthapiṇḍika. There the Buddha addressed the bhikkhus, "Bhikkhus." "Lord," replied those bhikkhus to the Buddha. The Buddha said: "Bhikkhus, I know not any other single sight that seizes and exhausts the mind of a man as the sight of a woman. Bhikkhus, the sight of a woman seizes and exhausts the mind of a man."

The Aṅguttara Nikāya Commentary (Manorathapūraṇī)[2] *Ekakanipāta, Rūpādivagga, 1st Sutta.*

The Sight of a Woman

This religious discourse, the First Sutta, was set forth by the Buddha for the benefit of men who thought highly of the sight of a woman.

"I know not any other single sight" means "I see not any other single sight apart from that of a woman"—"Bhikkhus, even though I ponder with my Omniscience (*Sabbaññutañaṇa*), I see not any other single sight apart from that of a woman."

"... that seizes and exhausts the mind of a man" means the sight of a woman seizes and exhausts the wholesome consciousness of four spheres[3] in the man who thinks highly of the sight of a woman by way of preventing it (wholesome consciousness) from arising.

"... the sight of a woman" means the physical form of a woman as produced by four causes namely (*kamma, citta, utu* and *āhāra*) kamma, mind, temperature and nutrition.

---

1. Aṅguttara Nikāya, Ekakanipāta. Rūpādi-Vagga, pg. 1, 6th. Syd. Edn.
2. Aṅguttara Nikāya, Ekakanipāta. Rūpādivaggavaṇṇaṇā, pg. 15, Vol. I, 6th. Syd. Edn.
3. Cātubhūmika Kusala Citta, = *Kāma* - (1) Sensual sphere, (2) *Rūpa* - form sphere, (3) *Arūpa* - formless sphere, (4) *Lokuttara* - Supramundane sphere.

Furthermore, *the sight of a woman* means her dress, ornaments, unguents, flowers and other adornments connected with her body.

The Story of Citta Thera

Once upon a time King Mahādāṭhikanāga, having built a huge pagoda on the top of Cetiya-gīri, a hill with mango trees, made a great adoration to the pagoda. He often went there with a big retinue and gave offerings on a grand scale to the bhikkhus.

Usually in a crowd all are not mindful.

The king had a queen named Damiḷha Devī who was young, beautiful and lovely. Then Citta Thera, who became a bhikkhu late in life, without restraining his sense of sight, looked at that queen, took delight in her beautiful form, became as if mad and while standing and sitting he murmured, "O, Damiḷha Devī, Damiḷha Devī" and roamed about. From that time the novices called him 'the mad Citta Thera'.

Then the queen died. A group of bhikkhus went to the cemetery. On their return the novices approached Citta Thera and said, "Venerable Sir, you are merely murmuring about the queen, Damiḷha Devī. As for us we have just come back from her grave."

Even then being unable to believe them, he retorted saying, "You must have gone to a grave of some other woman. Your faces look like smoke," as a mad man might say.

This is how the sight of a woman seized and exhausted the mind of the mad Citta Thera.

The Story of a Certain Young Bhikkhu

One day, King Saddha Tissā came to a monastery with his retinue. Then a young bhikkhu standing at the door of Lohapāsāda Monastery, looked at a woman among the King's retinue without restraining his sense of sight. That woman also stopped and looked at him. Both of them were burnt by the fire of lust which arose in them and died. Thus, the sight of a woman seized and exhausted the mind of the young bhikkhu.

Another story runs thus:

The Story of a Young bhikkhu from the Kalyāṇiya Monastery

A young bhikkhu from the Kalyāṇiya Monastery went to a monastery near the gate of the village, Kāḷadīghavāpī, to learn the teachings of the Buddha.

After the completion of his studies, without obeying the words of his teachers who were desirous of his welfare, he went out for alms thinking: "Wherever I go I may have to tell the position of the village to the novices who may ask me about it."

Taking the object of perception of beauty of the opposite sex, that young bhikkhu went back to his dwelling place. He recognised the dress worn by that woman and on asking the elder monk where he got it, he learnt the death of that woman. While he was thinking that such a woman had died on account of him, the fire of lust arose in him and burnt him to death.

Thus, the sight of a woman seized and exhausted the mind of a man.

The Voice of a Woman

2. "Bhikkhus, I know not any other single voice that seizes and exhausts the mind of a man as the voice of a woman. Bhikkhus, the voice of a woman seizes and exhausts the mind of a man."

The Commentary on the 2nd Sutta

2. The voice of a woman

The Second Sutta, etc. was set forth by the Buddha in the interest of men who respectively thought highly of the voice, the odour, the savour and the physical contact of a woman.

In the Second Sutta, "the voice of a woman" means the voice caused by her mind in speaking or singing.

Moreover, the sounds produced by a woman's clothes and ornaments and the sound of a harp, conch and drum, etc. caused through a woman's effort should be regarded as *the voice of a woman*. All these seize and exhaust the mind of a man.

In this connection the stories of (1) 'The Golden Crab', (2) 'The Golden Peacock', and (3) 'The Young Bhikkhu' should be noted.

(1) The Golden Crab

Once there dwelt a large herd of elephants among the mountains. In the vicinity there was a big lake on which a great number of beings depended. There was a huge golden crab in it. The huge crab used to seize any being that entered the lake, in the leg with its claws as if with pincers, take it to his place and kill it.

The elephants which entered the lake roared about making a big bull elephant their chief. One day the huge crab seized the big bull elephant. The mindful big bull elephant, reflecting thus: "Were I to scream in fear, all of the elephants will run away without playing in the water to their heart's content", stood still there.

But when he knew that all the elephants had already got onto the shore, the big bull elephant, to make his wife-elephant know that the huge crab had seized it, said thus:

> "There is a huge golden crab which has claws like the horns of a beast, the strength of a lion or an elephant, wide and protruding eyes, and bony skin, which lives in the water and is hairless. I, being tortured by it, cry all alone. Please do not desert me who is like your life."

On hearing it she knew that her husband had been caught and said to him as well as to the crab, in order that he might be free from that danger:

> "The King of elephants who is declining in strength at sixties, wanders trumpeting with the voice of a heron, Lord, I will not desert you. In the land bounded by the four great oceans, I love you most.
>
> Of all the crabs in the ocean, and the Ganges and Jamuna, you the Golden Crab are the chief. Please release my crying husband."

On hearing the voice of the female elephant, the huge crab relaxed its claws.

Then the big bull elephant, knowing that it was a good opportunity, let one leg stand as it was caught, raised the second leg, trod upon and crushed the back shell of the crab, drew it out a little and threw it on the bank.

Then all the elephants, knowing that it was their enemy, assembled together and crushed it into pieces.

Thus, the voice of the female elephant seized and exhausted the mind of the golden crab.

(2) The Story of the Golden Peacock

Once there lived a Golden Peacock in the forest of Himalaya mountains. Always looking at the sun at the time of its rising and wishing to protect itself, the Golden Peacock uttered thus:

> "The sole ruler, this (sun) who has eyes, is golden hued and shines all over the Earth rises! I pay homage to you who are Golden hued and shines all over the Earth. I shall live under your protection the whole day long.
>
> I pay my homage to the Buddhas, the Purified, the Omniscience, who have mastered all the dhammas. May they protect me from dangers.

I pay my homage to Buddhas. I pay my homage to the Paths and the Fruitions. I pay my homage to those who have emancipated themselves. I pay my homage to emancipation."

Thus, making a protection (by reciting the verses) it wanders about looking for food.

"The sole ruler, this (sun) who has eyes is golden hued and shines all over the Earth sets! I pay my homage to you who are Golden hued and shines all over the Earth. I shall live under your protection the whole night long.

I pay my homage to the Buddhas, the Purified, the Omniscience, who have mastered all the dhammas. May they protect me from dangers.

I pay my homage to Buddhas. I pay my homage to the Paths and the Fruitions. I pay my homage to those who have emancipated themselves. I pay my homage to emancipation."

Thus, making a protection (by reciting the verses) it lived for the night.

700 years passed in this way. One day, the Golden Peacock heard the voice of a peahen before making a protection by reciting the Paritta, forgot to make a protection and fell into the hands of a hunter sent by the king of Banaras.

Thus, the voice of a peahen seized and exhausted the mind of the Golden Peacock.

(3) The Stories of the Two Bhikkhus

A young bhikkhu dwelling at Mt. Chāta, and another one dwelling at Sudhāmuṇḍaka came to ruin on account of the voice of a woman.

Here ends the Commentary on the Second Sutta.

The Odour of a Woman

3. "Bhikkhus, I know not any other single odour that seizes and exhausts the mind of a man as the odour of a woman. Bhikkhus, the odour of a woman seizes and exhausts the mind of a man."

The Commentary on the Third Sutta
The Odour of a Woman

In the Third Sutta, "the odour of a woman" means the odour of a woman which is produced by the four causes, (*Kamma, Citta, Utu and Āhāra*). The odour of a woman is a bad one.

But here it means the odour of unguents, etc. which have been applied to her body.

Some women have the odour of a horse, some have that of a goat, some have that of sweat, some have that of menses. Some foolish worldlings like such kind of women also.

From the body of the queen of Cakkavatin, the odour of sandal wood comes out. The odour of blue lotus comes out of her mouth. All women do not have such odours. Therefore, only the odour of unguents, etc. is referred to here.

The odour of the woman's body or that of the clothes she wears, the unguents she uses, the flowers she puts on her head,—all of them must be taken as "the odour of a woman".

The Savour of a Woman

4. Bhikkhus, I know not any other single savour that seizes and exhausts the mind of a man as the savour of a woman. Bhikkhus, the savour of a woman seizes and exhausts the mind of a man.

The Commentary on the Fourth Sutta
The Savour of a Woman

In the Fourth Sutta, "the savour of a woman" means the savour produced by the four causes (*Kamma, Citta, Utu and Āhāra*) Kamma, mind, temperature and Nutrition.

There is taste in saliva clinging to the lips of a woman: there is taste in rice gruel, etc. given to a husband by the wife—all of them are called "the savour of a woman".

Many people go to ruin as they take whatever are given by their wives with their hands as delicious. Here ends the Commentary on the fourth sutta.

The Physical Contact of a Woman

5. Bhikkhus, I know not any other single physical contact that seizes and exhausts the mind of a man as the physical contact of a woman. Bhikkhus, the physical contact of a woman seizes and exhausts the mind of a man.

Commentary on the Fifth Sutta
The Physical Contact of a Woman

In the Fifth Sutta, "the physical contact of a woman" means (1) the contact with the body of a woman and (2) the contact with clothes, ornaments, and flowers, etc. on her body.

All these seize and exhaust the mind of a man, as in the case of a bhikkhu whose mind was seized by the physical contact of the opposite sex, while reciting suttas in a group at Mahācetī Pagoda.

Thus, in accordance, with the respective propensity of men, the Buddha, taking one at a time out of *Rūpa*, etc., expounded thus:

"I know not any other single ...."

The sight of a woman can make the mind of a man (who thinks highly of the sight) to be restless, hindered, disturbed, bound, stupefied and entirely forgetful, but the remaining four objects such as the voice of a woman, etc. cannot make his mind likewise.

So also, the remaining four objects cannot *mutatis mutandis* affect the mind of a man who thinks highly of a woman's voice only.

Only one of the objects can seize and exhaust the mind of some men whereas two or three or four or five objects can seize and exhaust the mind of other men.

These five Suttas are set forth in accordance with the propensities of men who think highly of the five objects respectively—and not of men who think highly of all the five objects. However, the Pañcagaruka Jātaka[4] may be cited in support.

Pañca Garuka Jātaka

In that story of the five friends of the Great Man (Bodhisatta) who went about the stalls created by non-human beings (ogres) in the midst of a desert, one who thought highly of sight got infatuated with sight and perished and those who thought highly of voice, etc. got infatuated with voice, etc. respectively and perished.

Five Suttas for Women. The Sight of a Man.

6. "Bhikkhus, I know not any other single sight that seizes and exhausts the mind of a woman as the sight of a man. Bhikkhus, the sight of a man seizes and exhausts the mind of a woman."

The Voice of a Man

7. "Bhikkhus, I know not any other single voice that seizes and exhausts

---

4. Khuddaka-nikāya, Jātakaṭṭhakathaā Asampadāna-Vagga, Pañcagaruka (Bhīruka) Jātaka, Pg. 494, Vol, l, 6th Syd. Edn.

the mind of a woman as the voice of a man. Bhikkhus, the voice of a man seizes and exhausts the mind of a woman."

8. "Bhikkhus, I know not any other single odour that seizes and exhausts the mind of a woman as the odour of a man. Bhikkhus, the odour of a man seizes and exhausts the mind of a woman."

The Savour of a Man

9. "Bhikkhus, I know not any other single savour that seizes and exhausts the mind of a woman as the savour of a man. Bhikkhus, the savour of a man seizes and exhausts the mind of a woman."

The Physical Contact of a Man

10. "Bhikkhus, I know not any other single physical, contact that seizes and exhausts the mind of a woman as the physical contact of a man. Bhikkhus, the physical contact of a man seizes and exhausts the mind of a woman."

Commentary on the Five Suttas for Woman

Not only men think highly of the five objects but also women think highly of them. So, the Buddha set forth the five suttas for women. Also, with regard to the meaning of the Suttas refer to the Commentary above.

As regards stories with reference to the First Sutta, the story of a woman in the king's retinue, who died after looking at a young bhikkhu standing at the door of Lohapāsāda Monastery should be noted.

In the Second Sutta, the story of a courtesan, in Banaras, who was living on her beauty, should be noted.

The Story of a Courtesan

Once Guttila, the harper sent a thousand *kyats* (*kahāpaṇa*) to a courtesan. She snobbishly refused to accept it. Guttila reflecting thus: "In this connection I shall do what should be done". And towards the evening, he dressed himself well, sat at the door of a house facing that of the courtesan, adjusted the strings of the harp and sang without letting the music overwhelm the melody of the song.

The courtesan heard the song, and meant to go near him and lost her life in the air as she mistook the window for a door.

With reference to the Third Sutta, the odour of the body of King Cakkavatin is that of sandal wood; the odour of his mouth is that of the blue lotus.

At Sāvatthi, the husband of a daughter of a banker, after hearing the religious discourse of the Buddha, thought, "I am unable to practice this dhamma in the household life," and entered the Order under the preceptorship of an Elder who was practicing *piṇḍapātikaṅga Dhutaṅga* the ascetic practice of eating only food received in the alms-bowl.

Knowing that this woman had no husband, King Pasenadi Kosala ordered his men to bring her to his harem. One day, the king entered the harem bringing with him a bunch of blue lotus, ordered that a flower be given to each and every woman.

On distributing the flowers, two flowers fell into the hand of that woman. She showed a sign of gladness, but she wept bitterly after smelling them.

Seeing the two expressions on her face King Pasenadi Kosala ordered his men to bring her and asked her. The woman explained why she was glad and why she wept bitterly.

Even though she explained three times, the king did not believe her.

So on the next day, the king ordered his men to take all the sweet scented ones from among the unguents and the scented flowers in the palace, prepare seats for a group of bhikkhus headed by the Buddha, and offered a meal to the bhikkhus headed by the Buddha, and after the meal asked the woman, "Which is your bhikkhu?" and when she replied, "This" knowing him, paid homage to the Buddha, and said, "Lord, the other bhikkhus may return with you; this bhikkhu will deliver a religious discourse of rejoice to us." And the Buddha returned to the monastery leaving that bhikkhu behind.

As soon as the bhikkhu made an effort to deliver a religious discourse of rejoice, the whole of the palace became as if it was full of sweet scents.

The king was convinced that the woman had verily told the truth, and on the next day asked the Buddha what the reason for it was.

The Buddha said, "Once in the past when he was listening to a religious discourse, this bhikkhu listened to it respectfully saying 'Sadhu! Sadhu!' (Good! Good!). He got this distinction as a result thereof.

"From the mouth of the one who utters 'Sadhu! Sadhu!' at the time of listening to a religious discourse, sweet scent arises just as the blue lotus arises in the water."

Here ends the Commentary on the Rūpādi-Vagga.

2. NĪVARAṆAPPAHĀNA-VAGGA[5] (Abandoning of Hindrances)

1st Sutta

Pleasant Object

1. "Bhikkhus, I know not any other single thing that can be (i) the cause of arising of sensual desire that has not arisen, and (ii) the cause of more becoming and increase of sensual desire that has already arisen—as the pleasant object.

"In him, bhikkhus, who pays attention to pleasant object in an improper manner, sensual desire that has not arisen arises, and sensual desire that has already arisen becomes more and increases."

The Aṅguttara Nikāya Commentary on the[6] 1st Sutta

Sensual desire means hindrance which has already been explained as lust in sensuality, greed, longing, craving, etc.

'arises' means appears, comes into existence.

It should be understood that this sensual desire that has not arisen for lack of practice or for not having an enjoyable object arises. In reality, however, there is no sensual desire that has not arisen throughout the beginningless rounds of rebirths.

In the context 'Sensual desire that has not arisen', (i) defilement, sensual lust, does not arise in some who is performing his duties, (ii) sensual desire does not arise in some due to one of these reasons, namely learning the scriptures, practicing the ascetic practices, establishing concentration, developing insight (*vipassanā*) and performing new activities.

How is it so? Some bhikkhu is dutiful, and in him while performing the 82 minor duties or 14 major duties or duties at the pagodas and Bodhi tree or the duties with regard to water, drinking and using for various purposes, duties at the meeting chamber, duties at the consecrated place (*sīma*), duties towards bhikkhu-guests, and bhikkhu-travellers, there is no opportunity for

5. P.2, book One 6th Syd. Edn.
6. Aṅguttara-Nikāya Ekakanipātaṭṭhakathā, p. 23, Bk. II, 6th Syd. Edn.

the sensual lust to arise. But later on, he abandons his duties and in him while remaining without duties, defilement arises due to paying attention in an improper manner and heedlessness.

Thus, the sensual desire that has not arisen for lack of practice arises.

(a) Some bhikkhu learns the sacred texts, learns one of the Nikāyas or two or three or four or five of the Nikāyas

In him there is no opportunity for the defilements (*kilesa*) to arise while learning; reciting, teaching, preaching or explaining Tipiṭaka, the words of Buddha with regard to their meaning and *pāḷi* with regard to their connections and with regard to their preceding and following.

But later on, he abandons learning the scriptures, and in him while remaining lazily, the defilements arise due to paying attention in an improper manner and heedlessness.

Thus, too, the defilements that have not arisen for lack of practice, arise.

(b) Some bhikkhu practices the ascetic practice, and observes the 13 qualities of ascetic practices. In him while practicing the ascetic practices there is no opportunity for the defilements to arise.

But later on, he abandons the ascetic practices and in him while roaming about for the accumulation of requisites such as robes, the defilements appear due to paying attention in an improper manner and heedlessness.

Thus, too, the defilement that has not arisen for lack of practice arises.

(c) Some bhikkhu has mastery over the 8 attainments of *jhānas* (*samāpatti*). In him while dwelling on the first *jhāna* and so on with regard to mastery in adverting, etc., there is no opportunity for the defilements to arise. But later on, having fallen from the *jhānas*, or having abandoned the *jhānas*, defilements arise in him while indulging in talking and so on, due to paying attention in an improper manner, and heedlessness.

Thus also, the sensual desire that has not arisen for lack of practice arises.

(d) Some bhikkhu contemplates *vipassanā* insight. He dwells in contemplating over the seven kinds of *Anupassanā* (contemplation) and eighteen chief kinds of *vipassanā* insight (*Mahā-vipassanā*). In such a person living thus there is no opportunity for the defilements to arise.

But later on, in him having abandoned the contemplation of insight (*vipassanā*) while making very strong in the body the defilements arise due to paying attention in an improper manner and heedlessness.

Thus, also the sensual desire that has not arisen for lack of practice, arises.

(e) Some bhikkhu performs some new work; he makes others build some consecrated place (*sīma*), dining hall, etc. In him while thinking about the means of their completion there is no opportunity for the defilements to arise.

But later on, after the completion of the work, or after he has abandoned the work, in him there appear the defilements due to paying attention in an improper manner and heedlessness.

Thus, also the sensual desire that has not arisen for lack of practice, arises.

(f) Moreover, some person who came from the *brahma* world is pure. As he had no habit of indulging in sensual pleasures in previous existence, there is no opportunity for the defilement to arise in him.

But later on, having the habit of indulging in sensual desires, the defilement arises in him due to paying attention in an improper manner and heedlessness.

Thus, also the sensual desire that has not arisen for lack of practice, arises.

It should thus be noted at first that the sensual desire that has not arisen for lack of practice, arises.

How does the sensual desire that has not arisen for not having an enjoyable object, arise?

In this world some person has got some lovely objects such as sight that has never been experienced before. Sensual desire arises in him due to paying attention to such objects in an improper manner and heedlessness. Thus, the sensual desire that has not arisen for not having an enjoyable object, arises.

"that has already arisen" means that has occurred, that has appeared.
"for more becoming" means for becoming again and again.
"for increase" means for accumulation.

In the context "for more becoming and increase" there is no such a case as sensual desire that has once arisen will not cease; sensual desire that has once ceased will arise again.

When sensual desire has ceased, there is indeed more becoming and increase of sensual desire in succession for the same object or for any other object.

"Pleasant object" means the object that is the cause of sensual lust.

Herein desirable object which is the cause of sensual lust is required as "the pleasant object."

In the context: "In him who pays attention in an improper manner", what is paying attention in an improper manner?

(i) Paying attention to impermanence as permanence, (ii) suffering as pleasure, (iii) impersonality as personality, (iv) unpleasantness as pleasantness—this is paying attention in an improper manner. This is paying attention in a wrong way.

Moreover, in a manner contrary to the penetration of the Four Noble Truths, (i) advertence of the mind towards the object, (ii) contemplating on the object again and again, (iii) mindfulness of the object, (iv) directing one's mind towards the object, (v) setting of the mind to the object—all this is called "paying attention in an improper manner."

For those who pay attention in such a way, sensual desire that has not arisen, arises.

Here ends the Commentary on the 1st Sutta.

2nd Sutta

Hateful Object

"Bhikkhus, I know not any other single thing that can be (i) the cause of arising of ill will that has not arisen, and (ii) the cause of more becoming and increase of ill will that has already arisen—as the hateful object.

In him, bhikkhus, who pays attention to hateful object in an improper manner, ill will that has not arisen, arises, and ill will that has already arisen becomes more and increases.

The Commentary on the 2nd Sutta

In the 2nd Sutta, ill will means the wrong state of mind—just as the rottenness of the rice—the abandoning of the original state of mind.

In this context, "what is ill will". It is the name of the hindrance of ill will which has already been explained thus that there arises malice that "some harm has been done to me" and so on. Repulsive object (*paṭigha-nimitta*) is undesirable object. It is the name of hatred (*dosa*) as well as repulsive object.

"Hatred itself is repulsive object and the phenomenon which is the cause of hatred is also, repulsive object (*paṭigha-nimitta*)," thus stated in the old Commentary.

Here ends the Commentary on the 2nd Sutta.

3rd Sutta

Dullness of the mind

"Bhikkhus, I know not any other single thing that can be (i) the cause of arising of sloth and torpor (*thīna-middha*) that has not arisen, and (ii) the cause of more becoming and increase of sloth and torpor that has already arisen—as weariness, laziness, stretching of the limbs in sleepiness, drowsiness after meals, and dullness of the mind.

In him, bhikkhus, who has dullness of the mind, sloth and torpor that has not arisen arises, that has already arisen increases."

The Commentary on the 3rd Sutta

In the 3rd Sutta, "sloth and torpor" means stolidity and drowsiness. Therein the lack of workableness of consciousness is sloth (*thīna*). It is the name of the state of being lazy.

The lack of workableness of the three mental aggregates[7] is torpor (*middha*). It is the name of the state of a person who is dosing and blinking in drowsiness.

"In 'sloth and torpor', what is meant by 'sloth' (*thīna*)? Unwholesomeness and unworkableness of consciousness, shrinking and stolidity of consciousness—such a state of consciousness is called sloth. In sloth and torpor; what is meant by torpor (*middha*)? It is lack of pliancy and workableness, shrouding and cloudiness of the three mental aggregates. Thus, the explanation of the two should be noted.

The state of weariness, etc., should be noted as already explained in detail in Vibhaṅga Pāḷi. It is truly said, 'In the context: weariness and laziness, etc.', what is meant by 'weariness (*Arati*)'? In secluded places, or in one or the other of the higher wholesome phenomena (calmness and insight) weariness, the state of utter weariness, discontent, the state of discontent, dissatisfaction, the state of longing for something—all this is called weariness.

In the context, what is meant by 'laziness (*tandī*)'? Laziness, the state of laziness, the state of mind oppressed by laziness, the lazy mood, the state of mind caused by laziness—all this is called laziness.

In the context, what is meant by 'trembling (*vijambhitā*)'? The trembling of the body, the trembling of the body again and again, the bending of the body forward and backward and to all sides, keeping the body upright, the state of being upset—all this is called trembling.

---

7. *vedanā, saññā, saṅkhāra-kkhandhas.*

In the context, what is meant by 'drowsiness after meals? (*Battasammado*) drowsiness after taking food, uneasiness, burning in stomach, unworkableness of the body—all this is called drowsiness after meals.

In the context, what is meant by 'dullness of the mind (*cetaso ca līnattaṃ*)'? Unwholesomeness, unworkableness of the mind shrinking and, utter shrinking of the mind, shrinkage, the state of shrinking, mode of shrinking, hardness, hard mood, the state of being hardness of the mind—all this is called dullness of the mind."

In this context, the former four things namely, weariness, laziness, trembling, and drowsiness after meals condition the hindrance of sloth and torpor by way of appearing together (*sahajātavasena*) and also by way of basis (*upanissaya-vasena*). Dullness of the mind itself does not appear as co-nascence but indeed it appears by way of basis.

Here ends the Commentary on the 3rd Sutta.

4th Sutta

The Uncalmed Mind

4. Bhikkhus, I know not any other single thing that can be (i) the cause of arising of restlessness and worry that has not arisen, and (ii) the cause of more becoming and increase of restlessness and worry that has already arisen—as the uncalmed mind.

In him, bhikkhus, who has uncalmed mind, restlessness and worry that has not arisen arises, restlessness and worry that has already arisen becomes more and increases."

The Commentary on the 4th Sutta

In the Fourth Sutta, "restlessness and worry" means restlessness as well as worry. In the context 'restlessness' means the wavering state of mind.

'Worry (*kukkucca*)' means remorse over the good that has not been done and the evil that has been committed.

'The uncalmed mind' is the name of restlessness and worry. 'Who has uncalmed mind' means who has the mind which has not been calmed by ecstasy (*jhāna*) or by insight (*vipassanā*).

This uncalmed mind indeed conditions restlessness and worry basically.

Here ends the Commentary on the 4th Sutta.

5th Sutta

Paying Attention in an Improper Manner

5. "Bhikkhus, I know not any other single thing that can be (i) the cause of arising of sceptical doubt that has not arisen and (ii) the cause of more-becoming and increase of sceptical doubt that has already arisen—as paying attention in an improper manner.

In him, bhikkhus, who pays attention in an improper manner, sceptical doubt that has not arisen arises, sceptical doubt that has already arisen becomes more and increases.

The Commentary on the 5th Sutta

In the 5th Sutta, sceptical doubt (*vicikicchā*) is the hindrance of sceptical doubt as already explained in detail (in Dhammasaṅgaṇī) thus: "Doubt about the Buddha" etc.

'Paying attention in an improper manner' has the same characteristic as explained before.

Here ends the Commentary on the 5th Sutta.

6th Sutta

The Unpleasant Object

6. "Bhikkhus, I know not any other single thing that can be (i) the cause of non-arising of sensual desire that has not arisen, and (ii) the cause of abandoning of sensual desire that has already arisen—as the unpleasant object.

In him, bhikkhus, who pays attention to unpleasant object in a proper manner, sensual desire that has not arisen does not arise, and sensual desire that has already arisen is abandoned."

The Commentary on the 6th Sutta[8]

In the 6th Sutta, 'the sensual desire that has not arisen does not arise' means the sensual desire that has not arisen by two causes, namely, for lack of practice and also for having not an enjoyable object, does not arise. It is as it has already been abandoned; it does not get either the regenerative cause (*janaka*) or the supporting cause (*upathambhaka*). Herein lack of practice should be understood to be due to performing of the duties, etc. Indeed, there is no opportunity for the sensual lust to arise in some bhikkhu

8. Aṅguttara Aṭṭhakathā, p. 27, Vol-l, 6th Syd. Edn.

while performing duties only in the said manner. By performing duties, the sensual lust is abandoned. The bhikkhu, having thus abandoned the sensual lust, makes himself free from the rounds of defilements (*vaṭṭa*) and attains Sainthood (*Arahatta*) as Milakkhatissa Thera did.

The Story of Milakkhatissa Thera

Milakkhatissa Thera was born in a family of hunters, at the Rohaṇa Janapada, the grazing of Gameṇḍavāla Mahāvihāra, (the place for bhikkhu's almsround). Having attained the age of puberty and been married, he thought: "I am to support the children and wife," and placed one hundred traps, arranged one hundred nooses, and set up one hundred pecks, thus he committed much evil; one day taking fire and salt from home, he went into the forest, killed the deer caught in the trap, and ate the meat baked by embers; being so thirsty he went into Gameṇḍavāla Mahāvihāra, but did not get any sufficient water even to quench his thirst, from the ten pots on the water stand, so he tried to rebuke: "How is it? In a dwelling place of such a number of bhikkhus, there is no water even to quench the thirst of those who come through thirst."

On hearing his words, Cūḷapiṇḍapātikatissa Thera went to him; but on seeing that the ten pots on the water-stand were full of water, the Thera thought, "This man might be a ghost (*peta*) even while alive," and lifted the pot and poured water down into his hands saying, "Upāsaka, if you are thirsty, drink water." As a result of his misdeed (*kamma*), all the water he drank vanished as if it were poured down into a red-hot-pot. Even though he drank the whole lot from all the pots, his thirst was not quenched.

Then the Thera said to him, "Upāsaka, you have done so cruel a misdeed (*kamma*); even now you have become a ghost (*peta*), what will the result be?"

On hearing the words of the Thera, he repented, paid homage to him, destroyed the traps, etc., went home in great haste, looked at his children and wife, destroyed the instruments, set decoy deer and birds free in the forest, approached the Thera and asked for his ordination.

"Difficult, Upāsaka, is the ascetic life (as a bhikkhu). How will you take up the ascetic life?" asked the Thera.

He replied, "Venerable Sir, having seen such a condition for myself, how should I not take up the life of a bhikkhu?"

The Thera gave him *tacapancaka*[9] meditation, and ordained him as

---

9. The five dermatic constituents of the body such as hair, etc., with skin as the fifth.

a novice. Being rejoiced in performing duties, he learnt the words of the Buddha; one day he heard this passage from the Devadūta Sutta, Discourse on Death's Messengers: "Bhikkhus, the guardians of the hell throw that evil-doer again into the Great Hell," and said, "They again throw such a being who has suffered such a great deal of pain into the Great Hell."

"Yes, novice, very grave indeed is the Greater Hell," replied the Thera.

"Venerable Sir, is it possible to see the Great Hell?" asked the novice.

"Hard it is to see. I shall show you one thing to make a resemblance of the sight," said the Thera and ordered him to assemble the novices and make a heap of green firewood on the rock. He made them do accordingly. The Thera, even while sitting, exercised his psychic power, took out from the Great Hell a small particle of fire about the size of a firefly or a glow-worm, and threw it into the heap of firewood while he was looking at it. No sooner did the small particle of fire fall into the heap then it burned to ashes.

Seeing that, he asked, "Venerable Sir, how many burdens (*dūra*) are there in this Sāsana?"

"My dear, there are the burden of practicing insight (*vipassanā*) and the burden of learning the texts," replied the Thera.

"Venerable Sir, learning the texts is the work of the one who is able to do so. But my confidence is based on seeing suffering; I shall take the burden of practicing *vipassanā*; please give me the object of meditation," said he, paid homage to the Thera and sat down.

The Thera, thinking: 'This bhikkhu is dutiful' and emphasizing the importance of duties, gave him a talk on meditation.

The bhikkhu, taking the meditation, practiced *vipassanā* and also fulfilled the duties.

One day he performed his duties at Cittalapabbata Mahāvihāra, one day at Gameṇḍa Mahāvihāra, and one day at Gocaragāma Mahāvihāra.

Fearing to be slack in performing his duties while feeling stolid and drowsy, he wetted a bundle of straw and put it on his head and sat dipping his feet in the water.

One day, after performing his duties at Cittalapabbata Mahāvihāra for the two watches of the night; at about dawn, when he tried to sleep, putting the wet bundle of straw on the head and sat, he heard a novice on the slope of the east hill reciting Aruṇavatiya Suttanta:

"Make an effort in Calmness and Insight etc., try hard, set forth energy in the Teachings of the Buddha. Thus, you destroy the army of Death as the bull elephant does the reed-house. He who is heedful in this *dhamma-vinaya* will abandon the rounds of rebirth and make an end to suffering."

He then thought: 'This Sutta might have been set forth by the Buddha for such an energetic bhikkhu like me', and having a zest he developed the *jhāna* ecstasy. Taking it as a basis he established himself in the fruition of Never-returner (*Anāgāmiphala*) and successively made an effort, and attained the Fruition of Arahatta together with the Four-fold Analytical Knowledge (*Paṭisambhidā*). Even at the time of *parinibbāṇa*, he, wishing to reveal that happening, uttered the following:

> "Putting the wet bundle of straw on the head I walked. The third stage (*Anāgāmiphala*) have I attained. Doubt on this have I none,"

Thus, in such a person the defilement is abandoned as it has been abandoned by performing duties.

The Story of Maliyadevatthera

There is no opportunity for defilements (*kilesa*) to arise in some bhikkhu while learning, reciting, teaching, preaching or explaining the texts. The defilement is abandoned by way of (learning, etc.) texts. The bhikkhu, having abandoned the defilement in this way, makes himself free from the rounds of rebirth and attains the Fruition of Arahatta as Maliyadevatthera did.

He, at his third rainy season (*vasa*) in bhikkhuhood, learned the brief text (*uddesa*) at Maṇḍalārāma Mahāvihāra in the village of Kalla, and also practiced *vipassanā*. One day while he was going out, he was asked by a laywoman, "Son, which village do you live in?" "Upāsika," he said, "I am learning the texts at Maṇḍalārāma Mahāvihāra."

"If so, son, as long as you learn the texts, please always take meals here," said the laywoman.

He accepted it and had his regular meals there.

After meals, wishing to say thanks, he uttered the two lines: "May you be happy. May you be free from suffering." and went away. For the three months of the rainy season, he, wishing to do her a great favour, respected the rice by way of ending the defilements within him, and attained the Fruition of Arahatta together with the Four Analytical Knowledge at the end of the rainy season when a kind of function known as *Pavāraṇā* is performed.

The resident Mahāthera said, "My dear Mahādeva, there will be a big gathering of people today at the monastery. Bestow upon them the gift of dhamma." The Thera consented to do so.

The young novices gave hints to the laywoman, "Your son will deliver the religious discourse today. Go to the monastery and listen to it."

She said, "Sons, by no means do all bhikkhus know how to deliver the religious discourse. For such a long time, when delivering the religious discourse, my son used to utter the only two lines thus: 'May you be happy. May you be free from suffering.' Sons, please don't make fun."

They said, "Upāsika, please don't mind whether they know or not. Go to the monastery and listen to the dhamma."

Taking flowers and unguents, the laywoman paid homage and sat on one side of the assembly to listen to the dhamma.

The day-time preacher and the pāḷi-text reciter knew their time and rose from their seats.

Then, Maliyadeva Thera, sitting on the preacher's seat, holding a wonderful fan, delivered a series of dhamma. Thinking, "I have said grace to the Upāsika with the two lines for the last three months. Today, I shall explain the meaning of the two lines: 'May you be happy. May you be free from suffering,' in consultation with Tipiṭaka, he set forth the dhamma and continued for the whole night. At dawn, at the end of the religious discourse, the great Upāsika attained the Fruition of *Sotāpanna*.

At that great monastery, another one named Tissabhūtitthera was learning Vinaya. At the time of going for almsround, he went into the village, and looked at the object of the opposite sex; sensual desire arose in him: he did not move his foot from the place it stood, and poured down the rice-gruel from his bowl into the bowl of his attendant-novice thinking, "If this thought develops, it will cause me to sink deep in the Four states of Misery (*Apāya*)," he returned from there and went to his teacher, paid homage to him, sat at one side and said, "I have an illness; if I am unable to cure this, I shall come back; otherwise, I shall not come back. You should consider me and set aside the day study and the evening study and not the morning study." Having said thus, he went to Malayavāsi Mahāsaṅgharakkhitatthera.

The Thera, making the walls of his own leaf roofed hut, even without looking at him, said, "My dear, keep your bowls and robes in order."

"Venerable Sir, I have an illness; if you can cure it, I shall keep my bowl and robes in order," he said.

"My dear, you have come to him who can cure the illness, keep them in order," said the Thera.

The obedient bhikkhu, thinking: "Our teacher would not say like this without knowing it," kept the bowl and robes in order, performed duties to the Thera, paid homage to him and sat at one side.

The Thera, knowing that he was of lusty nature, told him the meditation on an unpleasant object (*asubha kammaṭṭhāna*). He stood up, put the bowl and robes over his shoulder, and paid homage to the Thera again and again.

The Thera asked him, "Dear Mahābhūti, how is it that you show the most respectful action?"

"Venerable Sir, if I were able to do my work, it will do good. If not, this will be my last homage," said he.

"Go, Dear Mahābhūti, for such an energetic son of a good family, ecstasy (*jhāna*) or Insight (*vipassanā*) or Path or Fruition is not difficult," said the Thera.

Hearing the words of the Thera, and showing the manner of respect, he went to the foot of the leafy *sepanni* bush which he noticed when he came. Sitting cross-legged, he took the meditation on unpleasant object as a basis, developed the Insight, attained the Fruition of Arahatta, and fulfilled the learning of Vinaya, *uddesa*, at dawn.

In such persons, the defilements are abandoned as they have been abandoned by learning texts.

In some bhikkhus, while practicing the ascetic practices in the aforesaid way, there is no opportunity for defilement; it has been abandoned by the ascetic practice. He, having thus abandoned the defilements, and freed himself from the rounds of rebirth, attains the Fruition of Arahatta like Gāmantapabbhāravāsī Mahāsivatthera. The Thera living at Tissa-mahāvihāra, the big monastery in the big village, taught the 18 sects the Tipiṭaka with regard to its meaning (*aṭṭhakathā*) and Pāḷi.

Depending upon the Thera's instruction, 60,000 bhikkhus reached the state of *Arahatta*. A certain bhikkhu among them, felt very happy about his realisation of the dhamma, and thought: 'Is there any bliss of this kind in our teacher?' On reflection he knew that the Thera was still in a state of worldling, and thought: 'I am to make the Thera get alarmed (*saṃvega*) by some means,' and went out from his dwelling place to the Thera, paid homage to him, showed him his duties and sat.

Then the Thera asked him, "My dear, Piṇḍapātikā, why have you come here?"

"Venerable Sir, I have come here with a thought: 'If you would allow me, I should like to learn a certain dhamma.'"

"My dear, there are many things to learn; there will be no opportunity for you (to learn)," said the Thera. Being unable to get the opportunity for all the days and nights, he said, "Venerable Sir, if there is no opportunity as such, how can death get the opportunity?"

Then the Thera thought: 'This bhikkhu has come here not for learning pāḷi (*uddesa*); indeed, he has come here to cause me to be alarmed."

That Thera (Piṇḍapātikā) also said, "Venerable Sir, a bhikkhu should certainly be like me," paid homage to him, rose up into the crystal blue sky and went away.

From the time of his departure, the Thera, getting alarmed, taught the pāḷi in the day time and in the evening kept his bowl and robe at the side of his hand,[10] took them and descended together with the bhikkhu who learned the pāḷi at dawn and descended.

He fully observed the 13 ascetic qualities, went to the monastery in the valley near the village, cleaned it, set the couch upright, and thought: 'I will not stretch my limbs (lie down) on the couch, without attaining the state of Arahatta, and with such a firm determination he walked up and down meditating. While striving with diligence: 'Today I will attain the state of Arahatta: today I will attain the state of Arahatta? There came the time of Pavāraṇā.'[11]

Coming close to the time of *Pavāraṇā*, he felt very tired with the thought: 'I am to abandon the state of a worldling and make the *Visuddhipavāraṇā*.'[12]

Being unable to attain the Path and the Fruition for that *pavāraṇā* he said, "Even a person like me strenuously contemplating *vipassanā* Insight does not attain it: hard indeed is this state of Arahatta to attain." Saying in this way, he kept a constant practice on standing and walking postures, observed the dhamma of the bhikkhu for thirty rainy seasons, and in the middle of *Pavāraṇā* ceremony he looked at the full moon considering: 'Which is purer? The full moon or my moral conduct? There appears the sign of a rabbit in the moon.'

---

10. *Hattha-pāsa*—approximately within a distance of 1-1/2 cubits or 2-1/4 feet.

11. A mutual invitation among the bhikkhus to point out one another's guilt if seen, heard or suspected with the intention of expiating an offence. This is a kind of function solely meant for the bhikkhus and conducted by them every year in the consecrated places (*sīma*) on the *full-moon* day of Thadingyat, the end of *vassa* (rainy season), approximately in October, as laid down in the rules of *Vinaya-dhamma*.

12. An *arahatta's* invitation as above.

'Whereas in my moral conduct, since the time of my bhikkhu ordination up to this day, there is not a single stain as big as a mole and not even a stain as small as a blackhead'; he was very pleased, and his wisdom being fully developed, he abandoned the zest (*pīti*) and attained the state of Arahatta together with the Four Analytical Knowledge (*paṭisambhidā*).

In such a person the defilement is abandoned as has been abandoned by the ascetic practices.

There is no opportunity for the defilement to arise in a bhikkhu who dwells in the first *Jhāna* etc. in the said manner; the defilement has already been abandoned by the Attainments (*samāpatti*).[13] He thus abandons the defilement, frees himself from the rounds of rebirth and attains the state of *Arahatta* as Mahātissa Thera (did).

Mahātissa Thera attained the Eight Attainments (*samāpatti*) since he was in his eighth *vassa*[14] (rainy season) as a bhikkhu.

He having no defilements that have been dispelled by *Samāpatti* and by learning and questioning on the Texts, talked about *Ariya Magga*, the Noble Path. Even though he was in his 60th *vassa*, he did not realize his own state of being worldling.

One day a company of bhikkhus from Tissa Monastery at Mahāgāma village sent a message to Dhammadinnā Thera who lived in Talaṅgara, saying: "Dhammadinnā Thera may please come and deliver a religious discourse to us."

Dhammadinnā Thera accepted and thought: 'I have no elder bhikkhu near me; but Mahātissa Thera is my meditation instructor; I shall go to them making him the chief (Saṅgha Thera);' and he, accompanied by a group of bhikkhus, went to the Thera's Monastery, showed him his duties at his daytime dwelling place and seated himself at one side.

The Thera asked, "Dhammadinnā, why do you come here after so long a time?"

"Yes, Venerable Sir, bhikkhus from Tissamahāvihāra monastery sent a message to me. I do not want to go alone, as I should like to go with you, I come to you," said Dhammadinnā.

---

13. 'Attainments', *Samāpatti* is a name for the 8 *Jhānas* of the Fine-material and Immaterial spheres (*rūpa* and *arūpa*).

14. *vassa* literally means 'rainy season'. It is a common practice of a bhikkhu to count his age as a bhikkhu from the time of his ordination, in terms of rainy seasons. Hence eighth *vassa* means eighth year—8 years after his ordination.

Having conversation worth remembering for the whole life and developing it, Dhammadinnā asked the Thera, "Venerable Sir, when did you realize this dhamma?"

"My dear Dhammadinnā, 60 years ago," replied the Thera.

"Ven'ble Sir, can you enjoy the Attainments (*samāpatti*)?"

"Yes, I can," said the Thera.

"Ven'ble Sir, can you create a pond?"

"My dear, it is not a burden," replied the Thera, and created a pond in front of him.

When he asked, "Ven'ble Sir, please create a bush of lotuses in it?" the Thera did too.

"Now, Ven'ble Sir, please show a big flower in the bush of lotuses," he asked. The Thera showed it too.

"Please show me the appearance of a girl of sixteen years of age," he asked, and the Thera showed him too.

Then he asked the Thera, "Ven'ble Sir, please pay attention to it again and again. As a pleasant object;" the Thera, while looking at the image created by himself. craving arose in him. Then he knew that he was still in a state of worldling, and said, "Virtuous one, may you be my guide." So saying he sat down squatting (a special manner of sitting), near the pupil (Dhammadinnā).

"Ven'ble Sir, I come here for this purpose only," said Dhammadinnā, and made him light by means of meditation on an unpleasant object (*asubha*) showed him meditation and went out, to let the Thera have an opportunity (to complete).

Immediately after Dhammadinnā had gone out of the day resort, the Mahāthera who had already pondered over the compounded things (*saṅkhāra*) attained the state of *Arahatta* together with the Four Analytical Knowledge.

Then, Dhammadinnā, making Mahātissa Thera the chief of Saṅgha, went to Tissa Monastery and delivered the religious discourse.

In such a bhikkhu the defilement is abandoned as has already been abandoned by *samāpatti*.

There is no opportunity for the defilement to arise in a bhikkhu, while contemplating *vipassanā* insight: the defilement has been abandoned by means of *vipassanā* insight. He thus abandons the defilements, makes himself free from the rounds of rebirth and attains the state of *Arahatta*, just like 60 bhikkhus who ardently contemplated on *vipassanā* insight at the time of the Buddha.

Those bhikkhus, having taken the meditation from the Buddha, entered in to a quiet grove and developed the *vipassanā* insight. As there were no defilements arising during *vipassanā* meditation, they thought that they have penetrated the Path and Fruition, so they did not strive for the Path and Fruition. They then went to the Buddha with the thought: 'We are going to tell the dhamma penetrated by us to the Buddha.'

Before they had come to Him, the Buddha said to Ānanda, "Ānanda, those who are practicing the principal action (*padhāna kamma*), i.e. meditation, will come to see me today. Don't give them permission to see me, but send them to a cemetery to develop their meditation on the fresh corpse (*asubha bhāvanā*).

When they came, Ānanda told them what the Buddha had said. They thought thus: 'The Tathāgata will never speak without knowing. Indeed, there will be some reason,' and went to the cemetery. While they were looking at a fresh corpse, craving arose in them and they thought: 'The Fully Enlightened One indeed might have foreseen this' and got alarmed and strove to develop the meditation that had been practiced right from the beginning.

The Buddha, knowing that they were now contemplating on *vipassanā* insight, and sitting in the scented chamber, uttered the following enlightening verse (*obhāsa gāthā*):

"What benefit will there be to you enjoying the five sensual pleasures on seeing the bones that have the colour of the pigeon's leg, and are like gourds thrown away in the month of November (*Sārada*)."

At the end of the verse, they attained the State of *Arahatta*.

For such bhikkhus, the defilements are completely abandoned as have already been abandoned by means of *vipassanā* insight.

The Story of Cittalapabbata Tissatthera

There is no opportunity for the defilement to arise in a bhikkhu who in the aforesaid manner is performing new work; the defilement is abandoned by means of performing new work. He abandons the defilement and makes himself free from the rounds of rebirth and attains the state of *Arahatta* just as Cittalapabbata Tissatthera did.

It is said that unhappiness arose in him at his eighth rainy season (*vassa*) of his ordination: he, being unable to get rid of it, washed and dyed his robe, baked his bowl, shaved his head (hair), and stood paying homage to his preceptor.

Then the Thera said to him, "How, my dear Mahātissa, you seem to be unhappy?"

He replied, "Yes, Ven'ble Sir, unhappiness arose in me; I am unable to get rid of it."

The Thera, pondering over his innate disposition, saw his suffering condition for Arahatship, said to him out of compassion, "My dear Tissa, we are getting old, please make a dwelling place for us."

The bhikkhu who had never been spoken twice readily agreed by saying, "Yes, Ven'ble Sir."

Then the Thera said to him, "My dear, while performing new work, do not abandon the pāḷi series; be mindful of the meditation also, and do the preparatory work of *kasina*[15] from time to time."

He replied, "Ven'ble Sir, I shall do as you say," and paid homage to the Thera, looked at a suitable place and thought: 'It is possible to make a dwelling place here.' He then filled the place with firewood, burnt, cleaned it, surrounded the place with bricks for the walls, put doors and windows, and together with a well-built wall and ground for a walking place, etc. he completed the cave.

Having laid the couch, he went to the Thera, paid homage to him and said, "Ven'ble Sir, the work at the cave has been completed; please live in it."

The Thera replied, "My dear, you have done this work through trouble; today, you alone may live in for the whole day."

He accepted by saying, "Yes, Ven'ble Sir," and after paying homage to the Thera, he washed his feet, entered the cave, sat cross-legged, reflected over his completed work. While thinking: 'I have done a pleasant manual job for my preceptor,' zest (*pīti*) arose in him. But he abandoned it and contemplated over the *vipassanā* insight, attained to the highest Fruition, the state of *Arahatta*.

In such a bhikkhu, the defilement is completely abandoned as has already been abandoned by performing new work.

Moreover, a bhikkhu who came from the brahma world is pure. As he had no habit of indulging in sensual pleasures in previous existence, there is no opportunity for the defilement to arise in him; the defilement is abandoned through his existence; having abandoned the defilement, he makes himself free from the rounds of rebirth and attains the state of *Arahatta* as the Ven'ble Mahākassapa.

The venerable did not enjoy the sensual pleasures even amidst such pleasures of the household life, abandoned his great wealth; lead an ascetic

15. *Kasina* – literally means 'all, the whole'; is the name for a purely external device for *samatha* (calm) meditation to concentrate the mind and attain the 4 *jhānas*, Ecstatic states.

life. Having renounced his worldly life, he on his way found the Buddha coming to welcome him, paid homage to Him; received Bhikkhu ordination by following the three instructions, and on the eighth dawn attained the state of *Arahatta* together with the Four Analytical Knowledge.

In such a bhikkhu, the defilement is completely abandoned as has already been abandoned through his past existence.

Moreover, a bhikkhu gets an object as visual and so on, that has not appeared before, and contemplates the *vipassanā* insight on that very object, makes himself free from the rounds of rebirth and attains the state of *Arahatta*; in such a bhikkhu, the sensual desire that has not appeared before does not arise as has not arisen.

In the context: "Sensual desire that has already arisen is abandoned," that has already arisen means that has already come into existence, become, appeared.

"Is abandoned" means is abandoned by these five kinds of abandonment namely: (i) temporarily abandonment, (ii) a long-time abandonment, (iii) complete abandonment by destruction, (iv) abandonment by tranquillization, and (v) abandonment by deliverance; it means the sensual desire does not arise again.

Of these five, the *vipassanā* insight which temporarily abandons the sensual lust, should be noted as the temporarily abandonment.

But, as the Attainment (*Samāpatti*) abandons the sensual lust for a long time, it should he noted as a long-time abandonment.

The Path appears by overcoming the defilements completely; the Fruition by tranquillization; Nibbāna is the release (deliverance) from all defilements; so, these three are called: abandonment by complete destruction, abandonment by tranquillization, abandonment by deliverance from all defilements respectively.

It means: is abandoned by these five kinds of mundane and supramundane abandonment.

"Unpleasant object" means the first *jhāna* which takes the object that appears in the ten kinds of loathsomeness (*asubha*). Therefore, the ancient sages said: "The sign of unpleasantness means not only the unpleasantness but also the things that have the unpleasant object."

"Paying attention in a proper manner" means paying attention in a manner as has already been stated, "Therein, what is paying attention in a proper manner? Paying attention to impermanence as impermanence etc."

"The sensual desire that has not arisen does not arise" means it does not arise as has not arisen.

"The sensual desire that has already arisen is abandoned" means the sensual desire that has already arisen is abandoned' by the five kinds of abandonment.

Moreover, there are six kinds of things (*dhamma*) that are for the abandonment of the sensual desire—namely (1) taking note of the sign of unpleasantness, (2) practice of meditation on unpleasantness, (3) being well-guarded at the six sense doors, (4) knowing the right amount of food (to eat), (5) being associated with good friends and (6) suitable religious talk (*on dhamma*).

Furthermore, even in him who studies the ten signs of unpleasantness, the sensual desire is abandoned; also, in him who meditates on them; in him who is guarding the six sense doors; also, in him who is in the habit of keeping his body by drinking water whenever there is an opportunity (for him) to take four or five morsels of food before he finishes his meal and thereby knows the proper amount of food. Therefore, it is thus said:

> "Water should be taken instead of taking four or five morsels of food. The feeling of easiness is well deserved for him who tends his mind toward nibbāna."

The sensual desire is abandoned in him who associates with a good friend, who takes delight in *asubha-bhāvanā* like Tissatthera, the practicer at the unpleasantness; it is also abandoned by a suitable talk based on the ten kinds of unpleasantness while standing, sitting, etc. So, it is said: "The six things (*dhamma*) are for the abandonment of sensual desire."

AṄGUTTARA NIKĀYA, EKAKANIPĀTA PĀḶI
(The Book of the Ones)

2. NĪVARAṆAPPAHĀNA-VAGGA[16]
(Abandoning of Hindrances)

7th Sutta

Loving-Kindness, The Emancipation of Mind

7. "Bhikkhus, I know not any other single thing that can be (i) the cause of non-arising of ill will that has not arisen, and, (ii) the cause of abandoning of ill will that has already arisen—as loving-kindness that is deliverance of mind.

"In him, bhikkhus, who pays attention to loving-kindness that is deliverance of mind, in a proper manner, ill will that has not arisen does not arise and ill will that has already arisen is abandoned."

The Commentary on the 7th Sutta[17]

In the 7th Sutta, "loving-kindness that is deliverance of mind" means the loving-kindness that promotes the welfare of all beings. As the mind which is associated with loving-kindness is free from adverse hindrances etc., it is called deliverance of mind. Moreover, as it is especially free from the arising of all ill will, it should be noted as the deliverance of mind.

In the context: "Loving-kindness that is deliverance of mind" by mere loving-kindness is meant the neighbourhood of ecstatic concentration. But as "deliverance of mind" is mentioned the ecstatic concentration, by way of threefold and fourfold *Jhānas*, is required here.

"In him who pays attention in a proper manner" means in him who pays attention to loving-kindness that is deliverance of mind in such a proper manner, the characteristic of which has already been said.

Moreover, the 6 things are for the abandonment of ill will, namely: (i) practicing to take the object of loving-kindness; (ii) practicing meditation on loving-kindness, (iii) reflecting on the fact that one's deed is one's possession,

---

16. Aṅguttara Nikāya, p. 3, Vol. 1, 6th Syd Edn.
17. Aṅguttara Aṭṭhakathā, p. 36, Vol. 1, 6th Syd. Edn.

(iv) considering much the ill-consequence of hatred and the good-consequence of loving-kindness, (v) association with good friends, and (vi) suitable words or speech for loving-kindness.

Ill will is abandoned in him who is taking the object of loving-kindness towards beings either in a particular direction or any other direction.

Ill will is also abandoned in him who is cultivating loving-kindness towards beings either in a limited direction or unlimited directions.

Ill will is also abandoned in him who is reflecting that his deed is his possession and the deed of others are their possessions thus: "What will you do to that person through anger? How can you break his morality, etc.? Have you not come by your own kamma and will you not go by your own kamma alone? Feeling angry with others is like the desire of the one who takes hold of burning ember, red-hot iron rod, filth, etc., to beat others. What will that person do to you through his anger? Can he break your morality, etc.? He has come by his own kamma and will go by his own kamma alone. Just as the present unaccepted by others and just as the dust thrown against the wind, his anger will fall upon his own head."

Ill will is abandoned in him who is considering: (i) kamma as the property of both his own and others (ii) the ill-consequence of anger and good-consequence of loving-kindness.

Ill will is abandoned also in him who associates with the good friend like Assagutta Thera who takes pleasure in the development of loving-kindness.

Ill will is also abandoned through listening to suitable talks relating to loving-kindness, while standing, sitting, etc.

Hence it has been said: "Six things are for the abandonment of ill will."

8th Sutta

The Effort

8. "Bhikkhus, I know not any other single thing that can be (i) the cause of non-arising of sloth and torpor that has not arisen and, (ii) the cause of abandoning of sloth and torpor that has already arisen—as the initial effort, the medium effort and the supreme effort.

"In him, bhikkhus; who is energetic, the sloth and torpor that has not arisen does not arise, and the sloth and torpor that has already arisen is abandoned."

The Commentary on the 8th Sutta

In the 8th Sutta, in the context: "the initial effort" means the first effort that is put forth, As the medium effort overcomes laziness it is more vigorous than the first. As the supreme effort overcomes the successive stages, it is still more vigorous than the medium effort.

But in the Great Commentary it has been stated: "The first effort is for the mind to abandon sensual lust. The medium effort is for the mind to unfasten the bolt of ignorance. The supreme effort is for the mind to cut fetters. And those three kinds of efforts are also called the most strenuous effort."

"In him who is energetic" means in him who has strenuous effort and also upholding effort.

In the context: "in him who is energetic", the effort, free from the four kinds of defects, should be called effort. It is of two kinds, physical and mental.

Of these two, in this Sāsana, a bhikkhu cleanses his mind from hindrances through walking and sitting. Thus, the effort of him who exerts physically for five watches of the night and day should be noted as the physical effort.

By limiting the place thus: "I will not get out of this cave until and unless my mind is free from the *āsavas* without being attached to anything", or by limiting the postures, sitting, etc. "I will not change my cross-legged sitting until and unless my mind is free from *āsavas,* without being, attached to anything," the effort thus exerted by him with a fixed mind should be noted as the mental effort.

Herein, both the physical effort and mental effort are essential.

In him, who has these two kinds of effort, the sloth and torpor that has not arisen does not arise, the sloth and torpor that has already arisen is abandoned, just as in Milakkhatissa Thera Gāmantapabbhāravāsi Mahāsiva Thera, Pītimallaka Thera and Tissatthera, the son of a rich man.

Out of these four Theras, the former three Theras and others like them have physical effort. Tissatthera, the son of a rich man and others like him, have the mental effort. Mahānāga Thera, dwelling at Uccāvāḷuka Monastery, has both physical and mental effort.

Mahānāga Thera meditated on walking for a week, on standing for a week, on lying for a week. There was not even a single posture that did not suit him. On the fourth week, he developed the *vipassanā* insight and attained the Fruition of Arahatta.

Moreover, the six things are for the abandonment of sloth and torpor, namely: (i) taking caution in eating much food, (ii) frequent changing of postures, (iii) paying attention to the perception of light, (iv) staying in the open space, (v) having a good friend, (vi) suitable speech for the abandonment of sloth and torpor.

In him who takes food like Āharahatthaka brahmin, Buttavamitaka brahmin, Taṭṭravattaka brahmin, Alansāṭaka brahmin, Kākamāsaka brahmin, etc., sits down at the places prepared for spending day and night, and practices the dhamma of a bhikkhu, sloth and torpor overwhelms him as a great elephant does. (i) In him, who is in the habit of having aside four or five morsels of food and drinking water, sloth and torpor does not arise. Thus, by taking caution in eating much food, sloth and torpor is abandoned.

In him, (ii) who is frequently changing from one posture that causes sloth and torpor to arise to the other; (iii) in him who is paying attention to the moon light, the torch (the lamp light), the star light at night and the sunlight in the day time, sloth and torpor is abandoned.

(iv) Also in him, who is dwelling in the open space sloth and torpor is abandoned.

(v) Also in him, who is associated with a good friend like Mahākassapa Thera who had abandoned sloth and torpor, sloth and torpor is abandoned; (vi) also through suitable words or speech relating to ascetic practices, sloth and torpor is abandoned.

Hence it is said. "Six dhammas are for the abandonment of sloth and torpor."

9th Sutta

Calmness of the Mind

9. "Bhikkhus, I know not any other single thing that can be (1) the cause of non-arising of restlessness and worry that has not arisen and; (ii) the cause of the abandonment of the restlessness and worry that has already arisen.

"In him, bhikkhus, who has calmness of the mind, the restlessness and worry that has not arisen does not arise, the restlessness and worry that has already arisen is abandoned."

The Commentary on the 9th Sutta

In the 9th Sutta, "In him who has calmness of the mind" means in him, who has calmness of the mind through ecstasy (*jhānas*) or insight (*vipassanā*).

Moreover, the six things are for the abandonment of restlessness and worry, namely: (i) having great knowledge, (ii) having much discussion and asking questions, (iii) proficiency in the *vinaya-dhamma* (bhikkhus' disciplinary code), (iv) association with elderly people, (v) having good friends, (vi) suitable speech for the abandonment of restlessness and worry.

Through a great knowledge, (i) in him, who learns one, two, three, four, or five *nikāyas* with regard to pāḷi and the meaning, restlessness and worry is abandoned. (ii) In him, who has much discussion and asking questions about suitability and unsuitability, (iii) also in him, who has reached mastership in the *vinaya* rules, (iv) also in him, who approaches the elderly Theras, (v) also in him, who associates with a good friend like Upālitthera, who is expert in *vinaya-dhamma*, restlessness and worry is abandoned.

(vi) While standing, sitting, etc., by suitable speech relating to suitability and unsuitability, restlessness and worry is abandoned.

Thus, the Buddha said, "Six things are for the abandonment of restlessness and worry."

10th Sutta

Paying Attention in a Proper Manner

10. "Bhikkhus, I know not any other single thing that can be (i) the cause of non-arising of sceptical doubt and, (ii) the abandonment of sceptical doubt that has already arisen as paying attention in a proper manner.

"In him, bhikkhus, who is paying attention in a proper manner, the sceptical doubt that has not arisen does not arise, the sceptical doubt that has already arisen is abandoned."

The Commentary on the 10th Sutta

In the 10th Sutta, "In him who pays attention in a proper manner" means in him who pays attention in such a proper manner as stated above.

Moreover, the six dhammas are for the abandonment of sceptical doubt: (i) having a great knowledge, (ii) having much discussion and asking questions, (iii) proficiency in the *vinaya-dhamma*, (iv) having much confidence in the three jewels, (v) having good friends and (vi) suitable speech for the abandonment of sceptical doubt.

Through a great knowledge, (i) in him, who learns one, two, three, four or five *nikāyas* with regard to pāḷi and the meaning, the sceptical doubt is abandoned.

(ii) In him, who has much discussion and asking questions about the three jewels (Buddha, Dhamma and Saṅgha), (iii) also in him, who has reached mastership in *vinaya*, (iv) also in him, who has a firm confidence in the three jewels, (v) also in him, who associates with a good friend like Vakkali Thera who has a great confidence in the Buddha, the sceptical doubt is abandoned.

While standing, sitting, etc., also by the suitable words or talks relating to the qualities or the three jewel, the sceptical doubt is abandoned.

Here the Buddha has said: six dhammas are for the abandonment of sceptical doubt.

In this Nīvaraṇappahāna-Vagga, the rounds of rebirth and the deliverance from the rounds of rebirth are expounded.

Here ends the Nīvaraṇappahāna-Vagga (Abandoning of Hindrances).

3. AKAMMANĪYA-VAGGA[18] (Unadaptable)

1st Sutta

The Undeveloped Mind

1. "Bhikkhus, I know not any other single thing that is so undeveloped and unadaptable as the undeveloped mind. Bhikkhus, the mind if undeveloped is (indeed) unadaptable."

2nd Sutta

The Developed Mind

2. "Bhikkhus, I know not any other single thing that is so developed and adaptable as the developed mind. Bhikkhus, the mind if developed is (indeed) adaptable."

The Commentary on the 1st and 2nd Suttas[19]

In the 1st Sutta of the 3rd Vagga "undeveloped" means not developed by calm-development (*samatha-bhāvanā*) and insight-development (*vipassanā-bhāvanā*). "Is unadaptable" means is not workable and suitable for calm-development and insight-development.

The meaning in the 2nd Sutta should be understood the other way round. The difference is that in the 1st Sutta of the two, "mind" means the mind which has arisen by way of rounds of existence (*vipāka-vaṭṭa*). In the 2nd Sutta, "mind" means the mind which has arisen by way of absence of rounds of existence.

In the context: "the thing which has arisen by way of rounds of existence and the thing which has arisen by way of absence of defilements", this fourfold should be noted: (i) *vaṭṭa*, (ii) the cause of *vaṭṭa*, (iii) *vivaṭṭa*, and (iv) the cause of *vivaṭṭa*.

(i) *Vaṭṭa* is the rounds-of-results (*vipāka-vaṭṭa*) which happens in the three planes of existence (i.e. *karma*, *rūpa* and *arūpa*).

---

18. Vol. 1, Pg. 4, 6th Syd Edn.
19. Manorathapūraṇī, Aṅguttaraṭṭhakathā, Vol. I, Pg. 40, 6th Syd. Edn.

(ii) The cause of *vaṭṭa* is the volition (*kamma*) which causes the rounds-of-results to arise.
(iii) *Vivaṭṭa* is the nine supramundane states (*lokuttara*).
(iv) The cause of *vivaṭṭa* is the volition (*kamma*) which causes emancipation from the rounds of birth.

Thus, *vaṭṭa* and *vivaṭṭa* is expounded in these Suttas.

3rd Sutta

3. "Bhikkhus, I know not any other single thing so conducive to great loss as the mind undeveloped. Bhikkhus, the mind if undeveloped (indeed) conduces to great loss."

4th Sutta

4. "Bhikkhus, I know not any other single thing so conducive to great benefit—as the mind developed. Bhikkhus, the mind if developed (indeed) conduces to great benefit."

The Commentary on the 3rd and 4th Suttas

In the third Sutta, the mind which arises by way of rounds-of-results should be noted. "Conduces to great loss" means even though it gives the attainments of human beings; celestial beings, the rulerships of Māra and Brahma, it again and again gives birth, decay (old age), disease, death, sorrow, lamentation, pain, grief, despair and also the five aggregates or existence, elements, *āyatana* sense-bases, the chain of causal existence, so it really gives all that suffering, it is therefore said: "conduces to great loss".

In the 4th Sutta, "mind" means the mind which arises by way of absence of rounds of existence.

5th Sutta

5. "Bhikkhus, I know not any other single thing so conducive to great loss as the mind undeveloped, has not become manifest. Bhikkhus, the mind if undeveloped, has not become manifest (indeed) conduces to great loss."

6th Sutta

6. "Bhikkhus, l know not any other single thing so conducive to great benefit as the mind developed, has become manifest. Bhikkhus, the mind if developed, has become manifest (indeed) conduces to great benefit."

The Commentary on the 5th and 6th Suttas

In the 5th and 6th Suttas, this context: "that is undeveloped, not made clear", is the difference.

In the context: "is not undeveloped", the explanation of it is as follows: The mind which has arisen by way of vaṭṭa (rounds of existence), occurs in the three moments, but it is not yet developed by way of concentration, does not become manifest. Why? Because it is unable to get into the *jhāna* which is the foundation of supramundane, insight, path, fruition and Nibbāna (Supreme Bliss).

The mind which has arisen by way of absence of rounds of existence (*vivaṭṭa*) is the one which has been developed, has become manifest. Why? Because it is able to get into these states (*dhamma*). Sumitta Thera, dwelling at Kurundaka said: "My dear, the only Path-consciousness is the one that is developed, becomes manifest."

7th Sutta

7. "Bhikkhus, I know not any other single thing so conducive to great loss as the mind that is undeveloped, not frequently practiced. Bhikkhus, the mind if undeveloped, not frequently practiced, conduces to great loss."

8th Sutta

8. "Bhikkhus, I know not any other single thing so conducive to great benefit as the mind developed, frequently practiced. Bhikkhus, the mind if developed, frequently practiced, conduces to great benefit."

The Commentary on the 7th and 8th Suttas

In the 7th and 8th Suttas, the context: "is not frequently practiced", means is not practiced again and again. The two kinds of mind expounded in these 7th and 8th Suttas should be understood to be the minds that have arisen by way of *vaṭṭa* and *vivaṭṭa*.

* * *

9th Sutta

9. "Bhikkhus, I know not any other such single thing that leads to suffering as the mind undeveloped, not frequently practiced. Bhikkhus, the mind if developed, not frequently practiced, indeed leads to suffering."

10th Sutta

10. "Bhikkhus, I know not any other such single thing that leads to happiness as the mind developed, frequently practiced. Bhikkhus, the mind if developed, frequently practiced (indeed) leads to great happiness."

The Commentary on the 9th and 10th Suttas

In the 9th Sutta, as it leads to suffering that has already been explained, "rebirth is also suffering and so on", it is said bringing to suffering. There is also the pāḷi word *dukkhādhivāhaṃ*. The meaning of it runs thus: As it brings sufferings against the noble *dhammas* such as *jhānas*, the foundation of supramundane, it is said, "bringing to suffering". This is also the mind which has arisen by way of rounds-of-existence. Even though that mind gives the said attainments (*samāpatti*) of celestial and human beings etc, it leads to birth etc, it is said, "leading to suffering". As it also leads away from the attainment of the noble dhammas, it is said, "leading to suffering".

In the 10th Sutta, the mind is that which arises by way of *vivaṭṭa*. As the mind which arises by way of *vivaṭṭa* (free from defilements) leads to the attainment of celestial being (*deva*) rather than the attainment of human being, the bliss of *jhāna* rather than that of *deva*, the bliss of *vipassanā* rather than that of *jhāna*, the bliss of the path (*magga*) rather than that of *vipassanā* insight, the bliss of Fruition rather than that of the Path, the bliss of Nibbāna rather than that of the Fruition, it is said, bringing happiness (*sukhādhivāhaṃ*).

As the mind which arises by way of *vivaṭṭa* leads to the noble dhammas such as *jhāna*, the foundation of supramundane, and as it is similar to (*vajira*), the weapon of the king of devas, that has been shot out, it should also be called, bringing great happiness (*sukhādhivāhaṃ*).

In this Akammaniya-Vagga too *vaṭṭa* and *vivaṭṭa* are expounded.

Here ends the Commentary on the Akammaniya-Vagga.

AṄGUTTARA NIKĀYA, EKAKANIPĀTA PĀḶI
(The Book of the Ones)

4. ADANTA-VAGGA (The Untamed)

1st Sutta

The Untamed Mind

1. "Bhikkhus, I know not any other single thing so conducive to great loss as the untamed mind. Bhikkhus, the mind if untamed (indeed) conduces to great loss."

2nd Sutta

The Tamed Mind

2. "Bhikkhus, I know not any other single thing so conducive to great benefit as the tamed mind. Bhikkhus, the mind if tamed (indeed) conduces to great benefit."

3rd Sutta

The Uncontrolled Mind

3. "Bhikkhus, I know not any other single thing so conducive to great loss as the uncontrolled mind. Bhikkhus, the mind if uncontrolled (indeed) conduces to great loss."

4th Sutta

The Controlled Mind

4. "Bhikkhus, I know not any other single thing so conducive to great benefit as the controlled mind. Bhikkhus, the mind if controlled (indeed) conduces to great benefit."

5th Sutta

The Unguarded Mind

5. "Bhikkhus, I know not any other single thing so conducive to great loss as the unguarded mind. Bhikkhus, the mind if unguarded (indeed) conduces to great loss."

6th Sutta

The Guarded Mind

"Bhikkhus, I know not any other single thing so conducive to great benefit as the guarded mind. Bhikkhus, the mind if guarded (indeed) conduces to great benefit."

7th Sutta

The Unrestrained Mind

7. "Bhikkhus, I know not any other single thing so conducive to great loss as the unrestrained mind. Bhikkhus, the mind if unrestrained (indeed) conduces to great loss."

8th Sutta

The Restrained Mind

8. "Bhikkhus, I know not any other single thing so conducive to great benefit as the restrained mind. Bhikkhus, the mind if restrained (indeed) conduces to great benefit."

9th Sutta

9. "Bhikkhus, I know not any other single thing so conducive to great loss as the mind that is untamed, uncontrolled, unguarded and unrestrained. Bhikkhus, the mind if untamed, uncontrolled, unguarded and unrestrained (indeed) conduces to great loss."

10th Sutta

10. "Bhikkhus, I know not any other single thing so conducive to great benefit as the mind that is tamed, controlled, guarded and restrained. Bhikkhus, the mind if tamed, controlled, guarded and restrained (indeed) conduces to great benefit."

The Commentary on the Suttas 1 to 10

In the 1st Sutta of the 4th Vagga, "untamed" means wild, like the untamed elephant, horse, etc. "Mind" means the mind which has arisen by way of the rounds of existence (*vaṭṭa*).

In the 2nd Sutta, "tamed" means not wild, like the tamed elephant, horse, etc. In both of these suttas, the mind which has arisen by way of *vaṭṭa* and *vivaṭṭa* is expounded. As is expounded here thus so in other suttas.

In the 3rd Sutta, "uncontrolled' means unwatched, lack of restraint in mindfulness like an uncontrolled elephant, horse, etc.

In the 4th Sutta, "controlled" means watched, no lack of restraint in mindfulness like the controlled elephant, horse, etc.

The 5th and the 6th Suttas are expounded in terms "unguarded and guarded" in accordance with the wish of those who may understand them. The meaning here however is the same as the previous ones.

So is with the 7th and 8th Suttas too. In this context, the simile of the unguarded house door, etc. should be noted.

The 9th and 10th Suttas are expound ed by mixing the four words. In this *vagga* also, the mind is expounded only by way of *vaṭṭa* and *vivaṭṭa*.

Here ends the Commentary on the Adanta-Vagga.

5. PAṆIHITAACCHA-VAGGA (The Mind) Well-Directed

1st Sutta

Ill-Directed Mind

1. "Suppose, bhikkhus, the ill-directed spike of bearded rice or wheat be pressed by hand or foot, it cannot possibly pierce hand or foot and draw blood. Why? Because the spike is ill directed.

"Just so, bhikkhus, it cannot be that a bhikkhu with his ill-directed mind will indeed pierce ignorance, draw knowledge and realize Nibbāna. Why? Because his mind is ill directed."

2nd Sutta

Well-Directed Mind

2. "Suppose, bhikkhus, the well-directed spike of bearded rice or wheat be pressed by hand or foot, it is certain that it will pierce hand or fort and draw blood. Why? Because the spike is well directed.

"Just so, bhikkhus, it is certain that a bhikkhu with his well-directed mind will indeed pierce ignorance, draw knowledge and realize Nibbāna. Why? Because his mind is well directed."

The Commentary on the 1st and 2nd Suttas

In the 1st Sutta of the 5th Vagga, there is an expression of comparison. The Exalted One, in certain cases, shows certain similes adorning with the meaning of Suttas as in Vattha Sutta, Pāricchattakopama Suttas etc. In certain cases, the Exalted One shows the meaning of Suttas, adorning with certain similes as in Loṇambila Sutta, Suvannakāra Sutta or Suriyopama Sutta etc. While in this Sālisukopama, the Exalted One, wishing to show the meaning adorning with the simile, said: "Suppose bhikkhus etc."

In the context, "the spike of bearded rice" means the spike of bearded rice grain. So, with the spike of bearded wheat meaning the spike of bearded wheat grain.

"III-directed" means wrongly placed; that is the spike of bearded rice or wheat grain is not placed upward so as to pierce (hand or foot).

"pierce" means prick; that is penetrate through the skin (and flesh).

"With the ill-directed mind" means with the improperly kept mind. It is said with reference to the mind which has arisen by way of *vaṭṭa*.

"Ignorance" means the great ignorance which is utterly ignorant of eight conditions, such as the Four Noble Truths, past, etc.

In the context: "Will draw knowledge" means the Arahatta Magga Ñāṇa.

"Nibbāna" means the immortal state that is said to be free from lust (*taṇhā vāṇa*).

"Will realize" means will see as real.

In the 2nd Sutta, "well-directed" means properly placed; the spike of bearded rice or wheat is placed upward so as to pierce (hand or foot).

In the context: "Pressed (*akkanta*) stepped upon", "stepped upon" only by foot and pressed by hand. But symbolically only *akkanta* (stepped upon) is said. This indeed is the usage of the Nobles.

Why are the other big thorns such as *sepannika, madana*, etc. not taken here and why only the minute weak thorn of rice or wheat is taken? Because it is to show that even a small amount of wholesome kamma can be for *vivaṭṭa.*

All kinds of thorns, whether it be minute thorn of rice or wheat, whether it be the big thorns of *sepannika, madana*, etc., if placed improperly cannot pierce hand or foot and draw blood.

But only when placed properly it can pierce hand or foot and draw blood.

Just so the wholesome kamma whether it be a small offering a handful of grass or a big offering given by Velāma Brahmina, etc; if ill directed by longing for, and depending on *vaṭṭa*, it can lead only to *vaṭṭa*, and not to *vivaṭṭa*. If it be well directed by longing for, and depending on *vivaṭṭa* thus: "May my offering lead to Nibbāna, the complete extinction of *āsava*", it indeed can lead to the attainment of Arahatta Phala or silent *Buddha Ñāṇa*, or Omniscience (*Sabbaññuta Ñāṇa*). In fact, it is said that the Fourfold Analytical Knowledge, the Eightfold Deliverance, Perfect Discipleship, silent Buddhahood and the Supreme Buddhahood—all these can be obtained by the merit of offering.

In both of these Suttas, too, *vaṭṭa* and *viraṭṭa* are expounded.

3rd Sutta

The Corrupt Mind

3. "In this world, bhikkhus, with my thought (Supernormal knowledge) perceiving his, I know a person whose mind is corrupted by hatred. If this person were to die at this moment, he would fall into Purgatory as if he were brought and put down there. Why? Because of his corrupt mind.

"In the same way, bhikkhus, it is due to a corrupt mind that some beings in this world when body breaks up, after death, are reborn in the miserable state, the woeful course, the downfall, in Purgatory."

4th Sutta

The Clear Mind

4. "In this world, bhikkhus, with my thought (Supernormal Knowledge), perceiving his, I know a person whose mind is pure. If this person were to die at this moment, he would get into heaven (the deva abode) as if he were brought up to it. Why? Because of the purity of his mind.

"In the same way, bhikkhus, it is due to pure mind that some beings in this world when body breaks up, after death, are reborn in the happy state, in the Heaven world (deva abode)."

The Commentary on the 3rd and 4th Suttas

In the 3rd Sutta, "corrupted mind" means the mind that is corrupted by anger (hatred).

"With my thought perceiving his" means with my own thought embracing his thought.

"As if he were brought and put down" means as he was brought and placed.

"Thus, he would fall into Purgatory" means so he would be put into Purgatory.

"The miserable state, etc." are all the synonyms of Purgatory.

"As Purgatory is indeed devoid of happiness or bliss", it is called the miserable state. It, being the course of woe, is called the woeful course of existence. As the wrong doers have to fall down without their consent, it is called "the downfall".

It, being devoid of anything enjoyable, is called "Purgatory (Niraya)".

The Commentary on the 4th Sutta

In the 4th Sutta, "pure" means pure with confidence and gratification. ""Happy course of existence" means the course of happiness. ""Heaven World (Deva abode)" means the abode which is very excellent in the attainment of beautiful appearance, etc.

5th Sutta

The Turbid State of Mind

5. "Suppose, Bhikkhus, a pool of water is turbid, stirred up and muddy; a man who has eyes to see, while standing on the bank, cannot see the oysters and the shells, the pebbles and the gravel as they lie, or the shoals of fish that dart about. Why not? Bhikkhus, because of the turbid state of the water.

"Just so, bhikkhus, it is impossible for the bhikkhu, with his turbid state of mind to understand (i) his own benefit, (ii) the benefit of others and (iii) the benefit of both and (iv) to realize the States (the Jhāna, the path and the fruition) surpassing the 10 types of wholesome course of action of ordinary lay men, and discernible by special knowledge and insight of the noble ones. Why? Bhikkhus, because of the turbid state of mind."

6th Sutta

The Clearness of the Mind

"Suppose, bhikkhus, a pool of water is clear, fresh, free from mud; a man who has eyes to see, while standing on the bank, can see the oysters and the shells, the pebbles and the gravel as they lie, and the shoals of fish that dart about. Why? Bhikkhus, because of the clearness of the water.

"Just so, bhikkhus, it is possible for the bhikkhu, with his clear mind indeed to understand (i) his own benefit, (ii) the benefit of others, (iii) the benefit of both and (iv) to realize the states (the jhāna, the path and the fruition) surpassing the 10 types of wholesome course of action of ordinary laymen, and discernible by special knowledge and insight of the noble ones. Why? Bhikkhus, because of the clearness of the mind."

The Commentary on the 5th and 6th Suttas

In the 5th Sutta, "A pool of water" means a lake. "Turbid" means not clear. "Stirred up" means not stable. "Muddy" means full of mud. "The oyster shells" means the Oysters and the shells. "The pebbles gravel" means the pebbles and the gravel. "The shoals of fish" mean groups of fish.

In the context: "as they lie ... that dart about" only the pebbles and the gravel that lie, the others lie and also dart about. Just as referring to the cows that are going about, all the other cows are said to be going about, even though the others are standing or sitting or lying. So also referring to the pebbles and the gravel that lie, the other two are said to lie. Returning to the other two that are going about, the pebbles and the gravel are also said to be going about.

"Turbid" means covered up with the five kinds of hindrances in the context: "His benefit" etc., his own benefit that is the mixture of mundane and supramundane in this existence is indeed called his own benefit.

One's own benefit that is the mixture of mundane and supramundane in the next existence is indeed called "the benefit of the other". Such benefit of the other is so called. Such benefit of both is "the benefit of both".

Or his own benefit that is mundane and supramundane in this existence and the next, is indeed called "his own benefit". Such benefit of others is indeed called the benefit of others. Such benefit of both is also called the benefit of both.

"Surpassing the Dhamma of ordinary laymen" means surpassing the ten types of wholesome course of action of laymen.

As the people, being frightened by the end of the period of slaughter (*Satthantrakappa*), observe the ten dhammas by themselves of their own accord, without the instigation of an instructor, these ten dhammas are called the tenfold wholesome course of action of ordinary laymen. The Jhāna, Insight, the Path and the fruition should be noted as the dhamma surpassing them.

"Discernible by the special knowledge and insight of the Noble ones" means the special knowledge and insight that is suitable for the Noble ones or that can lead one to the state of being a Noble one. Knowledge itself being in the sense of knowing is called knowledge and in the sense of insight it should also be noted as sight. This "knowledge Insight" is the name of the Divine-eye, the Insight, the Path and the Fruition, and the Retrospective Knowledge.

In the 6th Sutta "Clear" means not thick; bright is also suitable. "Fresh" means perfectly bright. "Free from mud" means not muddy; pure is meant. It means free from foams, water-bubbles, moss and fern.

"Clear" means free from the five hindrances. The rest is the same, as the way explained in the 4th Sutta.

In both of these Suttas are also expanded only *vaṭṭa* and *vivaṭṭa*.

7th Sutta

The Developed Mind

7. "Just as, bhikkhus, there are all kinds of trees. Among them, the *phandana*, being pliable and adaptable, is regarded as the best.

"Even so, bhikkhus, I know not any other single thing that is pliable and adaptable as the mind that is developed and made much of. Bhikkhus, the mind that is developed and made much of, is indeed pliable and adaptable."

The Commentary on the 7th Sutta

In the 7th Sutta, "Among them" means among all kinds of trees. "Being pliable" means bring in a state of pliability. A certain kind of tree excels in colour (sight), some excels in odour, some in taste, some in hardness. But phandana tree is said to excel in pliancy and adaptability.

In the context: "Bhikkhus, the mind that is developed, made much of", the mind that is developed and made much of by Calm and Insight is meant. But Kurundavāsi Phussamitta Thera said: "My dear, the mind that is pliable and adaptable" is indeed the 4th Jhāna consciousness which is the foundation of Supernormal powers.

8th Sutta

The Changeable Mind

8. "Bhikkhus, I know not any other single thing so quick in changing as the mind. Bhikkhus, the mind indeed is so quick in changing that it is not so easy to illustrate it by any example."

The Commentary on the 8th Sutta

In the 8th Sutta, "So quick in changing" means arising quickly and vanishing quickly.

"Mind" means "subconscious mind", said some teachers at first. Rejecting that, it is said: "Herein, mind means any consciousness, at least even eye-consciousness should be taken as the mind."

In connection with this meaning also, King Milinda asked Nāgasena Thera, the preacher: "Venerable Nāgasena, if the mind-formations appearing at a moment of a finger's snap be material things how great would the heap be?"

The Thera replied, "Your Majesty, one hundred cart loads of grain, half of that amount, seven *ambana*[20] and two *tumba*[21] of grain—(all of them) are not equal to the mind appearing at a moment of a finger's snap. They are not equal to one-sixteenth part of it even." Then why does the Buddha say: "It is not so easy to illustrate it by any example?" Even rejecting such example, the longevity of the world cycle (*kappa*) is illustrated by an example of a mountain of one *yojana*[22] in length, breath and height, or of an area of one *yojana* filled with mustard seeds: the state of suffering in Purgatory (*niraya*) is illustrated by an example of piercing with hundred spears; the bliss of celestial abode is illustrated by an example of the attainment of *Cakkavatti*; in the same way, here too, should it not be illustrated by an example? There the example was given for the question: "Ven'ble Sir, can it be illustrated by an example?"

In this Sutta, as there appears no question, it is not illustrated by an example. This Sutta is expounded at the end of the discourse. Thus, in this Sutta aggregation of consciousness is indeed expounded.

9th Sutta

Subconscious Mind

9. "This mind, bhikkhus, is luminous. Even then, it becomes turbid due to temporary mental defilements (at the evil impulsive moment.)"

10th Sutta

10. "This mind, bhikkhus, is luminous. It indeed is free from temporary mental defilements (at the good impulsive moment)."

The Commentary on the 9th Sutta

In the 9th Sutta, "Luminous" means pure. "Mind" means subconscious mind. How is it? Has the mind any colour? No, it has not. Anything whether it be of a certain colour such as blue, etc. or of no colour, can be said "luminous" as it is pure. This mind too is called "luminous" because it is free from mental defilements.

"That mind" means that subconscious mind.

---

20. *Ambana* is a kind of measure used in olden days which is equivalent to 2-3/4 baskets (present measure) of grains.

21. *Tumba* is (also a kind of measure) used in olden days as well as the present days which is equal to one-sixteenth part of a basket-measure.

22. *Yojana*, a distance of about 7 miles.

"Temporary" means appearing temporarily at the impulsive moment.

"Mental defilements" means: The mind being clouded with sensual lust etc. is called "defilement".

How is it? Just as it is through the unvirtuous, ill-behaved and undutiful sons or pupils, students that the virtuous parents or teachers or the preceptors, get bad reputation that "they do not threaten, make learn, advise or teach their sons or pupils and students". Just so this parable should be noted. The subconscious mind should be noted as the virtuous parents or teachers or the preceptors. Just as on account of their sons, etc. the parents etc. get bad reputation, even so at the impulsive moment, the naturally pure subconscious mind is defiled by the temporary mental defilements that arise owing to the thoughts that are accompanied by lust, etc. which are of greedy, destructive and delusive nature.

The Commentary on the 10th Sutta

In the 10th Sutta too, the subconscious mind is, indeed taken as "the mind".

"Free" means at the impulsive moment the mind that is not greedy, not destructive and not delusive, and that arises owing to the wholesome state of the three root-conditions accompanied by knowledge etc. is free from temporary defilements. Herein just as the mother etc., owing to the virtuous and well-behaved sons gain good reputation that "They are splendid; they make their sons etc. learn, advice and teach them." Just so this subconscious mind is said to be free from the temporary mental defilements owing to the wholesome thought that arise at the impulsive moment.

Here ends the Commentary on the Paṇihitaaccha-Vagga.

TIKA-NIPĀTA, DUTIYA-PAṆṆĀSAKA

Brahmaṇa-Vagga, Nibbuta Sutta[23]

Discourse on Nibbāna

Now, the brahmin Jāṇussoni approached to where the Buddha was. Having approached, he paid respects, sat at one side and asked the Buddha:

"O Gotama, it is said, 'Nibbāna can be visualised by oneself; Nibbāna can be visualised by oneself?' (1) In what respect, O Gotama, can Nibbāna to be visualised by oneself? (2) In what respect can Nibbāna be attained simultaneously (with *magga*)? (3) In what respect does Nibbāna invite everyone to come and see it? (4) In what respect can Nibbāna be attained by proper practice? (5) In what respect can Nibbāna be realized or experienced by the wise?"

"O brahmin, he who takes delight in lust, is overcome by lust, and having lost control over his mind plans harm to himself to others and to both. He experiences painful and unpleasant mental feelings. When lust is extinguished, he does not plan harm to himself, to others or to both. He does not experience painful and unpleasant mental feelings. Thus, O brahmin, is Nibbāna visualised by oneself.

"O brahmin, he who is defiled by ill will, is afflicted by it, having lost control over his mind he plans harm to himself, to others and to both. He experiences painful and unpleasant mental feelings. When ill will is extinguished, he does not plan harm to himself, to others or to both. He does not experience painful and unpleasant mental feelings. Thus, O brahmin, is Nibbāna visualised by oneself.

"O brahmin, he who is bewildered with delusion, is overcome by it, and having lost control over his mind plans harm to himself to others and to both. He experiences painful and unpleasant mental feelings. When delusion is extinguished, he does not plan harm to himself, to others or to both. He does not experience painful and unpleasant mental feelings. Thus, O brahmin, is Nibbāna visualised by oneself.

"O brahmin, because he enjoys the extinction of lust without any remainder, the extinction of ill will without any remainder, the extinction

23. Saṅgāyanā Edition Vol. I. p. 158.

of delusion without any remainder, thus, O brahmin, is Nibbāna visualised by himself, can be attained simultaneously (with *magga*) invites everyone to come and see it, can be realized and experienced by the wise."

"Wonderful indeed, O Gotama. Delightful indeed, O Gotama. Just as, O Gotama, one should set upright that which is upset, or one should reveal that which is covered, or one should point out the way to one who has gone astray, or should hold a lamp in the darkness with the intention, 'those who have eyes may see', in the same way, the Buddha expounds the Dhamma in various ways.

"I take refuge in the Buddha, in the Dhamma and in the Saṅgha. May the Venerable Gotama receive me as a disciple who has taken refuge in the Three Jewels from this day onwards up to the end of my life."

TIKA-NIPĀTA, MAHĀVAGGA
Titthāyatana-Sutta
Discourse on Heretical Views

Three Kinds of Wrong Views

"Monks, there are three kinds of wrong views, which although fully enquired into, deeply considered and discussed by recluses and brahmins, nevertheless they go to extremes and become *akiriya-diṭṭhi* (holders of the 'View of the Inefficacy of action')."

"What are these three?"

"Monks, there are some recluses and brahmins who set forth and hold the following view:

'All bodily and mentally agreeable sensations, all bodily and mentally disagreeable sensations and all indifferent sensations experienced by beings in the present existence are caused and conditioned only by the volitional actions done by them in their past existences.'"[24]

"Monks, there are some recluses and brahmins who set forth and hold the following view:

'All bodily and mentally agreeable sensations, all bodily and mentally disagreeable sensations and all indifferent sensations experienced by beings in the present existence are created by a Supreme Being.'"[25]

"Monks there are some recluses and brahmins who set forth and hold the following view:

'All bodily and mentally agreeable sensations all bodily and mentally disagreeable sensations and all indifferent sensations experienced by beings in the present existence are uncaused and unconditioned.'"[26]

"Now, monks, as to those recluses and brahmins who set forth and hold the first of these three wrong views,—that all bodily and mentally agreeable sensations, all bodily and mentally disagreeable sensations, and all indifferent sensations experienced by beings in the present existence are caused and conditioned solely by volitional actions done by them in their past

24. Pubbekata-Hetu-Diṭṭhi.
25. Issaranimmāna-Hetu-Diṭṭhi.
26. Ahetu-Apaccaya-Diṭṭhi.

existences—I approach them and say: 'Friends, is it true that you set forth and hold the wrong view that all bodily and mentally agreeable sensations, all bodily and mentally disagreeable sensations and all indifferent sensations are caused and conditioned solely by the volitional actions done by beings in their past existences?'

"To this those recluses and brahmins reply: 'Yes, Venerable Sir.'

"I then declare: 'Friends, if that be the case there will be persons who, conditioned by the volitional actions done by them in their past existences:

(1) kill any living being;
(2) steal;
(3) tell lies;
(4) practice illicit sexual intercourse;
(5) slander;
(6) use harsh language;
(7) foolishly babble;
(8) are avaricious;
(9) maintain ill will against others;
(10) maintain Wrong Views.'

"Monks, indeed in those who believe only in the volitional actions done by beings in their past existences and hold this view, there cannot arise such mental factors as *chanda* (Desire-to-do) and *viriya* (Energy), to differentiate between what actions should be done and what actions should be refrained from.

"Monks, indeed, in those who cannot truly and firmly differentiate between what actions should be done and what actions should be avoided, and who live without the application of mindfulness and self-restraint, there cannot arise righteous beliefs that are conducive to the cessation of Defilements.

"Monks, this is the first factual statement to refute the heretical views advanced by those recluses and brahmins who maintain that all sensations experienced by beings in the present life are caused and conditioned only by the volitional actions performed by them in their past existences."

Refutation of Issaranimmāna View

"Monks, of these three wrong views, there are some recluses and brahmins who hold the following view:

'All bodily and mentally agreeable sensations, all bodily and mentally disagreeable sensations and all indifferent sensations experienced by beings in the present life are created by a Supreme Being or God.'"

"I approach them and ask: 'Friends, is it true that you hold and set forth the following view that all bodily and mentally agreeable sensations, all bodily and mentally disagreeable sensations and all indifferent sensations experienced by beings in the present life are created by a Supreme Being or God?'

"To this those recluses and brahmins reply: 'Yes, Venerable Sir.'

"I then declare: 'Friends, if that be the case, there will be persons, who, owing to the creation of a Supreme Being or God:

(1) kill any living being;
(2) steal;
(3) tell lies;
(4) practice illicit sexual intercourse;
(5) slander;
(6) use harsh language;
(7) foolishly babble;
(8) are avaricious;
(9) maintain ill will against others;
(10) maintain Wrong Views.'

"Monks, indeed, in those who believe only in the creation of a Supreme Being or God, there cannot arise such mental factors as Desire-to-do and Energy to differentiate between what actions should be done and what actions should be refrained from.

"Monks, indeed, in those who cannot truly and firmly differentiate between what actions should be done and what actions should be refrained from, and who live without the application of mindfulness and self-restraint, there cannot arise righteous belief that are conducive to the cessation of Defilements.

"Monks, this is the second factual statement to refute the heretical beliefs and views advanced by those recluses and brahmins who maintain that all sensations experienced by beings in the present existence are created by a Supreme Being or God."

Refutation of Ahetu-Apaccaya View

"Monks, of these three wrong views, there are some recluses and brahmins who set forth and hold the fallowing view:

'All bodily and mentally agreeable sensations, all bodily and mentally disagreeable sensations and all indifferent sensations experienced by beings in the present existence are uncaused and unconditioned.'"[27]

27. I.e. beings in the present life come into existence of their own accord and without

"I approach them and ask: 'Friends, is it true that you hold and set forth the following view that all bodily and mentally agreeable sensations, all bodily and mentally disagreeable sensations and all indifferent sensations experienced by beings in the present existence are uncaused and unconditioned?'

"To this those recluses and brahmins reply: 'Yes, Venerable Sir.'

"I then declare: 'Friends, if this be the case, there will be persons, who, without any cause or condition (or without the Generative and Sustaining Kammas),

(1) kill any living being;
(2) steal;
(3) tell lies;
(4) practice illicit sexual intercourse;
(5) slander;
(6) use harsh language;
(7) foolishly babble;
(8) are avaricious;
(9) maintain ill will against others;
(10) maintain Wrong Views.'

"Monks, indeed, in those who believe only in the 'Uncausedness and Unconditionality' of existence, there cannot arise such mental factors as Desire-to-do and Energy to differentiate between what should be done and what should be avoided.

"Monks, indeed, in those who cannot truly and firmly differentiate between what should be done and what should not be done, and who live without the application of mindfulness and self-restraint, there cannot arise righteous beliefs that are conducive to the cessation of Defilements.

"Monks, this is the third factual statement to refute the heretical beliefs and views advanced by those recluses and brahmins who maintain that all sensations experienced by beings in the present existence are uncaused and unconditioned.

"Monks, these are the three wrong views, which although fully enquired into, deeply considered and discussed by recluses and brahmins, nevertheless they go to extremes and become *akiriya-diṭṭhi* (holders of the 'View of the Inefficacy of action').

"Now, monks, this Dhamma do I teach, one not refuted, pure, unblamed, uncensured by intelligent recluses and brahmins. And what is this Dhamma?

---

the help of the Generative and Sustaining Kammas.

"These are the six elements—that Dhamma do I teach, one not refuted, pure, unblamed, uncensured by intelligent recluses and brahmins.

"These are the six sense organs of contact—that Dhamma do I teach, one not refuted, pure, unblamed, uncensured by intelligent recluses and brahmins.

"These are the eighteen *manopavicārā* (things with which the mind preoccupies itself)—that Dhamma do I teach, one not refuted, pure, unblamed, uncensured by the intelligent recluses and brahmins.

"Monks, I teach the six elements as the Dhamma, one not refuted, pure, unblamed, uncensured by the intelligent recluses and brahmins. Depending upon what do I teach them?

"Monks, these six elements are the element of extension, the element of cohesion, or the holding, the fluid, the element of kinetic energy, the element of motion, the element of space and the element of consciousness. ...

"And depending upon what do I teach these sense organs of contact?

"The six sense organs of contact are these: The organ of eye-contact, that of ear-contact, nose-contact, tongue-contact, body-contact, and the organ of mind-contact. ...

"And depending upon what do I teach these eighteen applications of mind? ...

"Seeing an object with the eye one's thoughts are concerned with the object, whether it gives ground for agreeable, disagreeable or indifferent sensation. The same as regards ear, nose, tongue and other sense organs ... Contacting a mental object with the mind one's thoughts are concerned with the object, whether it gives ground for agreeable, disagreeable or indifferent sensation.

"This is what I mean when I teach the eighteen applications of mind.

"And as to these four Noble Truths, depending upon what do I teach?

"Conditioned by the six elements, conception in the womb arises. This conception taking place, Mind and Form come into existence. Through the Mental and Physical Phenomena, the 6 Bases are conditioned. Through the 6 Bases Contact is conditioned. Through Contact Sensation is conditioned. Now to him who has sensation, monks, I make known: This is Suffering. I make known: This is the Origin of Suffering. I make known: This is the Extinction of Suffering. I make known: This is the Path leading to the Extinction of Suffering.

"And what, monks, is the noble truth of the Suffering?

"Birth is suffering, decay is suffering, death is suffering; sorrow, lamentation, pain, grief and despair are suffering; in short, the 5 groups of existence connected with clinging are suffering.

"And what, monks, is the noble truth of the Origin of Suffering?

Through Ignorance Kamma formations are conditioned;

Through Kamma formations Consciousness is conditioned;

Through Consciousness Mental and Physical Phenomena are conditioned;

Through Mental and Physical Phenomena, the 6 Bases are conditioned;

Through the 6 Bases Contact is conditioned;

Through Contact Sensation is conditioned;

Through Sensation Craving is conditioned;

Through Craving Clinging is conditioned;

Through Clinging the Process of Becoming is conditioned;

Through the Process of Becoming Rebirth is conditioned;

Through Rebirth are conditioned Old Age and Death (sorrow, lamentation, pain, grief and despair. Thus arises the whole mass of suffering again in the future).

"This, monks, is called the noble truth of the Origin of Suffering.

"And what, monks, is the noble truth of the Extinction of Suffering?

"From the utter fading out and extinction of Ignorance comes the extinction of Kamma-formations; from the extinction of Kamma-formations, the extinction of Consciousness; from the extinction of Consciousness, the extinction of the Mental and Physical Phenomena; from the Mental and Physical Phenomena, the extinction of the 6 Bases; from the extinction of the 6 Bases, the extinction of the Contact, from the extinction of the Contact, the extinction of Sensation; from the extinction of the Sensation, the extinction of Craving; from the extinction of Craving, the extinction of Clinging; from the extinction of Clinging, the extinction of the Process of Becoming; from the extinction of the Process of Becoming, the extinction of Rebirth; from the extinction of Rebirth, the extinction of Old Age and Death (sorrow, lamentation, pain, grief and despair. Thus ceases the whole mass of suffering).

"This, monks, is called the noble truth of the Extinction of Suffering.

"And what, monks, is the Path leading to the Extinction of Suffering?

"It is just this Eightfold Noble Path namely, Right View, Right Aim, Right Speech, Right Action, Right Living, Right Effort, Right Mindfulness,

Right Concentration. This is called the noble truth of the Path leading to the Extinction of Suffering.

"This Dhamma, monks, do I teach, these four Noble Truths, Dhamma not refuted, pure, unblamed, uncensured by intelligent recluses and brahmins."

CATUKKANIPĀTA DUTIYAPAṆṆĀSAKA PUÑÑĀBHISANDA-VAGGA

Paṭhama-saṃvāsa Sutta[28]

Discourse on Living Together as Husband and Wife

On one occasion, the Buddha was travelling between Madhura and Verañja. Many householders and their wives were also on the same journey. The Buddha then went and sat down at the foot of a certain tree by the side of the road; the householders and their wives saw the Buddha sitting there, approached him, paid homage to him and sat down at one side. The Buddha said to them while they were sitting there. "O householders, there are four ways of men and women living together. What are the four?

(1) A dead man[29] lives with a dead woman.

(2) A dead man lives with a *devī*.[30]

(3) A *deva* lives with a dead woman.

(4) A *deva* lives with a *devī*.

1. "O, householders, how does a dead man live with a dead woman? In this case, the husband is one who takes the life of sentient beings, takes what is not freely given, indulges in sexual misconduct, tells lies, partakes of intoxicants, is vicious, is wicked, lives the householder life with his mind agitated by the evil of selfishness, and abuses and threatens monks and brahmins.

"His wife also is one who takes the life of sentient beings, takes what is not freely given, indulges in sexual misconduct, tells lies, partakes of intoxicants, is vicious, is wicked, lives the household life with mind agitated by the evil of selfishness, and abuses and threatens monks and brahmins.

"Thus, O householders, a dead man lives with a dead woman.

2. "O householders, how does a dead man live with a *devī*? In this case, householders, the husband is one who takes the life of sentient beings, takes what is not freely given, indulges in sexual misconduct, tells lies, partakes of intoxicants, is vicious, is wicked, lives the householder life with mind agitated by the evil of selfishness, and abuses and threatens monks and brahmins.

---

28. Saṅgāyanā Edition, Vol. I. p. 368.

29. "Dead" because his or her good qualities are dead.

30. God (*deva*) or Goddess (*devī*) because his or her qualities are divine.

"But his wife refrains from taking the life of sentient beings, refrains from taking what is not freely given, refrains from indulging in sexual misconduct, refrains from telling lies, refrains from partaking of intoxicants, is virtuous and of good conduct, lives the householder life with her mind free from the evil of selfishness, and does not abuse nor threaten monks and brahmins.

"In this way, householders, a dead man lives with a *devī*.

3. "O householders, how does a *deva* live with a dead woman? O householders, in this case, the husband refrains from taking the life of sentient beings, refrains from taking what is not freely given, refrains from indulging in sexual misconduct, refrains from telling lies, refrains from partaking of intoxicants, is virtuous and of good conduct, lives the householder life with mind free from the evil of selfishness, and does not abuse nor threaten monks and brahmins.

"But his wife is one who takes the life of sentient beings, takes what is not freely given, indulges in sexual misconduct, tells lies, partakes of intoxicants, is vicious, is wicked, lives the householder life with mind agitated by the evil of selfishness, and abuses and threatens monks and brahmins.

"In this way, householders, a *deva* lives with a dead woman.

4. "O householders, how does a *deva* live with a *devī*? In this case, householders, the husband refrains from taking the life of sentient beings, refrains from taking what is not freely given, refrains from indulging in sexual misconduct, refrains from telling lies, refrains from partaking of intoxicants, is virtuous and of good conduct, lives the householder life with mind free from the evil of selfishness, and does not abuse nor threaten monks and brahmins.

"His wife also refrains from taking the life of sentient beings, refrains from taking what is not freely given, refrains from indulging in sexual misconduct, refrains from telling lies, refrains from partaking of intoxicants, is virtuous and of good conduct, lives the householder life with mind free from the evil of selfishness, and does not abuse nor threaten monks and brahmins.

"In this way, householders, a *deva* lives with a *devī*. These are the four ways of living together.

1. "Both are vicious, stingy and abusers. They are husband and wife living together as dead persons.

2. "The husband is vicious, stingy and abusive; the wife is virtuous, liberal, and free from selfishness. That wife is a *devī* who lives with a dead husband.

3. "The husband is virtuous, liberal and free from selfishness; the wife is vicious, stingy and an abuser; she is a dead person who lives with a *deva* as her husband.

4. "Both have faith and are liberal; they have self-control, they live righteously and speak pleasantly to each other. There is so much prosperity for the couple who are equally virtuous, and there is so much happiness in their life that people who are unfriendly to them are displeased.

"The couple having morality equally practice the Dhamma in this world and rejoice in the deva world enjoying the pleasures of the senses."

PANCAKA-NIPĀTA, PAṬHAMA PAṆṆĀSAKA, SUMANA-VAGGA, UGGAHA SUTTA, page 30, 6th Synod Edition

A Housewife's Fivefold Duty

On one occasion the Exalted One was staying at Jātiyā Wood in Bhaddiya. At that time, Uggaha, the grandson of Meṇḍaka the millionaire, approached Him and, after paying his veneration to Him, sat down on one side. So seated, he addressed the Exalted One:

"Venerable Sir, let the Exalted One accept a meal for four including the Exalted One at my house tomorrow."

The Exalted One accepted the invitation by remaining silent.

Then Uggaha, Meṇḍaka's grandson, knowing that the Exalted One had accepted, rose from his seat, paid his veneration to Him, and departed, keeping Him on the right.

When night passed, the Exalted One, robing Himself in the morning, took His bowl, went to Uggaha's house, and sat on the seat specially prepared for Him.

And Uggaha, Meṇḍaka's grandson, offered the delicious food to the Exalted One to His satisfaction, until He refused to take any more. After the Exalted One had finished His meal and withdrawn His hands from His bowl, Uggaha sat down on one side and said:

"Lord, these young maidens of mine will be going to their husbands' houses; let the Exalted One admonish and advise them. Such admonition and advice will be conducive to their progress and prosperity for a great length of time."

Then the Exalted One said to the young maidens:

Fivefold discipline

I. "Wherefore in this matter, maidens, you should train yourselves in this manner:

   'To whatever husbands we shall be given out of compassion by our parents who are our well-wishers, who desire to promote our welfare and who are compassionate to us, we shall (1) get up before him, (2) go to bed after him, (3) always consider what work there is to be done, (4) always try to please him, and (5) always speak affectionately.' Maiden, you should train yourselves in this manner.

II. Honour those to whom honour is due:

"And again maidens, you should train yourselves in this manner: 'We will revere, esteem, venerate and honour all whom our husbands revere, whether mother, father, *samaṇa* or *brāhmaṇa*, and when they come, we will offer them a seat and water.' Maidens, you should train yourselves in this manner.

III. Handicraft:

"And again, maidens, you should train yourselves in this manner: 'We will be skilful and active at our husbands' domestic works, whether it relates to wool or cotton. We shall find ways and means and make ourselves efficient to do it ourselves and to supervise others.' Maidens, you should train yourselves in this manner.

IV. Household Management:

"And again, maidens, you should train yourselves in this manner: 'Whoever may be inmates of our husbands' household as servants, messengers or workmen, we will know what amount of work each has done and what amount of work each has left undone; we will know the strength and weakness of the sick among them; we shall provide them with food according to what they deserve.' Maidens, you should train yourselves in this manner.

V. Thrift and Economy:

"And again, maidens, you should train yourselves in this manner: 'Money, corn, silver, and gold that our husbands bring to us, we will keep them securely and guard them properly; we will not squander them by way of robbing, stealing and taking intoxicating drinks.' Maidens, you should train yourselves in this manner.

VI. "Indeed, maidens being possessed of these five qualities, a housewife, on the dissolution of her body after death, will be reborn among the Manāpakāyika Devas.

"A husband always strives hard and with care maintains his wife. A good wife should not slight such a husband who provides her with all her needs.

"A good wife shall not rouse her husband's anger by jealousy; and a wise housewife should revere all whom her husband reveres.

"A housewife is active and heedful; and she also has attendants who are well maintained.

"She behaves herself in such a way as to please her husband, and properly looks after the property which has been earned by him.

"A housewife who lives in this manner complying with her husband's wishes will be reborn in the Manāpa Devas' abode (Nimmānarati)."[31]

---

31. Please see Suttanta Piṭaka, Pāthikā-vagga, Siṅgāla Sutta, page 146, 6th Synod Edition; and Pāthikā-vagga Aṭṭhakatha, Siṅgāla Sutta Vaṇṇaṇā, page 124, 6th Synod Edition.

PAÑCAṄGUTTARA, NIRAYA SUTTA

Discourse on Hell

"O monks, one who has the following five vices arises in hell as if he were taken and thrown there. What five?

"He kills a living being; he takes what is not given; he indulges in sexual misconduct; he tells lies; and he partakes of intoxicants.

"O monks, one who has these five vices arises in hell as if he were taken and thrown there.

"O monks, one who has the following five virtues arises in heaven as if he were taken and placed there. What five?

"He abstains from killing any living being; he abstains from taking what is not given; he abstains from indulging in sexual misconduct; he abstains from telling lies; and he abstains from partaking of intoxicants.

"O monks a lay adherent who has these five virtues arises in heaven as if he were taken and placed there."

PAÑCAKA NIPĀTA, CĀTUTTHA-PAṆṆĀSAKA, UPĀSAKA-VAGGA, VISĀRADA SUTTA

Discourse on Self-Confidence

Thus, I have heard. On one occasion the Buddha was staying at Jeta's Grove in the monastery of Anāthapiṇḍika at Sāvatthi. There the Buddha addressed the monks, "O monks." "Yes, Revered Sir," answered those monks to the Buddha.

"O monks, a lay adherent who has the following five vices lives the home-life without self-confidence. What five?

"He takes life; he takes what is not given; he indulges in sexual misconduct; he tells lies; and he partakes of intoxicants.

"O monks, a lay adherent who has these five vices lives the home-life without self-confidence.

"O monks, a lay adherent who has the following five virtues lives the home-life with self-confidence. What five?

"He abstains from killing any living being; he abstains from taking what is not given; he abstains from sexual misconduct; he abstains from telling lies; and he abstains from intoxicants.

"O monks, a lay adherent who has these five virtues lives the home-life with confidence."

PAÑCAKA-NIPĀTA, CATUTTHA-PAṆṆĀSAKA, UPĀSAKA-VAGGA, VERA SUTTA

Discourse on the Five Things Which Are Dangers and Enemies

Now the householder, Anāthapiṇḍika, visited the Buddha, paid homage to Him and sat down at one side; and the Buddha spoke to the householder, thus seated, saying:

"Householder, he who has not got rid of the five dangers and enemies is called 'vicious' and arises in hell. What five?

"Killing living beings, taking what is not given, sexual misconduct, telling lies, partaking of intoxicants.

"Householder, in not getting rid of these five dangers and enemies a man is termed 'vicious', and he arises in hell.

"Householder, he who has got rid of these five dangers and enemies is called 'virtuous' and arises in the happy plane of existence. What five?

"Killing living beings, taking what is not given, sexual misconduct, telling lies, partaking of intoxicants.

"Householder, in having got rid of these dangerous things, he is called 'virtuous' and arises in the happy plane of existence.

"When, householder, the killer of a living being, by reason of his killing, breeds hatred in this very life or breeds hatred in the life hereafter, he feels in his mind pain and grief; but he who abstains from killing living beings breeds no hatred in this life, nor in the life hereafter, nor does he feel in his mind pain and grief; thus, for one who abstains from killing living beings, danger is dispelled.

"When, householder, the thief, by reason of his stealing, breeds hatred in this very life and the life hereafter, he feels in his mind pain and grief; but he who abstains from stealing, breeds no hatred in this life, nor in the life hereafter; nor does he feel in his mind pain and grief; thus, for one who abstains from stealing danger is dispelled.

"When, householder, the indulger in sexual misconduct, by reason of his sexual misconduct, breeds hatred in this life and the life hereafter, he feels in his mind pain and grief, but he who abstains from sexual misconduct breeds no hatred in this life, nor in the life hereafter, nor does he feel in his mind pain and grief; thus, for one who abstains from sexual misconduct, danger is dispelled.

"When, householder, the liar, by reason of his telling lies, breeds hatred in this very life and the life hereafter he feels in his mind pain and grief; but he who abstains from telling lies, breeds no hatred in this life, nor in the life hereafter, nor does he feel in his mind pain and grief; thus, for one who abstains from telling lies danger is dispelled.

"When, householder, the drinker, by reason of his partaking of intoxicants, breeds hatred in this very life and the life hereafter, he feels in his mind pain and grief; but he who abstains from intoxicants breeds no hatred in this life, nor in the life hereafter, nor does he feel in his mind pain and grief; thus, for one who abstains from intoxicants danger is dispelled.

"One who kills a living being, takes what is not given, indulges in sexual misconduct, tells lies, and partakes of intoxicants, on account of his not having got rid of these five dangers and enemies is said to be 'vicious'. On the dissolution of the body after death, that unwise man is reborn in hell.

"One who abstains from killing living beings, abstains from taking what is not given, abstains from sexual misconduct, abstains from telling lies, and from intoxicants, on account of his abstinence from these five dangerous things, is called 'virtuous'. On the dissolution of the body after death he arises in the Happy Course of Existence."

GAVESĪ SUTTA[32]

Thus, I have heard. On one occasion the Exalted One toured through the kingdom of Kosala with a great company of brethren. And as He went along the highway, He saw a place where a big grove of sal trees grew; and seeing it there, He moved down from the road and having approached that grove, He smiled at a certain place.

Then the Venerable Ānanda thought: What is the cause of the Exalted One's smiling? What is the reason? Tathāgatas do not smile for nothing. And the Venerable Ānanda asked the Exalted One: "Lord, what is the cause of the Exalted One's smiling? What is the reason? Tathāgatas do not smile for nothing."

Then the Exalted One replied: "At this place, Ānanda, in ancient

---

32. Aṅguttara Nikāya, Pañcaka-Nipāta, Catuttha-paṇṇāsaka, 3. Upāsaka-vagga, 10. Gavesī Sutta, page 189, 6th Syn Edn.

times there was a rich and flourishing city inhabited by many people; and by the city, there dwelt the Exalted One, Kassapa, Arahat, Supremely Enlightened. At that time Gavesī was a lay-disciple of the Exalted One, Kassapa, Arahat, Supremely Enlightened; but he did not keep the moral precepts. Ānanda, the lay-disciple Gavesī incited other five hundred persons who did not keep the moral precepts, to declare themselves as 'lay-devotees' and become lay-devotees."

1. "Ānanda, Gavesī then thought thus: 'I have been of great service to these five hundred lay-disciples; I have been their leader; and I have caused them to become lay-disciples. Yet, I do not keep the moral precepts nor do these five hundred lay disciples. I am on the same level as they and do not surpass them, in any way. Now, I shall practice myself so that I may surpass them.'

"Then Ānanda, Gavesī went to the five hundred and said: 'Sirs, from today please recognise me as one who keeps the moral precepts.'

"Now, Ānanda, those five hundred lay disciples thought to themselves: "'Master Gavesī has been of great service to us; he has been our leader; and he has caused us to become lay-disciples. He will now keep the moral precepts. Why then not we too?'"

"Then, Ānanda, those five hundred lay disciples went to Gavesī and said: "'Master Gavesī, from today please recognise us five hundred lay-disciples as those who keep the moral precepts.'

2. "Then, Ānanda, Gavesī thought thus: 'I have been of great service to those five hundred lay-disciples; I have been their leader; and I have caused them to become lay-disciples. Now, I am keeping the moral precepts, and they too are doing so. I am on the same level as they and do not surpass them in anyway. I shall now practice so that I may surpass them.'

"Ānanda, Gavesī then went to those five hundred lay-disciples and said, 'Sirs, from today please recognise me as one who practices to live a pure life, one who practices to live a life (free from vices), and one who abstains from having sexual intercourse which is the habit of the village folks.'

"Then, Ānanda, those five hundred lay disciples thought thus: 'Master Gavesī has been of great service to us; he has been our leader, and he has caused us to become lay disciples. He is now practicing to live a pure life, is practicing to live a life (free from vices), and is abstaining from having sexual inter-course which is the habit of village folks. Why not we too?'

"Then, Ānanda, those five hundred lay disciples went to Gavesī and said: 'Master Gavesī, from today please recognise us five hundred lay-disciples as those who are practicing to live a pure life, those who are practicing to live a life (free from vices) and those who are abstaining from sexual intercourse which is the habit of the village folks.'

3. "Then, Ānanda, Gavesī thought thus: 'I have been of great service to those five hundred lay-disciples; I have been their leader; and I have caused them to become lay-disciples. I have kept the moral precepts, and they too have done so. I am practicing to live a pure life; I am practicing to live a life (free from vices); and I am abstaining from sexual intercourse which is the habit of the village folks. They too are now practicing so. I am on the same level as they and do not surpass them in any way. Now, I shall practice myself so that I may surpass them.'

"Ānanda, Gavesī then went to those five hundred lay-disciples and said: 'Sirs, from today please recognise me as one who takes one meal a day, and one who abstains from taking meals at night or after midday.'

"Ānanda, then those five hundred lay disciples thought to themselves: 'Master Gavesī has been of great service to us; he has been our leader; and he has caused us to become lay-disciples. Now he even is one who takes only one meal a day, and one who abstains from taking meals at night or after midday—why not we too?'

4. "Ānanda, Gavesī thought thus: 'I have been of great service to those five hundred lay disciples; I have been their leader; and I have caused them to become lay-disciples. I have kept the moral precepts and they also have done so. I have practiced to live a pure life; I have practiced to live a life (free from vices); and I have abstained from sexual intercourse which is the habit of village folks. They too have done the same. I have been one who takes only one meal a day, and one who abstains from taking meals at night or after midday. They also have done the same. I am on the same level as they and do not surpass them in any way. Now, I shall practice so that I may surpass them.'

"And, Ānanda, the lay-disciple Gavesī went to the Exalted One, Kassapa, Arahat, Supremely Enlightened, and, having approached Him, said to Him: 'Lord, grant me an ordination as a sāmaṇera and then a full ordination as a Bhikkhu.'

"Ānanda, the lay-disciple Gavesī obtained ordination as a sāmaṇera and then as a Bhikkhu under the preceptorship of the Exalted One, Kassapa, Arahat, Supremely Enlightened.

5. "Ānanda, not long after his being ordained, Gavesī, dwelling solitary, detached, earnest, ardent and aspiring, attained that goal for which the sons

of good families rightly leave home for the homeless life, even that unrivalled goal[33] or righteous living, attained it in that very life, and knowing it for himself lived in full realisation thereof: 'Rebirth is no more; I have lived the pure life. I have done all that ought to be done; I have nothing more to do for Arahatship.'

"And the Venerable Gavesī was another of the Arahats.

"Then, Ānanda, those five hundred lay disciples thought thus: 'Master Gavesī has been of great service to us; he has been our leader; and he has caused us to become lay disciples. Now, even Master Gavesī has had his hair and beard shaved off, donned the yellow robe, and gone forth from the home to the homeless life; why then not we too?'

"Ānanda, those five hundred lay-disciples then approached the Exalted One, Kassapa Arahat, Supremely Enlightened and addressed Him: 'Lord, may the Exalted One be pleased to ordain us as sāmaṇeras and then as Bhikkhus.'

"Ānanda, those five hundred lay-disciples obtained ordination as sāmaṇeras and then as Bhikkhus under the preceptorship of the Exalted One, Kassapa, Arahat, Supremely Enlightened.

"Ānanda, then Bhikkhu Gavesī thought thus: 'I, verily, have obtained this unsurpassed bliss of liberation at will, with ease, and without difficulty; it would be a good thing if those five hundred Bhikkhus obtain this unsurpassed bliss of liberation at will, with ease, and without difficulty, in like manner.'

"Ānanda, then those five hundred lay-disciples, dwelling solitary, detached, earnest ardent and aspiring, attained that goal for which the sons of good families rightly leave home for the homeless life, even that unrivalled goal of righteous living, attained it in that very life, and knowing it for themselves lived in full realisation thereof: 'Rebirth is no more; we have lived the pure life; we have done all that ought to be done; we have nothing more to do for Arahatship.'

"Thus, Ānanda, those five hundred Bhikkhus with Gavesī as their leader, in striving from higher things to higher, from nobleness to nobleness attained in this very life that incomparable bliss of liberation—*Arahatta-phala*.

"Wherefore, Ānanda, you should train yourselves in this way: From higher things to higher, from nobleness to nobleness, we will strive and will come to realize that bliss of liberation—*Arahatta-phala* in this very life.

"Well, Ānanda, you should train yourselves in this way."

---

33. The 'goal' means *Arahatta-phala* (Fruition of Holiness).

"Bhikkhus, these are known as *kāma-guṇa*, but in the teaching of Ariyās *kāma-guṇa* are not *kāma*.[34]

(1) "*Saṅkappa-rāga*—lust which arises from impure thought is called *kāma*. Pretty objects in the world are not *kāma*, Pretty objects stand in this world, as they are and yet wise man get rid of desire for them.

(2) "Bhikkhus, what is the origin of *kāma* (sensuality)?

"Bhikkhus, *phassa* (contact) is the origin of sensuality.

(3) "Bhikkhus, what is the variety of sensuality?

"Bhikkhus, one kind of sensuality is with regard to visible objects, another with regard to sounds, another with regard to smells, another with regard to tastes, another with regard to physical contacts. This, Bhikkhus, is called the variety of sensuality.

(4) "Bhikkhus, what is the resultant of sensuality?

"Bhikkhus, whatever being is brought into existence in the planes of merits or in the planes of demerits by *kāma* as its offspring is the resultant of *kāma* (sensuality).[35]

(5) "Bhikkhus, what is the cessation of sensuality?

"Bhikkhus, the cessation of contact is the cessation of sensuality.

(6) "Bhikkhus, what is the practice leading to the cessation of sensuality?

"The Noble Eightfold Path, namely, Right Understanding, Right Thinking, Right Speech, Right Action, Right Livelihood, Right Effort, Right Mindfulness, Right Concentration, is the practice leading to the cessation of sensuality.

"And when the Noble disciple thus understands sensuality, the origin of sensuality, the variety of sensuality, the resultant of sensuality, the cessation of sensuality, and the practice leading to the cessation of sensuality, he understands this *nibbedhikabrāhmacariya* (Noble practice which explodes masses of *lobha*, *dosa* and *moha*).

---

34. There are two kinds of *kāma*, viz:

(i) *Vatthu-kāma* – Objects of sensuality, and

(ii) *Kilesa-kāma* – Sensuality itself

What has to be got rid of is *kilesa-kāma*.

The teaching of Ariyās is the Buddha Sasana.

35. Those who long for *dibba-kāma* (the pleasure of *devas*) and practice virtues are reborn in the planes of *devas*. Those who fall into vice (in their quest for pleasure) are reborn in the Apāya (planes of demerits, etc.).

"Bhikkhus, it is said: 'Sensuality should be understood; the origin of sensuality should be understood; the variety of sensuality should be understood; the resultant of sensuality should be understood; the cessation of sensuality should be understood; the practice leading to the cessation of sensuality should be understood;—and because of this it is said."

II. VEDANĀ

(1) "Bhikkhus, it is said: 'Feeling should be understood; the origin of feeling should be understood; the variety of feeling should be understood; the resultant of feeling should be understood; the practice leading to the cessation of feeling should be understood'—and wherefore is this said?

"Bhikkhus, feelings are these three: (i) Agreeable feeling, (ii) disagreeable feeling, (iii) indifferent feeling.

(2) "Bhikkhus, what is the origin of feeling? Bhikkhus, *phassa* (contact) is the origin of feeling.

(3) "Bhikkhus, what is the variety of feeling?

"Bhikkhus, (i) there are agreeable feelings associated with *kilesa* (defilement); (ii) there are agreeable feelings not associated with *kilesa*, (iii) there are disagreeable feelings associated with *kilesa*; (iv) there are disagreeable feelings not associated with *kilesa*; (v) there are indifferent feelings associated with *kilesa*; (vi) there are indifferent feelings not associated with *kilesa*. This Bhikkhus, is the variety of feeling.

(4) "Bhikkhus, what is the resultant of feeling?

"Bhikkhus, whatever being is brought into existence in the plane of merits or in the plane of demerits by feeling as its offspring is the resultant of feeling.

(5) "Bhikkhus, what is the cessation of feeling?

"Bhikkhus, the cessation of *phassa* (contact) is the cessation of feeling.

(6) "Bhikkhus, what is the practice leading to the cessation of feeling?

"Bhikkhus, This Noble Eightfold Path, namely, Right Understanding, Right Thinking, Right Speech, Right Action, Right Livelihood, Right Effort, Right Mindfulness, Right Concentration, is the practice leading to the cessation of feeling.

"And when the noble disciple understands feeling, the origin of feeling, the variety of feeling, the resultant of feeling, the cessation of feeling, the practice leading to the cessation of feeling, he understands this *nibbedhikabrāhmacariya* (Noble Practice which explodes masses of *lobha*, *dosa* and *moha*).

"Bhikkhus, it is said: 'Feeling should be understood; the origin of feeling should be understood; the variety of feeling should be understood; the resultant of feeling should be understood; the cessation of feeling should be understood: the practice leading to the cessation of feeling should be understood—and because of this it is said."

III. SAÑÑĀ

(1) "Bhikkhus, it is said: 'Perception should be understood; the origin of perception should be understood; the variety of perception should be understood; the resultant of perception should be understood; the cessation of perception should be understood; the practice leading to the cessation of perception should be understood'—and wherefore is this said?

"Bhikkhus, there are six kinds of perceptions. They are: (i) *rūpa-saññā* (perceptions having visible things as its objects), (ii) *sadda-saññā* (perception having sounds as its objects), (iii) *gandha-saññā* (perception having smells as its objects), (iv) *rasa-saññā* (perception having tastes as its objects), (v) *phoṭṭabba-saññā* (perception having physical contacts as its objects), (vi) *dhamma-saññā* (perception having mental states as its object).

(2) "Bhikkhus, what is the origin of perception?

"Bhikkhus, *phassa* is the origin of perception

(3) "Bhikkhus, what is the variety of perception?

"Bhikkhus, there is one kind of perception with regard to visible objects, another with regard to sounds, another with regard to smells, another with regard to tastes, another with regard to physical contacts and another with regard to mental states. This, Bhikkhus, is called the variety of perception.

(4) "What is the resultant of perception?

"Bhikkhus, perception gives rise to conventional term. A certain thing is perceived and is cognized by a conventional term. Thus, the conventional term is the resultant of perception.

(5) "Bhikkhus, what is the cessation of perception?

"Bhikkhus, the cessation of *phassa* is the cessation of perception.

(6) "Bhikkhus, what is the practice leading to the cessation of perception?

"Bhikkhus, this Noble Eightfold Path, namely, Right Understanding,

Right Thinking, Right Speech, Right Action, Right Livelihood, Right Effort, Right Mindfulness, Right Concentration, is the practice leading to the cessation of perception.

"And when the Noble disciple understands perception, the origin of perception, the variety of perception, the resultant of perception, the cessation of perception and the practice leading to the cessation of perception, he understands this *nibbedhikabrāhmacariya* (Noble practice which explodes masses of *lobha*, *dosa* and *moha*).

"Bhikkhus, it is said: 'Perception should be understood; the origin of perception should be understood; the variety of perception should be understood; the resultant of perception should be understood; the cessation of perception should be understood; the practice leading to the cessation of perception should be understood'—and because of this it is said"

IV. ĀSAVA

(1) "Bhikkhus, it is said: '*Āsavas* should be understood; the origin of *āsavas* should be understood; the variety of *āsavas* should be understood; the resultant of *āsavas* should be understood; the cessation of *āsavas* should be understood; the practice leading to the cessation of *āsavas* should be understood'—and wherefore is this said?

"Bhikkhus, there are three kinds of *āsavas*, namely, (i) *kāmāsava* (mental impurities of sensuality), (ii) *bhavāsava* (mental impurities for existence), (iii) *avijjāsava* (mental impurities of ignorance).

(2) "Bhikkhus, what is the origin of *āsavas*?

"Bhikkhus, *avijjā* (ignorance) is the origin of *āsavas*.

(3) "Bhikkhus, what is the variety of *āsavas*?

"Bhikkhus, there are the following:

(i) *āsavas* that bear fruit in hell.

(ii) *āsavas* that bear fruit in the animal world.

(iii) *āsavas* that bear fruit in the Peta world.

(iv) *āsavas* that bear fruit in the world of men.

(v) *āsavas* that bear fruit in the *deva loka*. This, Bhikkhus, is the variety of *āsavas*.

(4) "Bhikkhus, what is the resultant of *āsavas*?

"Bhikkhus, whatever being is brought into existence in the plane of merits or in the plane of demerits by *āsavas* as its offspring is the resultant of āsavas.

(5) "Bhikkhus, what is the cessation of *āsavas*?

"Bhikkhus, the cessation of *avijjā* is the cessation of *āsavas*.

(6) "What is the practice leading to the cessation of *āsavas*?

"Bhikkhus, this Noble Eightfold Path, namely, Right Understanding, Right Thinking, Right Speech, Right Action, Right Livelihood, Right Effort, Right Mindfulness, Right Concentration, is the practice leading to the cessation of *āsavas*.

"And when the Noble disciple understands *āsavas*, the origin of *āsavas*, the variety of āsavas, the resultant of *āsavas*, the cessation of *āsavas*, the practice leading to the the cessation of *āsavas*, he understands this *nibbedhikabrāhmacariya* (Noble Practice which explodes masses of *lobha*, *dosa* and *moha*).

"Bhikkhus, it is said: '*Āsavas* should be understood; the origin of *āsavas* should be understood; the variety of *āsavas* should be understood; the resultant of *āsavas* should be understood; the cessation of *āsavas* should be understood; the practice leading to the cessation of *āsavas* should be understood'—and because of this it is said."

V. KAMMA

(1) "Bhikkhus, it is said: '*kamma* should be understood; the origin of *kamma* should be understood, the variety of *kamma* should be understood; the resultant of *kamma* should be understood; the cessation of *kamma* should be understood; the practice leading to the cessation of *kamma* should be understood'—and wherefore is this said?

"The volition, Bhikkhus, do l call *kamma*. Through volition one performs *kamma* (wholesome or unwholesome) by means of body, speech and mind.

(2) "Bhikkhus, what is the origin of *kamma*?

"Bhikkhus, *phassa* (contact) is the origin of *kamma*.

(3) "Bhikkhus, what is the variety of *kamma*?

"Bhikkhus, there are the following:

(i) *kamma* that bears fruit in hell.

(ii) *kamma* that bears fruit in the animal world.

(iii) *kamma* that bears fruit in the Peta world.

(iv) *kamma* that bears fruit in the world of men.

(v) *kamma* that bears fruit in the deva loka. This, Bhikkhus, is the variety of *kamma*.

(4) "Bhikkhus, what is the resultant of *kamma*?

"Bhikkhus, there are three kinds of *kamma*-resultants:

(i) *kamma* bearing fruit during life-time;

(ii) *kamma* bearing fruit in the next life; and

(iii) *kamma* bearing fruit in later lives.

This Bhikkhus, is called the resultant of *kamma*.

(5) "Bhikkhus, what is the cessation of *kamma*?

"Cessation of *phassa* (contact), Bhikkhus, is the cessation of *kamma*.

(6) "Bhikkhus, what is the practice leading to the cessation of *kamma*?

"Bhikkhus, this Noble Eightfold Path, namely, Right Understanding, Right Thinking, Right Speech, Right Action, Right Livelihood, Right Effort, Right Mindfulness, Right Concentration, is the practice leading to the cessation of *kamma*.

"And when the Noble disciple understands *kamma*, the origin of *kamma*, the variety of *kamma*, the resultant of *kamma*, the cessation of *kamma*, the practice leading to the cessation of *kamma*, he understands this *nibbedhika-brāhmacariya* (Noble Practice which explodes masses of *Lobha*, *dosa* and *moha*).

"Bhikkhus, it is said: '*Kamma* should be understood; the origin of *kamma* should be understood; the variety of *kamma* should be understood; the resultant of *kamma* should be understood; the cessation of *kamma* should be understood; the practice leading to the cessation of *kamma* should be understood'—and because of this it is said."

VI. DUKKHA

(1) "Bhikkhus, it is said: '*Dukkha* should be understood; the origin of *dukkha* should be understood; the variety of *dukkha* should be understood; the resultant of *dukkha* should be understood; the cessation of *dukkha* should be understood; the practice leading to the cessation of *dukkha* should be understood'—and wherefore is this said?

"Bhikkhus, Birth is Suffering; Old Age is Suffering; Disease is Suffering; Death is Suffering; Sorrow, Lamentation, Pain, Grief and Despair are Suffering; not getting what one wants is Suffering. In short, the five constituent groups of existence which are the objects of Clinging are Suffering.

(2) "Bhikkhus what is the origin of *dukkha*?

"Bhikkhus, craving is the origin of *dukkha*.

(3) "Bhikkhus, what is the variety of *dukkha*?

"Bhikkhus, (i) Suffering that is above measure; (ii) Suffering that is trifling; (iii) Suffering that is slow to disappear; (iv) Suffering that is quick to disappear. This, Bhikkhus, is the variety of *dukkha*.

(4) "Bhikkhus, what is the resultant of *dukkha*?

"Bhikkhus, in the world, some people being oppressed by suffering (*dukkha*) and mentally worn out, grieve, mourn, lament, beat their breasts and become bewildered.

"Or, being oppressed by this Suffering, they seek outside (the Sāsana) saying to themselves, 'Who will be able to know a word or two to put an end to this *dukkha* (suffering)?' Bhikkhus, I say that Suffering leads to bewilderment and search for such a person.

"This, Bhikkhus, is the resultant of *dukkha*.

(5) "Bhikkhus, what is the cessation of *dukkha*?

"Bhikkhus, the cessation of craving is the cessation of *dukkha*.

(6) "Bhikkhus, what is the practice leading to the cessation of *dukkha*?

"Bhikkhus, this Noble Eightfold Path, namely, Right Understanding, Right Thinking, Right Speech, Right Action, Right Livelihood, Right Effort, Right Mindfulness, Right Concentration, is the practice leading to the cessation of *dukkha*.

"And when the Noble disciple understands *dukkha*, the origin of *dukkha*, the variety of *dukkha*, the resultant of *dukkha*, the cessation of *dukkha* and the practice leading to the cessation of *dukkha*, he understands this *nibbedhika-brāhmacariya* (Noble Practice which explodes masses of *lobha*, *dosa* and *moha*).

"Bhikkhus, it is said: '*Dukkha* should be understood; the origin of *dukkha* should be understood; the variety of *dukkha* should be understood; the resultant of *dukkha* should be understood; the cessation of *dukkha* should be understood and the practice leading to the cessation of *dukkha* should be understood'—and because of this it is said.

"Verily, Bhikkhus, such is this dhamma discourse on the way to explode (masses of *lobha*, *dosa* and *moha*)."

AṬṬHAKA-NIPĀTA, PAṬHAMA-PAṆṆĀSAKA, GAHAPATI-VAGGA, ANURUDDHA-MAHĀVITAKKA SUTTA

Discourse on the Great Reflections of Venerable Anuruddha

On one occasion the Bhagavā was staying at the Deer Park in Bhesakaḷa grove at Saṃsumāgiri in the kingdom of Bhagga. At that time the Venerable Anuruddha was dwelling in the Eastern Bamboo Forest in the kingdom of Ceti. Then the Venerable Anuruddha, being in a secluded place, reflected:

'This Buddha-Dhamma is for one whose wants are few, this Buddha-Dhamma is not for one whose wants are many. This Buddha-Dhamma is for the contented, not for the discontented. This Buddha-Dhamma is for one who practices seclusion, not for one fond of society. This Buddha-Dhamma is for one who is energetic, not for one who is indolent. This Buddha-Dhamma is for one who is setting up mindfulness, not for one who is heedless. This Buddha-Dhamma is for one who has composure of mind, not for one whose mind is confused. This Buddha-Dhamma is for the wise; not for the unwise.'

Now the Buddha, knowing these reflections of Anuruddha, by His higher spiritual power, just as a strong man might stretch forth and bend back his arm, travelled from Bhesakaḷa Grove in Bhagga to the Eastern Bamboo Forest, appeared before the Venerable Anuruddha and sat down on the seat specially prepared for Him. Then the Venerable Anuruddha made obeisance to the Buddha and sat at one side. When Anuruddha was thus seated, the Buddha addressed him

"Well done! Well done, Anuruddha! You have entertained the thoughts of a superman: 'This Buddha-Dhamma is for one whose wants are few, this Buddha-Dhamma is not for one whose who wants are many. This Buddha-Dhamma is for the contented, not for the discontented. This Buddha-Dhamma is for one who practices seclusion, not for one fond of society. This Buddha-Dhamma is for one who is energetic, not for one who is indolent. This Buddha-Dhamma is for one who is setting up mindfulness, not for one who is heedless. This Buddha-Dhamma is for one who has composure of mind, not for one whose mind is confused. This Buddha-Dhamma is for the wise; not for the unwise.' As you have reflected so far Anuruddha, you should reflect on this eighth thought of a superman: 'This Buddha-Dhamma is for one who is free from Hindrances and who delights in things which are free from Hindrances, not for one, who indulges in sensuous pleasures and who delights in things that impede spiritual progress.'

"Anuruddha, when you entertain these eight thoughts of a superman, at that time you will be devoid of sensuous pleasures and evil thoughts and abide in the first Jhana,[36] which is accompanied by Thought conception and Discursive thinking, is born of Detachment, and filled with Rapture and Joy.

"Anuruddha, when you entertain these eight thoughts of a superman, at that time you will, after the subsiding of Thought conception and Discursive thinking, abide in the second Jhāna, which is born of Concentration, and accompanied by Rapture and Joy.

"Anuruddha, when you entertain these eight thoughts of a superman, at that time you will, after the fading away of rapture, dwell in equanimity, be mindful and clearly conscious; and will experience in your person that ease which the Noble Ones talk of when they say: 'Happy lives the man of equanimity and attentive mind'; thus will you enter the third Jhāna.

"Anuruddha, when you entertain these eight thoughts of a superman, at that time, after having given up pleasure and pain, and through the disappearance of the previous joy and grief which you had, you will enter into a state beyond pleasure and pain, into the fourth Jhāna, a state of pure Equanimity and clear mindfulness.

"Anuruddha, when you entertain the eight thoughts of a superman, at that time whenever you will, you can enjoy these Jhānas according to your wish, without difficulty and pain, bringing comfort here and now. Then Anuruddha, just as a box containing multicoloured clothes is an object of delight to some householder or householder's son; you who are contented with any clothing will contemplate that this robe which is besmeared with dust serves you as an object of delight in the sense that you use this robe simply as a requisite, that you have no attachment for this robe, and that it will lead you to the portals of emancipation.

---

36. *Jhāna* has been variously translated as "Ecstasy", "Rapture", "Absorption" (Nyanatiloka); and the latter, though best, does not give a completely satisfactory definition. It is a state which supervenes on the practice of "awareness" of "setting up of mindfulness" and so the opposite of a hypnotic "trance". There is only one way to arrive at the meaning of the word and that is to enter the state.

"Anuruddha, when you entertain these eight thoughts of a superman, at that time, whenever you will, you can enjoy these four Jhānas according to your wish, without difficulty and pain, bringing comfort here and now. Then, Anuruddha, just as a meal of rice served with deliciously cooked curries is an object of delight to some householder or householder's son; the alms-food which you receive by begging from door to door will be an object of delight to you in the sense that you simply take food as a requisite, that you have no attachment for that meal, and that it will lead you to the portals of emancipation.

"Anuruddha, when you entertain these eight thoughts of a superman, at that time, whenever you will, you can enjoy these four Jhānas according to your wish, without difficulty and pain, bringing comfort here and now. Then, Anuruddha, just as a gabled house, plastered both inside and outside, with doors barred and shutters closed, and draught-free, is an object of delight to some householder or householder's son; the place at the foot of some tree will be an object of delight to you who are contented with dwelling, in the sense that you simply use the foot of the tree as a requisite, that you have no attachment for this dwelling, and that it will lead you to the portals of emancipation.

"Anuruddha, when you entertain these eight thoughts of a superman, at that time, whenever you will, you can enjoy these four Jhānas according to your wish, without difficulty and pain, bringing comfort here and now. Then, Anuruddha, just as a place with fleecy cover, woollen cloth or coverlet, spread with rugs of deer-skins, with awnings over it, with crimson cushions at either end, is an object of delight to some householder or householder's son; to you who are contented with bed and seat, this bed and seat, made of grass will be an object of delight in the sense that you simply use it as a requisite, that you have no attachment for it, and that it will lead you to the portals of emancipation.

"Anuruddha, when you entertain these eight thoughts of a superman, at that time, whenever you will, you can enjoy these four Jhānas according to your wish, without difficulty and pain, bringing comfort here and now. Then, Anuruddha, just as the variegated medicines: butter pure and fresh, oil, honey and treacle, are objects of delight to some householder or householder's son: to you who are contented, this medicine made of cattle urine will be an object of delight in the sense that you simply use it as a requisite, that you have no attachment for it and that it will lead you to the portals of emancipation.

"Wherefore, Anuruddha, stay here in this Eastern Bamboo Grove in Ceti during the coming Vassa."

And the Venerable Anuruddha replied: "Yes Lord."

Then the Buddha, having given His advice to the Venerable Anuruddha, just as a strong man might stretch his arm and bend it back, returned by His power and appeared at Bhesakaḷa Grove in Bhagga. Now the Buddha sat down on the seat specially prepared for Him and addressed the monks as follows:

"Monks, I shall declare the 'Discourse on the eight thoughts of a superman'. Listen to me."

"Yes, Lord" the monks replied, and the Buddha said:

"This Buddha-Dhamma is for one whose wants are few, this Buddha-Dhamma is not for one whose wants are many. This Buddha-Dhamma is for the contented, not for the discontented. This Buddha-Dhamma is for one who practices seclusion, not for one fond of society. This Buddha-Dhamma is for one who is energetic, not for one who is indolent. This Buddha-Dhamma is for one who is setting up mindfulness, not for one who is heedless. This Buddha-Dhamma is for one who has composure of mind, not for one whose mind is confused. This Buddha-Dhamma is for the wise not for the unwise. This Buddha-Dhamma is for one who is free from Hindrances and who delights in things which are free from Hindrances, but not for one who indulges in sensuous pleasures and who delights in things that impede spiritual progress.

"O monks! This Buddha-Dhamma is for one whose wants are few, this Buddha-Dhamma is not for one whose wants are many, thus it is said. But why is this said?

"Herein, monks, a monk wanting little does not wish: 'May they know me as wanting little; may they know me as contented; may they know me as practicing seclusion; may they know me as energetic; may they know me as setting up mindfulness; may they know me as composed; may they know me as wise: may they know me as one who is free from Hindrances and who delights in things that are free from Hindrances.'

"O monks! This Buddha-Dhamma is for one whose wants are few, this Buddha-Dhamma is not for one whose wants are many so, what is said, is said on this account.

"O monks! This Buddha-Dhamma is for the contented, not for the discontented, thus it is said. But why is this said?

"Herein, monks, a monk is contented with such requisites—robe, alms, dwelling, medicine for illness.

"O monks! This Buddha-Dhamma is for the contented, not for the discontented—so, what is said, is said on this account.

"O monks! This Buddha-Dhamma is for one who practices seclusion, not for one fond of society, thus it is said. But why is this said?

"Herein, monks, while a monk practices seclusion, there come to him visitors such as monks, nuns, male and female devotees, kings and their chief ministers, heretics and their disciples. Then the monk with his mind inclined towards seclusion, leaning towards seclusion, abiding in seclusion and delighting in the life of a recluse, entirely confines his talk to that which encourages him to live in a place free from all worldly troubles.

"O monks! This Buddha-Dhamma is for one who practices seclusion, not for one fond of society—so, what is said, is said on this account.

"O monks! This Buddha-Dhamma is for one who is energetic, not for one who is indolent, thus it is said. But why is this said?

"Herein, monks, a monk strives energetically to avoid unwholesome deeds and to perform wholesome ones; firm and steadfast, he does not lay aside the yoke of performing wholesome actions—so, what is said, is said on this account.

"O monks! This Buddha-Dhamma is for one who is setting up mindfulness, not for one who is heedless, thus it is said. But why is this said?

"Herein, monks, a monk sets up mindfulness, he is endowed with supreme intentness of mind and discrimination; he recollects and remembers both the doings and sayings of long ago—so, what is said, is said on this account.

"O monks! This Buddha-Dhamma is for one who has composure of mind, not for one whose mind is confused; thus it is said. But why is this said?

"Herein, monks, a monk having got rid of sensuous desires ... enters and abides in ... the first ... second ... third ... and fourth Jhāna—so, what is said, is said on this account.

"O monks! This Buddha-Dhamma is for the wise not for the unwise, thus it is said. But why is this said?

"Herein, monks, a monk is wise; is endowed with a knowledge by means of which he is able to see the physical and mental phenomena as they really are, and is also able to penetrate into the complete destruction of suffering—so, what is said, is said on this account.

"O monks! This Buddha-Dhamma is for one who is free from Hindrances and who delights in things which are free from Hindrances, not for one who indulges in sensuous pleasures and delights in things that impede spiritual progress, thus it is said. But why is this said?

"Herein, monks, a monk's mind is at the portals of emancipation, becomes calm, composed and free. This Buddha-Dhamma is for one who is free from Hindrances and who delights in things which are free from Hindrances, not for one who indulges in sensuous pleasures and who delights in things that impede spiritual progress—so, what is said, is said on this account."

And the Venerable Anuruddha spent his Vassa at Ceti in the Eastern Bamboo Forest.

There, dwelling alone, solitary earnest, strenuous, resolute, he attained not long after, in this world, by the knowledge gained in the practice of meditation, the realization of the *cessation of suffering*, for the sake of which householders rightly go forth from their homes to the homeless life. He realized: 'Rebirth is no more; I have lived the pure life; I have done what ought to be done; I have nothing more to do for the realisation of Arahatship.'

And the Venerable Anuruddha was numbered among the Arahats.

Now at the time of his attaining Arahatship, the Venerable Anuruddha uttered these verses:

> 'The Master knew what thoughts were in my mind.
> With Power supreme He then appeared before me.
> Great were the thoughts I'd had anent the goal,
> But what was still unthought He taught to me.
> He who had first attained defilement's end,
> Taught me the way to reach that self-same goal.
> Hearing, I followed close the Path He showed:
> Won is the Threefold Knowledge[37] by His Way,
> Done is the task the Buddha set for me!'

---

37. *Tisso vijjā* = *Te-vijjā*: Three-fold knowledge:
(1) Remembrance of former births, (2) Insight into the arising and passing away of all beings, (3) Full recognition of the origin of Suffering and of the Way to its removal which culminates in the Extinction of all Biases.

AṬṬHAKANIPĀTA, DĀNA-VAGGA, DUCCARITA-VIPĀKA SUTTA

Discourse on Bad Effects of Evil Deeds

(1) "Monks, killing a living being, when practiced, developed, and repeatedly performed, causes one to arise in hell, in the world of animals, and in the world of *Petas*;[38] the very least result of taking life is the shortening of one's life when reborn as a man.

(2) "Monks, stealing, when practiced, developed, and repeatedly performed, causes one to arise in hell, in the world of animals, and in the world of *Petas*; the very least result of stealing is loss of one's wealth when reborn as a man.

(3) "Monks, sexual misconduct, when practiced, developed, and frequently performed, causes one to arise in hell, in the world of animals, and in the world of *Petas*; the very least result of practicing sexual misconduct is that one will breed rivalry and hatred when reborn as a man.

(4) "Monks, telling lies, when practiced, developed, and repeatedly performed, causes one to arise in hell, in the world of animals, and in the world of *Petas*; the very least result of telling lies is that one will be falsely accused when reborn as a man.

(5) "Monks, backbiting, when practiced, developed, and repeatedly performed, causes one to arise in hell, in the world of animals, and in the world of *Petas*; the very least result of backbiting is the breaking up of one's friendship when reborn as a man.

(6) "Monks, harsh speech, when practiced, developed, and repeatedly performed, causes one to arise in hell, in the world of animals, and in the world of *Petas*; the very least result of harsh speech is that one will possess an unpleasing voice when reborn as a man.

(7) "Monks, frivolous talk, when practiced, developed, and repeatedly performed, causes one to arise in hell, in the world of animals, and in the world of *Petas*; the very least result of frivolous talk is that one's words will be not accepted by others, when reborn as a man.

---

38. Ghosts.

(8) "Monks, partaking of intoxicants, when practiced, developed, and repeatedly performed, causes one to arise in hell, in the world of animals; and in the world of *Petas*; the very least result of partaking of intoxicants is that one will be afflicted with insanity when reborn as a man."

AṬṬHAKA NIPĀTA, PAṬHAMA-PAṆṆĀSAKA UPOSATHA-VAGGA, SAṄKHITTŪPOSATHA SUTTA

Discourse on Observing the Precepts in Brief

Thus, I have heard. On one occasion the Bhagavā[39] was staying at Jeta's Grove in the monastery of Anāthapiṇḍika at Sāvatthi. There the Bhagavā addressed the monks. "O monks." "Yes, Lord," answered the monks to the Bhagavā.

"Monks, the observance of the Eight Precepts on Fasting Day is very fruitful, of great merit, of great splendour, and radiantly shining.

"Monks, how are they observed and kept?

1. "Herein, monks, a Noble disciple reflects: 'All their lives Arahats desist from taking life and refrain therefrom; they lay aside stick and weapon; they are compassionate to all beings; and they look to the welfare of all beings. I, too, now, during this night and day, will desist from taking life and refrain therefrom; I will lay aside stick and weapon; I will be compassionate to all beings; and I will look to the welfare of all beings, and thus in this way, I shall follow the example of Arahats and observe this Precept.' This is the first of the Precepts in which he establishes himself.

2. 'All their lives Arahats desist from taking what is not given; they take only what is given; they desire to take only what is given; they dwell with a body clean and untainted with the speck of stealing. I, too, now, during this day and night, will desist from taking what is not given; I will take only what is given; I will desire to take only what is given; I will dwell with a body clean and untainted with the speck of stealing, and thus in this way, I shall follow the example of Arahats and observe this Precept.' This is the second of the Precepts in which he establishes himself.

3. 'All their lives Arahats desist from living unchastely; living the chaste life, abiding apart, they refrain from sexual practices which are indulged in by the village folk. I, too, now during this night and day, will live the chaste life; abiding apart, I will refrain from the practices of the village folk, and

39. A title of the Buddha: Variously translated as "Exalted one", "Fortunate one", "Sublime one", "Illustrious one."

thus following the example of Arahats I shall observe this Precept.' This is the third of the Precepts in which he establishes himself.

4. 'All their lives Arahats desist from telling lies and refrain therefrom; they speak the truth; they are bondsmen to truth; they speak honestly; they speak believable words; they deceive no one in the world. I, too, now, during this day and night, will speak the truth; will be bondsman to truth; will speak honestly; will speak believable words; will deceive no one in the world, and thus in this way, I shall follow the example of Arahats and observe this Precept.' This is the fourth of the Precepts in which he establishes himself.

5. 'All their lives Arahats desist from sloth-producing intoxicants and refrain therefrom. I, too, this night and day, will desist from intoxicants, and thus in this way, I shall follow the example of Arahats and observe this Precept.' This is the fifth of the Precepts in which he establishes himself.

6. 'All their lives Arahats take but one meal a day, and refrain from taking food after noon and at night. I, too, now, during this night and day, will act just as Arahats and observe this Precept.' This is the sixth of the Precepts in which he establishes himself.

7. 'All their lives Arahats refrain from dancing, singing, music, and unseemly shows; from the use of garlands, perfumes and unguents; and from things that tend to beautify and adorn the person. I, too, now, during this night and day, shall follow the example of Arahats and observe this Precept.' This is the seventh of the Precepts in which he establishes himself.

8. 'All their lives Arahats desist from using high and luxurious seats and refrain therefrom; they lie on low beds, couches or on strewn grass. I, too, now, during this night and day, shall follow the example of Arahats and observe this Precept.' This is the eighth of the Precepts in which he establishes himself.

"Monks, the observance of these Eight Precepts on Fasting Day is very fruitful, of great merit, of great splendour, and radiantly shining."

KHUDDAKA NIKĀYA

TIROKUṬṬA SUTTA

Suttanta Piṭaka, Khuddaka Nikāya, Khuddakapāṭha Pāḷi

—Page 8, 6th Synod Edition

Verse I

Tirokuṭṭesu, tiṭṭhanti, sandhisiṅghāṭakesu ca.
Dvārabāhāsu tiṭṭhanti, āgantvāna sakaṃ gharaṃ.

Outside the walls they stand, at the crossways and
leaning on the doorposts, to their own home returning.

Verse II

Pahūte annapānamhi khajjabhojje upaṭṭhite.
Na tesaṃ koci sarati, sattānaṃ kammapaccayā.

But when a plenteous meal is spread, or food and drink,
no one remembers them (the dead) on account of their (bad) *kamma*.

Verse III

Evaṃ dadanti ñātinaṃ, ye honti anukampakā.
Suciṃ paṇitaṃ kālena, kappiyaṃ pāṇabhojanaṃ.

Wherefore do those who have pity on their kin make offerings;
of pure, savoury and suitable food and drink at seasonable times.

Verse IV

Idaṃ vo ñātinaṃ hotu, sukhitā hontu ñātayo.
Te ca tattha samāgantvā, ñātipetā samāgatā

Be this a gift to our kinsmen—may our kinsmen be happy.
Then those *Peta* kinsmen come and gather there.

Verse V

Pahūte annapānamhi, sakkaccaṃ anumodare.
Ciraṃ jivantu no ñāti, yesaṃ hetu labhāmase.

They rejoice with due faith and earnestness at the plenteous food and drink.
Long live our kinsmen, of whom we get this.

Verse VI

Amhākañca kata pujā, dāyaka ca anipphalā.
Na hi tattha kasi atthi, gorakkhettha na vijjati.

To us this offering with honour is made; and it is not without fruit to the donor.
For there is—no ploughing—no cattle-keeping in the *Peta*-world.

Verse VII

Vaṇijjā tādisī natthi, hiraññena kayokayaṃ.
Ito dinnena yāpenti, petā kālaṅkatā tahiṃ

There is no trading—buying or selling—with gold or the like.
Petas live and subsist either on what normally is food for *Petas* or what reaches them through offerings made here (for their benefit by their friends and relatives.)

Verse VIII

Unname udakaṃ vuṭṭhaṃ, yathā ninnaṃ pavattati.
Evameva ito dinnaṃ, petānaṃ upakappati.

Even as water rained on high ground flows down to a lower level,
So, offerings given here reach the *Petas*.

Verse IX

Yathā vārivahā pūrā, paripūrenti sāgaraṃ.
Evameva into dinnaṃ petānaṃ upakappati.

Just as rivers which are full, fill the sea,
even so offerings given here reach the *Petas*.

Verse X

Adāsī me akāsi me, ñātimittā sakhā ca me.
Petānaṃ dakkhinaṃ dajjā, pubbe katamanussaraṃ.

'He gave me gifts, he did things for me. They were my kinsmen,
friends and companions'—
Thus, mindful of past deeds let a man make offerings for the
sake of the *Petas*.

Verse XI

Na hi ruṇṇaṃ vā soko vā, yā caññā paridevanā.
Na taṃ petānamatthāya, evaṃ tiṭṭhanti ñātayo.

Weeping or sorrowing or any other manner of lamenting
is not for the benefit of the *Petas*, the kinsmen (*Petas*) remain as they were.

Verse XII

Ayañca kho dakkhīṇā dinnā, saṃghamhi suppatiṭṭhitā.
Dīgharattaṃ hitāyassa, ṭhānaso upakappati.

Moreover, this offering which has been made is firmly established
in the Order,
reaches the *Petas* immediately and will be for their benefit for a
long time.

Verse XIII

So ñātidhammo ca ayaṃ nidassito,
Petāna pūjā ca katā uḷārā.
Balañca bhikkhunamanuppadīnnaṃ
Tumhe hi puññaṃ pasutaṃ anappakkanti.

The duty of relatives to make offering for the sake of the deceased has been demonstrated: offering with honour and liberality has been, made to the *Petas*, physical strength has been given to Bhikkhus; and you also have earned great merit.

COMMENTARY ON TIROKUṬṬA SUTTA[1]

The Story of those *Petas*[2] who had once been King Bimbisāra's Relatives

Q. Who delivered this Tirokuṭṭa Sutta? Where, when and on what account?

A. The Master gave this religious discourse on the second day of His arrival at Rājagaha, in appreciation of the meritorious deeds done by King Bimbisāra. Herein is the sequence of the narration:

Ninety-two *kappas* (world cycles) ago, there was a city named Kāsi, which was ruled over by King Jayasena. His chief queen was called Sīrimā. The embryo named Phussa was conceived in her womb, and in due course of time he attained Supreme Enlightenment and became a *sammā sambuddha* (Supremely Enlightened Buddha).

King Jayasena saying: "My son has renounced the world and now become a Supreme Buddha. This is my Buddha, Dhamma and Saṅgha only" attended on the Buddha personally without allowing others to do so.

At that time Buddha Phussa's three younger half brothers said to themselves: "Buddhas arise for the benefit of all mankind; they will not arise for the welfare of a single person. Our father does not allow others to attend on the Buddha. What shall we do so that we may be able to attend on the Buddha? Then the thought, 'We shall use a tactic' arose in their mind. These three younger half brothers caused a sham rebellion in the suburb of the city.

When the king heard about the rebellion, he sent for his three sons and sent them to the suburb of the city to suppress the rebellion.

When the three brothers returned to the city after suppressing the rebellion, the king was much pleased and granted them a boon saying, "Take any kind of reward you like."

They submitted: "We desire to attend on Buddha Phussa."

The king replied: "Ask for any other reward."

When the three brothers said that they did not desire any other reward, the king said: "Well then, you may attend on the Buddha by fixing a period."

---

1. Khuddaka-pāṭha, 7. Tirokuṭṭa Sutta p. 8, 6th Syn. Edn.
Khuddaka-pāṭha Aṭṭhakathā; Tirokuṭṭa Sutta. Vaṇṇaṇā, P 168; 6th Syn. Edn.
Tirokuṭṭa: On the other side of the wall; outside the wall.
2. *Petas*: Inhabitants of one of the Four Lower Regions.

Then they asked for a period of seven years. The King did not agree to their proposal. Then they reduced the period to six years, five years, four, three, two, one year, seven months, six months, five months, four months and finally to three months. To it the king gave his assent.

The three brothers being much pleased with this reward, approached the Buddha and having paid their obeisance to Him, addressed Him as follows: "Venerable Sir, we desire to attend on the Exalted One for a period of three months. May the Exalted One be pleased to spend the *Vassa* (the three month Season of Rains) here."

The Exalted One accepted by His silence.

After that the three brothers sent the following message to their royal agent in the suburb: "We shall attend on the Buddha for a period of three months. Kindly do the needful beginning with the building of a *vihāra* (monastery)." That royal agent accordingly accomplished his task and sent a reply to the three brothers to that effect. They put on yellow robes and together with 2500 attendants approached the Buddha, and having conveyed Him to the *vihāra* in the suburb of the city, requested Him to reside there.

Their treasurer and his wife had great *saddhā* (faith) in the Buddha, and they respectfully made offerings to the Saṅgha headed by the Buddha.

The royal agent sent for that treasurer and caused him to respectfully make offerings to the Saṅgha headed by the Buddha with eleven thousand men. Some of these people from the suburb had corrupt minds. They caused danger to *dāna* (almsgiving) by partaking of the gifts themselves and by setting fire to the dining hall.

After performing the *Pavāraṇā*[3] (the ceremony performed at the termination of the *Vassa*), the princes paid their deepest respects to the Buddha and went to their father's palace with the Buddha at their head. In due course of time, Buddha Phussa attained *Mahāparinibbāna*.

As time passed, the king, the princes, the royal agent in the suburb, the treasurer and the 2500 attendants died and were reborn in the heavenly abodes. Those people who had corrupt minds were reborn in hell. These two groups wandered, one, from one heavenly abode to another, and the other, from one hell to another. Thus, they went on for ninety-two *kappas* (world cycles).

---

3. Inviting admonishment from one another.

During Buddha Kassapa's Time

When Buddha Kassapa arose in this *Bhadda kappa* (*Bhadda* good world cycle), those people who had corrupt minds were reborn in the *Peta*-world.

At that time people made *dāna* (almsgiving) for the sake of their deceased relatives who were reborn in the *Peta*-world, with the definite intention: "May this *dāna* be also that of our relatives." Those *Petas* attained happiness accordingly. When the *Petas* (of Buddha Phussa's time) saw this, they approached Buddha Kassapa and said: "Venerable Sir, can we not attain such happiness?"

Buddha Kassapa replied: "You cannot get such a bliss now. But in the future, Buddha Gotama will arise in this world. At that time there will be a king named Bimbisāra. That king was your relative ninety-two world cycles ago. He will make offerings to the Buddha with the object of sharing his merits with you. Then you will attain such a bliss."

Buddha Kassapa's words appeared to them as if they would attain that bliss the next day.

During Buddha Gotama's Time

After the interim period between the arisings of the two Buddhas had expired, Buddha Gotama arose in this world. The three princes and their 2500 attendants having passed away from the heavenly abodes were reborn in the world of men as *brahmins* of Magadha. Subsequently, they led an ascetic life and became known as the three ascetics of Gayāsisa.[4] The treasurer became Visākha the millionaire. His wife became Dhammadinnā,[5] the daughter of a millionaire. Similarly, the rest of the attendants became the king's retinue.

After attaining the Supreme Enlightenment, Buddha spent His "seven weeks period" and went to Benares to deliver His First Sermon[6] to the group of the Five Ascetics at Sarnath. (He then went to Gayāsisa and delivered the Great Fire[7] Sermon to the three ascetics and their 2500 followers.) Thence

---

4. Uruveḷa Kassapa, Gayā Kassapa and Nādi Kassapa.
5. Majjhima Nikāya, Mūlapaṇṇāsa-5. Cūḷayamaka-vagga, 4. Caḷavedalla Sutta, pages 373-9; 6th Syn. Edn.
Please see *The Light of the Dhamma*, Vol. VI-No. 4, p. 38.
6. Dhammacakkappavattana Sutta-Vinaya Piṭaka, Mahāvagga, 6. Pañcavaggiyakathā, p. 14. 6th Syn. Edn.
7. Saṃyutta Nikāya, Saḷāyatana Saṃyutta, 3. Sabba-vagga, 6. Āditta Sutta, p. 251, 6th Syn. Edn.

He went to Rājagaha with the three ascetics and 2500 followers of theirs. On the very day of his arrival at Rājagaha, He delivered a discourse at the end of which King Bimbisāra and one hundred and eleven thousand inhabitants of Magadha—*brahmins*, bankers and commoners—became Sotāpannas (Stream-winners).

Then King Bimbisāra invited the Buddha to the morning meal on the following day and He accepted the invitation. On the second day He entered Rājagaha and went to the king's palace to accept the great offering made by the king. The Sakka—king of Devas—accompanied the Buddha going ahead as His guide and uttering the following stanza:

"*Danto dantehi saha purāṇajaṭilehi,*
Vippamutto vippamuttehi. Siṅgīnikkhasavaṇṇo,
Rājagahaṃ pāvisi bhagavā ti."

(One who has tamed himself, One who is absolutely free from all defilements and One whose complexion resembles the colour of *Siṅgani* gold, enters Rājagaha along with former ascetics who have been tamed and are free from all defilements.)

The above-mentioned *Petas* surrounded (the king's palace) and stood with the expectation, 'The king will make *dāna* for our sake; the king will now aim at us in making his *dāna*.'

After presenting his gifts to the Buddha, the king's mind was occupied with only one thought: 'Where should the Buddha stay?' He did not make his offering for the sake of anybody. When the *Petas* found that their hope had been frustrated, they went to the king's palace at night and made a dreadful noise. When the king heard this, he was frightened, startled and stricken with fear.

The next morning, he went to the Buddha and said: "Venerable Sir, I heard such a noise. What will happen to me?"

The Buddha replied: "O king! nothing will happen to you. In fact, your former relatives were reborn in the *Peta*-world. During the interim period between the arising of the two Buddhas, they wandered with the hope: 'The king will make an offering for our sake'; but you did not specify them when you made your offering the other day. Their hope having been frustrated these *Petas* made that dreadful noise."

"Lord, can they attain happiness if I make an offering now?"

"Yes, O king!"

"May the Exalted One be pleased to accept this morning's meal from me. I shall offer it for their sake."

The king returned to his palace and having made all preparations for the offering, invited the Buddha. The Buddha went to the palace and sat on the seat specially prepared for Him.

With the hope: 'Today's offering may be for us' those *Petas* stood outside the wall, etc. (*tirokuṭṭa*). The Buddha made the king see them clearly.

Then the king poured the water of libation and shared his merits with the *Petas* saying:

"May this offering of mine be for the sake of my relatives (who are reborn as *Petas*)." At that very moment there appeared for them ponds of water covered with lotuses. They bathed in them and drank the water from them. They satiated their thirst, and became free from anxiety and distress. Their complexion changed into a golden colour.

The king offered eatables for their sake. At that very moment there appeared for them nectar and ambrosia. They ate the food and regained vigour.

The king offered clothes and seats for their sake. At that very moment there appeared for them nectar and ambrosia. They ate the food and regained vigour.

The king offered clothes and seats for their sake. At that very moment there appeared for them celestial apparel, celestial vehicles, celestial mansions, celestial lodgings, etc. The Buddha made the king see all their prosperity clearly. The king was very pleased.

Then the Buddha having finished His meal and said that He did not require any more, uttered the verse beginning with "*Tirukuṭṭesu tiṭṭhanti*"', so that the king (of Magadha) might rejoice at his offering.

With these words, the question "Who delivered this Tirokuṭṭa Sutta? Where, when and on what account?" has been fully explained.

Verse I

"*Tirokuṭṭesu tiṭṭhanti, sandhisinghātakesu ca.*
Dvārabāhāsu tiṭṭhanti, āgantvāna sakaṃ gharaṃ."

Outside the walls they stand, at the cross-ways and
leaning on the door-posts, to their own home returning.

There (in the verse):

Āgantvāna sakaṃ gharaṃhiti: "To their own home returning." The house which belonged to the relatives in a former existence, or the house which belonged to one in former existences is spoken as "one's own house." Hence the expression "to their own home returning."

Verse II

"Pāhute annapānamhi, khajjabhojje upaṭṭhite.
Na tesaṃ koci sarati, sattānaṃ kamma-paccayā."

But when a plenteous meal is spread, of food and drink,
no one remembers them (the dead) on account of their (bad) *kamma*,

"Although the *Petas* had not resided in the house before, but as the house belonged to their relatives, they went to King Bimbisāra's house (palace) as if it was their own.

Of these, some *Petas* as a result of their *issā* (envy) and *macchariya* (selfishness) during their existence as human beings, have long beards, distorted faces, loose and drooping jaws, lean, coarse and dark-coloured parts of the body, resembling burnt trees or palm trees.

Some *Petas* being much oppressed with great hunger, their mouths emit flames just as a firelathe emits flames.

Some *Petas* having an abdomen as big as a mountain and a throat about the size of a needle-eye, cannot take food to their satisfaction, although they obtain food, and so are greatly oppressed with hunger.

Some *Petas*, not being able to obtain any other food, joyfully eats pus, impure blood and mucus coming out of pimples, boils, etc. of their fellow *Petas* or other creatures, and thus have ugly-looking and dreadful bodies."

The Exalted One desiring to show these *Petas* to the king declared:

"Outside the walls they stand, at the cross-ways and leaning on the door-posts, to their own home returning."

Again, in order to show the severity of these *Peta's* past *kammas*, He uttered the Second Verse:

> "But when a plenteous meal is spread, of food and drink, no one remembers them (the dead) on account of their (bad) *kamma*.

There (in the verse):

Four kinds of food have been classified: (1) That can be eaten, (2) that can be drunk, (3) that can be chewed, and (4) that can be licked.

Kamma paccayā: Owing to their own *kammas*.

In their previous existences they did not make *dāna* through stinginess;

they prevented others from making *dāna*. Their own bad *kammas* prevented their relatives from remembering them.

Verse III

"*Evaṃ dadanti ñātinaṃ, ye honti anukampakā.*
Suciṃ paṇitaṃ kālena, kappiyaṃ pana-bhojanaṃ."

(Wherefore do those who have pity on their kin make offerings of pure, savoury and suitable food and drink at seasonable times.) There (in the verse):

The Buddha uttered the Third Verse, in appreciation of the *dāna* made by King Bimbisāra for the sake of those former relatives who were reborn in the *Peta*-world.

There (in the verse):

"Food and drink" are mentioned as the beginning, so it should be understood that all articles which can be subject matter of gift are included.

First line of Verse IV

"*Idaṃ vo ñātīnaṃ hotu, sukhitā hontu ñātayo.*"

(Be this a gift to our kinsmen—may our kinsmen be happy!)

The Buddha desired to show that the offering made by the King of Magadha was intended for his kinsmen *Petas*.

Second line of Verse IV and first line of Verse V

"*Te ca tattha samagantvā, ñātipetā samagatā.*"

(Then those *Peta* kinsmen come and gather there.)

This line should be read in conjunction with the first line of Verse IV, when it will read:

'Be this a gift to our kinsmen—may our kinsmen be happy!'

Then those *Peta* kinsmen come and gather there.

It is true that the wholesome volitional actions[8] done by one cannot give result to another, but, in this case, the wholesome volitional actions done by King Bimbisāra leads to the wholesome volitional actions on the part of the *Petas*. Owing to this gift the kinsmen *Petas* are able to do wholesome volitional

8. *Pattānumodana*: Rejoicing at wholesome volitional actions done by others.

actions (by saying *Sādhu*), which bear fruit immediately. In order to show this the Buddha uttered:

"*Te ca tattha samagantvā, ñātipetā samāgatā.*"

(Then do those *Peta* Kinsmen come and gather there.)

First line of Verse V

"*Pāhute annapānamhi, sakkaccaṃ anumodare.*"

(They rejoice with due faith and earnestness at the offering of plenteous food and drink.)

By gathering at the king's palace and by rejoicing at the offering made by the king for their benefit (by saying '*Sādhu*') the *Petas* have also performed wholesome volitional actions which bear fruit immediately.

Second line of Verse V and first line of Verse VI

When the *Petas* attained happiness immediately after their saying 'Sadhu' and rejoicing at the offering made by the King of Magadha, they thanked him and earnestly wished for his long life and prosperity saying: "The offering with honour, is made for our benefit; we have enjoyed immediate bliss; and the doer of the deed has earned great merit." In order to show this the Buddha declared the following two lines:

"*Ciraṃ Jīvantu no ñātī, yesaṃ, hetu labhāmase.*"

(Long live our kinsmen, on account of whom we get this!)

"*Amhākañca katā pūjā, dāyakā ca anipphalā.*"

(To us this offering with, honour is made; and it is not without fruit to the donor.)

The *dāna* (almsgiving) will be effective only if the following three conditions are fulfilled:

(1) *Petas* must actually rejoice in the gift;
(2) The gift must be made for their sake;
(3) The donee must be virtuous.

If these three conditions are fulfilled, the *Petas* attain immediate bliss.

Of these three conditions, the doer of the deed is the most essential. Hence the declaration:

"On account of whom get this."

Here, one may ask: "How is it? Can only those relatives who are born in the world of *Petas* attain happiness? A brahmin named Jānussoṇi[9] asked the Buddha the same question, and the Buddha replied as follows. So, there is nothing to be said by us.

Brahmin Jānussoṇi asked the Buddha:

"Venerable Gotama! We brahmins present gifts and make offerings saying: 'Be this a gift to our relatives. May they enjoy it.'

"O Venerable Gotama! How is it? Will this gift reach our relatives who are dead? Will they enjoy it?"

The Exalted One replied: "O brahmin, it will reach them if they are in an opportune place, but not otherwise."

Jānussoṇi: "Venerable Gotama! What is meant by an 'opportune place' and what by an 'inopportune place'?"

Inopportune Places

The Buddha replied:

I) "O Brahmin! In this world there are some people who are in the habit of (1) taking life, (2) taking what is not given, (3) indulging in improper sexual intercourse, (4) telling lies, (5) slandering, (6) using harsh or impolite speech, (7) talking frivolously and senselessly, (8) entertaining covetousness, (9) entertaining malevolence, and (10) holding wrong views. On the dissolution of their bodies after death, they are reborn in hell. There they have what is food for hell-beings. They live and subsist on it. O brahmin! That place (hell) is an inopportune place where the gift cannot reach (or benefit) them.

II) "O Brahmin! In this world there are some people who are in the habit of (1) taking life, (2) taking what is not given, (3) indulging in improper sexual intercourse, (4) telling lies, (5) slandering, (6) using harsh or impolite speech, (7) talking frivolously and senselessly, (8) entertaining covetousness, (9) entertaining malevolence, and (10) holding wrong views. On the dissolution of their bodies after death, they are reborn in animal-world. There they have what is food for animals. They live and subsist on it. O brahmin! That place (animal-world) is an inopportune place where the gift cannot reach (or benefit) them.

III) "O Brahmin! In this world there are some people who abstain from (1) taking life, (2) taking what is not given, (3) improper sexual intercourse,

---

9. Aṅguttara Nikāya, Dasaka Nipāta, 11. Jānussoṇi Sutta, p. 478, 6th Syn: Edn.

(4) telling lies, (5) slandering, (6) using harsh or impolite speech, (7) frivolous and senseless talk, (8) entertaining covetousness, (9) entertaining ill will, and (10) holding wrong views. On the dissolution of their bodies after death, they are reborn in the world of men. There they have what is food for men. They live and subsist on it. O brahmin! That place (world of men) is an inopportune place where the gift cannot reach (or benefit) them.

IV) "O brahmin! In this world there are some people who abstain from (1) taking life, (2) taking what is not given (3) improper sexual intercourse, (4) telling lies, (5) slandering, (6) using harsh or impolite speech, (7) frivolous and senseless talk, (8) entertaining covetousness. (9) entertaining ill will, and (10) holding wrong views. On the dissolution of their bodies after death, they are reborn in the heavenly abodes as the companions of the *devas*. There they have what is food for *devas*. They live and subsist on it. O brahmin! That place (heavenly abodes) is an inopportune place where the gift cannot reach (or benefit) them.

Opportune Place

"O brahmin! In this world there are some people who are in the habit of (1) taking life, (2) taking what is not given, (3) indulging in improper sexual intercourse, (4) telling lies, (5) slandering, (6) using harsh or impolite speech, (7) talking frivolously and senselessly, (8) entertaining covetousness, (9) entertaining ill will, and (10) holding wrong views. On the dissolution of their bodies after death, they are reborn in the *Peta*-world. There they have their own food, and they have to live and subsist on that food; or in the alternative, they live and subsist there on what reaches them through offerings made for their benefit by their friends and relatives. That place (*Peta*-world) is an opportune place where the gift can reach them."

Jānussoṇi: "If none of the relatives arises in the *Peta*-world, who will enjoy the benefits of that gift?"

"O brahmin! Other relatives who are reborn in the *Peta*-world will enjoy it" replied the Buddha.

Jānussoṇi: "Venerable Gotama! Supposing neither the relative nor any other relative is in the *Peta*-world, who will enjoy it?"

"O brahmin! The *saṃsāra* has been so long that it is impossible for the *Peta*-world to be devoid of your relatives. Besides, O brahmin! the donor himself is not without any benefit."

Second line of Verse VI and Verse VII

In the *Peta*-world as there are no such occupations as cattle rearing, cultivation, trading-buying or selling with gold or the like, *Petas* cannot earn anything there. They can only attain what reaches them as shares of merits done by their friends and relatives here, for their benefits. So the Buddha uttered following three lines:

"*Nahi tattha kasi atthi, gorakkhettha na vijjati.*
Vāṇijjā tādisi natthi, hiraññena kayokayaṃ.
Ito dinnena vāpenti, petā kālaṅkatā tahiṃ."

Verses VIII and IX

Again, the Buddha desiring to explain it with further examples, uttered the Eighth and the Ninth Verse.

Verse VIII

"*Unname udakaṃ vuṭṭhaṃ, yathā ninnaṃ pavattati.*
Evemeva ito dinnaṃ, petānaṃ upakappati."

Even as water rained on high ground flows down to a lower level, so offerings given here reach the *Petas*.

Verse IX

"*Yathā vārivahā pūrā, paripūrenti sāgaraṃ.*
Evemeva ito dinnaṃ, petānaṃ upakappati."

Just as rivers which are full, fill the sea even so offerings given here reach the *Petas*.

(*Peta*-world being one of the Four Lower Regions, is compared to a lower level and the world of men is compared to a higher level.) Just as rain fallen on the higher ground flows down to a lower level, the merits done by the friends and relatives of the *Petas* reach them, and enable them to enjoy immediate bliss.

Or in other words, just as water collected in the lakes, creeks and rivulets on a higher level flows into the rivers and thence into the ocean, the offerings made by the friends and relatives of the *Petas* reach them and enable them to enjoy immediate bliss.

Hence the Buddha declared that the *Peta*-world is the Opportune Place.

Verse X

"*Adāsi me akāsi me, ñātimittā sakhā ca me.*
Petānaṃ dikkhinaṃ dajjā, pubbe katamanussaraṃ."

'He gave me gifts; he did things for me. They were my kinsmen, friends and companions'—thus mindful of past deeds let a man make offerings for the sake of the *Petas.*

So after explaining that the *Petas* live and subsist there on what is given here for their benefit, the Buddha uttered this verse: to show that for the said reason a good relative should make offerings remembering these things as reminders about them.

Although the *Petas* go to the houses of their relatives hoping that they would get something there, they cannot ask (for anything) saying, 'Please give such and such a thing.'

The meaning of the verse is: Offerings should be made for the benefit of *Petas* remembering, 'He gave me this property; he gave me this paddy; he had personally attended to my work; he was my relative either from the father's or the mother's side; he was my intimate friend; he was my playmate and companion.'

Verse XI

After showing that people should make offerings specially intended for *Petas* with the thought 'I had been given such and such a thing, etc. in former days', the Buddha uttered the Eleventh Verse to show that the weeping, sorrowing, etc., of those who are oppressed by weeping, sorrowing, etc. at the death of their relatives but do not make any offering for their benefit, merely cause their own suffering and that they do not do any good to the *Petas.*

"*Na hi ruṇṇaṃ vā soko vā, yā caññā paridevanā.*
Na taṃ petānamatthāya, evaṃ tiṭṭhanti ñātayo."

Weeping or sorrowing or any other manner of lamentation is not for the benefit of the *Petas*; and they (the *Petas*) remain as they were.

Verse XII

The Buddha uttered the Twelfth Verse, to show that the offering made by Bimbisāra, King of Magadha, is of great benefit.

"*Ayañca kho dakkhiṇā dinnā, saṅghamhi suppatiṭṭhitā.*
Dīghasattaṃ hitāyassa, ṭhānasa upakappati."

Moreover, this offering which has been made and firmly established in the Order, reaches the *Petas* immediately and will be for their benefit for a long time.

The following is what the Buddha meant to say: "O king! As the *Bhikkhu-Saṅgha* is the best soil for meritorious deeds, the offering, which you have made today for a group of your relatives is well established in the *Bhikkhu-Saṅgha* and it reaches the *Petas* immediately for their long benefit."

Upakappati means reaches immediately at that very moment and not after some delay.

What is meant is that the offering immediately reaches (and benefits) various kinds of *Petas*, such as, *Khuppipāsika Petas* (starving Petas), *Vaṇtāsa Petas* (Petas who eat what has been vomited by others), *Paradattūpajīvita Petas* (Petas who have to live on what is given for them by others), *Nijjhāmataṇhika Petas* (Petas who are very furiously burnt with the fire of *lobha-taṇhā,* etc.). They all are said to benefit by that gift of the king.

Verse XIII

"So ñātidhammo ca ayaṃ nidassito,
Petāna pūjā ca kata uḷārā.
Balañca bhikkhūnamanuppadinnaṃ
Tumhe hi puññaṃ pasutaṃ anappakanti."

The duty of relatives to make offering for the sake of the deceased has been demonstrated; offering with honor and liberality has been made to the *Petas*; physical strength has been given to Bhikkhus; and you also have earned great merit.

The Buddha uttered the Thirteenth Verse praising the king on his real qualities as he (1) has demonstrated the duty of a relative towards the deceased by making the said offering and made it clear to the people at large that they also should fulfil their duty to deceased relatives in the same manner and that they should not make themselves miserable with useless weeping, etc., (2) has made liberal offering to the *Petas* by making them attain the prosperity of *Devas* (gods), (3) has given strength to the Bhikkhus by letting them take food and drink to their satisfaction and (4) has acquired great merit by generating the desire to give charity which is accompanied by such good qualities as compassion and so on.

At the end of the discourse, 84000 beings, who were terrified when the Buddha explained the horrors of rebirth in the *Peta*-world, practiced Insight and realized the Four Noble Truths.

On the second day also, the Buddha delivered the same Sutta to the *devas* and men. Thus, Realization of the Truths in the same manner went on up to seven days.

SUTTA-NIPĀTA, CULAVAGGA

Āmagandha[10] Sutta

Ascetic Tissa

"Millet, beans and peas, edible leaves and roots, the fruit of any creeper; the holy men who eat these, obtained lawfully, do not seek pleasures nor speak vainly.

"O Kassapa! Thou who eatest whatsoever food is given by others, which is well-prepared, daintily garnished, pure and excellent; he who enjoys such food served with rice, he eats uncleanness.

"O Brahmin![11] You say that the charge of uncleanness does not apply to you who eat rice tastily cooked with birds' flesh. O Kassapa! I enquire the meaning from you, please define 'Uncleanness'."

Buddha Kassapa

"Taking life, beating, cutting, binding, stealing, lying, fraud, deceiving, pretended knowledge, adultery; this is uncleanness and not the eating of flesh. When men are unrestrained in sensual pleasures, are greedy in tastes, are associated with impure actions, are of nihilistic views, crooked, obscurantist; this is uncleanness and not the eating of flesh.

"When men are rough and harsh, backbiting, treacherous, without compassion, haughty, ungenerous and do not give anything to anybody; this is uncleanness and not the eating of flesh.

"Anger, pride, obstinacy, antagonism, hypocrisy, envy, ostentation, pride of opinion, intercourse with the unrighteous; this is uncleanness and not the eating of flesh.

"When men are of bad morals, refuse to pay their debts, slanderers, deceitful in their dealings, pretenders, when the vilest of men commit foul deeds; this is uncleanness and not the eating of flesh.

---

10. Āmagandha – lit. 'Odors of flesh' which had the connotation of 'putridity' and 'the repugnant sense of uncleanness'.

11. The Buddha Kassapa was a Brahmin by birth.

"When men attack living beings either because of greed or hostility, and are always bent upon evil, they go to darkness after death and fall headlong into hell; this is uncleanness and not the eating of flesh.

"Abstaining from fish or flesh, nakedness, shaving of the head, wearing the hair matted, smearing with ashes, wearing rough deer skins, attending the sacrificial fire, all the various penances performed for immortality; neither incantations, oblations, sacrifices nor observing seasonal feasts, will cleanse a man who has not overcome his doubt.

"He who lives with his senses guarded and conquered, and is poised in the Law, delights in uprightness and gentleness, who has gone beyond attachments and has overcome all sorrows; that wise man does not cling to what is seen and heard."

Thus, the Blessed One preached this again and again, and that Brahmin who was well-versed in the ancient lore, understood it; for the Sage free from defilement, detached and hard to track, uttered this in beautiful verses. Having listened to the well-preached word of the Buddha, which is free from defilement and which ends all misery, he paid homage to the Tathāgata with humble spirit and begged to be admitted into the Order at that very place.

ABHIDHAMMA PIṬAKA-VIBHAṄGA

Sacca-Vibhaṅga Suttantabhājanīya

The Four Noble Truths

There are Four Noble Truths. They are:

The Noble Truth of Suffering,

The Noble Truth of the Origin of Suffering,

The Noble Truth of the Extinction of Suffering,

The Noble Truth of the Path leading to the Extinction of Suffering.

1. The Noble Truth of Suffering

What is the Noble Truth of Suffering?

Birth is suffering; Decay is suffering; Death is suffering; Lamentation, Pain, Grief and Despair are suffering; association with those one does not love is suffering; to part with those one loves is suffering; not to get what one desires, is suffering; in short, the Five Groups of Existence, which are the objects of clinging are suffering.

What, now, is Birth (Jāti)?

i) The birth of beings belonging to this or that order of beings or planes (*jāti*), ii) being born with full development (*sañjāti*), iii) their conception (*okkanti*), iv) coming into existence (*abhinibbatti*), v) the arising of the constituent groups of existence (*khandhānaṃ pātubhavo*), and vi) the appearance of sense organs (*āyatānanaṃ paṭitabho*) is called Birth.

And what is Decay (Jarā)?

The decay of beings existing in this or that order of beings; their getting aged, becoming toothless, grey-haired and wrinkled; the failing of their vital force, the wearing out of the senses; this is called decay.

What is Death (Maraṇa)?

i) Passing away (*cuti*),[12] of beings out of this or that order of beings, ii) the state of passing away (*cavanatā*), iii) the destruction of the

12. Vibhaṅga pp. 104, 6th Syn. Edition.

i) *Jāti* is the initial formation of the body at the beginning of its conception. It is the stage of becoming but the sense organs are not yet formed.

groups of existence (*bhedo*), iv)disappearance of the groups of existence (*antaradhāna*),[13] v) dying (*maccu-maraṇa*), vi) making an end of life (*kalakirirvā*), vii) dissolution of five groups of existence (*Khandhānaṃ bhedo*),[14] viii) discarding of the body (*Kaḷevarassa nikkhepo*),[15] and ix) the cessation of the vital force (*Jivitindriyassa upacchedo*)[16] is called Death.

What is Sorrow (Soka)?

Sorrow (*soka*), sorrowfulness (*socana*), the state of being sorry (*socitatta*), inward sorrow (*antosoko*), inward woe (*antoparisoko*), inward burning sorrow

---

ii) *Sañiāti* is the full development of sense organs.

iii) *Okkanti* is taking conception in the womb in the form of *andaja* (born from egg) and *jalabuja* (born from womb).

iv) *Abhinibbatti* is coming into existence in the form of *saṃsedaja* (born from moisture) and *opapātika* apparitional or spontaneous birth as an adult.
These four are in the conventional sense *Sammuti katha*).

v) *Khandhānaṃ pātubhayo* refers (1) to the appearance of the Corporeality-group in the case of a *brahmā* of the plane of non-perception, (2) the appearance of the Mentality group in the case of a *brahmā* of the formless Sphere and (3) the appearance of the five groups of existence in the case of beings belonging to the sense sphere.

vi) *Khandhānaṃ pātubhayo* and *Āyatanānaṃ pātitabho* are called Birth in the philosophical sense.

As birth in the ultimate analysis is the arising of the constituent groups of existence and the appearance of sense organs—and not the arising or appearance of an individual. (*Sammoha vinodani attagatha*).

Cuti is the general term for the dissolution of: (a) one Khanda Corporeality-group in the case of a *brahmā* of the plane of Non-perception (b) four Khandhas four mentality groups in the case of a *brahmā* of the Formless Sphere and five Khandhas five constituent groups of existence of a being belonging to the Sense-sphere.

13. *Antaradhāna* is the disappearance of the groups of existence.

14. *Khandhānaṃ bhedo* refers to the dissolution: (a) of four groups of existence in the case of a *brahmā* of the Formless Sphere and (b) of five groups of existence (in the case of beings belonging to the sense-sphere).

15. *Kalevarassa nikkhepo* – Discarding of the body refers to discarding (a) one group of existence (in the case of a brahma in the plane of non-perception) and (b) the five groups of existence (1n the case of beings belonging to the Sense sphere).

16. *Jivitindriyassa upacchedo* – The cessation of the vital force refers only to the death of all animate beings. There is no death (*maraṇa*) for inanimate things.

Numbers i to vi are in the conventional sense (*samutikathā*). The last three Nos. vii, viii and ix are in the philosophical sense. Death in the ultimate analysis is mere dissolution and discarding of the groups of existence and cessation of the vital force. It is not the passing away of any individual. (*parmatthakathā*).

(*cetaso-parijjhayana*), distress (*domanassa*), the arrow (pang) of sorrow (*sokasalla*)—which arises through: 1) loss of relatives, 2) loss of property, 3) loss of health, 4) loss of virtue, 5) loss of right view, 6) any other loss (or ruin) or 7) any other suffering; this is called sorrow.

What is Lamentation (Parideva)?

The moaning for the loss (e.g. of children etc., calling their names) (*ādevo*), wailing and lamenting, mentioning their respective qualities (*paridevo*), the state of such moaning (*ādevanā*), the state of such wailing and lamentation (*paridevanā*), the state of being a bemoaner (*ādevitattā*), the state of being such a wailer or lamenter (*paridevitatta*) talking vainly (*vācāpalāpo*), talking incoherently (*vippalāpo*), repeated grumbling (*lalappo*), the act of repeated grumbling (*lālappana*), the state of being one who grumbles repeatedly (*lālāppita*), which arises through: 1) loss of relatives, 2) loss of property, 3) loss of health, 4) loss of virtue, 5) loss of right views, 6) any other loss (or ruin), or 7) any other suffering; this is called lamentation.

And what is pain (dukkha)?

Bodily pain and unpleasantness, the painful and unpleasant feeling produced by bodily contact; this is called pain.

And what is grief (domanassa)?

Mental pain and unpleasantness, the painful and unpleasant feeling produced by mental contact; this is called grief.

And what is despair (upāyāsa)?

Mental suffering (*āyāso*), intense mental suffering (*upāyāso*) the state of having mental suffering (*āyāsitatta*), the state of having intense mental suffering (*upāyāsitatta*) which arises through: 1) loss of relatives, 2) loss of property, 3) loss of health, 4) loss of virtue, 5) loss of right view, 6) any other loss (or ruin), or 7) any other suffering; this is called Despair.

And what is suffering due to Association with those who do not love?

There are six classes of sense objects, which are undesirable, disagreeable and not appealing to mind. To see, hear, smell, taste and contact physically or mentally such objects is suffering.

Or, there are persons who cause our disadvantage, who desire to see that we encounter misfortunes and danger, and who do not desire to see that we are prosperous. To associate with, to mingle with, to stay with and to be in union with such persons is suffering. This is suffering of association with those we do not love.

And what is suffering due to Separation from those we love?

There are six classes of sense objects which are desirable, agreeable and appealing to mind. Not to see, not to hear, not to smell, not to taste and not to contact such sense objects is suffering. Or, there are persons who are working for our good and benefit; who desire to see us in prosperity and in safety, such as our dear and near ones such as parents, brothers, sisters, relations and friends. To dissociate with, part with, not to stay with or not to be in union with such persons is suffering. This is known as suffering due to separation from those we love.

And what is suffering of not getting what one desires?

To beings subject to birth there comes the desire: 'O that we were not subject to birth. O, that no new birth was before us'. Subject to decay; disease, death, sorrow, lamentation, pain, grief, and despair, the desire comes to them: 'O, that we were not subject to these things. O, that these things were not before us.' But this cannot be got by mere desiring; this is known as suffering of not getting what one desires.

And in short, what five groups of existence which form the objects of Clinging are suffering?

Corporeality; feeling, perception, mental formations and consciousness; these five groups of existence are suffering. This is the Noble Truth of Suffering.

2. The Noble Truth of the Origin of Suffering

What, now, is the Noble Truth of the Origin of Suffering?

It is that craving which gives rise to fresh rebirth, and, bound up with pleasure and lust, now here, now there, finds ever fresh delight. That *taṇhā* (craving)—is of three kinds namely the Sensual Craving (*kāmataṇhā*), the Craving for Eternal Existence (*bhavataṇhā*), the Craving for Self-Annihilation (*vibhavataṇhā*).

Where does this craving arise and take root?

This craving arises and takes root in whatever is delightful, attractive and pleasurable.

What is attractive and pleasurable in this world?

SIX INTERNAL BASES:

1.	*Cakkhu*	(Eye-base)
2.	*Sota*	(Ear-base)
3.	*Ghāna*	(Nose-base)
4.	*Jivhā*	(Tongue-base)
5.	*Kāya*	(Body-base)
6.	*Mano*	(Mind-base)

Each of the above objects is attractive and pleasurable. This craving arises and takes root in whatever is delightful, attractive and pleasurable.

SIX EXTERNAL BASES:

1.	*Rūpa*	(Visible objects)
2.	*Sadda*	(Sounds)
3.	*Gandha*	(Smells)
4.	*Rasa*	(Tastes)
5.	*Phoṭṭhaba*	(Contacts)
6.	*Dhamma*	(Mental objects)

Each of the above objects is attractive and pleasurable. This craving arises and takes root in whatever is delightful, attractive and pleasurable.

SIX KINDS OF CONSCIOUSNESS:

1.	*Cakkhu-viññāṇaṃ*	(Eye-consciousness)
2.	*Sota-viññāṇaṃ*	(Ear-consciousness)
3.	*Ghāna-viññāṇaṃ*	(Nose-consciousness)
4.	*Jivhā-viññāṇaṃ*	(Tongue-consciousness)
5.	*Kāya-viññāṇaṃ*	(Body-consciousness)
6.	*Mano-viññāṇaṃ*	(Mind-consciousness)

Each of the above objects is attractive and pleasurable. This craving arises and takes root in whatever is delightful, attractive and pleasurable.

SIX KINDS OF CONTACTS:

1.	*Cakkhu-samphasso*	(Eye-contact)
2.	*Sota-samphasso*	(Ear-contact)
3.	*Ghāna-samphasso*	(Nose-contact)
4.	*Jivhā-samphasso*	(Tongue-contact)
5.	*Kāya-samphasso*	(Body-contact)
6.	*Mano-samphasso*	(Mind-contact)

Each of the above objects is attractive and pleasurable. This craving arises and takes root in whatever is delightful, attractive and pleasurable.

SIX KINDS OF SENSATION:

1. *Cakkhu-samphassa-vedanā* (Sensation conditioned by eye-contact)
2. *Sota-samphassa-vedanā* (Sensation conditioned by ear-contact)
3. *Ghāna-samphassa-vedanā* (Sensation conditioned by nose-contact)
4. *Jivhā-samphassa-vedanā* (Sensation conditioned by tongue-contact)
5. *Kāya-samphassa-vedanā* (Sensation conditioned by body-contact)
6. *Mano-samphassa-vedanā* (Sensation conditioned by mind-contact)

Each of the above objects is attractive and pleasurable. This craving arises and takes root in whatever is delightful, attractive and pleasurable.

SIX KINDS OF PERCEPTION:

1. *Rūpa-saññā* (Perception having visible things as its objects)
2. *Sadda-saññā* (Perception having sounds as its objects)
3. *Gandha-saññā* (Perception having smells as its objects)
4. *Rasa-saññā* (Perception having tastes as its objects)
5. *Phoṭṭhaba-saññā* (Perception having contacts as its objects)
6. *Dhamma-saññā* (Perception having mental things as its objects)

Each of the above objects is attractive and pleasurable. This craving arises and takes root in whatever is delightful, attractive and pleasurable.

SIX KINDS OF VOLITION:

1. *Rūpa-sañcetanā* (Volition having visible things as its objects)
2. *Sadda-sañcetanā* (Volition having sounds as its objects)
3. *Gandha-sañcetanā* (Volition having smells as its objects)
4. *Rasa-sañcetanā* (Volition having tastes as its objects)
5. *Phoṭṭhaba-sañcetanā* (Volition having contacts as its objects)
6. *Dhamma-sañcetanā* (Volition having mental things as its objects)

Each of the above objects is attractive and pleasurable. This craving arises and takes root in whatever is delightful, attractive and pleasurable.

SIX KINDS OF CRAVING:

1. *Rūpa-taṇhā* (Craving for visible objects)
2. *Sadda-taṇhā* (Craving for sounds)
3. *Gandha-taṇhā* (Craving for smells)
4. *Rasa-taṇhā* (Craving for tastes)

5. *Phoṭṭhaba-taṇhā* (Craving for contacts)
6. *Dhamma-taṇhā* (Craving for mental objects)

Each of the above objects is attractive and pleasurable. This craving arises and takes root in whatever is delightful, attractive and pleasurable.

SIX KINDS OF THOUGHT CONCEPTION: (*Vitakka*)

Vitakka is the directing of mental factors towards an object.

1. *Rūpa-vitakko* (Thought-conception of visible objects)
2. *Sadda-vitakko* (Thought-conception of sounds)
3. *Gandha-vitakko* (Thought-conception of smells)
4. *Rasa-vitakko* (Thought-conception of tastes)
5. *Phoṭṭhaba-vitakko* (Thought-conception of contacts)
6. *Dhamma-vitakko* (Thought-conception of mental objects)

Each of the above objects is attractive and pleasurable. This craving arises and takes root in whatever is delightful, attractive and pleasurable.

SIX KINDS OF DISCURSIVE THINKING: (*Vicāra*)

(*Vicāra* is the continued exercise of the mind on the same object).

1. *Rūpa-vicāro* (Discursive thinking of visible objects)
2. *Sadda-vicāro* (Discursive thinking of sounds)
3. *Gandha-vicāro* (Discursive thinking of smells)
4. *Rasa-vicāro* (Discursive thinking of tastes)
5. *Phoṭṭhaba-vicāro* (Discursive thinking of contacts)
6. *Dhamma-vicāro* (Discursive thinking of mental objects)

Each of the above objects is attractive and pleasurable. This craving arises and takes root in whatever is delightful, attractive and pleasurable.

This is called the Noble Truth of the Origin of Suffering.

3. The Noble Truth of the Extinction of Suffering

What, now, is the Noble Truth of the Extinction of Suffering? It is the complete fading away and extinction of this craving, its forsaking and giving up, the liberation and detachment from it.

But where may this craving vanish, where may it be extinguished?

Whatever in this world is attractive and pleasurable, there it may vanish and be extinguished.

SIX INTERNAL BASES:

1. *Cakkhu* (Eye-base)
2. *Sota* (Ear-base)
3. *Ghāna* (Nose-base)
4. Jivhā (Tongue-base)
5. *Kāya* (Body-base)
6. *Mano* (Mind-base)

Each of the above objects is attractive and pleasurable. This craving may vanish and be extinguished in whatever is delightful, attractive and pleasurable.

SIX EXTERNAL BASES:

1. *Rūpa* (Visible objects)
2. *Sadda* (Sounds)
3. *Gandha* (Smells)
4. *Rasa* (Tastes)
5. *Phoṭṭhaba* (Contacts)
6. *Dhamma* (Mental objects)

Each of the above objects is attractive and pleasurable. This craving may vanish and be extinguished in whatever is delightful, attractive and pleasurable.

SIX KINDS OF CONSCIOUSNESS:

1. *Cakkhu-viññāṇaṃ* (Eye-consciousness)
2. *Sota-viññāṇaṃ* (Ear-consciousness)
3. *Ghāna-viññāṇaṃ* (Nose-consciousness)
4. *Jivhā-viññāṇaṃ* (Tongue-consciousness)
5. *Kāya-viññāṇaṃ* (Body-consciousness)
6. *Mano-viññāṇaṃ* (Mind-consciousness)

Each of the above objects is attractive and pleasurable. This craving may vanish and be extinguished in whatever is delightful, attractive and pleasurable.

SIX KINDS OF CONTACTS:

1. *Cakkhu-samphasso* (Eye-contact)
2. *Sota-samphasso* (Ear-contact)
3. *Ghāna-samphasso* (Nose-contact)
4. *Jivhā-samphasso* (Tongue-contact)
5. *Kāya-samphasso* (Body-contact)
6. *Mano-samphasso* (Mind-contact)

Each of the above objects is attractive and pleasurable. This craving may vanish and be extinguished in whatever is delightful, attractive and pleasurable.

SIX KINDS OF SENSATION:

1. *Cakkhu-samphassa-vedanā* (Sensation conditioned by eye-contact)
2. *Sota-samphassa-vedanā* (Sensation conditioned by ear-contact)
3. *Ghāna-samphassa-vedanā* (Sensation conditioned by nose-contact)
4. *Jivhā-samphassa-vedanā* (Sensation conditioned by tongue-contact)
5. *Kāya-samphassa-vedanā* (Sensation conditioned by body-contact)
6. *Mano-samphassa-vedanā* (Sensation conditioned by mind-contact)

Each of the above objects is attractive and pleasurable. This craving may vanish and be extinguished in whatever is delightful, attractive and pleasurable.

SIX KINDS OF PERCEPTION:

1. *Rūpa-saññā* (Perception having visible things as its objects)
2. *Sadda-saññā* (Perception having sounds as its objects)
3. *Gandha-saññā* (Perception having smells as its objects)
4. *Rasa-saññā* (Perception having tastes as its objects)
5. *Phoṭṭhaba-saññā* (Perception having contacts as its objects)
6. *Dhamma-saññā* (Perception having mental things as its objects)

Each of the above objects is attractive and pleasurable. This craving may vanish and be extinguished in whatever is delightful, attractive and pleasurable.

SIX KINDS OF VOLITION:

1. *Rūpa-sañcetanā* (Volition having visible things as its objects)
2. *Sadda-sañcetanā* (Volition having sounds as its objects)
3. *Gandha-sañcetanā* (Volition having smells as its objects)
4. *Rasa-sañcetanā* (Volition having tastes as its objects)
5. *Phoṭṭhaba-sañcetanā* (Volition having contacts as its objects)
6. *Dhamma-sañcetanā* (Volition having mental things as its objects)

Each of the above objects is attractive and pleasurable. This craving may vanish and be extinguished in whatever is delightful, attractive and pleasurable.

SIX KINDS OF CRAVING:

1. *Rūpa-taṇhā* (Craving for visible objects)
2. *Sadda-taṇhā* (Craving for sounds)
3. *Gandha-taṇhā* (Craving for smells)
4. *Rasa-taṇhā* (Craving for tastes)

5. *Phoṭṭhaba-taṇhā* (Craving for contacts)
6. *Dhamma-taṇhā* (Craving for mental objects)

Each of the above objects is attractive and pleasurable. This craving may vanish and be extinguished in whatever is delightful, attractive and pleasurable.

SIX KINDS OF THOUGHT CONCEPTION: (*Vitakka*)

1) *Rūpa-vitakko* (Thought-conception of visible objects)
2) *Sadda-vitakko* (Thought-conception of sounds)
3) *Gandha-vitakko* (Thought-conception of smells)
4) *Rasa-vitakko* (Thought-conception of tastes)
5) *Phoṭṭhaba-vitakko* (Thought-conception of contacts)
6) *Dhamma-vitakko* (Thought-conception of mental objects)

Each of the above objects is attractive and pleasurable. This craving may vanish and be extinguished in whatever is delightful, attractive and pleasurable.

SIX KINDS OF DISCURSIVE THINKING: (*Vicāra*)

1. *Rūpa-vicāro* (Discursive thinking of visible objects)
2. *Sadda-vicāro* (Discursive thinking of sounds)
3. *Gandha-vicāro* (Discursive thinking of smells)
4. *Rasa-vicāro* (Discursive thinking of tastes)
5. *Phoṭṭhaba-vicāro* (Discursive thinking of contacts)
6. *Dhamma-vicāro* (Discursive thinking of mental objects)

This is the Noble Truth of the Extinction of suffering.

4. The Noble Truth of the Path Leading to the Extinction of Suffering

What, now, is the Noble Truth of the Path leading to the Extinction of Suffering?

It is the Noble Eightfold Path, the way that leads to the extinction of suffering. What are its constituents? They are:

1) *Sammā-diṭṭhi* (Right Understanding)
2) *Sammā-saṅkappa* (Right Thought)
3) *Sammā-vācā* (Right Speech)
4) *Sammā-kammanta* (Right Action)
5) *Sammā-ājiva* (Right Livelihood)
6) *Sammā-vāyāma* (Right Effort)
7) *Sammā-sati* (Right Mindfulness)
8) *Sammā-samādhi* (Right Concentration)

What, now, is Right Understanding?

1. To understand suffering. 2. To understand the origin of suffering. 3. To understand the extinction of suffering. 4. To understand the path leading to the extinction of suffering. This is called Right Understanding.

What, now, is Right Thought?

1) *Nekkhama-saṅkappa* (Thoughts free from lust)
2) *Avyapāda-saṅkappa* (Thoughts free from ill will)
3) *Avihimsa-saṅkappa* (Thoughts free from cruelty)

This is called Right Thought.

What, now, is Right Speech?

1) Speech free from lying
2) Speech free from tale bearing
3) Speech free from harsh language
4) Speech free from vain talk

This is called Right Speech.

What, now, is Right Action?

1) Action free from killing
2) Action free from stealing
3) Action free from sexual misconduct

This is called Right Action.

What, now, is Right Livelihood?

When the noble disciple, avoiding a wrong way of living, earns his livelihood in a proper manner, this is called Right Livelihood.

What, now, is Right Effort?

There are Four Great Efforts: the effort to avoid, the effort to overcome, the effort to develop, and the effort to maintain.

1) The disciple incites his will to avoid the arising of evil, unwholesome things that have not yet arisen; and he strives, puts forth his energy, strains his mind struggles vigilantly,
2) The disciple incites his will to overcome the evil, unwholesome things that have already arisen; and he strives, puts forth his energy, strains his mind and struggles vigilantly.[17]

---

17. He does not harbour any thought of sensual lust, ill-will, grief or malice; he

3) The disciple incites his will to arouse wholesome things that have not yet arisen; and he strives, puts forth his energy, strains his mind and struggles vigilantly.
4) The disciple incites his will to maintain the wholesome things that have already arisen, and not to let them disappear, but to increase, to bring them to growth, to maturity and to the full perfection of development; and he strives, puts forth his energy, strains his mind and struggles vigilantly. This is called Right Effort.

What, now, is Right Mindfulness?

Here, the disciple dwells in contemplation of the Body, Sensation, Mind, and Mental Objects, ardent, clearly comprehending them and mindful, after putting away worldly greed and grief.

This is called Right Mindfulness.

What, now, is Right Concentration?

(1) Detached from sensual objects, detached from evil things, the disciple enters into the first *jhāna*, which is accompanied by thought conception and discursive thinking, is born of detachment, and filled with rapture and joy.

(2) After the subsiding of thought conception and discursive thinking, and by gaining tranquillity and oneness of mind, he enters into a state free from thought conception and discursive thinking, the second *jhāna*, which is born of concentration, and filled with rapture and joy.

(3) After the fading away of rapture, he dwells in equanimity, being mindful and clearly conscious; and he experiences in his person that ease which the Noble Ones talk of when they say: "Happy lives the man of equanimity and attentive mind'. He enters the third *jhāna*.

(4) After having given up pleasure and pain, and through the disappearance of the previous joy and grief which he had, he will enter into a state beyond pleasure and pain, into the fourth *jhāna*, a state of pure equanimity and clear mindfulness.

This is called Right Concentration.

This is called the Noble Truth of the Path leading to the Cessation of Suffering.

---

abandons such thoughts, dispels them, conquers them and makes them disappear.

PAṬICCASAMUPPĀDA VIBHAṄGA (SUTTANTABHĀJANĪYA)

Analytical Exposition of the Dependent Origination (Analysis as in Suttas) —Abhidhamma Piṭaka, Vibhaṅga, 6th Synod Edition, pages 142–45

1) Through *Avijjā* (Ignorance) *Saṅkhārā* (Kamma-formations) arise;
2) Through *Saṅkhārā* (Kamma-formations) *Viññāṇaṃ* (Consciousness) arises;
3) Through *Viññāṇaṃ* (Consciousness) *Nāmarūpaṃ* (Mental and Physical Phenomena) arise;
4) Through *Nāmarūpaṃ* (Mental and Physical Phenomena) *Saḷāyatanaṃ* (the 6 Bases) arise;
5) Through *Saḷāyatanaṃ* (the 6 Bases) *Phasso* (Contact) arises;
6) Through *Phasso* (Contact) *Vedanā* (Sensation) arises;
7) Through *Vedanā* (Sensation) *Taṇhā* (Craving) arises;
8) Through *Taṇhā* (Craving) *Upādānaṃ* (Clinging) arises;
9) Through *Upādānaṃ* (Clinging) *Bhavo* (Volitional action and further existence) arises;
10) Through *Bhavo* (Volitional action and further existence) *Jāti* (Rebirth) arises;
11) Through *Jāti* (Rebirth) there arise *Jarā, Maraṇa Soka Parideva Dukkha Domanassa, Upāyāsa* (Old Age, Death, Sorrow, Lamentation, Pain, Grief and Despair).

Thus arises the unalloyed mass of Suffering.

I. *Avijjā paccayā saṅkhārā* (Through Ignorance, Kamma-formations) arise

Avijjā **(Ignorance):**

What is meant by *Avijjā*?

Avijjā means

1) not knowing the Noble Truth of Suffering,
2) not knowing the Noble Truth of the Origin of Suffering,
3) not knowing the Noble Truth of the Extinction of Suffering, and
4) not knowing the Noble Truth of the Path leading to the Extinction of Suffering.

What is meant by *Avijjā paccayā saṅkhārā* (Through Ignorance, Kamma-formations arise)?

There are six kinds of *saṅkhāras*. They are:

1) *Puññābhisaṅkhāra* (formations of merit),
2) *Apuññābhisaṅkhāra* (formations of demerit),
3) *Āneñjābhisaṅkhāra* (formations of the imperturbable),
4) *Kāyasaṅkhāra* (the bodily formations),
5) *Vacīsaṅkhāra* (the verbal formations), and
6) *Cittasaṅkhāra* (the mental formations).

1. What are *Puññābhisaṅkhāra*?

The following are *Puññābhisaṅkhāra:*

Wholesome volitions in the Sensuous Sphere (*Kamāvacara*) and the Form Sphere (*Rupāvacara*) culminating in *dāna* (almsgiving), *sīla* (morality) and *bhāvanā* (practice of mental concentration) are *Puññābhisaṅkhāra.*

2. What are *Apuññābhisaṅkhāra*?

Unwholesome volitions are *Apuññābhisaṅkhāra.*

3. What are *Āneñjābhisaṅkhāra*?

Wholesome volitions in practicing mental concentration in the Formless Sphere (*Arūpāvacara*) are *Āneñjābhisaṅkhāra.*

4. What are *Kāyasaṅkhāra, Vacisaṅkhāra* and *Cittasaṅkhāra*?

- Volitions connected with physical action are *Kāyasaṅkhāra.*
- Volitions connected with speech (such as thought-conception and discursive thinking) are *Vacīsaṅkhāra.*
- Volitions that arise only in the mind (and not connected with the bodily and verbal functions) are *Cittasaṅkhāra.*

II. *Saṅkhāra paccayā viññāṇaṃ* (Through Kamma-formations, Consciousness arises)

The following Consciousness arise through Kamma-forrnations:

1. *Cakkhu-viññāṇaṃ* (Eye-consciousness)
2. *Sota-viññāṇaṃ* (Ear-consciousness)
3. *Ghāna-viññāṇaṃ* (Nose-consciousness)
4. *Jivhā-viññāṇaṃ* (Tongue-consciousness)
5. *Kāya-viññāṇaṃ* (Body-consciousness)
6. *Mano-viññāṇaṃ* (Mind-consciousness)

III. *Viññāṇa paccayā nāmarūpaṃ* (Through Consciousness, Mental and Physical Phenomena arise)

There are Mental Phenomena as well as Physical Phenomena.

The following are the Mental Phenomena:

1. *Vedanākkhandha* (Sensation-group)
2. *Saññākkhandha* (Perception-group)
3. *Saṅkhārakkhandha* (Kamma-formations-group)
4. *Viññāṇakkhandha* (Consciousness-group)

The following are the Physical Phenomena:

(i) The Four Great Primaries (*Mahābhūta*)—Element of Extension, Element of Liquidity or Cohesion, Element of Kinetic Energy and Element of Support or Motion.

(ii) The twenty-four *Upādāyarūpāni* (Forms which are derived from and dependent on the Four Great Primaries), namely, (1) eye basis, (2) ear basis, (3) nose basis, (4) tongue basis, (5) body basis, (6) heart basis, (7) male sex, (8) female sex, (9) vital force, (10) nutrition, (11) visible form, (12) sound, (13) odour, (14) savour, (15) element of space, (16) intimation through body, (17) intimation through speech, (18) lightness, (19) pliancy, (20) adaptability, (21) growth of Corporeality, (22) continuance, (23) decay and (24) impermanence.

IV. *Nāmarūpa paccayā saḷāyatanaṃ* (Through Mental and Physical Phenomena, the six Bases arise)

There are six kinds of Bases. They are:

1. *Cakkhāyatanaṃ* (Eye-base)
2. *Sotāyatanaṃ* (Ear-base)

3. *Ghānāyatanaṃ* (Nose-base)
4. *Jivhāyatanaṃ* (Tongue-base)
5. *Kāyāyatanaṃ* (Body-base)
6. *Manāyatanaṃ* (Mind-base)

V. *Saḷāyatana paccayā phasso* (Through the six Bases, Contact arises)

There are six kinds of Contact. They are:

1. *Cakkhu-samphasso* (Eye-contact)
2. *Sota-samphasso* (Ear-contact)
3. *Ghāna-samphasso* (Nose-contact)
4. *Jivhā-samphasso* (Tongue-contact)
5. *Kāya-samphasso* (Body-contact)
6. *Mano-samphasso* (Mind-contact)

VI. *Phassa paccayā vedanā* (Through Contact, Sensation arises)

There are six kinds of Sensations. They are:

1. *Cakkhu-samphassajā-vedanā* (Sensation caused by eye-contact)
2. *Sota-samphassajā-vedanā* (Sensation caused by ear-contact)
3. *Ghāna-samphassajā-vedanā* (Sensation caused by nose-contact)
4. *Jivhā-samphassajā-vedanā* (Sensation caused by tongue-contact)
5. *Kāya-samphassajā-vedanā* (Sensation caused by body-contact)
6. *Mano-samphassajā-vedanā* (Sensation caused by mind-contact)

VII. *Vedanā paccayā taṇhā* (Through Sensation, Craving arises)

There are six kinds of Craving. They are:

1) *Rūpa-taṇhā* (Craving for visible objects)
2) *Sadda-taṇhā* (Craving for sounds)
3) *Gandha-taṇhā* (Craving for smells)
4) *Rasa-taṇhā* (Craving for tastes)
5) *Phoṭṭhaba-taṇhā* (Craving for contacts)
6) *Dhamma-taṇhā* (Craving for mental objects)

VIII. *Taṇhā paccayā upādānaṃ* (Through Craving, Clinging arises)

There are four kinds of Clinging. They are:

1) *Kāmupādānaṃ* (Clinging to sensual pleasure)

2) *Diṭṭhupādānaṃ* (Clinging to wrong views)
3) *Sīlabbatupādānaṃ* (Clinging to rites and rituals)
4) *Attavādupādānaṃ* (Clinging to personality-belief)

IX. *Upādāna paccayā bhavo* (Through Clinging, Volitional action and further existence arise)

There are two kinds of *bhavas*, namely,

1) *Kamma-bhava* (*Kamma* – volitional action which leads to future existence), and
2) *Upapatti-bhava* (Existence "i.e. life after death")

Kamma-bhava consists of (1) *Puññābhisaṅkhāra* (2) *Apuññābhisaṅkhāra*, and (3) *Āneñjābhisaṅkhāra*, mentioned above.

Upapatti-bhava comprises:

1) *Kāma-bhava* (Existence in the Sphere of Sensual Pleasure),
2) *Rūpa-bhava* (Existence in the Form Sphere),
3) *Arūpa-bhava* (Existence in the Formless Sphere).
4) *Saññā-bhava* (Existence in the Sphere of Consciousness),
5) *Asaññā-bhava* (Existence in the Sphere of Non-consciousness),
6) *Neva-saññā-nā-saññā-bhava* (Existence in the Sphere of Neither-perception-nor-non-perception),
7) *Ekavokāra-bhava* (Existence where there is only One Constituent Group of Existence),
8) *Catuvokāra-bhava* (Existence where there are Four Constituent Groups of Existence), and
9) *Pañcavokāra-bhava* (Existence where there are Five Constituent Groups of Existence).[18]

X. *Bhava paccayā jāti* (Through Volitional action and further existence, Rebirth arises)

Jāti of beings belonging to this or that order of beings means:

(1) *Jāti* (The first appearance of one or more *khandhas* or constituent groups of existence);
(2) *Sañjāti* (Their first appearance simultaneously with all the sense organs):

---

18. See Appendix on *Bhava* (existence).

(3) *Okkanti* (Entering the womb or shell of an egg at the time of conception);
(4) *Abhinibbatti* (Arising straightaway as a full-grown individual as in the case of *devas* and *Brahmās*);
(5) *Khandhānaṃ patubhāvo* (Arising of *khandhas* or constituent groups of existence) and
(6) *Āyatānānaṃ paṭilābho* (Attainment or appearance of sense organs).[19]

XI. *Jāti paccayā jara maraṇaṃ* (Through Rebirth, there arise Old Age, Death, Sorrow, Lamentation, Pain, Grief and Despair)

Jarā means the decay of beings in this or that order of beings (*jarā*), their getting aged (*jiraṇatā*), becoming toothless (*khandiccaṃ*), grey-haired (*pāliccaṃ*), wrinkled (*valittacatā*), general decrease in the vigour of life (*āyunosaṃhāni*) decrepitude of their sense-bases (*indriyānaṃ-pāripako*).

Maraṇaṃ (death) means (1) *cuti* (passing away), (2) *cavanatā* (the state of passing away), (3) *bhedo* (breaking-up), (4) *antara-dhānaṃ* (disappearance of the groups of existence), (5) *maccumaraṇaṃ* (death), (6) *kālakiriyā* "life being put an end to (by *kāla*, i.e. death)", (7) *khandhānaṃ bhedo* (dissolution of the groups of existence), (8) *kalevarassanikkhepo* (discarding of the body), and (9) *jivitindriyassa upacchedo*[20] (the cessation of life or vital energy).

What is Soka (Sorrow)?

Soka (sorrow), *socanā* (sorrowfulness), *socitattaṃ* (the state of being sorry), *antosoko* (inward sorrow), *anto parisoko* (inward woe), *cetaso parijjhāyanā* (inward burning sorrow), *domanassa* (mental distress), *sokasalla* "the arrow (pang) of sorrow which arises through (1) loss of relatives, (2) loss of property, (3) loss of health, (4) loss of virtue, (5) loss of right views, (6) any other loss (or ruin), or (7) any other suffering"; this is called Sorrow.

---

19. *Khandhānaṃ pātubhāvo* and *Āyatanānaṃ paṭilābho* are called birth in the philosophical sense.

As birth in the ultimate analysis is the arising of the constituent groups of existence and the appearance of sense organs and not the arising or appearance. (*Sammoha Vinodanī Aṭṭhakathā*)

20. Death in the ultimate analysis is mere dissolution and discarding of the groups of existence and cessation of life or vital energy. It is not the passing away of any individual.

What is Parideva (Lamentation)?

Ādevo (the mourning for the loss, e.g. of children, etc.), *paridevo* (wailing and lamenting, mentioning their respective names and qualities), *ādevanā* (state of such mourning), *paridevanā* (state of such wailing and lamentation), *ādevitattaṃ* (state of being a mourner), *paridevitattaṃ* (state of being such a wailer or lamenter), *vācāpalāpo* (talking vainly), *vippalāpo* (talking incoherently), *lālappo* (repeated grumbling), *lālappitattaṃ* (state of repeated grumbling), which arise through (1) loss of relatives, (2) loss of property, (3) loss of health, (4) loss of virtue, (5) loss of right views, (6) any other loss (or ruin), or (7) any other suffering; this is called Lamentation.

What is Dukkha (Pain)?

Bodily pain and unpleasantness, the painful and unpleasant feeling produced by bodily contact; this is called Pain.

What is Domanassa (Grief)?

Mental pain and unpleasantness, the painful and unpleasant feeling produced by mental contact; this is called Grief.

What is Upāyāsa (Despair)?

Āyāso (mental suffering), *upāyāso* (intense mental suffering), *āyāsitattaṃ* (the state of having mental suffering), *upāyāsitattaṃ* (the state of having intense mental suffering) which arise through (1) loss of relatives, (2) loss of property, (3) loss of health, (4) loss of virtue, (5) loss of right views, (6) any other loss (or ruin), or (7) any other suffering; this is called Despair.

Thus, the unalloyed mass of Suffering arises. Thus, the unalloyed mass of Suffering unites, assembles, combines and becomes manifest.

APPENDIX ON BHAVAS (EXISTENCES)

Kāmabhava is existence in the four Lower Regions, or as a man, or as a deva.

Rūpabhava is existence as a Brahmā in the Form-Sphere.

Arūpabhava is existence as a Brahmā in the Formless-Sphere.

These three *Bhavas* are reclassified first with reference to consciousness and absence of consciousness and then with reference to the number of constituent groups of existence.

Saññabhava covers all existences except *Asaññabhava,* i.e. existence as an *Asaññasatta* Brahmā in the Form-Sphere and *Neva-saññā-nāsaññā-bhava,* i.e. existence as a *Neva-saññā-nāsaññā-bhava* Brahmā in the Formless-Sphere.

Ekavokāra-bhava is existence as an *Asaññasatta* Brahmā with only one Khandha (constituent group of existence), i.e. the Form-group.

Catuvokāra-bhava is existence as a Brahmā in the Formless-Sphere with four groups of existence, i.e. (1) *Vedanākkhandha* (Sensation-group), (2) *Saññakkhandha* (Perception-group), (3) *Saṅkhārakkhandha* (Kamma-formations-group), and *Viññāṇakkhandha* (Consciousness-group).

Pañcavokāra is existence with all the five constituent groups of existence and it covers all the remaining existences.

APPENDIX ON SAṄKHĀRAS

1) *Puññābhisaṅkhāra* in the Sensuous Sphere, such as *dāna* (almsgiving) and *sīla* (morality) will ordinarily lead to *kāmabhava,* i.e. to existence as man or *deva* in that Sphere and cause *viññāṇa* (consciousness) to arise there.
2) *Puññābhisaṅkhāra* in the Form-Sphere, such as *bhāvanā* (mental contemplation) will ordinarily lead to existence as a Brahmā in that Sphere and cause *viññāṇa* (consciousness) to arise there.
3) *Apuññābhisaṅkhāra,* such as murder and theft, will ordinarily lead to the lower form of *kāmabhava,* i.e. to existence in hell, animal world, *peta* world or *asurakāya* world and cause *viññāṇa* (consciousness) to arise there.
4) *Āneñiābhisaṅkhāra,* such as practice of meditation on infinity of space, will ordinarily lead to existence as a Brahmā in the Formless Sphere and cause *viññāṇa* (consciousness) to arise therein.

APPENDIX ON BHAVACAKKA (THE VICIOUS CIRCLE OF EXISTENCE)

Soka, etc. are not only bound up with *Avijjā*, but also arise through *Āsava* (Fluxions).

For instance:

1) Sorrow for separation from cherished objects arise through *Kāmāsava* (Fluxion of Sensual Pleasure);
2) Sorrow of one who regards the body as "I" or "Mine" for its change for the worse arises through *Diṭṭhāsava* (Fluxion of Wrong View); and
3) Sorrow of one who notices signs of his approaching death arises through *Bhavāsava* (Fluxion of Attachment to Existence).

As *Soka*, etc. arise through *Āsava*, where there are *Soka*, etc. there also is *Āsava*; and *Avijjā* arises through *Āsava* (*Āsava samudayā avijjā samudayo*).

So, the vicious circle of existence (*bhava-cakka*) is complete and the process of *saṅkhāra* arising through *avijjā*, etc. continues ad infinitum, i.e. till the attainment of Nibbana.

* * *

DUTIES AND RULES OF TRAINING OF A SĀMAṆERA

There are two degrees of ordination into the Noble Order of Buddhist monks, the *saṅgha*, that of a *sāmaṇera*, a novice, and that of a *bhikkhu*, one who has been fully ordained.

It is possible for any male person, even in early childhood, to become a *sāmaṇera*, provided he has his parents' consent, is sane, is not suffering from certain physical deformities or diseases and is not bound by obligations to the State (e.g. government service) or if so can obtain consent, and provided he is accepted by the Order.

Only one who has reached the age of twenty years can receive full ordination; and full ordination requires a preliminary period (which may be a matter of days or may extend to years depending on circumstances) as a *sāmaṇera*.

A *sāmaṇera*, and a *bhikkhu*, can leave the Order at any time as there is no vow of lifelong service.

In addition to certain duties and observances a *sāmaṇera* has to observe '75 Rules of Training' which also form part of the 227 Rules undertaken by a *bhikkhu*. These Rules of Training, as the name implies, are to train the *sāmaṇera* in the discipline and department befitting his high vocation and to help him in leading the religious life.

Formula for Sāmaṇera

Any layman who wishes to be initiated as a *sāmaṇera* has first to get permission from has parents or guardians, and having approached a *bhikkhu* with the 8 requisites for a *bhikkhu*,[21] he informs the *bhikkhu* of his desire for initiation. When the order agrees to initiate him, his head is to be shaved by a *bhikkhu* or a layman.

During this shaving of the head, he meditates on the first five of the constituent parts of the body (in the canonical enumeration) namely hair, body-hair, nails, teeth and skin and reflects: "These are mere filth as regards colour, shape, smell and location. These are not "I", not "mine", not a soul or a being, but are impermanent, a cause of suffering and not self (*anicca, dukkha, anattā*)."

21. Eight requisites for a *bhikkhu*: a full set of robes (3 robes), a girdle, a bowl, a razor, a needle and a filter.

Having his head shaved and washed, he squats on the ground with palms together and makes a request in the following manner: "Revered Sir, may you be pleased to take the yellow robe from me and out of compassion for me, initiate me as a novice so that I may be able to overcome all the suffering in the round of rebirths, and attain *Nibbāṇa*." Then he offers his robe to the *bhikkhu*.

He then recites a formula thrice requesting that his robe be returned:

"Revered Sir, may you be pleased to give me the robe and out of compassion for me, may you initiate me as a novice so that I may be able to overcome all the suffering in the round of rebirths and attain *Nibbāṇa*.

"Revered Sir, I ask for initiation in order to enable me to escape from the troubles of *samsara*. For the second time, Revered Sir, I ask you for initiation. For the third time, Revered Sir, I ask you for initiation."

Then he is given the yellow robe to wear and he takes refuge in three Jewels saying:

"I take refuge in the Buddha,
I take refuge in the Dhamma,
I take refuge in the Saṅgha."

For the second and third time also, he recites the formula of Refuge. At the end of the third recitation, he becomes a novice. He is received into the Order.

As soon as he becomes a novice, he has to ask one of the monks to be his instructor by reciting the formula:

"Revered Sir, may you become my instructor. For the second time, Revered Sir, may you become my instructor. For the third time also, Revered Sir, may you become my instructor."

His instructor then advises him to behave well in order to inspire respect and to fulfill the threefold Teaching (i.e. *Pariyatti, Paṭipatti* and *Paṭivedha*). The novice promises to act according to his advice.

In order to enable the novice to learn the Texts and practice *Paṭipatti*, the instructor excuses him from performing certain duties as a disciple. The disciple also requests the instructor to live according to his own wishes and not to burden himself with his personal obligations as a teacher.

Ten Precepts

As a novice, he has to observe ten precepts. They are:

(1) Abstaining from taking the life of sentient beings.
(2) Abstaining from taking what is not freely given.
(3) Abstaining from sexual misconduct.
(4) Abstaining from telling lies.
(5) Abstaining from partaking of intoxicants.
(6) Abstaining from taking food after midday.
(7) Abstaining from dancing, singing playing music and witnessing show or entertainments.
(8) Abstaining from wearing flowers, using scents and unguents and beautifying with ointments.
(9) Abstaining from using high and large beds.
(10) Abstaining from accepting gold and silver.

Fourfold Reflection

Besides these ten precepts he has to carry out certain duties as a novice and reflect attentively. This reflection is fourfold.

(1) Reflecting attentively will I wear the robe only for the purpose of protection from cold, heat, from dangers of gadflies; mosquitoes, snakes, from wind and sun, for the purpose of covering the body out of a sense of decency.
(2) Reflecting attentively will I partake of food not for the purpose of playing, not for taking pride in strength, not for the growth of the parts of the body (to have charm), not for beautification, but for support and maintenance of the body, for keeping it unharmed, for enabling the practice of the (*Brahmacariya*) religious life; and thus by taking food, I may dispel the former painful feelings and will not cause new ones to arise There will be for me, support of life; faultlessness and living without discomfort.
(3) Reflecting attentively will I use lodgings in order to protect from cold, heat, danger of gadflies, mosquitoes, snakes, for the purpose of dispelling the dangers of season and for retirement for meditation.
(4) Reflecting attentively will I use medicines for removing painful feelings that have arisen and the purpose of freedom from illness and disease.

Ten Acts for which a Novice may be Punished

He should avoid performing ten immoral acts and if he has committed one of them, he should be given penance in the form of carrying water and bags of sand, etc.

These ten improper acts for which the penance is imposed are:

(1) Taking food after midday.
(2) Indulging in dancing, singing, playing music and witnessing shows.
(3) Wearing flowers, using scents and unguents and beautifying with ointments.
(4) Using high and luxurious beds.
(5) Accepting gold and silver.
(6) Attempting to prevent monks from getting offerings.
(7) Attempting to cause harm to monks.
(8) Attempting to cause monks to be without lodgings.
(9) Abusing monks.
(10) Causing disunion among monks.

Ten Acts for which a Novice must be Expelled

There are another 10 immoral acts for which the novice is to be defrocked and expelled from the Order.

(1) Taking the life of sentient beings.
(2) Taking what is not freely given.
(3) Leading an unchaste life.
(4) Telling lies.
(5) Partaking of intoxicants.
(6) Speaking in dispraise of the Buddha.
(7) Speaking in dispraise of the Dhamma.
(8) Speaking in dispraise of the Saṅgha.
(9) Holding false views.
(10) Seducing nuns.

SEKHIYA (RULES FOR TRAINING)

These are the 75 Rules of a Sāmaṇera (Novice) which form part of the 227 Rules for a Bhikkhu.

1) 'I will dress with the inner robe hanging evenly around me' is a training to be observed.
2) 'I will put on the upper robe hanging evenly around me', is a training to be observed.
3) 'Properly clad will I go in the villages', is a training to be observed.
4) 'Properly clad will I sit down in the villages', is a training to be observed.
5) 'Well-controlled will I go in the villages', is a training to be observed.
6) 'Well-controlled will I sit down in the villages', is a training to be observed.
7) 'With the eyes cast down will I go in the villages', is a training to be observed.
8) 'With the eyes cast down will I sit down in the villages', is a training to be observed.
9) 'Not lifting up the robes will I go in the villages', is a training to be observed.
10) 'Not lifting up the robes will I sit down in the villages', is a training to be observed.
11) 'Not with loud laughter will I go in the villages', is a training to be observed.
12) 'Not with loud laughter will I sit down in the villages', is a training to be observed.
13) 'With little noise will I go in the villages', is a training to be observed.
14) 'With little noise will I sit down in the villages', is a training to be observed.
15) 'Not swaying the body will I go in the villages', is a training to be observed.
16) 'Not swaying the body will I sit down in the villages', is a training to be observed.
17) 'Not swaying the arms will I go in the villages', is a training to be observed.
18) 'Not swaying the arms will I sit down in the villages', is a training to be observed.
19) 'Not swaying the head will I go in the villages', is a training to be observed.
20) 'Not swaying the head will I sit down in the villages', is a training to be observed.

21) 'Not with arms akimbo will I go in the villages', is a training to be observed.
22) 'Not with arms akimbo will I sit down in the villages', is a training to be observed.
23) 'Not covering the head will I go in the villages', is a training to be observed.
24) 'Not covering the head will I sit down in the villages', is a training to be observed.
25) 'Not walking on the heels or toes will I go in the villages', is a training to be observed.
26) 'Not with knees raised and clasped or wound round with the upper robe will I sit down in the villages', is a training to be observed.
27) 'Attentively will I accept alms food', is a training to be observed.
28) 'Mindful of the bowl will I accept alms food', is a training to be observed.
29) 'With a proportionate amount of curry will I accept alms food', is a training to be observed.
30) 'Only up to the inner ring of the bowl will I accept alms food', is a training to be observed.
31) 'Attentively will I eat alms food', is a training to be observed.
32) 'Mindful of the bowl will I eat alms food', is a training to be observed.
33) 'In orderly manner will I eat alms food', is a training to be observed.
34) 'With a proportionate amount of curry will I eat alms food', is a training to be observed.
35) 'Not pressing down the top will I eat alms food', is a training to be observed.
36) 'Desiring something more I will not cover up the soup and curry and the condiment with rice', is a training to be observed.
37) 'If not ill, I will not ask for food for myself and eat it', is a training to be observed.
38) 'Not with a captious mind will I look at another's bowl', is a training to be observed.
39) 'I will not make up too large a mouthful', is a training to be observed.
40) 'I will make each mouthful round', is a training to be observed.
41) 'I will not open the mouth till the mouthful is brought close', is a training to be observed.
42) 'I will not put the fingers into the mouth while eating', is a training to be observed.
43) 'I will not talk with the mouth full', is a training to be observed.

44) 'I will not eat tossing the rounds of food into the mouth', is a training to be observed.
45) 'I will not eat breaking up the rounds', is a training to be observed.
46) 'I will not eat stuffing the cheeks', is a training to be observed.
47) 'I will not eat shaking the hands about', is a training to be observed.
48) 'I will not eat scattering grains of rice', is a training to be observed.
49) 'I will not eat putting out the tongue', is a training to be observed.
50) 'I will not eat smacking the lips', is a training to be observed.
51) 'I will not eat making a hissing sound', is a training to be observed.
52) 'I will not eat licking the fingers', is a training to be observed.
53) 'I will not eat scraping the bowl', is a training to be observed.
54) 'I will not eat licking the lips', is a training to be observed.
55) 'I will not touch a drinking cup, my hands soiled with food', is a training to be observed.
56) 'I will not throw out in the village, rinsings of the bowl containing rice', is a training to be observed.
57) 'I will not preach Dhamma to one who is not ill and yet has a sunshade in his hand', is a training to be observed.
58) 'I will not preach Dhamma to one who is not ill and yet has a staff in his hand', is a training to be observed.
59) 'I will not preach Dhamma to one who is not ill and yet has a knife in his hand', is a training to be observed.
60) 'I will not preach Dhamma to one who is not ill and yet has a bow in his hand', is a training to be observed.
61) 'I will not preach Dhamma to one who is not ill and yet is wearing sandals', is a training to be observed.
62) 'I will not preach Dhamma to one who is not ill and yet is wearing shoes', is a training to be observed.
63) 'I will not preach Dhamma to one who is not ill and yet is in a vehicle', is a training to be observed.
64) 'I will not preach Dhamma to one who is not ill and yet is on a bed', is a training to be observed.
65) 'I will not preach Dhamma to one who is not ill and yet is sitting with knees raised and clasped or wound round with the upper robe', is a training to be observed.

66) 'I will not preach Dhamma to one who is not ill and yet is wearing headgear (which covers all his head)', is a training to be observed.
67) 'I will not preach Dhamma to one who is not ill and yet has his head covered up', is a training to be observed.
68) 'While sitting on the ground myself, I will not preach Dhamma to one who is not ill and yet is sitting on a seat', is a training to be observed.
69) 'I will not preach Dhamma, while sitting on a low seat myself, to one who is not ill and yet is sitting on a high seat' is a training to be observed.
70) 'I will not preach Dhamma standing, to one who is not ill and yet is sitting down', is a training to be observed.
71) 'I will not preach Dhamma following one who is not ill and yet is going in front', is a training to be observed.
72) 'I will not preach Dhamma walking at one side of a path, to one who is not ill and yet is walking along the path', is a training to be observed.
73) 'I will not ease myself standing if not ill', is a training to be observed.
74) 'I will not ease myself or spit on living plants if not ill', is a training to be observed.
75) 'I will not ease myself or spit on potable water, if not ill', is a training to be observed.

INTRODUCTION TO THE TWO HUNDRED AND TWENTY-SEVEN RULES OF VINAYA

"PATIMOKKHA"

Two kinds of *Pātimokkha*:

Pātimokkha meaning "excellent", "foremost", "chief", is the code of discipline for the bhikkhus. There are really two kinds of *Pātimokkha*.

(1) *Sīla Pātimokkha*

(2) *Gantha Pātimokkha*

(1) Sīla Pātimokkha

It protects (*Pāti, rekkhati*) one who guards or observes *sīla* from pain and suffering and prevents him from falling to lower states of existences (*mokkheti, mocayati*). So it is known as "*Sīla Pātimokkha*."

(2) Gantha Pātimokkha

The Text (*gantha*) which points out *sīla* is called "*Gantha Pātimokkha*". *Sīla Pātimokkha* is the root cause for all mundane and supramundane benefits, and *Gantha Pātimokkha* points out *Sīla* which is to be practiced.

Sīla Pātimokkha is of two kinds.

(a) Ovāda Pātimokkha

(b) Āṇā Pātimokkha

Ovāda Pātimokkha is set forth in three gāthās.

These Gāthās are:

183. *Sabbapāpassa akaraṇaṃ,*
kusalassa upasampadā,
sacitta-pariyodapaṇaṃ,
etaṃ Buddhāna sāsanaṃ.

Not to do any evil, to cultivate good,
to purify one's mind, this is the Teaching of the Buddhas.

184. *Khantīparamaṃ tapo-titikkhā.*
Nibbānaṃ paramaṃ vadanti Buddha.
Na hi pabbajito parūpaghāti
Samaṇo hoti paraṃ viheṭhayanto.

Forbearance is the highest patience, Nibbāna is supreme, so declared the Buddhas. He is not a monk indeed who injures others. One is not a monk who hurts another.

185. *Anūpavādo, anūpaghāto,*
Pātimokkhe ca saṃvaro,
mattaññutā ca bhattasmiṃ,
pantañ ca sayanāsanaṃ,
Adhicitte ca āyogo,
etaṃ Buddhāna sāsanaṃ.

Non-abusing, non-injuring, restraint, according to the *Pātimokkha* rules, moderation in food, staying in a remote place, devotion to higher thought, this is the Teaching of the Buddhas.

Āṇā Pātimokkha—The 227 Rules of training for monks contained in *Bhikkhu Vibhaṅga Pāḷi* is known as *Āṇā Pātimokkha.*

Gantha Pātimokkha—The separate text formed by collecting the 227 Rules of training from the *Saṅgāyana* Canonical texts in order to make it easy in reciting them on *Uposatha* days.

How the Religion cannot last long without the *Āṇā Pātimokkha.*

While the Buddha was residing at Verañja, to the Venerable Sariputta, who lived alone in seclusion, occurred the idea: 'Whose religious Teachings last long and whose Teachings do not long endure?' With this thought he rose from his seat, went to the Buddha, paid respects to Him, sat at one side and enquired: "O Revered Sir, whose religious Teachings last long and whose do not endure?"

The Buddha replied, "The Teachings of Vipassī Buddha, Sikhī Buddha and Vessabhū Buddha did not last long but those of Kakusamda Buddha, Koṇāgomana Buddha and Kassapa Buddha did exist for a long time."

Again, the Venerable Sariputta asked, "Revered Sir, why is it that the Teachings of Vipassī, Sikhī and Vessabhū Buddhas did not last long?"

"O Sariputta, these Enlightened Buddhas—Vipassī, Sikhī and Vessabhū —had not put forth effort to propound the doctrine in detail to the people.[22] There were only a few *Suttas, Geyyas, Veyyākaranas, Gāthas, Udānas, ltivuttakas, Jātakas, Abbhutas* and *Vedallas*. They did not promulgate the *Āṇā Pātimokkha.*[23] When those Omniscient Buddhas passed away and when their chief disciples also breathed their last, the successor monks of different classes caused the disappearance of the religious teachings in a short time.

"O Sariputta, just as various flowers which are kept on a board without being threaded, are scattered, whirled and destroyed by the wind, in the same way the religious Teachings were destroyed by the monks of various classes after the passing away of the Omniscient Buddhas and their true disciples."

Then the Venerable Sariputta raised a further question: "Revered Sir, what is the reason for the long endurance of the Teachings of Kakusanda, Konāgamana and Kassapa Buddhas?"

"O Sariputta, Kakusanda, Konāgamana and Kassapa Buddhas preached the Dhamma in detail and their discourse of *Suttas, Geyyas, Veyyākaranas, Gāthas, Udānas, ltivuttakas, Jātakas, Abbhutas* and *Vedallas* were numerous. They pointed out the *Āṇā Pātimokkha* to their disciples. After the disappearance of these Buddhas and their chief disciples, the successor monks of various classes preserved the Teachings and protected them for a long time.

"Just as, O Sariputta, various flowers kept on a board but well threaded are not scattered, not whirled, not destroyed by the wind, so also the Teachings lasted long, because the successor monks of various classes preserved them after the passing away of the Buddhas and their noble disciples."

When the Rules should be laid down

When the Buddha explained this to Sariputta, the Venerable Sariputta rose from his seat, placed the robe on his left shoulder, paid respects to Him and requested the Buddha, "For the long endurance of this Teaching, may the

22. During the time of Vipassī, Sikhī and Vessabhū Buddhas, beings had little dust of *kilesas* and when they came to hear even a stanza of the four Noble Truths, insight arose in them. It was not necessary to expound the Dhamma to them in detail. So, the *Suttas, Geyyas, Veyyakaranas*, etc. given in brief by these Buddhas were short and few.

23. As the disciples of these Buddhas were of good conduct and as they committed no breaches, there arose no occasion on which the rules had to be laid down. So *Āṇā Pātimokkha* was not promulgated by those Buddhas.

Revered Buddha prescribe the Rules to the monks. It is time, Reverend Sir, to make know the *Pātimokkha* Rules."

"Wait, O Sariputta, wait, only the Buddha knows the proper time for promulgation of the *Pātimokkha* Rules. O Sariputta, so long as, in this Teaching there appear no offences committed due to defilements, the Buddhas never point out the *Āṇā Pātimokkha* Rules to the disciples. Only when there appear offences in the Order due to defilements, do the Buddhas lay down the *Āṇā Pātimokkha* Rules to ward off these offences.

"O Sariputta, so long as the number of monks of long-standing do not increase, the Order has not developed and so long as the Order has not received great gain and offerings, there occur no offences in the order due to defilements.

"When the number of monks of long-standing increases, when the Order develops and when to the monks accrue great gains and offerings, then occur in the order some breaches due to the existence of defilements. Then in order to ward off these offences, the Buddhas lay down the *Āṇā Pātimokkha* Rules for the disciples.

"Now, O Sariputta, the order is free from vice, danger and defilement; it is pure and has the essence of *sīla*. O Sariputta, among these 500 disciples, a monk of the lowest stage is a *Sotapanna*, who will not be born in hell but is destined to rise to higher stages (i.e. *Sakadāgami*, *Anāgāmi* and *Arahatta*)." (Pārāsika Pāḷi, 11-6th Syn Edn.)

Thus, the *Pātimokkha* Rules were not laid down when the disciples were of good conduct and committed no breaches. Only when they became corrupted and committed offences, were these Rules laid down from time to time.

Ten Points for the Promulgation of Pātimokkha Rules

The Buddha pointed out the rules for these ten objects.

1. To be practiced by the Order
2. For the welfare of the Order
3. To suppress those who break *sīla*
4. To enable them to live safely and happily
5. To restrain the existing tendencies to evil
6. To prevent the arising of new tendencies
7. To develop faith in those who do not believe in the Teaching
8. To increase faith in those who have belief already

9. For long endurance of the Good Law
10. For protection of the Vinaya Rules

Recitation of Pātimokkha on an Uposatha Day

A monk who knows all these rules has to recite in a *Sīma* on an *Uposatha* Day (Fasting Day) and this recitation and meeting of the Order is called the 'Performance of *Uposatha* or 'Pointing out the *Pātimokkha* Rules'. Even the *arahats* had to attend the *Uposatha* Ceremony.

Once the Buddha, having read the mind of Venerable Mahā Kappina who was living alone in seclusion, went to him and said, "Have you not a reflection: 'Shall I go to the Performance of *Uposatha* or not? Shall I go to the *Saṅgha Kamma* or not? Indeed, I have attained perfect purification?'" The Venerable Mahā Kappina answered in the affirmative. Then the Buddha told him, "If you, who have attained purification do not revere, honour, esteem and pay respect to the performance of *Uposatha* then who will revere, honour, esteem and pay respect to it? Go to the performance of *Uposatha* and to the *Saṅgha Kamma*. Don't remain absent." (Vinaya Mahavagga, p. 148)

If a monk, having given his consent with reference to the *Saṅgha Kamma* and having declared his purity, does not take part in the performance of *Uposatha*, he does not commit an offence. He who does not take part in it without giving his consent and without declaring his purity, commits a *Dukkata* offence.

By pointing out the *Pātimokkha* Rules, the following 18 assertions will not appear.

1) Asserting that which is not Dhamma to be Dhamma
2) Asserting that which is Dhamma to be not Dhamma
3) Asserting that which is not *Vinaya* to be *Vinaya*
4) Asserting that which is *Vinaya* to be not *Vinaya*
5) Asserting that which is not expounded to be expounded
6) Asserting that which is expounded to be unexpounded
7) Asserting that which was not practiced by the Buddha as being practiced
8) Asserting that which was practiced by the Buddha to be not practiced
9) Asserting that which is not prescribed by the Buddha to be prescribed
10) Asserting that which is prescribed by the Buddha to be unprescribed
11) Asserting that which entails offence as not entailing offence

12) Asserting that which does not entail offence as entailing offence
13) Asserting a light offence to be a grave one
14) Asserting a grave offence to be a light one
15) Asserting an offence which destroys the remaining observances as not destroying them
16) Asserting an offence which does not destroy the remaining observances to be destroying them
17) Asserting a disgusting offence to be not disgusting
18) Asserting an offence which is not disgusting, to be disgusting

By pointing out the *Pātimokkha* Rules, monks who do not know the Rules come to know them, and those who know them already, remember them; it yields good results such as unity of the Saṅgha, purity of *Sīla,* etc., up to the attainment of Nibbāna.

THE TWO HUNDRED AND TWENTY-SEVEN RULES[24] OF VINAYA Compiled from Vinaya Piṭaka and Commentaries

Note: The 75 Rules of Training of a novice also apply to *Bhikkhus*. These rules were published in Vol. V. No. 4. of *The Light of the Dhamma.*

I. PĀRĀJIKA

Four Offences which entail loss of monkhood

1. A monk who, undertaking the Rules of Discipline and not having disavowed his Training and not having declared his unwillingness to stay as a *Bhikkhu*, indulges in any kind of sexual intercourse commits an offence entailing loss of monkhood and he is not to be associated with.
2. A monk who either in a village or elsewhere, takes with the intention of stealing what has not been given to him, where the theft is such that rulers, catching a thief, would flog him or imprison him or banish him, saying "You are a robber, you are wicked, you are stupid, you are a thief", commits an offence entailing loss of monkhood, and he is not to be associated with.
3. A monk who intentionally deprives a human being of his life or provides the means for suicide, or praises death, or incites him to commit suicide saying "Of what use to you is this evil difficult life? Death is better for you than life", thus having his mind set on the other's death and with the idea that he should die, praises death in various ways or incites him to commit suicide, commits an offence entailing loss of monkhood and he is not to be associated with.

---

24. The rules are very much like brief headnotes to long judgments and there is a detailed account behind each rule and behind each exception to a rule.

The facts and circumstances which led to the Rules and exceptions being made, the occasions on which they were made and the aims and objects for which they were made are set Out at length in the respective accounts.

These accounts as well as explanations of the technical terms used in the rules are contained in the Vinaya Piṭaka which runs into as many as five big volumes.

The term *Pārājika* is applicable both to the offence and the offender. (Pārājika Aṭṭhakathā Vinaya Piṭaka Pārājikakaṇḍa-Aṭṭhakathā (I) Pārājikakaṇḍa (I) Paṭhamapārājika Padabhājanīya-vaṇṇanā. 6th Syn. Edn. Vol I. pp. 22:23-24.)

4. A monk who boasts with reference to himself, of clear knowledge and insight which are preventive or destructive of *kilesas* (defilements) and which are the attributes of those who have attained *jhāna*, *magga* and *phala*, without having such knowledge or insight, as well as a monk who having been guilty of contravention of this rule (and having lost his monkhood) and being desirous of the clean status of a novice or a layman,[25] confesses[26] subsequently, on being examined or without being examined: "Sir, I said 'I know' without really knowing and 'I see' without really seeing. I have made an empty boast and told a lie", commits an offence entailing loss of monkhood and he is not to be associated with, provided that it was not under a delusion.[27]

II. SANGHĀDISESA

Thirteen Offences which require Formal Meetings of the Order for their Exoneration

1) Intentional emission of semen is an offence requiring formal meetings of the Order for its exoneration.
2) A monk who with sexual desire and a perverse intention contacts a woman holding her hand or holding a braid of her hair or rubbing against any part of her body, commits an offence requiring formal meetings of the Order for its exoneration.
3) A monk who with sexual desire and a perverse intention makes suggestions to a woman with lewd words just as a young man makes suggestions to a young woman with words relating to sexual intercourse, commits an offence requiring formal meetings of the Order for its exoneration.

   A monk who with sexual desire and a perverse intention speaks in praise of ministering to his sexual pleasures in the presence of a woman, saying "Sister, this is the highest kind of ministration that a woman should

---

25. A monk, who has committed an offence entailing loss of monkhood, cannot attain any *jhāna*, *magga* or *phala* or be reborn in any higher plane if he does not leave the Order; but he can attain them and be reborn there, if he becomes a novice or a layman.
26. The monk having committed the offence and lost his monkhood as soon as he made an empty boast, his subsequent confession cannot exonerate him.
27. A monk may really be under the delusion of having attained *jhāna*, *magga* or *phala*. Such delusion is known as *Adhimāna*.

minister with to one who is virtuous, of good conduct, and leading the holy life like me," commits an offence requiring formal meetings of the Order for its exoneration.

4) A monk who acts as a go-between telling a man's desire to a woman or a woman's desire to a man in order to bring about their union as husband and wife or otherwise or to bring about their union even for a moment commits an offence requiring formal meetings of the Order for its exoneration.

5) A monk who builds a hut or a small monastery or has it built without a donor by his own begging and for his own advantage, should make it or have it made according to the measure. This is the measure: twelve *sugata* spans[28] in length and seven such spans in width. Monks should be brought to mark out the site. A site which is not unsafe[29] and which has an open space[30] round it, should be marked out by the monks.

   a. If a monk builds a hut or a small monastery or has it built by his own begging on a site which is unsafe and which has no open space round it, or if he does not bring the monks for marking out the site, or if he exceeds the measure, he commits an offence requiring formal meetings of the Order for its exoneration.

6) If a monk is building a big monastery for his own use, having a donor, monks should be brought to mark out a site, which is not unsafe and which has an open space round it, and it should be marked out by those monks.

   a. If a monk builds a big monastery on a site which is not safe and which has no open space round it, or if he does not bring monks to mark out the site, he commits an offence requiring formal meetings of the Order for its exoneration.

7) A monk who, being angry, malicious and malignant, makes against another monk an unfounded charge of an offence entailing loss of monkhood thinking 'Thus perhaps may I drive him away from this holy life', the charge being unfounded, and who subsequently confesses his wrong doing on being examined or without being examined, commits an offence requiring formal meetings of the Order for its exoneration.

---

28. *Sugata* span—A span of the Buddha.

29. An unsafe site is a site where there are ants, or white-ants, or rats, snakes, scorpions, centipedes, elephants, horses, lions, tigers, leopards, bears, hyenas, or any other animals; a site near paddy-fields, near fields of grain; near a slaughtering place, near an execution-block, near a cemetery, near a garden, near a king's property, near an elephant stable, horse stable, prison, tavern, meat stall, carriage-road, cross-roads, near a meeting place, near a blind alley. Pārājika Pāḷi, p. 226.

30. 'Wide enough for a yoked cart to be driven round it.'

8) A monk, who, being angry, malicious and malignant, accuses another monk of an offence entailing loss of monkhood making use of only some of the facts, those facts really concerning some other being[31] thinking 'Thus perhaps may I drive him away from this holy life', and the accusation being based on some facts relating to some other being, though he subsequently confesses[32] his wrong doing, on being examined or without being examined, commits an offence requiring formal meetings of the Order for its exoneration.
9) If a monk tries to cause a schism of the united Order or persists in taking up and advocating a cause which will lead to a schism, other monks should say to him, "Do not, Venerable One, try to cause a schism of the united Order or persist in taking up and advocating a cause which will lead to a schism. Let the Venerable One be united with the Order. The Order, which is united, lives happily, rejoicing, without disputing and under the same code."

    And if that monk, after he has been spoken to thus by the other monks, persists as before, the other monks should admonish him up to three times to desist from his endeavour.

    If he desists after having been admonished up to three times, that is well and good. If he does not desist, he commits an offence requiring formal meetings of the Order for its exoneration.

11. lf a monk (i.e., a monk who is attempting to cause a schism) has one, two or three monks who follow his leadership and speak for disunity, and if these should say, "Sirs, please do not say anything to this monk; this monk is one who speaks Dhamma; this monk is one who speaks Vinaya this monk speaks after ascertaining our wishes and views. He speaks with us; and what he does has our approval." The monks should say to them, "Do not speak thus. This monk is not one who speaks Dhamma; this monk is not one who speaks Vinaya. Please do not let a schism in the Order seem good to the Venerable Ones. Let the Venerable Ones be at one with the Order. The Order which is united, lives happily, rejoicing and without disputing and under the same code."

---

31. For instance, a person or animal which has or is given a name similar to that of a monk might do something which a monk should not do. Speaking of this it might, with evil intent, be made to appear it was done by that monk.

32. Confession is not an essential ingredient of the offence. Confession is mentioned just to make it clear that it cannot exonerate the offence.

If those monks, having been spoken to thus, up to three times, should desist, that is well and good.

If they should not desist, they commit an offence requiring formal meetings of the Order for its exoneration.

12. If a monk is by nature difficult to advise and being spoken to by the monks according to the Vinaya Rules, he makes himself one not to be spoken to, saying, "Do not say anything to me, Venerable Ones, either good or bad, and I will not say anything to the Venerable Ones, either good or bad. Refrain, Venerable Ones, from speaking to me," then the monks should say to him, "Do not, Venerable One, make yourself one not to be spoken to, let the Venerable One make himself one to be spoken to; let the Venerable One speak to the monks according to the Vinaya Rules; the monks will then speak to the Venerable One according to the Vinaya Rules. The number of the Buddha's disciples increases in this manner by mutual advice and mutual help to rise above offences."

    If that monk after having been admonished up to three times desists, that is well and good.

    If he does not desist, he commits an offence requiring formal meetings of the Order for its exoneration.

13. If a monk, who lives depending on a village or a little town, is one who spoils families (by making them lose faith and veneration) and is of improper conduct[33] and his improper conduct is seen and heard and families which are spoiled by him are seen and heard, let the monks say to him, "The Venerable One is one who spoils families and is of improper conduct. The Venerable One's improper conduct is seen and heard and the families which are spoilt by the Venerable One are seen and heard. Let the Venerable One depart from this residence. Enough of his living here!"

    If this monk, having been spoken to thus by the monks should say, "The monks are given to favouritism and the monks act unjustly out of hatred and stupidity and fear; they banish some for such an offence; they do not banish others," the monks should say to him, 'Venerable One, do

---

33. *Kuladūsako*—He spoils families by giving them flowers, fruits, face-powder, soap-clay, tooth-sticks bamboos, medical treatment and by going on errands. Pārājika Pāḷi Chattha Sangiti. Edn. p. 281.

Improper Conduct – is the growing of flower-plants, causing others to grow, sprinkling water, causing others to sprinkle, plucking flowers, causing others to pluck, threading flowers (making garlands), and causing others to thread. Ibid p. 281.

not speak thus. The monks are not given to favouritism and the monks are not acting unjustly out of hatred and stupidity and fear. The Venerable One is one who spoils families and is of improper conduct. The Venerable One's improper conduct is seen and heard and the families which are spoilt by the Venerable One, are seen and heard. Let the Venerable One depart from this residence. Enough of his living here!"

If after having been admonished thus up to three times he desists that is well and good.

If he does not desist, he commits an offence requiring formal meetings of the Order for its exoneration.[34]

III. ANIYATA[35]

Offences which are not fixed (i.e., offences the nature of which have to be determined according to the following Rules of Procedure)

1) If a monk sits down together with a woman on a seat which is secluded, hidden from view, and convenient for an immoral purpose and if a trustworthy woman lay-follower seeing him, accuses him of any one of three offences, namely: (1) an offence entailing loss of monkhood,[36] (2) an offence requiring formal meetings of the Order for its exoneration,[37] or (3) an offence of slackening or backsliding[38] *and the monk himself confesses that he was so sitting,* he should be found guilty of one of those three offences (i.e. of the offence of which he is accused by her).
2) If the seat is not hidden from view and is not convenient for an immoral purpose but is sufficiently so for speaking to a woman with lewd words, then if a monk sits down on such a seat together with a woman the two alone, and a trustworthy woman lay-follower seeing him accuses him of one of two offences, namely: (1) an offence requiring formal meetings

34. Spoiling families is only a minor offence namely *Dukkata*; but in this case the monk commits the offence of *Sanghādisesa* as he persists in recriminations of the other monks. Pārāiika Aṭṭhagata II, p. 202, 6th Syn. Edn
35. These Rules do not create any new offence.
36. I.e. the offence of sexual intercourse.
37. I.e. the offence of physical contact with a woman or a girl.
38. I.e. the offence of sitting with a woman on a seat which is secluded and out of view.

of the Order for its exoneration[39] or (2) an offence of slackening or backsliding[40] and *the monk himself confesses that he was so sitting down*[41] he should be found guilty of one of the two offences.

IV. NISSAGGIYA-PĀCITIIYA[42]

1. A monk who keeps an extra robe for more than ten days after the robe is finished and after the *Kathina* privileges are withdrawn, commits a *Nissaggiya Pācittiya* offence.
2. After the robe is finished and the *Kathina* privileges are withdrawn, a monk who stays away from his three robes, even for one night, except by special permission of the Saṅgha, commits a *Nissaggiya Pācittiya* offence.
3. If non-seasonal[43] material for a robe arises for a monk after the robe is finished and after the *Kathina* privileges withdrawn and if the monk wishes to accept it, he may do so. However, having accepted it he should make a robe quickly.[44] If the material be not sufficient for a robe, it may be laid aside by that monk for a month at the most provided that he has expectation for a supply of the deficiency. If he lays it aside longer than a month, even if there is such expectation, he commits a *Nissagiya Pācittiya* offence.
4. If a monk gets an old robe[45] washed or dyed or beaten by a nun who is not his relation, he commits a *Nissaggiya Pācittiya* offence.
5. If a monk accepts a robe except in exchange, from the hand of a nun who is not his relation, he commits a *Nissaggiva Pācittiya* offence.

---

39. I.e. the offence of physical contact with a woman or a girl or the offence of lewd words.
40. I.e. offence of sitting with a woman on a seat which is secluded.
41. Confession is essential in this case.
42. *Pācittiya* (the offence of slackening or back-sliding) falls into two categories, viz. *Nissaggiya Pācittiya* and *Suddha* (ordinary er Simple) *Pāicittiya*.

If the *Kathina* ceremony is not held, the "Robe Season" (*Cīvarakāta*) lasts for one month. Starting from the 1st day after the full-moon of *Kattika* (October) to the full-moon day of *Māgasira* (November). Thus, the remaining 11 months are the wrong season.

If the *Kathina* ceremony is held; the robe season extends to 5 months, i.e. starting from the 1st day after the full-moon of *Kattika* to the full-moon day of *Phaggana* (March). The remaining 7 months are the wrong season.

43. *Akātacīvara* – a robe offered out of time.
44. I.e. within ten days. Pārājika Pāḷi, p. 304, 6th Syn. Edn.
45. Even a robe, which has been worn only once, is an old robe for this purpose.

6. If a monk asks a man or woman householder, who is not his relation, for a robe, otherwise than on a proper occasion, he commits a *Nissaggiva Pācittiya* offence. This is a proper occasion—when the monk has been robbed of his robe or his robe has been lost or destroyed.
7. If a man or a woman householder who is not a relation of that monk i.e. the monk whose robe has been stolen or destroyed, brings many robes and invites him to accept them, he should accept at the most an inner robe and an upper robe. If he accepts more than these; he commits a *Nissaggiya Pācittiya* offence.
8. If a man or a woman householder who is not a relation has set aside the price in cash or kind of a robe saying, "I will get a robe with this and offer it to the monk whose name is so and so," then if the monk out of desire for something better, approaches him or her without having been invited before and makes special arrangements with regard to the robe saying "I ask you, please buy a robe like this or like that with this price and offer it to me," he commits a *Nissaggiya Pācittiya* offence.
9. If two men or two women householders who are not related to the monk concerned set aside the prices for two separate robes saying, "We will buy separate robes with these separate prices and offer them to the monk whose name is so and so," then if the monk, out of desire for something better, approaches them without having been invited and makes special arrangements with regard to a robe saying, "I ask you, please combine and buy a robe like this or like that with those separate prices and offer it to me jointly," he commits a *Nissaggiya Pācittiya* offence.
10. If a king or one in the service of a king or a brahmin or a householder sends the price of a robe for a monk by a messenger saying, "Buy a robe with this price and offer it to the monk whose name is so and so," and if the messenger approaches the monk and says, "Venerable Sir, this price of a robe is brought for the Venerable One, let the Venerable One accept it," then the messenger should be told by the monk, "Brother (*Āvuso*), we do not accept the price of a robe; but we do accept a robe, if it is at the right time and if it is suitable." If that messenger says to the monk, "Is there someone who is the Venerable One's attendant?", then the caretaker of the monastery or a lay-devotee should be pointed out as an attendant by the monk who wants the robe; saying, 'This person is the attendant of the monks." If that messenger after instructing the attendant, approaches the monk and says, "Venerable Sir, I have instructed the person whom the Venerable One

pointed out as an attendant; let the Venerable One approach at the right time; he will offer you the robe; then the monk who wants the robe should approach the attendant and ask and remind him two or three times saying, "Brother I am in need of a robe." If after asking and reminding two or three times he succeeds in obtaining the robe, that is good.

If he does not succeed in obtaining the robe, he should stand silently for it four times or five times or six times at the most. If he succeeds in obtaining that robe standing silently for it four times or five times or six times at the most, that is good.

If he, after trying more than that, succeeds in obtaining that robe, he commits a *Nissaggiya Pācittiya* offence.

If he does not succeed at all in obtaining it, he should either go himself to the place from where the price of the robe was brought or send a messenger[46] to say, "That price of a robe which you sent for a monk has not done any good to that monk. Please ask for return of your property. Please do not let your property be lost." This is the proper procedure in such a case.

11. If a monk makes[47] or causes to be made a rug mixed with silk he commits a *Nissaggiya Pācittiya* offence.
12. If a monk makes or causes to be made a rug of pure black wool, he commits a *Nissaggiya Pācittiya* offence.
13. A monk who is making a new rug or causing a new rug to be made, should take two portions of pure black wool, a portion of white wool and a portion of reddish-brown wool. If a monk makes or causes to be made a new rug without taking two portions of pure black wool, a portion of white wool and a portion of reddish-brown wool, he commits a *Nissaggiya Pācittiya* offence.
14. Having made or caused to be made a new rug a monk should keep it for 6 years, and if, either after abandonment of that rug or without having abandoned it, he makes or causes to be made a new rug, within six years except by special permission of the Saṅgha, he commits a *Nissaggiya Pācittiya* offence.
15. A monk who makes or causes to be made a new seat rug (*Nisīdana*) should take a piece about a *sugata*-span from all round the old one, in order to

46. If he neither goes himself nor sends a messenger, he commits the offence of *Vatta-bhedadukkata* (breach of duty)—

47. If he makes or causes to be made a rug mixed even with a single filament of silk, he commits the offence of *Dukkata*.

disfigure the new one. If the monk makes or causes to be made a new seat-rug without taking a piece about a *sugata*-span from all round the old one, he commits a *Nissaggiya Pācittiya* offence.

16. Wool may accrue to a monk while he is on a long journey. It may be accepted by that monk, if he wishes but having accepted it, he should carry it by himself for three yojanas[48] at the most, if there are no carriers. If he carries it further than that, even if there are no carriers, he commits a *Nissaggiya Pācittiya* offence.
17. A monk who gets wool washed or dyed or combed by a nun who is not a relation, commits a *Nissaggiya Pācittiya* offence.
18. A monk, who accepts gold or money[49] or gets another to accept it for him, or acquiesces in its being put near him,[50] commits a *Nissaggiya Pācittiya* offence.
19. A monk who makes a sale or an exchange of one of various kinds[51] of things in respect of gold and money commits a *Nissaggiya Pācittiya* offence.
20. A monk, who makes barter of one of various kinds,[52] commits a *Nissaggiya Pācittiya* offence.
21. An extra bowl may be kept for ten days at the most. A monk who keeps it longer commits a *Nissaggiya Pācittiya* offence.
22. If a monk who has a bowl which has been mended in less than five places asks for and gets a new bowl, he commits a *Nissaggiya Pācittiya* offence.

    That new bowl should be surrendered by the monk to an assembly of monks and the last bowl[53] of that assembly of monks should be given to the monk saying, "Monk, this for you is a bowl, which should be used till it breaks." This is the proper procedure in such a case.

---

48. A *yojana* is about seven miles.
49. I.e. any coin or paper currency which is used in buying and selling. *Vinaya Pitaka; Pārājika Pāḷi. p. 345.*
50. With the implication: 'Let it be yours.'—Ibid. 346.
51. Vinaya Pitaka, Pārājika Pāḷi, (4) Nissaggiyakaṇḍa, (2) Kosiyavagga, (9) Rupiyasamvohara-sikkhapada, p. 348, 6th Syn. Edn.
52. Vinaya Pitaka, Pārājika Pāḷi, (4) Nissaggiyakaṇḍa, (2) Kosiyavagga, (10) Kayavikkaya sikkhapada, p. 351, 6th Syn. Edn.
53. All monks should assemble bringing their bowls. The monks should be asked in order of seniority to take the surrendered bowl. If a senior monk takes it his bowl should in turn be offered to the other monks in order of seniority and so on till the most junior monk has taken a bowl, then the bowl which remains, i.e., the last bowl, should be given to the offender.

23. A monk who has accepted medicines which may be partaken of by sick monks, that is to say, ghee, fresh butter, oil, honey, molasses, may store and use them for seven days at the most. If he exceeds that period, he commits a *Nissaggiya Pācittiya* offence.
24. A monk should look for a robe for the rainy season when there remains only one month of the hot season[54] and he should wear or begin to wear it, when there remains only half a month of the hot season.

    If he looks for a robe for the rainy season earlier than a month before the end of the hot season or if he makes and wears a robe for the rainy season earlier than half a month before the end of the hot season, he commits a *Nissaggiya Pācittiya* offence.
25. A monk who having given a robe to another monk takes it back by force or causes it to be taken back by force as he is angry and displeased, commits a *Nissaggiya Pācittiya* offence.
26. A monk who asks for yarn himself and has robe material woven with it by weavers, commits a *Nissaggiya Pācittiya* offence.
27. A man or a woman householder who is not a relation may have robe material woven for a monk. Then, if that monk not having been invited before, approaches the weavers and makes special arrangements with regard to the robe material saying, "Now, sirs, this robe material is being specially woven for me. Make it long, wide and thick, and make it well woven, well scraped and well combed. I may be able to give you something," and if that monk, so saying, gives anything—even some food, he commits a *Nissaggiya Pācittiya* offence.
28. If an "urgent"[55] robe accrues to a monk ten days before the full moon of *Kattika*, *Temāsika*, and if he knows of the emergency, he may accept it. Having accepted it, he may keep it until the robe season. But if he keeps it longer than that, he commits a *Nissaggiya Pācittiya* offence.
29. A monk who lives up to the full moon of *Kattika,*[56] after he has spent the Lent there, in such jungle lodgings as are regarded as insecure and dangerous may, if he wishes to do so, keep one of his three robes in a

54. I.e., between the first day after the full moon of *Jettha* (June) and the full moon of *Asāḷha* (July)—Pātimokkha-medinā p. 269.

55. "Urgent robe" is a robe offered e.g., as the donor is a (a) about to go to the battle-front, (b) about to go to a distant place, (c) sick or (d) pregnant or (e) as the donor has just been converted to Buddhism. *Parajika Pali*—ps) 375 6th Syn. Edition.

56. The period of Lent ends with the first *Khattika*—Pātimokkhamedinī, p. 285.

village; and if there be any reason for doing so, he may live without that robe for six nights at the most.

If he lives without it longer than that except with the permission of the monks, he commits a *Nissaggiya Pācittiya* offence.

30. A monk who knowingly[57] causes diversion of any offering from the Saṅgha to himself, commits a *Nissaggiya Pācittiya* offence.[58]

V. SUDDHA PĀCITTIYA

1. Telling a conscious lie is a *Pācittiya* offence.
2. Insulting or abusive speech is a *Pācittiya* offence.
3. Speech calculated to estrange friendly monks[59] from each other is a *Pācittiya* offence.
4. If a monk teaches the Dhamma to one, who is not a monk, uttering letters of the alphabet, syllables, words or phrases[60] simultaneously with him, he commits a *Pācittiya* offence.[61]
5. A monk who lies down with one who is not a monk for more than two or three nights[62] in the same building with a roof and walls which are complete or almost, complete[63] commits a *Pācittiya* offence.[64]
6. A monk who lies down with a female in the same building with a roof and walls which are complete or almost complete, commits a *Pācittiya* offence.[65]

---

57. I.e. with the knowledge of the donor having declared his intention to make the offering to the Saṅgha. Pārājika Pāḷi—p. 380 6th Syn. Edn.

58. If he does not get it, he commits only a *Dukkata* offence. Pārājika Pāḷi—p. 380 6th Syn. Edn.

59. Speech calculated to estrange other friendly persons from each other is only a *Dukkata* offence—Pātimokkhamedinī, p. 286.

60. Pācittiya Pāḷi—Chattha Sangīti Edn. p. 25 and Pactiyadi Atthakatha, same edn. p. 81.

61. Because such practice affects the pupils' respect for and obedience to the teacher. See Pācittiya Pāḷi—Chattha Sangīti Edn. p. 25.

62. I.e. for more than three nights consecutively. Change of place and change of companion do not make any difference—Pātimokkhamedinī, p. 301.

63. Pācittiya Pāḷi—Chattha Sangīti Edn. p. 28.

64. If the place is only partially roofed or walled in, he commits only a *Dukkata* offence. Ibid, p. 28.

65. If the place is only partially roofed or walled in, he commits only a *Dukkata* offence. Ib, p. 31.

7. A monk who preaches Dhamma to women in more than five or six words[66] except in the presence of a man of understanding; commits a *Pācittiya* offence.
8. If a monk informs one, who is not a monk, of his having attained *jhāna*, *magga* or *phala* even though it is true[67] he commits a *Pācittiya* offence.
9. If a monk informs one who is not a monk of another monk's disgusting offence,[68] except by special permission of the Saṅgha, he commits a *Pācittiya* offence.
10. A monk who digs the ground or causes it to be dug, commits a *Pācittiya* offence.
11. Destruction[69] of vegetable growth is a *Pācittiya* offence.
12. A monk who evades questions or harasses the monks by remaining silent[70] commits a *Pācittiya* offence.
13. Speech which makes other monks look down upon another monk[71] as well as speech which is merely defamation of that monk is a *Pācittiya* offence.
14. A monk who puts, or causes to be put, in the open air a couch or a chair or a mattress or a stool belonging to the Order; and goes away without taking it back and without having it taken back[72] and without informing any monk, novice or caretaker, commits a *Pācittiya* offence.
15. A monk who spreads a mat or has it spread in a monastery[73] belonging to the Order, and goes away without removing it or without having it removed, and without informing any monk, novice or caretaker, commits a *Pācittiya* offence.

---

66. See Pātimokkhamedinī, p. 305.

67. If it be not true, the offence will be the fourth *Pārājika* unless the monk is under delusion (*adhimāna*).

68. I.e. a Sanghādisesa offence. Pactiyadi Atthakatha, same edn. p. 19.

69. E.g., by cutting or breaking or by causing it to be cut, or broken. Pacittiya-Pali, Chattha Sangīti Edn. p. 52.

70. I.e., when he is examined in the presence of monks as to whether he has committed any offence. Pācittiya Pāḷi, Chattha Sangīti Edn. p. 55.

71. Pācittiya-Pāḷi, Chattha Sangīti Edn. p. 57. If the victim is not a monk; the offence is onlv *Dukkata*. Ibid.

The first part of the rules refers to cases in which defamatory words are spoken to other monks. The second part thereof refers to cases in which they are merely said within the hearing of other monks without being addressed to them. Patimokkhammedini.

72. See Pācittiya Pāḷi, Chattha Sangīti Edn. p. 61.

73. Or within its precincts—see Pācittiya Pāḷi, Chattha Sangīti Edn. p. 61.

16. A monk who in a monastery belonging to the Order knowingly encroaches upon the space of a monk who has arrived there before him thinking, 'He who finds the space too narrow will go away,' and without any other reason commits a *Pācittiya* offence.
17. A monk who being angry or displeased, drags a monk out of a monastery belonging to the Order, or causes him to be dragged out therefrom, commits a *Pācittiya* offence.
18. A monk who sits or lies (throwing himself down) heavily on a couch or a seat, the legs of which protrude between the crossbeams in an upper storey of a monastery belonging to the Order, commits a *Pācittiya* offence.[74]
19. A monk who is building a big monastery should have mortar applied thickly in order that the door frame, the door leaves, the parts of the wall which may be hit by the door leaves when the door is opened, the windows and the parts of the wall which may be hit by their door leaves,[75] may be strong; and he should, standing where there are no green crops, give instructions for roofing it with two or three layers of roofing material.

    If he gives instructions for roofing it with more than three layers, he commits a *Pācittiya* offence even though he gives them standing where there are no green crops.[76]
20. A monk who throws on grass or ground, water which to his knowledge contains insects, commits a *Pācittiya* offence.[77]
21. A monk who without having been authorized by the monks gives advice to ordained nuns[78] with reference to the eight *garudhammas*,[79] commits a *Pācittiya* offence.
22. A monk who gives advice to ordained nuns with reference to any

---

74. The object is to prevent accidents as there was a case of a leg falling on the head of a monk in the lower storey. See Pācittiya Pāḷi, Chattha Sangīti Edn. p. 66.

75. See Pācittiya Atthakatha, Chattha Sangīti Edn. p. 50.

76. The objects are:

1. to prevent accidents, as there was a case of a monastery having collapsed on account of heavy roofing, and 2. to prevent damage to green crops. See Pācittiya Pāḷi, Chattha Sangīti Edn. pp. 67–68.

77. The object is that the insects may not die on account of the water drying up or getting muddy. Patimokkhamedini, p. 337.

78. There is no ordained nun, now. Those who are called nuns; now are mere laywomen who are observing the eight or ten precepts.

79. *Garudhammas* are eight of the Special Rules of Discipline which were prescribed for ordained nuns. See Pācittiya Pāḷi, Chattha Sangīti Edn. p. 74.

Dhamma[80] at or after sunset, commits a *Pācittiya* offence even though he has been authorized by other monks to exhort them.

23. A monk who approaches a monastery of ordained nuns and gives them advice with reference to the eight *garudhammas*, except on a suitable occasion, commits a *Pācittiya* offence.

    A suitable occasion is when an ordained nun is sick.

24. A monk who says, "The elder monks give advice to ordained nuns for the sake of gain," commits a *Pācittiya* offence.

25. A monk who gives a robe to an ordained nun who is not a relation, except in exchange, commits a *Pācittiya* offence.

26. If a monk sews or causes to be sown a robe for an ordained nun who is not a relation, he commits a *Pācittiya* offence.

27. A monk who having arranged with an ordained nun goes on a journey even to a neighbouring village, except on a suitable occasion, commits a *Pācittiya* offence.

    A suitable occasion is when the journey must be performed in the company of merchants and others when the way is unsafe and dangerous.

28. A monk who having arranged with an ordained nun, gets into a boat going either upstream or downstream, except for going across to the other bank, commits a *Pācittiya* offence.

29. A monk who eats what, to his knowledge, is food which an ordained nun has prepared or requested householders to offer him, commits a *Pācittiya.* offence, except where those others have prepared the food for him before her request.[81]

30. A monk who sits down in a secluded place together with an ordained nun, commits a *Pācittiya* offence.

31. A monk who is not sick may take one meal at a public rest house, a pandal, the foot of a tree, or an open space[82] where there is food prepared for unspecified travellers, patients, pregnant women and monks.[83] If he eats more than that, he commits a *Pācittiya* offence.

---

80. Pācittiya Pāḷi, Chattha Sangīti Edn. p. 7.

81. The rule does not apply to food offered by a relation or one who has invited the monk before. Pācittiya Pāḷi, Chattha Sangīti Edn. p. 93.

82. Pācittiya Pāḷi, Chattha Sangīti Edn. p. 97.

83. Pācittiya Atthakatha, Same Edn. p. 76.

32. *Gaṇabhojana* (eating together in a group),[84] except on a proper occasion, is a *Pācittiya* offence. There is proper occasion in this case:

    (1) When one is ill, (2) When robes are being offered, (3) When robes are being made, (4) When one is travelling,[85] (5) When one is embarking[86] (6) When food sufficient for more than three monks cannot be obtained and (7) When food is offered by a *Paribbājaka*.[87]

33. *Paramparabhojana* (eating a meal out of turn)[88] except on a proper occasion is a *Pācittiya* offence.[89]

    There are proper occasions in this case:

    (1) When one is ill, (2) When robes are being offered and (3) When robes are being made.

34. In case a monk who has approached a family be invited to take as much as he likes[90] of cakes or sweetmeats (i.e., of any food which has been prepared for presentation or for use on a journey)[91] he may if he wishes to do so, accept two or three bowlfuls. If he accepts more than that, he commits a *Pācittiya* offence.

    Having accepted two or three bowlfuls, he should take them from there and share them with the monks.[92] This is a proper course in this case.

35. If a monk who has, while eating, refused to have any more when food has been brought within two and a half cubits of him,[93] afterwards chews or eats any food, hard or soft, which has not been formally declared by

84. *Gaṇabhojana* is a group of four or more monks eating a meal together (1) to which they have been invited in unsuitable terms or (2) for which one of them, at least has asked in unsuitable terms. Patimokkhamedinī, p. 357. See also Pācittiya Atthakatha, Chattha Sangīti Edn. p. 78.

85. I.e., when one is about to go on a journey, is on a journey or has just finished a journey Pācittiya Pāḷi, Chattha Sangīti Edn. p. 101.

86. I.e., when one is about to embark, has embarked, or has just disembarked. lb. p. 101.

87. A Paribhājaka is one who has given up the household life to seek the Truth but is neither a monk nor a novice (*Samanera*). Pācittiya Pāḷi, Chattha Sangīti Edn. p. 123.

88. Paramparabhojana (eating a meal out of tum) means eating a meal other than the meal to which one has already been invited. Pācittiya Pāḷi, Chattha Sangīti Edn. p. 105.

89. Because there was a case in which the donor was displeased with some of the monks, whom he had invited to a meal, as they came to it after having had a meal elsewhere. Ibid p. 103.

90. Pācittiya Pāḷi, Chattha Sangīti Edn. p. 108.

91. Ibid.

92. On seeing other monks, he should tell them that he has got the food from that place and ask them not to go and get any more from there. Ibid. p. 109.

93. Pācittiya Pāḷi, Chattha Sangīti Edn. p. 111.

another monk to be surplus or which is not what is left after a sick monk has had his meal,[94] he commits a *Pācittiya* offence.

36. If a monk produces food, hard or soft, which is not surplus, and invites another monk who, to his knowledge has while eating refused to have any more, saying, "O Monk, chew or eat" with the object of bringing him into disrepute,[95] he commits a *Pācittiya* offence.
37. A monk, who eats any hard food or soft food[96] out of time i.e. after noon and before dawn,[97] commits a *Pācittiya* offence.
38. A monk who eats any hard food or soft food that has been stored[98] commits a *Pācittiya* offence.
39. There are sumptuous foods, namely foods mixed[99] with ghee, butter, oil, honey, molasses, fish, milk and curd; and a monk who, though not sick, asks for such sumptuous foods for himself and eats them commits a *Pācittiya* offence.
40. A monk, who puts in his mouth,[100] any nutriment, which has not been proferred[101] to him, commits a *Pācittiya* offence. This Rule does not apply to water and tooth-cleaner.
41. A monk who gives food to a naked ascetic or a *Pācittiya* male or female with his own hand, commits a *Pācittiya* offence.
42. A monk who having said to another monk, "Friend, we will go into a village or a small town for alms-food," tells him after causing something to be given to him or without having caused anything to be given to him, 'Go away, friend, there is no happiness for me in talking to or sitting with you. There is happiness for me in talking and sitting alone, 'for that reason only and not for any other reason, commits a *Pācittiya* offence.

---

94. Ibid.
95. e.g., by charging him subsequently with contravention of the previous rule. Pācittiya Pāḷi, Chattha Sangīti Edn. p. 114.
96. Such food does not include: (1) Yāmakālika, i.e., eight kinds of drinks, (2) Sattāhakālika such as butter, (3) Yavajivika i.e., medicine. Pācittiya Pāḷi, Chattha Sangīti Edn. p. 115.
97. Ibid.
98. Stored food means food which is accepted on one day and eaten on another day. See Pācittiya Pāḷi, Chattha Sangīti Edn. p. 117
99. Pācittiya Atthakatha, Chattha Sangīti Edn. p. 106.
100. Patimokkha-medini, p. 391.
101. It must be proferred to him by one who is within two and a half cubits of him, even though it is his own property. Ibid 387. See also Pacittiya Pali, Chattha Sangīti Edn. p. 121.

43. A monk who intrudes into and sits down in a house where husband and wife are by themselves[102] enjoying each other's company, commits a *Pācittiya* offence.
44. A monk who sits down together with a woman on a seat which is secluded and hidden from view, commits a *Pācittiya* offence.
45. A monk who sits together with a woman—the two alone on a seat which is secluded, commits a *Pācittiya* offence.
46. A monk who has been invited to a meal and goes out to other houses[103] either before or after having that meal without informing another monk who is present commits a *Pācittiya* offence,[104] except on suitable occasions; and suitable occasions are when robes are being offered and when robes are being made.
47. A monk who is not ill and who has been invited to ask for medicines should, unless the invitation is made again or is a permanent one, accept it and ask for medicines for four months.[105]

    If he accepts it for a longer period, i.e., if he asks for medicine after four months, he commits a *Pācittiya* offence.
48. A monk who goes without any particular reason to see an army marching, commits a *Pācittiya* offence.
49. A monk who has some reason for going to an army may stay with the army for two or three nights. If he stays longer than that, he commits a *Pācittiya* offence.
50. If a monk who is staying with an army goes to a place where there is a fight, sham or real, or where the troops are being counted, or where positions for military operations or manoeuvres are being assigned to troops, or goes to see any array of troops, he commits a *Pācittiya* offence.

---

102. Pacittiya Pali, Chattha Sangīti Edn. p. 127.

103. (1) That part of the rule which relates to going round to other houses before a meal was made in connection with a case in which a monk arrived at the house to which he had been invited very late much to the inconvenience of the other invitees (2) That part of the rule which relates to going out after a meal was made in connection with a case in which food, sent by a donor to be offered to other monks after it had been shown to a certain monk, had to be sent back to the donor as that monk was out till afternoon.

104. The object of these exceptions is that monks may not lose opportunities to get robes and sewing material. Pārājika Pāḷi, Chattha Sangīti Edn. p. 133.

105. This is only a general rule. If the invitation is limited by the donor in respect of medicine or time or both, the limitations must be observed. Pācittiya Pāḷi, Chattha Sangīti Edn. p. 138.

51. Drinking intoxicants[106] is a *Pācittiya* offence.
52. Tickling another monk[107] with fingers is a *Pācittiya* offence.
53. Playing in water is a *Pācittiya* offence.
54. Disrespect[108] is a *Pācittiya* offence.
55. A monk who startles or attempts to startle[109] another monk, commits a *Pācittiya* offence.
56. If a monk who is not ill kindles a fire or causes a fire to be kindled as he wants to warm himself and without any other reason,[110] he commits a *Pācittiya* offence.
57. A monk who bathes at intervals of less than half a month, except on suitable occasions, commits a *Pācittiya* offence.

    This is a suitable occasion in this case: (1) When it is the hot season, i.e., the last one and a half months of summer. (2) When it is hot (and humid) i.e. the first month of the rainy season. (3) When the monk is sick. (4) When the monk has done some work. (5) When the monk is travelling.[111] and (6) When there is storm or rain.[112]
58. A monk who gets a new[113] robe must use one of the three means of disfigurement[114]—dark green, muddy or black (or black and gold).

---

106. It does not make any difference even if (1) the quantity is as small as a drop on the of a blade of grass and (2) the monk drinks it as he thinks that it is not an intoxicant. Pācittiya Pāḷi, Chattha Sangīti Edn. p. 146.

107. Pācittiya Pāḷi, Chattha Sangīti Edn. p. 147.

108. Disrespect may be:
    (1) to a monk who speaks to him according to the Rules of *Vinaya* or
    (2) to the Rules themselves.

109. If the monk does anything wishing to startle the other monk, it will not make any difference even though the other monk is not startled. Pācittiya Pāḷi, Chattha Sangīti Edn. p. 151.

110. E.g. to take a bowl. Pācittādi Atthakathā, Chattha Sangīti Edn. p. 130.

111. He can bathe when he is about to travel or is travelling and when he has just arrived at his destination. Pācittiya Pāḷi, Chattha Sangīti Edn. p. 157.

112. I.e., when the storm has raised dust. Ib.

113. A robe which really is an old one, e.g., having been worn by a novice, is a new one for the purpose of this Rule if it has not been "disfigured".

114. "Disfigurement" is not of the whole robe but only of one, two, three or four corners thereof. Only one circular dot, about the size of a peacock's eye, should be made at a corner. Pācityādi Atthakathā, Chattha Sangīti Edn. p. 131.

If he uses a new robe without having applied any of those three means disfigurements, he commits a *Pācittiya* offence.[115]

59. If a monk who has himself given or assigned[116] a robe to a monk, an ordained nun or a novice uses it again without its having been given back to him and otherwise than as an intimate friend, he commits a *Pācittiya* offence.
60. A monk who hides or causes to be hidden another monk's bowl or robe or seat rug or needle case or girdle, even for fun, commits a *Pācittiya* offence.
61. A monk who knowingly and intentionally deprives any living being[117] of life, commits a *Pācittiya* offence.
62. A monk who knowingly makes use of water which contains insects, commits a *Pācittiya* offence.
63. A monk who knowingly reagitates a dispute which has been sett!ed according to the Dhamma commits a *Pācittiya* offence.
64. A monk who knowingly conceals another monk's disgusting offence[118] commits a *Pācittiya* offence.
65. If a monk knowingly ordains as a monk a person who is below twenty years of age, that person remains unordained (does not become a monk), other monks who take part are blameworthy[119] and that monk commits a *Pācittiya* offence.
66. A monk who knowingly makes arrangements with thieving merchants[120] and goes along the same road with them - even to a neighbouring village, commits a *Pācittiya* offence.
67. A monk who makes arrangements with a woman and goes together with her along the same road, even to a neighbouring village, commits a *Pācittiya* offence.

---

115. This rule was made in connection with a case in which monks and *Paribbājakas* who were travelling together, had been robbed of their robes and the monks were subsequently unable to identify their robes. Pācittiya Pāḷi, Chattha Sangīti Edn. p. 158.
116. I.e., having asked a third person to hand it over to a donee. Pācittiya Pāḷi, Chattha Sangīti Edn. p. 161.
117. I.e., other than a human being, since murder is a *Pārājika* offence.
118. i.e, a *Pārājika* offence or a Saṅghādisesa Offence. Pācittiya Pāḷi, Chattha Sangīti Edn. p. 168.
119. I.e. they commit a *dukkata* offence. Pācittiya Pāḷi, Chattha Sangīti Edn. p. 171.
120. I.e., merchants who have stolen or are about to steal government property or who are going to defraud government of its property or who are going to evade payment of taxes and duties. Pācittiya Pāḷi, Chattha Sangīti Edn. p. 172 and Pācityadi Atthakatta same Ed. p. 137.

68. If a monk says, "The things (*dhammas*) which the Buddha has declared to be obstructions[121] are not capable of obstructing one who has committed them (or is subject to them). I know that the Buddha has taught so," he should be told by the monks. "Sir, do not say so. Do not accuse the Buddha of having taught so. Accusation of the Buddha is not good. The Buddha surely could not have taught so. The Buddha has, in more ways than one, declared the obstructive things to be obstructions: and they really are capable of obstructing one."

    If he persists in holding the view, in spite of the monks telling him so, the monks should admonish him—up to three times—to give it up.

    If he gives it up when he is admonished up to three times, that is well and good.

    If he does not give it up, he commits a *Pācittiya* offence.

69. If a monk knowingly (1) associates with, in teaching the Dhamma or its Commentaries, (2) associates in reciting the *Pātimokkha* in the *Pāvarana*, or in any other affair of the Saṅgha, with or (3) lies down under the same roof with the monk,[122] who holds that view and who has not expiated the offence and given up the view, he commits a *Pācittiya* offence.

70. If a novice also says, "The things (*Dhammas*) which the Buddha has declared to be obstructions, are not capable of obstructing one who has committed them (or is subject to them.) I know that the Buddha has taught so," that novice should be told by the monks, "Novice, Sir, do not say so.

---

121. To rebirth in the *Devaloka* and attainment of *jhāna, magga, phala* and Nibbāna. There are five kinds of Obstruction:

(1) *Kamma* i.e., five evil deeds:

(a) Matricide, (b) Patricide, (c) Murdering an *Arahat*, (d) Act of extravasating the blood of the Buddha, (c) Causing a schism among monks.

(2) *Vipāka* – Consequence of evil deeds, e.g., being an animal a eunuch or a hermaphrodite, being born blind or dumb. (This, however, is not an obstruction to being born in the Devaloka.)

(3) *Kilesa* – i.e., holding one of the three wrong views which reject cause or effect or both, namely: (a) *Natthika*, (b) *Ahetuka* and (c) *Akiriya*.

(4) *Ariyapavāda* – i.e., wrong accusation or talking ill of Arahats. (This, however, is an obstruction only till pardon is asked for.)

(5) *Anavitikkama* – i.e. (in the case of monks) contravention of the Vinaya Rules. (*Pārājika* offence is an obstacle only so long as the offender continues to live in the Order; and the other offences can be expiated as provided in the Rules). See Pācityadi Atthakatta same Ed. p. 138.

122. Pācittiya Pāḷi, Chattha Saṅgīti Edn. p. 180.

Do not accuse the Buddha of having taught so. Accusation of the Buddha is not good. The Buddha surely could not have taught so. The Buddha has in more ways than one declared obstructive things to be obstructions; and they really are capable of obstructing one." If that novice persists in holding the view in spite of the monks telling him so, he should be told by the monks, "Novice, from this day forth you must not point out the Buddha as your Teacher; and you do not have the privilege, that other novices have, of sleeping under the same roof with monks for two or three nights. Go unwanted novice, and be ruined."[123]

A monk who knowingly:

(1) encourages[124] a novice who has been so ruined or

(2) allows such a novice to attend on him or

(3) gives him, or accepts from him, anything, or teaches him or makes him learn or

(4) lies down under the same roof with him, commits a *Pācittiya* offence.

71) If, on being admonished by the monks with reference to a rule of *Vinaya*, a monk says, "Sir, I shall not observe this rule till I have asked another monk who is experienced and learned in the Rules of *Vinaya*,"[125] he commits a *Pācittiya* offence.

A monk, who means to observe the Rules, should know the Rules, and should ask about and think over them. This is the proper procedure in the matter.

72) While the *Pāṭimokkha* is being recited if a monk disparages the rules saying, "What is the use of reciting these minor and more minor rules[126] which merely cause worry, distress and vexation," he commits a *Pācittiya* offence.

---

123. There are three kinds of ruin namely:

(1) *Samvasanasana*, i.e., loss of association,

(2) *Linganasana*, i.e., loss of the status of a novice and (3) *Dandakammanasana* i.e. forfeiture by way of punishment of the privilege to point the Buddha out as one's Teacher. The ruin prescribed in this rule is the third kind of ruin only. Pācittiya Atthakatta, Chattha Sangīti Edn. same Ed. p. 140.

124. Eg. Telling a novice that he would give him a bowl or a robe or that he would teach him the Dhamma and its commentaries. Pācittiya Pali, Chattha Sangiti Edn. p. 184.

125. A monk may say so just to evade Rule 54 above Pātimokkhamedini p. 381.

126. I.e., Rules relating to lesser offences.

73) If a monk, having contravened a rule,[127] says, while the *Pāṭimokkha* is being recited half monthly, "Only now do I know that this Rule also is set out and contained in the *Pāṭimokkha* and that it comes up for recitation every half month" and if other monks know about that monk, "This monk has sat down two or three times previously, while the *Pāṭimokkha* was being recited," not to say more often, there, for that monk, is no freedom from faults by reason of his pretended ignorance.

He should be required to act in accordance with the Rules of *Vinaya* for expiation of the offence which he has committed by contravening the Rule. Furthermore, his foolishness should be brought home to him saying "No gain[128] for you! No benefit from what you have acquired![129] Because you did not follow well, with respect and attention while the *Pāṭimokkha* was being recited."

Pretending further ignorance (after this)[130] is a *Pācittiya* offence.

74) A monk who being angry or displeased, hits another monk commits a *Pācittiya* offence.

75) A monk who being angry or displeased raises the palm of his hand to strike another monk, commits a *Pācittiya* offence.

76) A monk who accuses another monk with an unfounded charge of a *Saṅghādisesa* offence, commits a *Pācittiya* offence.

77) A monk who knowingly and intentionally arouses worry[131] in the mind of another monk with the object, "This will be unhappiness for him for at least a moment," for this reason only and for no other reason, commits a *Pācittiya* offence.

78) If a monk stands eavesdropping where he can hear monks who are quarrelling, disputing and arguing with each other with the object

---

127. Pācittiya Pali, Chattha Sangiti Edn. p. 190.

128. He would have gained knowledge of the Rules and merit for the *Saṃsāra* if he had been attentive while the Pāṭimokkha was being recited. Pāṭimokkha-Medinī pp. 455–456.

129. He has not derived full benefit from manhood and monkhood both of which he has acquired although they are so difficult to acquire. (Ibid p. 456)

130. Pretense of ignorance before such formal admonition is only a *dukkata* offence. Pācittiya Pali, Chattha Sangiti Edn. p. 191.

131. Eg. Telling him that he was ordained when he was less than twenty years of age and thereby making him worry as to whether his ordination was valid or not. Pācittiya Pali, Chattha Sangiti Edn. p. 195.

"I will hear what they say"—for that reason only, and not for any other reason,[132] he commits a *Pācittiya* offence.

79) A monk who having given consent to acts which are in accordance with the Rules of *Vinaya*, subsequently criticises them commits a *Pācittiya* offence.

80) A monk who while the Saṅgha is discussing how to decide a case (or a question) gets up from his seat and goes away without giving his consent,[133] commits a *Pācittiya* offence.

81) A monk who having given a robe together with other monks who are living harmoniously within the jurisdiction of the same *Sīma* (ordination hall),[134] subsequently criticises them saying, "The monks have disposed of the property of the Order in accordance with favouritism" commits a *Pācittiya* offence.

82) A monk who knowingly causes diversion of any offering from the Saṅgha to any individual, commits a *Pācittiya* offence.

83) A monk who crosses the threshold of the sleeping chamber of an anointed *Khattiya* king, from which the king has not gone out and the queen has not withdrawn, without previous intimation, commits a *Pācittiya* offence.

84) A monk who picks up or causes to be picked up any treasure or anything which is regarded as treasure,[135] within the precincts of a monastery or within the precincts of a building in which he is staying—commits a *Pācittiya* offence.

A monk who has picked up or caused to be picked up any treasure or anything which is regarded as treasure within the precincts of a monastery or within the precincts of the building where he is staying, should keep it with the intention, "He whose property it is will take it." This is the right course in such a case.

85) A monk, who goes into a village after noon and before dawn, without informing another monk who is present, commits a *Pācittiya* offence, unless there is something urgent to be done.[136]

---

132. Eg. With a view to stopping the quarrel or settling the dispute. Pācittiya Pali, Chattha Sangiti Edn. p. 198.

133. I.e. in order that the remaining monks may not be able to decide it. Eg. For want of a quorum. Pācittiya Pali, Chattha Sangiti Edn. p. 201.

134. Pācittiya Pali, Chattha Sangiti Edn. p. 272

135. Things which are regarded as treasure include all things; which are used by human beings. Pācittiya Pali, Chattha Sangiti Edn. p. 212.

136. Cp. Rule 46 which relates to going into the village after dawn and before noon.

86) A monk, who makes[137] a needle case or causes a needle case to be made of bone, ivory or horn, commits a *Bhedana Pācittiya* i.e., a *Pācittiya* offence which can be expiated only after the needle case has been broken.[138]

87) A monk who is making[139] or causing to be made a new couch or chair, should make it or cause it to be made with legs which are eight *sugata* finger breadths[140] in height excluding (i.e., up to) the lower edge of the frame.

If he exceeds that limit, he commits a *Chedanaka*[141] *Pācittiya* offence (i.e., a *Pācittiya* offence which can be expiated only after cutting it down to proper size).

88) A monk who makes or cause to be made a couch or a chair stuffed with *tūla*[142] commits an *Uddhālanaka Pācittiya* offence (i.e., a *Pācittiya* offence which can be expiated only after the stuff has been taken out).

89) A monk who is making or causing to be made a loin-cloth with fringe[143] should make it of a reasonable size. This is the reasonable size: In length, two *sugata* spans; in width, one and a half spans; a fringe of one span.

If he exceeds those limits, he commits a *Chedanaka Pācittiya* offence.

90) A monk who is making,[144] or causing to be made a piece of cloth to cover[145] skin diseases should make it of reasonable size. This is the reasonable size here: In length, four *sugata* spans; in width, two spans.

If he exceeds those limits, he commits a *Chedanaka Pācittiya* offence.

91) A monk in making[146] or causing to be made a cloth for the rainy season, should make it of reasonable size. This is the reasonable size here: In length, six *sugata* spans and in breadth, two and a half spans.

If he exceeds those limits, he commits a *Chedanaka Pācittiya* offence.

---

137. Pācittiya Pali, Chattha Sangiti Edn. p. 217.

138. Pāṭimokkhamedinī p. 480.

139. Pācittiya Pali, Chattha Sangiti Edn. p. 219.

140. Pāṭimokkhamedinī p. 482.

141. Pāṭimokkhamedinī p. 412.

142. Tūla is of three kinds viz:

1) Produced by trees and plants (eg. Cotton); 2) Produced by creepers and 3) Produced by a kind of grass. Pācittiya Pali, Chattha Sangiti Edn. p. 220.

143. Pācittiya Pali, Chattha Sangiti Edn. p. 222.

144. Pācittiya Pali, Chattha Sangiti Edn. p. 223.

145. This cloth is to cover skin disease and bleeding boils between the navel and the knees. Ibid. 223.

146. Pācittiya Pali, Chattha Sangiti Edn. p. 224.

92) A monk who makes[147] or causes to be made for himself a robe, which is of the size of the Buddha's robe or larger, commits a *Chedanaka Pācittiya* offence.

This is the size of the Buddha's robe: In length nine *sugata* spans, in breadth six spans. This is the size of the Buddha's robe

VI. PĀTIDESANIYA OFFENCES

1. If a monk accepts any food, hard or soft, from the hands of an ordained nun who has gone into a village and who is not related to him and chews or eats it, he should confess saying, "Sir, I have committed a blameworthy and unbecoming offence which must be confessed separately. I confess it."
2. Only invited monks have meals in the houses of families.[148] There an ordained nun stands saying, "Give curry here; give rice here" as if through favouritism.[149] She should be rebuked by those monks saying, "Keep away, Sister, while the monks eat."

   If even one of the monks does not say, "Keep away, Sister, while the monks eat," to rebuke her, all the monks should confess saying, "Sir, we have committed a blame worthy and unbecoming offence, which must be confessed separately. We confess it."
3. There are families which have been declared[150] to be *Sekkha* families.[151] If a monk, who has not been invited in advance[152] and who is not ill, accepts food, hard or soft, with his own hands, from such families and chews or eats it, he should confess saying, "Sir, I have committed a blameworthy and unbecoming offence, which must be confessed separately. I confess it."
4. There are such jungle lodgings as are regarded as insecure and dangerous.[153]

   If a monk, without having informed the donor beforehand of the lodgings being insecure or dangerous,[154] accepts food, hard or soft, within the precincts of such lodgings with his own hands and, although he is not

147. Pācittiya Pali, Chattha Sangiti Edn. p. 226.
148. Pācittiya Pali, Chattha Sangiti Edn. 2, p. 30.
149. Ibid.
150. I.e. by a formal declaration of the Saṅgha. Pācittiya Pali, Chattha Sangiti Edn. p. 233.
151. I.e. families with increasing generosity and decreasing financial position. Ibid.
152. Because there was a case of such a family having to go without a meal after offering a meal to an uninvited monk. Ibid. p. 231.
153. I.e. on account of thieves and robbers. Pācittiya Pali, Chattha Sangiti Edn. p. 236.
154. Ibid. 236.

ill, chews or eats it, he should confess[155] saying, "Sir, I have committed a blameworthy and unbecoming offence which must be confessed separately. I confess it."

VII. ADHIKARANASAMATHA DHAMMA

Seven Ways of Settling Disputes

For settlement of disputes which arise from time to time,

(1) *Sammukhā Vinaya* should be given;
(2) *Sati Vinaya* should be given;[156]
(3) *Amuḷha Vinaya* should be given;
(4) *Patiññāta karan* – Decision should be given according to confession;
(5) *Yebhuyyāsika kamma* – Decision should be given according to the vote of the majority;
(6) *Tassapāpiyāsikā kamma* should be performed;
(7) *Tiṇavatthāraka kamma* should be performed.

APPENDIX ON DISPUTES

There are four kinds of disputes, namely:

1. Vivādādhikarana – Disputes as to what is *dhamma*, what is not *dhamma*, what is *vinaya*, what is not *vinaya*, what the Buddha said, what the Buddha did not say, what is an offence, what is not an offence etc.
2. *Anuvādādhikarana* – Disputes (arising from accusations) as to whether a monk has fallen off or deviated from virtue, right practice, right view and right livelihood.
3. *Āpatāidhikarana* – Disputes (arising from accusations) as to whether a monk has contravened a Rule of *vinaya*.
4. *Kiccādhikarana* – Disputes with reference to the acts (or decisions) of the Saṅgha. Cūḷavagga Pāḷi, Chattha Sangīti Edn. pp. 211–212, and 220.

---

155. Because there was a case in which donors who brought meals to such a lodging in ignorance of the risk they were running were robbed on the way. Ibid. p. 235.
156. See Appendix on Ways of Settling Disputes.

APPENDIX ON WAYS OF SETTLING DISPUTES

1. "*Sammukhā Vinaya should be given*"—The monks should give a decision in accordance with the Rules of *vinaya* after making an inquiry to ascertain the facts in the presence of both parties.

A monk who performs any of the following acts, which involve decisions against another monk in his absence, commits a *Dukkata*[157] offence:

(a) *Tajjanīya kamma.*
(b) *Niyassa kamma.*
(c) *Pabbājanīya kamma.*
(d) *Patisāraniya kamma.*
(e) *Ukkhepaniya kamma.*

(a) *Tajjanīya kamma* is a decision by which the monks censure a monk in order that he may exercise self-control and abstain from contravening the Rules of vinaya in future.

(b) *Niyassa kamma* is a decision by which the monks advise a monk "to live depending on a teacher."

(c) *Pabbājaniya Kamma* is a decision by which the monks expel a monk from a place. (Cūḷavagga Pāḷi, Chattha Sangiti Edn. p. 28.)

(d) *Paṭisaraniya Kamma* is a decision by which the monks direct a monk to ask for pardon of a person whom he has offended. (Cūḷavagga Pāḷi, Chattha Sangiti Edn. p. 40.)

(e) *Ukkhepaniya Kamma* is a decision by which the monks declare that no monk should give anything to the monk against whom the declaration is made, accept anything from him, teach him anything or learn anything from him. Such a declaration is made when the monks find after due inquiry:

i) that a monk who has committed an offence does not regard it as such, or
ii) that a monk who has committed an offence has not taken any step to expiate it, or
iii) that a monk will not give up the wrong view e.g., that the Buddha did say what He did not say or that the Buddha did not say what He actually said. (Cūḷavagga Pāḷi, Chattha Sangiti Bein. p. 48.)

The monks can revoke a decision in (a), (b), (c), (d), or (e) by a subsequent declaration at the request of the monk concerned, if they are

157. Cūḷavagga Pāḷi, Chattha Sangīti Edn. p. 188.

satisfied that he has been penitent and that he has done the proper thing e.g., (1) that he has lived with a teacher and learnt the scriptures if the decision to be revoked is a *Niyassa Kamma*, (2) that he has asked pardon of the person whom he offended and the latter has pardoned him, if the decision to be revoked is a *Paṭisaraniya Kamma* or (3) that he has given up the wrong view, if the decision to be revoked is an *Ukkhepaniya Kamma* for not giving up that view.

However, before the decision is revoked, he must not (1) ordain any one as a monk, (2) act as a teacher of any monk, (3) allow any novice to attend on him, (4) accept nomination to give advice to nuns, and (5) must not advise them.

The monks cannot revoke a decision if he has, after that decision, (1) repeated the offence, (2) committed a similar offence, (3) committed a graver offence, (4) criticised the decision or (5) criticised the monks who gave the decision. (Cūḷavagga Pāḷi, Chatta Sangiti Edn. pp. 11, 21, 35, 46, 55, 66 and 77.)

2. If an *Arahat*, who has been accused of an offence and found by the monks after due inquiry to be innocent, and who has abundant caution, asks for a *Sativinaya*, it should be given to him. It is a declaration which will serve as a reminder to prevent all further accusations of the same offence. (Cūḷavagga Pāḷi, Chattha Sangiti Edn. p. 197.)
3. *Amuḷha Vinaya* is a declaration by the monks that another monk, who has been charged with contravention of a Rule of *vinaya* is unable to recollect it not because he is stupid but because he was insane at the time of contravening the rule. (Cūḷavagga Pāḷi, Chattha Sangiti Edn. p. 200.)
4. *Tassapāpiyāsika Kamma* is a declaration of "his being very bad" as, for instance, a monk has, in the course of his trial, confessed and retracted his confession, evaded questions and told conscious lies. (Cūḷavagga Pāḷi, Chattha Sangiti Edn, p. 205.)

   The declaration is made as the monk, if virtuous, would do the proper thing and get peace and, if bad, would remain "ruined" in that manner. (Cūḷavagga Atthakatha, Chattha Sangiti Edn. p. 43.)

   He would remain "ruined" as the other monks would not have anything to do with him. (Cūḷavagga-nissaya, Hanthawaddy, p. 48.)
5. *Tinavatthāraka Kamma*—i.e., "The act of covering up with grass."—It should be performed when the parties of monks, who have been quarrelling, disputing and arguing with each other, feel (1) that they have

said and done many things, which are unbecoming to monks, (2) that their controversy would become rough, frightful and disrupting if they were to accuse one another of contraventions of the Rules of *vinaya* and (3) that contraventions (if any) of the Rules should be covered up—(i.e., forgiven and forgotten) in the interests of all concerned. It has the effect of exonerating the offences of all monks who perform it except the offences of *Pārājika*, *Sanghādisesa* and offences in connection with laymen and laywomen. (Cūḷavagga Pāḷi, Chattha Sangiti Edn. pp. 235–237 and its Atthakatha, same Edn. p. 38.)

APPENDIX ON DISPUTES AND THE RESPECTIVE WAYS OF SETTLING THEM

1) *Vivādādhikarana* should be settled by (a) *Sammukhāvinaya* and (b) *Yebhuyyasika*.
2) *Anuvādādhikarana* should be settled by (a) *Sammukhāvinaya*, (b) *Sativinaya*, (c) *Amuḷhavinaya* and (d) *Tassapāpiyāsika*.
3) *Āpattādhikarana* should be settled by (a) Sammukhāvinaya, (b) *Paṭiññāta-karana* and (c) *Tinavatthāraka*.
4) *Kiccādhikarana* should be settled by *Sammukhāvinaya*. (Parivara Pāḷi, Chattha Sangiti Edn. p. 195.)

APPENDIX ON VISSASAGAHA

Vissāsagaha—A thing may be taken by virtue of intimacy if the following five conditions are fulfilled:

1) Being a friend who has seen the owner;
2) Being a close friend who has eaten together with the owner;
3) Having been told by the owner "Take what you want of my property";
4) The owner being alive at the time of taking and
5) Knowledge that the owner will be pleased.

—Mahavagga, Chattha Sangiti Edn. p. and its Commentary same Edn. p. 410.

APPENDIX ON ADHIMĀNA

Adhimāna is the delusion occurring to those people who misconceive themselves to have attained *jhāna*, *magga* and *phala*.

Such delusion occurs not to those foolish and ignorant persons who strive for worldly pleasures and not to the noble disciples. To a *Sotāpanna* the delusion that 'I am a *Sakadāgāmi*', does not occur. To a *Sakadāgāmi* the delusion that 'I am an *Anāgāmi'*, does not occur. To an *Anāgāmi*, the delusion that 'I am an *Arahat'* does not occur.

Such delusion occurs to one who discards *kilesas* by means of *samatha* or *vipassanā*, who is always bent on meditation and practice and is strenuous.

To one who does not perceive the arising of *kilesas* which he dispels by means of *samatha* or *vipassanā* the delusion such as 'I am a *Sotāpanna, Sakadāgāmi, Anāgāmi* or *Arahatta'* appears.

—*Majjhima Nikāya, Mūlapaññāsaṭṭhakatha,* (*1*) *Mūlapariyāya-Vagga,* (*8*) *Sallekha-Sutta vaṇṇanā*, p. 187.

FORMULA FOR A BHIKKHU

Any layman who wishes to become a monk (*bhikkhu*) has first to be initiated as a *samaṇera*. Having become a novice, he approaches his preceptor who points out his requisites and asks him to go apart from the assembled Order.

Then a monk who is given the authority by the Order to instruct him goes to him and says, "Now, listen to me. This is the time for you to speak the truth. When asked by the monks in the midst of the Order, you admit if there is any obstacle to your becoming a monk. If you are free from all obstacles, you say 'No'. Don't get confused and don't be at a loss. They will ask you in this way. 'Have you such diseases as leprosy, boils, eczema, consumption, epilepsy? Are you a human being? Are you a male? Are you a free man (not a slave or servant)? Are you free from debt? Are you free from government service? Have you your parents' consent? Have you attained the age of 20 years? Have you a full set of bowl and robes? What is your name, and what is your preceptor's name?'" Having instructed him the monk comes back to the assembled Order and says, "Revered Sirs please listen to me. Such and such a one wishes to be ordained as a *bhikkhu*. He has been instructed by me. If the Order deems fit let him come." The Order of the monks then says, "Come."

Now the *sāmaṇera* puts the upper robe on one shoulder, pays respect at the feet of the monks, squats on the floor and with palms together, requests ordination. "Revered Sirs, I ask you for ordination. Out of compassion for me, may you ordain me as a *bhikkhu*. For the second time, Revered Sirs, I ask you for ordination. For the third time, Revered Sirs, I ask you for ordination."

Then a wise and competent monk of the Order makes an announcement. "Revered Sirs, please listen to me. Such and such a novice of such and such a preceptor wishes to become a monk. If the Order of the monks deems it fit, I will question him as to obstacles." When the Order gives consent to do so, he asks the candidate in the same way as mentioned above. If the candidate has one of these obstacles, he is not to be ordained as a monk. But if he be free from all these obstacles, that monk announces his purity to the Order, "Revered Sirs, please listen to me. Such and such a candidate of such and such a preceptor wishes to become a monk. He is free from all the obstacles. He has a full set of bowl and robes. He asks for ordination through his preceptor. If the Order deems it fit, he should be ordained as a *bhikkhu*."

After this announcement, he makes a declaration three times in this way.

"Revered Sirs, please listen to me. Such and such a candidate of such and such a preceptor wishes to become a *bhikkhu*. He is free from all the obstacles, and he has a full set of bowl and robes. He asks for ordination through his preceptor and that the Order make him a monk. He who agrees to this may remain silent; but he who does not agree may speak out his own opinion. If there is no objection raised by the monks, the novice becomes a *bhikkhu* at the end of the third declaration."

As soon as he becomes a *bhikkhu*, the shadow should be measured (in order to know the time), the season, the portion of the day (whether morning, afternoon or evening), and the date should be explained to him (so that he may note the date and time of his monkhood).

Four Nissayas (Requisites)

He has four requisites to rely on. They are:

(1) As a monk he has to depend on the food acquired on his almsround. He should exert himself in this wise as long as he is in the Order. Exceptions are, a meal for the Order, a meal for a certain monk, a meal by invitation, (*salāka bhotta*) a meal by assignment, food offered on a waxing or waning day of the moon, on a fast day, and on the day after the fast day.

(2) As a monk he has to depend on robes made from discarded clothes. He should exert himself in this wise as long as he is in the Order. Exceptions are, robes made of linen, cotton, silk, wool coarse hemp or a mixture of any of these.

(3) As a monk he has to depend on living at the foot of a tree. He should exert himself in this wise as long as he is in the Order. Exceptions are, a

monastery, a building with a gable roof, a storied building, a flat-roofed building or a cave.

(4) As a monk he has to depend on cattle urine for medicine. He should exert himself in this wise as long as he is in the Order. Exceptions are ghee, butter, oil, honey and molasses.

Four Akaraniya Kammas

There are four acts (*Akaraniya Kammas*) which are not to be performed by a bhikkhu. They are:

(1) A monk shall not indulge in any kind of sexual intercourse. If he so indulges, he is no longer a monk, no longer a son of the *Sakyamuni*. Just as a man who has been beheaded is unable to be alive again, so also a monk who indulges in sexual intercourse can never be a monk, son of the *Sakyamuni*. Indulgence in sexual intercourse must be avoided throughout his life.

(2) He who has become a monk, shall not take what has not been given to him, with intention of stealing, even as much as a blade of grass, a quarter of a *Kahāpana*[158] or a thing worth that amount, or more than that. If he does so he is no longer a monk, no longer a son of the *Sakyamuni*. Just as a leaf which has f alien from its stalk can never become green, even so a monk who takes., with the intention of stealing, a quarter of a *Kahāpana* or a thing worth that amount or more than that, can never become a monk, son of the *Sakyamuni*.

This must be avoided throughout his life.

(3) He who has become a monk shall not intentionally deprive a being of life. He who intentionally deprives a human being of life, including the causing of abortion, is no longer a monk, no longer a son of the *Sakyamuni*.

Just as a big stone which has broken can never be joined again, so also, he who deprives a human being of life intentionally, can never become a monk, son of the *Sakyamuni*.

This must be avoided throughout his life.

(4) He who has become a monk shall not boast with reference to himself, of clear knowledge and insight; he should not even say, "I take delight in seclusion." He who, with evil intention and being overwhelmed by it, boasts with reference to himself, of clear knowledge and insight, of

158. A coin of ancient India.

overcoming defilements, concentration, attainment of *jhānas*, enjoyment of Paths and Fruitions without having attained them, is no longer a monk, no longer a son of the *Sakyamuni*.

Just as a palm tree with its top cut off can never grow again, so also, he who, with evil intention and being overwhelmed by it, boasts with reference to himself, of clear knowledge and insight without having such knowledge is no longer a monk, no longer a son of the *Sakyamuni*.

This boasting must be avoided throughout his life.

"This is reckoned to be lamentation in the discipline of the Noble, namely, singing. This is reckoned as causing madness in the discipline of the Noble, namely, dancing. This is reckoned as childishness in the discipline of the Noble, namely, immoderate laughter that displays the teeth."

—*Anguttara Nikāya*, Book of the Threes

Index

Symbols

(*maraṇa*), death 329
(*middha*), torpor 232
(*saṃvega*) get alarmed 239

A

a danger to your own selves 4
abandonment
  a long time 245
  by deliverance 245
  by tranquillization 245
  temporarily 245
ābhassara plane (plane of radiant Brahmā) 17
abides in the third Jhāna 36, 78, 112
absolutely agreeable 30, 50
abstained from unchastity 5, 66, 99
achieved Freedom through detachment 16, 21, 23, 27, 28, 29, 31, 32, 33, 35, 37, 38
acrobatic feats 7, 68, 101
actions, bodily, verbal and mental 118, 171, 175
active arguers 25
addicted to logic and investigating things 16, 20, 23, 28
adhimāna 365, 376, 394
adidcca samuppanna vāda (Beliefs that things arise without a cause) 27
  First View 27
  Second View 28
admit 34, 395
  the fact as right 4
admitted into an Order 63, 64
adopted son of Abhaya 53, 153, 156
adorning and beautifying themselves 9, 69, 103
advance their arguments 14, 29, 37, 38, 40, 42
advantages of a samaṇa's life 53, 65, 79, 80, 81
affirm 24
after death, is not subject to decay and is neither percipient nor impercipient 32, 51
aggimukha serpent 201
Ajātasattu, King of Magadha, son of Queen Videha 63, 64
Ajātasattu's Conversion 86
Ajita Kesakambala's Vew 58
  of the garment of hair 58
ākāsānañcāyatana Brahmā plane 34
ākiñcaññāyatana Brahma plane 34
akiriya-diṭṭhi 269, 272
akkhaṃ (games with balls of all sizes) 8, 68, 102
akkhānaṃ (telling stories with a mingling of doggerel and rhymes) 7, 68, 101
akkharikaṃ (a game where one has to find out the missing letter or letters) 8, 68, 102
all-seeing 18
altruistic joy 154, 159
amarāvikkhepa-vāda (Eel-wriggling) 24, 49
  First View 24
  Second View 24
  Third View 25
  Fourth View 26
ambalatthikā garden 3
ambana 265
ambaṭṭha 88, 89, 90, 91, 92
ambiguously give evasive replies in four ways 41
analytical knowledge (*paṭisambhidā*) 237, 241

Ānanda 43, 157, 165, 166, 169, 243, 285, 286, 287, 288
ānāpānassati (watching over in-and-out-breathing) 159
Anāthapiṇḍika at Sāvatthi 167, 283, 304
anattā: not-self 187
ancestor 92, 93, 94, 95
angry and hurt 4
anicca-saññā (contemplation of impermanence) 159
aniyata 369
annihilation 33, 35, 40, 41, 45, 51, 59, 145, 331
annihilationists 33, 35, 40, 41, 51
answer ambiguously and evasively 26
 equivocally and evasively 24, 25, 26, 49
antānanta vāda 21, 22, 23
 First View 22
 Second View 22
 Third View 22
 Fourth View 23
Anuruddha 157, 296, 297, 298, 299, 301
anusaya (inherent tendency) 150
apannaṭṭhika-bhāva (Nibbāna) 43
aparantakappika (Speculators on the Future) 29
 (Belonging to the Future) 50
apāya (the 4 Lower worlds) 165
appaṇihita-phassa (Contact with Freedom from Desire) 149
application of mindfulness 143, 270, 271, 272
appointed seat 3
arahat 88, 89, 141, 152, 197, 201, 203, 207, 286, 287, 288, 384, 392, 394
arahatship 86, 119, 120, 151, 169, 170, 189, 206, 244, 288, 301
ariya magga, the Noble Path 241
arūpa jhānas 171, 175
as a bird flies anywhere freely 75, 108
asaññi-vāda (8 views) 45
āsavas 85, 86, 119, 120, 249, 292
Ascetic Tissa 326
as the wriggling of eels 26
asubha bhāvanā 243, 246
asubhakammaṭṭhāna (reflections on the loathsomeness of the body) 159
attā and the *saññā* (perception after death) 30
attā and the world are partly eternal and partly not 17, 19, 20, 21, 39
attā and the world arise without a cause 27
attā breaks off and is destroyed 34, 35
attained the earthly Nibbāna 36
attainments (*samāpatti*) 241, 242, 256
attains Mindfulness and Clearness of Comprehension 65, 99
attain the highest earthly Nibbāna 36
attā – in the sense of a permanent unchanging entity 15
attā possessing the five sensuous pleasures fully enjoys them 35
attā (soul) 146, 167, 191
aṭṭhaka 123, 296
aṭṭhakathā (meaning) 239
 loke samaṇā-brāhmaṇā 46
 paro loko 46
 sattā opapātikā 46
 sukata dukkhaṭānaṃ kammānaṃ phalaṃ vipāko 46
aṭṭha padaṃ (games on chess boards or boards with eight rows of squares) 7
atthi mātā 46, 47
atthi pitā 46, 47
 dinnaṃ 47
 hutaṃ 47
 yiṭṭhaṃ 47
 has attained the earthly Nibbāna 36
 has attained the highest bliss in this life—the earthly Nibbāna 35
 is completely annihilated 33, 34
 is percipient 39, 41
avijjā (ignorance) 151, 292, 341
avijjānusaya (inherent tendency towards ignorance) 150, 151
avijjāsava (mental impurities of ignorance) 292
āyatana (bases) 186

B

bad effects of evil deeds 302
bamboo grove 145, 169
banaras at lsipatana in the Deer Park 187, 212
banishes sensual desire 75, 108
bank, other 205
becomes wearied of *rūpa* 189
being caught in a whirlpool 204, 205
beings that are born without the instrumentality of parents 26
belief that there exists no Perception after death 31
belief that there is earthly Nibbāna 37
be lifted up in mind 4
benefit 143, 195, 197, 219
betray you to the enemy 54
bhadda kappa 314
bhagavā 3, 4, 43, 44, 53, 62, 86, 87, 153, 154, 155, 156, 157, 162, 165, 167, 212, 296, 304
bhagga 296
bhavacakka (the vicious circle of existence) 349
bhava-taṇhā (craving for existence) 145, 214
bhavo (Through clinging "Volitional action and further existence") 341, 345
biases 85, 160, 301
Bimbisāra 312, 314, 315, 317
binds together those who are divided 5, 66, 100
birth (*jāti*) 328
blessed one 153, 210, 327
blowing through toy pipes made of leaves or papers 8, 68, 102
blue lotus 78, 112, 224, 226, 227
body-consciousness 181, 186, 332, 335, 343
born of Detachment 36, 77, 110, 339
boundary 22, 49
bows, toy 8
boxing 7, 68, 101
brahmacariya (practice of the Eightfold Path) 151
Brahmadatta, the youth 3
brahma-plane 158
Brahmā Sanañkumāra 98
break his word to the world 5, 66, 99
breaking up, the destruction, and the annihilation of a living being 33, 40, 41
breaks off and is destroyed on the dissolution of the body 33
bride or bridegroom 13, 73, 106
brief text (*uddesa*) 237
bring the four Applications of Mindfulness to full perfection 160, 161
Buddha 3
Buddha-Dhamma v, 296, 297, 299, 300, 301
Buddha Kassapa 314, 326
Buddha Phussa 312, 313, 314
burdens (*dūra*) 236
by means of zeal, earnestness, constant application, vigilance 14, 15

C

cakkavatin 224, 226
calling upon 53, 54
calm-development (*samatha-bhāvanā*) 253
calmness of the mind 251
caṇḍāla-vaṃsa-dhovanaṃ (acrobatic feats on the top of a hoisted bamboo pole) 7, 101
caraṇa (conduct) 98, 99, 111, 112
cūḷa-sīla (The Minor Morality) 99
carpets or coverlets 8, 69, 102
catusacca-sammā-diṭṭhi (4 kinds) 45
cause vexation 24, 25
causing physical injury to anyone 6, 67, 101
celestial being (*deva*) 256
celestial ear 82, 115
celestial eye 84, 117

cemetery 59, 75, 220, 243
cessation of suffering 128, 301, 340
cetovimutti 196, 197
chanda (intention) 24
change, not subject to 18
charms 11, 71, 72, 73, 105
  to understand the language of animals 72, 105
cheating with scales or coins or measures 6
cittalapabbata mahāvihāra 236
cittalapabbata tissatthera 243
citta (state of consciousness) 167
cleanses his mind from ill will 75
clear mind 261, 262
clever in argument 53
clinging 145, 146, 165, 166
cognises a mental object 74, 107, 133, 136, 196, 197
combats of elephants 7, 68, 101
compassion 75, 109, 154, 159
complete abandonment by destruction 245
completely annihilated 33, 34, 35
compounded things (*saṅkhāra*) 242
comprehensible only by the wise 14, 23, 27, 28, 29, 31, 32, 35, 37, 38
conceit (*māna*) 16, 21
concentration of mind 18, 19, 20, 22
conqueror 18, 90
consciousness 172, 173, 174, 177
  six kinds 178, (*viññāṇa*) 172
consciousness-group 168, 177, 348
consecrated place (*sīma*) 228, 230
constant application 14, 15, 18, 19, 20, 22, 27
constant meditation 65, 99
contact-three kinds
  Animmita-phassa 149
  Appaṇihita-phassa 149
  Suññata-phassa 149
contemplation 160
  of Sensation 274
  of the Body 160
  of the Mental Objects 161
  of the Mind 161
contented 296, 297, 298, 299
contented with robes 75, 108
continue after death 33, 34, 35
contradict 3, 4
controlled mind 257
conventional term 291
corporeality-group 145, 168, 177, 329
corporeality-perceptions 34
corrupt mind 261
covetousness and grief 74
cowherd 131, 137, 140
craving 16, 21, 23, 27, 28, 29, 31, 32, 35, 37, 38, 39, 40, 42, 43, 145, 146, 155, 158, 165, 166, 173, 174, 178, 211, 213, 214, 274, 294, 295, 331, 333, 334, 337, 341, 344
craving for existence (bhava-taṇhā) 213
creator 18
cruel thought 135
cūḷa sīla (The Minor Morality) 66
cultivating, loving-kindness 248
cunning ways of bribery, cheating and fraud 67, 101
cunning ways of bribery, cheating, and fraud 6
cymbals, *Vetālaṃ* (playing music by means of) 68

D

Damiḷha Devī 220
dāna (Almsgiving) 313, 314
dāna-kathaṃ (Discourse on Liberality) 127
danger is dispelled 284
dangers and enemies 284
dasavatthuka sammā-diṭṭhi 46
death (*maraṇa*) 328
decay and death 173
decay (*jarā*) 328
deduced by mere logic 14, 16, 23, 27, 28, 29, 31, 32, 33, 35, 37, 38
deer park at Isipatana 215, 216
deer park in Bhesakaḷa 296
defilements (*kilesa*) 229, 237
degraded to the lowest position 97, 98
degrades the Sākyas as lbbhās 92
dependent origination 42, 165
derogatory remarks 91
deserted village is a metaphor for the six somatic bases 200
desire-to-do and energy 271, 272
despair (*upāyāsa*) 330
destruction, and the annihilation of a living being 33, 35
destruction of life 5, 66, 99
Devadundubhi (a supernatural rumble) 12, 72, 106
deva planes 47
devas 19, 20, 43
dhamma 3
dhamma and *vinaya* 10
dhamma-eye 87
dhammakkhandhas 141, 142
dhamma-saññā 179, 291
dhammaṭṭhiti ñāṇa 171, 172
dhamma-vinaya (Teaching of the Buddha) 131, 178
dhamma-way 207, 208
dhātu (elements) 186
dibba-cakkhu 50
dice, Throwing 102
disā 93
disā-dāha ("sky-glow") 72, 106
discards the passion 173, 192
  know the ford 131, 133
disciplines himself in the rules 65
discursive thinking 77, 78, 110, 111, 148, 150
disputes 390, 391
dissolution of their bodies after death 84, 85, 117, 118
diṭṭhadhamma-nibbāna-vāda (5 views) 35, 45
diṭṭhi (wrong views) 16, 21, 23
divine ear 170, 174
doctrine and discipline (Dhamma Vinaya) 175
does not break his word to the world 5, 66, 99
does not dress the sore 131, 133, 138
  do most honour to them 144
  get rid of flies' eggs 131
  know the path 131, 139
  know whether water has been drunk 133
  make a smoke 142
  pay special honour 134
domanassa (Mentally Disagreeable Sensation or Grief) 151, 347
donee 319, 383
donor 144, 366, 390
dosa (hatred) 25, 154, 155
dress the sore 131, 135
drowsiness after meal 232, 233
dubbhagakaraṇaṃ (using charms to make people unhappy) 13, 73, 106
duggatiṃ (the four Woeful Courses of Existence 165
dukkha 47, 151, 350
dukkha nirodhagāmini paṭipadāya ñāṇaṃ 47
dukkha (pain) 347
dull and full of delusion 26
dullness of the mind 232, 233
dwells in equanimity 36, 78, 112, 339

E

ear-consciousness 181, 185, 332, 335
earned great merit 311, 319, 324
earnestness 14, 15, 18, 19, 20, 22, 27, 309, 319
earthly Nibbāna in this life 35, 36
Eastern Bamboo Forest 296, 301
ecstasy (*jhāna*) 233, 239
ehi bhikkhu 216
eighteen ways speculate on the past 39
eightfold noble path 159, 200, 203, 275
ekacca sassata vāda (First View) 17 (Second View) 19, (Third View) 19, (Fourth View) 20
element of cohesion 58, 200, 201
element of extension 58, 273, 343
element of motion 59, 273
eleven defects 131, 134
emancipation 16, 21, 23, 27, 28, 42, 141, 196, 197
end of the world 21, 39, 41, 49
enlightened and sublime 54
enlightened one is accomplished and worthy of offerings 88, 89
enlightened one, the exalted one 89, 98
enlightening verse (*obhāsa gāthā*) 243
enraptured in mind 162
equanimity 36, 37, 78, 79, 112, 151, 159, 297, 339, 340
equivocal and ambiguous reply 24, 25, 49
eternalists 15, 16, 19, 39
eternalists with regard to some 17, 21
eternity-belief 48
eternity-belief with regard to some 17, 19, 21
etymology 133, 136, 142
evasive answer 62, 94
even so I exist now 28
exalted 14, 16, 23, 27, 28, 29, 31, 32, 33, 35, 37, 38, 44, 128
exalted one 4, 65, 88, 89, 90, 91, 92, 93, 94, 95, 96, 98, 124, 125, 126, 127, 128, 131, 145, 146, 152, 165, 177, 182, 187, 189, 198, 204, 205, 206, 207, 208, 210, 211, 212, 215, 216, 260, 279, 285, 286, 287, 288, 313, 316, 317, 320
example of a farmer 64
example of freedom from ill will 76
example of freedom from restlessness and worry 76
example of freedom from sceptical doubt 76
example of freedom from sensual desire 75
example of freedom from torpor and languor 76
existence, *vaṭṭa* (rounds of) 255
exorcists 70, 104
experienced in the views maintained by others 25
extinction of *sakkāya* 146
extinction of suffering 273, 274
extinction of the *āsavas* 85, 119
eye-consciousness 181, 185, 332, 335
eye of wisdom 128

F

faithful and trustworthy 5, 66, 99
fall within the net of this Discourse 43
fearing and abhorring the speaking of falsehood 24, 25
feeding on *pīti* (rapture) 17
feel ill-will 4
feeling arising from body-contact 179
from ear-contact 178
from eye-contact 178, 183
from mind-contact 183
from nose-contact 183
from tongue-contact 183
feeling-group 177
feeling (*vedanā*) 172, 173, 191
filled with pleasure and gladness 4
finiteness and infinity of the world 21
finitude and infinitude of the world 22, 39, 41
first *jhāna* 36, 229, 241, 245, 339
first sermon 212, 314

first view 48
five constituent groups of existence 145, 146
five constituent groups of existence (form, feeling, perception, mental formations and consciousness) 192
five Mental Powers 158
five murderous enemies 199, 200, 201
five Spiritual Faculties 158
formula for a *bhikkhu* 394
formula for *sāmaṇera* 350
fortune telling 11, 71, 105
forty-four grounds 37
forty-four ways 29, 37, 40, 42
four analytical knowledge (*paṭisambhidā*) 241
four applications of mindfulness 134, 136, 143, 148, 158, 160
four carriers (with the bier as the fifth) 59
four causes of failure 120, 121, 122
fourfold *jhānas* 247
fourfold reflection 352
four great essentials 33, 58, 167
four great primaries 132, 135, 140, 178, 182, 343
four great root elements 79, 80, 113
four *nissayas* (requisites) 396
four noble truths 128, 177, 215, 216, 231
four realities or four great truths 46
four requisites—robe, food, lodging, and medicine 63, 64
four right efforts 148, 158
four roads to power 158
four serpents 201
four states of misery (*apāya*) 238
fourth *jhāna* 79, 112, 151, 297, 300
freed and the unfreed mind 170, 174
freedom 21, 28, 29, 171, 211, 386
freedom through detachment 29, 31, 32, 33, 35, 37
freedom through detachment as He has realized 38
frivolous talk 5, 66, 100, 302
full of miseries 36
full of solicitude for the welfare of all sentient beings 66
fully enlightened 54, 243
fulness of meaning in spirit and letter 88, 89
future existences 16, 21, 23

G

gāmantapabbhāravāsī mahāsivatthera 239
games and recreations 8, 68, 69, 101
games involving mimicry of deformities 8, 69, 102
games on chess boards 102
games somewhat akin to hopscotch 68, 102
games with balls of all sizes 8, 68
game where one has to find out the missing letter or letters 8, 68, 102
gandha-saññā 179, 184, 333, 336
ganges and jamuna 222
gavesī sutta 285
get rid of flies' eggs 131
getting rid of rudeness of speech 100
getting rid of slander 5
getting rid of the rudeness of speech 5
ghaṭikaṃ 8, 68
gītaṃ (singing of songs) 7, 67, 101
glad at heart, they exalted His word 44
glad to hear the Discourse 44
goal means 'Arahatta-phala' (Fruition of Holiness) 206
go forth from the household life into that of a recluse 18, 19, 20
golden crab 221, 222
'golden peacock' 221
granted them a boon 312
grasping (*upādāna*) 173
great brahmā 18
great reflections 296
'great river' is the metaphor for the four floods 202
greed (*rāga*) 151
grief (*domanassa*) 330
gross or subtle 172, 173, 189, 192
group of mental formations 168

guard his sense of sight 74, 107, 133
guessing others' thoughts 8
guttila, the harper 226

H

had never been formerly 28, 50
handicraft 280
happily attained 54, 65
happy course of existence 262, 285
happy lives the man of equanimity and attentive mind 112, 297, 339
happy states of existence 171, 175
hard to understand 14, 16, 23
harsh language 5, 66, 270, 271, 272, 338
has the fullness of meaning in spirit and letter 65, 98
hatred (*dosa*) 231
Hatthinika 93
have a grudge against 4
having himself realized them and seen them face to face 14, 17, 23
heaven world (deva abode) 261, 262
held and persisted in 16, 21, 23, 26
hell 50, 84, 85
high and luxurious resting places 8, 9, 69
higher and beiter advantages of a samaṇa's life 65
higher spiritual powers 47, 58
highest bliss in this very life 35, 52
highest earthly Nibbāna 36, 40
Himalaya mountains 222
Himalayas 93
hindrances 228, 247
'hither shore' is the metaphor for the groups of existence as objects of clinging 203
hoarded things 7, 67
holds the Right View and can therefore attain Nibbāna 42
holds the same view 33
hold that things arise without a cause 28
honour 131, 134, 136, 137
hopscotch 8, 68, 102
housewife's fivefold duty 279

I

ibbhā 91, 92
icchānaṅgala wood 88, 126
idha means "In this sāsana" 140
ill-consequence 248
ill-directed mind 259, 260
ill-will 4, 339
ill will is caused by *rāga* (greed), *dosa* (hatred) and *moha* (delusion) 154, 155
ill will means the wrong state of mind 231
immediate advantage 55, 62, 63
impression (*phassa*) 173
improper manner 228, 229
in-and out-breathing, is Kamma-formation of body 148
incomparable bliss of liberation—Arahatta-phala 288
incomparable leader of men to be tamed 54, 65, 88, 89, 207, 210
incomparable Supreme Enlightenment 177
indifferent sensation 149, 150
infinite and without a limit 22, 49
influenced by Craving and Bias 39, 40
in its real sense 24, 25
in like manner 26, 288
in praise of the Buddha, the Dhamma, and the Saṅgha 3, 4
insight-knowledge 120
insight (*vipassanā*) 229, 236, 239
instrumentality of the father and the mother 33
intention (*chanda*) 24
intoxicants 85, 276, 277
investigation of the dhamma 158, 161
isi (hermit) 95, 120
is not clever about grazing grounds 131
  is not conversant with rūpa 131
  is not skilful in distinguishing the *lakkhaṇa* 131

J

jāti (rebirth) 341
jātiyā wood in Bhaddiya 279
Jetavana Monastery of Anāthapiṇḍika, Jetas grove 219
jhāna 77, 78, 79, 297, 300, 339, 365
jhāna ecstasy 237
Jīvaka the doctor 153

K

kāma-guṇa 289
kāmāsava (mental impurities of sensuality) 292
kāma (sensuality) 289
kāma-taṇhā (Craving for Sensual pleasures) 145
kamma bandhū—Kamma alone is the real relative of all beings 46
kamma dāyādā—All beings are the heirs of their own kamma 46
kammānaṃ ādinavaṃ, okāraṃ saṃkilesaṃ (Discourse on the blemishes; meanness and vulgarity of sensuous pleasures) 127
kamma paccayā: Owing to their own kammas 317
kammappaṭisaraṇā—Kamma alone is the real Refuge of all beings 46
kammāsaddhamma 165
kammassakata-sammā-diṭṭhi (6 kinds) 45
kammaṭṭhāna (practice of meditations 141
kamma (volition) 254
kamma yoni—All beings are the descendants of their own kamma 46
kaṇha (blackies) 93
kaṇhāyana 92
karakaṇḍa 93
kasi 310, 322
Kassapa 314
kattika 370
kāya (life-continuum) 43
kevalino (those who have done all that ought to be done in this Sāsana) 178
khalikaṃ (throwing dice) 68
khiḍḍāpadosikā (debauched by pleasure) 19
kilesa (defilement) 229
kinetic energy 59, 273, 343
King Okkāka 92, 96
klaṇha lineage 93
knower of worlds 98, 207
knowledge and Conduct 98
knowledge and insight 262
knowledge of former existences 83, 116
knowledge of the minds of others 82, 115
kodañña 216
Kosala 122, 227, 285
Kosambi 204
kumbhathūnaṃ (playing drums) 68
Kurundavāsi Phussamitta Thera 264
kurus 165
kūṭāgāra 190

L

laid the stick and the weapon aside 5, 66, 99
lakkhaṇa (characteristics) 131, 134, 135
lamentation (*parideva*) 330
lamenting 311, 330, 347
languor, torpor and 75
laws of *paṭicca-samuppāda* (Dependent Origination) 42
lay-disciples 286
laziness (*tandī*) 232
least offences 65, 99
life-continua 46
life-continuum 43, 210
links of enlightenment 158, 161, 162
live a chaste and pure life in all its fulness 99
live in holy life 169, 170
livelihood, wrong means of 11, 12
lives in honesty and purity of heart 5, 66, 99
lives only on bulbs, roots and fruits. 120
live without the application of mindfulness 270, 271, 272

living being 5, 33
living by wrongful means 13, 73
loathsomeness (*asubha*) 245
lofty and spacious resting places 6, 67, 100
log of wood 204
Lohapāsāda Monastery 220, 226
lokāyataṃ (popular lore and custom) 13, 73, 106
lokāyata (sophistry) 89
loss 254
lost self-control 19
loving-kindness 144, 153, 154
  The Emancipation of Mind 247
low arts 11, 12, 13, 71, 72, 73, 104, 105, 106, 107
low talks 9, 70, 103
luminous 265

M

maddarūpī 95, 96
Madhura 276
magga-paññā (knowledge pertaining to the Holy Paths) 45
mahābhūta 343
Mahācetī Pagoda 225
mahāgopālaka sutta 131, 137
Mahākaccāna 194, 195, 196
Mahākassapa 157, 244, 250
Mahāsaṅgharakkhitatthera 238
mahā sīla (The Major Morality) 11, 71, 104
Mahātissa Thera 241, 242
maintain ill will against others 270, 271, 272
  beliefs in which they wriggle like eels 26
  the belief 27
Majjhima sīla (The Medium Morality) 7, 67
major morality 11, 71, 104
make a smoke 131, 133, 136, 138
make offerings 309, 310, 313, 314, 318
makkarakaṭa in the kingdom of Avanti 194
makkhali of the cow-pen 53, 57
  Gosāla's View 57
malevolent thought (*byāpāda vitakka*) 132
māna (conceit) 16, 21, 23, 27, 28, 29, 31, 32, 33, 35, 37, 38
manāpa devas' abode (Nimmānarati) 281
Mango Grove of Jīvaka 53, 153
manoeuvres 7, 68, 101, 382
mano (mind) 167
manopadosikā (Debauched in Mind) 20
manopadosikā devas (Devas debauched in Mind) 20
manorathapūraṇī 219, 253
mano-viññāṇaṃ (Mind-consciousness) 186
mantras 95, 96, 97
many a becoming or kappa (world cycle) 46
maraṇa (death) 328
Master Gavesī 286, 287, 288
material qualities 131, 132
meals offered for the benefit of the dead 96, 97
means for adorning and beautifying themselves 9, 69
mediators and messengers 10, 70, 104
medicine made of cattle urine 298
meditation on an unpleasant object (*asubha kammaṭṭhāna*) 239
medium morality 7, 67, 101
meṇḍaka 279
mental and physical phenomena 273, 274
mental creative powers 80, 113, 120
  Formations 145, 146, 147
merit is exhausted 17
meritorious deeds 62, 63, 64, 194, 312, 324
merry-making and pleasure 19
mettābhāvanā (development of all-embracing loving kindness) 159
micchā-diṭṭhi (wrong views) 48
midstream, sinking in 204
Milakkhatissa Thera 235, 249
milks dry 131, 134, 140, 144
mimicry of deformities 8, 69, 102
mind and body become tranquil 162
mind and matter 143, 168

mind, calmness of the 250
mind-continuum 168
mindfulness 270, 271
mindfulness and clearness of comprehension 65, 74, 75, 99, 108
mind well directed 259
minor morality-CŪLA SĪLA 5
monk Gotama 5, 7, 8
moral shame and dread 5, 66, 99
muddle-headed and ignorant 175
muditābhāvanā (development of altruistic joy) 159
multiformity-perceptions 34

N

na āsāṭikaṃ hāretā 142
na dhūmaṃ kattā hoti 142
na lakkhaṇakusalo hoti 138, 141
  rūpaññū hoti 140
  titthaṃ jānāti 142
  vanaṃ paticchādetā hoti 142
Nālanda 3
nāmarūpaṃ (Mental and Physical Phenomena) 341
name and form (*nāma rūpa*) 173
Nanda 205, 206
neither applauded nor rejected what he said 56, 58, 59, 60
  created nor caused to be created 59
  Devas nor men will behold Him 43
  know nor perceive 39
  made nor caused to be made 59
  Perception nor Non-perception after death 32
nekkhamme ānisaṃsaṃ (Discourse on the Advantages of Renunciation) 128
net of *attha* (Advantage) 43
nevasaññā nāsaññāyatana Brahmā plane 52
never-returner (*Anāgāmiphala*) 237
nibbāna 245, 246, 255, 256, 259, 260
nibbāna is the release (deliverance) from all defilements 245
nibbāna ñāṇa 171, 172
nibbedhikabrāhmacariya (Noble Practice) 289, 290, 292
niccaṃ (dances) 7, 67, 101
Nigaṇṭha Nāṭaputta 54, 60
  Nigaṇṭha Nāṭaputta's View 60
nikāya 145, 153, 157, 165, 167, 190, 194, 219, 228, 253, 257, 309
nimmānarati 215, 281
nissaggiya pācittiya offence 370, 371
noble eightfold path 134, 136, 143, 145, 146, 147, 178, 179, 180, 181, 183, 184, 185, 186, 213, 289, 290, 291, 293, 294, 295, 337
noble truth of the Path 213, 214, 275
non-eternalists, in regard to others 17
non-eternity-belief 19, 20
non-humans, seized by men or 204
nose-consciousness 181, 186, 332, 335, 343
not subject to change 19, 20, 21
not to be deduced by mere logic 16, 23, 27, 28, 29, 31
November (*Sārada*) 243

O

objectifying on 16
observing the precepts 304
offerings 11, 54, 91, 313
okkāmukha 93
old age and death sorrow, lamentation, pain, grief and despair 165, 166
omniscience 16, 43, 65, 88, 89, 98, 207, 219, 222, 223, 261
omniscient buddha 3, 4
one-pointedness of mind, is Mental Concentration 148
one worthy of offerings, the Supremely Enlightened Buddha 54
one worthy of veneration 3, 4
on the dissolution of the body 33, 34
opinions are based on personal experience 40
opportune place 320, 321, 322

oracular answers 13, 73, 106
ordinary crafts 55, 56, 57, 58, 59
origin of *sakkāya* 145
origin of suffering 273, 274, 301, 328
other bank 204, 378
other shore is the metaphor for nibbāna 203
outward appearance 133, 135, 136
overcome Sceptical Doubt 128

P

pain (*dukkha*) 347
Pakudha Kaccāyana 53, 60
Pakudha Kaccāyana's View 59
palmistry or chiromancy 11, 71, 105
pañca garuka jātaka 225
paṇissaraṃ (music attended by clapping) 7, 68, 101
paññāvimuttā 171
paññāvimutti 196
paññā (wisdom) 147
pārājika 364, 368
parideva (lamentation) 346
paritta 223
paro loko means the 4 Lower Worlds 47
Pasenadi Kosala 227
Pasenadi of Kosala 88
patchwork counterpanes 8, 69, 102
paṭibhāga (opposite) 151
paṭiccasamuppāda (dependent origination) 165, 168, 186
pātidesaniya offences 389
paṭigha 25, 151
paṭigha-nimitta 231
paṭighānusaya (Inherent tendency towards Friction) 150, 151
paṭiloma-paṭicca-samuppāda 42
pāṭimokkha 386
pavāraṇā 237, 240, 313
pavilion 3, 54, 55
paying attention in a proper manner 245, 251
peace 5
  loves peace 5
  makes peace 5
pekkaṃ (theatrical shows) 7, 68
penetrative insight into the truth of Suffering (*Dukkhe ñāṇaṃ*) 47
  the truth of the Extinction of Suffering 47
  the truth of the Origin of Suffering 47
perceive the truth 39, 40
perception after death 30, 31, 41, 50, 51
perception and sensation 148, 149
perception and sensation is Kamma-formation of mind 148
perception arises in them 27
perception-group 145, 343, 348
perception (*saññā*) 172, 192
percipient nor impercipient 32, 40
perfect one 65
perfect one, supremely enlightened, possessed of clear wisdom and action 65
period of slaughter (*Satthantrakappa*) 263
personality-belief 146, 147, 158, 345
petas 310, 311, 312, 314, 315, 316, 317, 318, 319, 320, 322, 323, 324
phala-paññā (knowledge pertaining to the Fruitions 45
phassa, *-o* (contact) 149, 341
phassa-paccaya (With the aid of Contact 40
philanthropic and generous 67, 68, 69, 70
phoṭṭhabba-saññā 179, 184
piṇḍapātikaṅga dhutaṅga 227
pisāca (demons) 93
playing with toy measures 8
play where the hand is dipped in dye and used as a brush 102
  with paper wind-mills 8
  with toy bow 68
  with toy chariots 102
pleasantness and unsatisfactoriness of *vedanā* (sensations) 16, 21, 23, 27
pleasant to the ear, lovely, reaching to the heart, polite 5, 66, 100
plenteous food and drink 309, 319
plunderers of villages 199, 200, 202, the metaphor for the six external bases 202

point out my errors 25
Pokkharasāti 88, 89, 90, 92, 122, 123, 125, 126, 127, 128
pondering 14, 15, 18, 19, 20, 22, 27, 243
possessed of clear vision and virtuous conduct 54
praise the Tathāgata in accordance with the truth 14
preceptor 243, 244, 394
preserve the foetus in cases of abortive women 13, 73, 106
principal action (padhāna kamma 243
process of becoming 274
proclaims the Dhamma to men 65, 88, 89, 98
profound 14, 16
profound, difficult to realize 16, 23, 27
psychic power 125, 127, 236
pubbantakappika (18 Views 14
pubbenivāsa-ñāṇa 45
Pūraṇa Kassapa 53, 56
purgatory (*niraya*) 262, 265
purified 37, 53, 54, 79
purified by equanimity and attentiveness 37
purify our minds 53
pūtimukha serpent 201
putting in bonds 6, 67

Q

Queen Videha 53, 63, 64
question is put to them on this and that 24
quilts 8, 69

R

'raft' is the metaphor for the Noble Eightfold Path 203
rāga (greed) 24, 154, 155
rāgānusaya (inherent tendency towards Sensuous Greed) 150
raise a quarrel against the people 5, 66, 100
Rājagaha 3, 53, 54, 145, 153, 169, 312, 315
rasa-saññā 179, 184, 333, 336
reaching to the heart 5, 66, 100
realization of the truths 325
realizes the Origin, Cessation, Pleasantness, and Unsatisfactoriness of the Six Bases of Contact 42
rebirth (*jāti*) 173
rebut their statement 4
recluses and Brahmins 7, 8, 9, 10, 11
reflex-perceptions 34
refrains from 66, 67
  falsehood 24
  partaking of intoxicants 277
  such low arts 72
  the destruction of life 5
  using harsh language 66
  vain conversation 66
refuge
  I take refuge in the Buddha, in the Dhamma and in the Saṅgha 268
regenerative cause (*janaka*) 234
relevant facts 10, 70
remember what had happened in the past existences 14
remembrance of former existences 116, 117
renounce the world 63, 64
renunciation 128, 160
replete with mindfulness and clearness of comprehension 75, 108
repulsive object 231
requisite food and shelter 63, 64
requisites-robe, alms, dwelling, medicine for illness 299
restrains his sense of sight 74, 107, 135
resultant of *āsavas* 292, 293
result of *phassa* (contact) 40
riding elephants 54
right action 146, 147, 179, 180
right effort 134, 146, 147, 159, 178, 179
rightly praise the Tathāgata in accordance with the truth 14, 17, 23, 27, 29
right mindfulness 147, 159, 178
right speech 134, 146, 147, 159, 178, 179
right understanding (*sammā-diṭṭhi*) 204

ripe experience 53
rotting inwardly 204, 205
rounds of defilements (*vaṭṭa*) 235
existence (*vipāka-vaṭṭa*) 253
results (*vipāka-vaṭṭa*) 253
royal rest house 3
rubbing scented powder on one's body 9, 69, 103
rudeness of speech 5, 66, 100
rugs with fur 8, 69, 102
rūpa and *arūpa* 141, 241
rūpa brahmā plane 34, 52
rūpa (forms) 131
rūpaññū 137
rūpa-saññā 179, 184, 291, 333, 336

S

sabbe sattā kammasakā 46
sacrifice of human blood to gods 71, 105
sadda-saññā 179, 184, 291, 333, 336
saddhā (faith) 313
sādhu sādhu 227
sagga-kathaṃ (Discourse on the Heavenly Abodes) 127
sainthood (*Arahatta*) 235
sakka 94, 315
sakkāya-diṭṭhi (Personality-belief) 146, 147
sakyamuni 396, 397
sākyan clan 88, 89, 207
sākyas 91, 92
saḷāyatanaṃ (the 6 Bases) 341
samādhi (Mental Concentration) 147
samaṇa 53, 55, 56, 58
samaṇas and *brāhmaṇas* 62, 65, 67, 68, 69
sammā-diṭṭhi (Right Understanding) 45, 337
sammapadhāna 203
saṃsāra (the Round of Rebirths) 165
samuṭṭhāna 140, 141
saṅgha 3
saṅghādisesa 383, 387
saṅkappa-rāga 289
saṅkhāra (kamma-activities) 187, (mental formation) 172
saññā-vedayita nirodha-sammāpatti (Attainment of Cessation of Perception and Sensation) 148
saññi-vāda (Belief that there is Perception after death) 30, 50
saññni-vāda (16 views) 45
sassata-diṭṭhi (Eternity belief) 45
sassata-vāda 48
First View 48
Second View 48
Third View 48
Fourth View 48
sassata-vāda (Eternity-Belief) 48
satthamukha serpent 201
sāvatthi 131, 157, 167, 177, 182, 226, 283, 304
scattered mind 82, 83
scented flowers 227
sceptical doubt 76, 109, 110, 128
seclusion 63, 64, 162, 296, 299
second *jhāna* 36, 52, 111, 297, 339
seen them face to face 14, 17, 23, 27
seer of the worlds 3, 4
seized by men or non-humans 204
sekhiya (Rules for Training) 354
self-annihilation (*vibhava-taṇhā*) 213
self-confidence 283
self-defence 7, 68, 101
self-restraint 74, 108, 270, 271, 272
semi-eternalists 39, 40
sensation-group 145, 168, 343
sensations (*vedanā*) 16
sense-bases 254
sense organs of contact 273
senses guarded and conquered 327
sensual craving (*kāma-taṇhā*) 213
sensual desire 228, 229
sensuous pleasures (kāma vitakka) 35, 36, 52, 132
sentient beings 99
separation from those we love 331
serpent, *pūtimukha* 201
servile duties 10, 70, 104
sets forth the following views and holds the same 35

set upright 156, 268
seven aspects 182, 186
seven great protuberances 57
seven ways of settling disputes 390
seven ways the breaking up 40, 41
sexual act which is the practice of the country folk 5, 66
sexual misconduct 276, 277
sham fights 7
she-elephants 54
sight of a woman 219, 220
sīla-katham (Discourse on Morality) 127
sīla (morality) 147, 342, 348
sīma 228, 230, 240, 362
six bases of contact 42
six external bases 200, 202
six internal bases 204, 332
six kinds of discursive thinking: (*vicāra*) 334, 337
six kinds of perception 179
  consciousness 181
  contacts 179
  craving 39
  feeling 162
  perception 30
  sensation 42
  volition 180
six kinds of thought conception: (*vitakka*) 334, 337
six sense bases (*saḷāyatana*) 173
skillful as hair-splitters 25
sloth and torpor 248, 249
  means stolidity and drowsiness 232
smashing to pieces 25
soaked with Rapture and Joy 77, 111
sobhanakaṃ (art exhibitions) 7, 68, 101
sofas 9
solicitude for the welfare of all sentient beings 5, 66
solicitude—full of solicitude 99
sorrow, lamentation, pain, grief and despair 165
sorrow (*soka*) 329, 346
sotāpanna 211
soul 14
soul and the world are eternal 15
spacious couch 8, 69, 102
speak against 4
speak ill of 4
speak only things of small value 5
speaks the truth and nothing but the truth 5
speculate on the future "world cycles" 29
speculate on the past "world cycles" 29
speculations are concerned with the past 40, 41
speculators and investigators 49
speculators on the past or the future "World cycles" 43
sphere of form (*rūpa*) 171, 175
sphere of neither-perception-nor-non-perception 34
sphere of unbounded consciousness 34
sphere of unbounded space 34
spiritual progress 297
spontaneously-manifesting beings 47
stranded upon land 204
stream-winner 211
street talks 9, 70
striving with arms and legs 199, 200
subconscious mind 264
subhagakaraṇaṃ (using charms to make people happy) 73, 106
subject to change 172
subject to craving and bias (*taṇhā* and *diṭṭhi*) 39, 40
subject to decay 50, 51
subtle 14
subtle, comprehensible only by the wise 14, 23
such games played by imagining such boards in the air 8
suddha pācittiya 375

su'dhāvāsa Brahma-plane (Abode of Purity) 158
suffer heart-burning 4
suitable religious talk 246
sukha (bodily agreeable sensation 151

sukhādhivāhaṃ 256
Sumitta Thera 255
suññata-phassa (contact with the devoid) 149
superman 296, 297
supernormal knowledge 81, 114, 117, 118
supernormal powers 81, 264
suppiya, the wandering religious mendicant 3
supporting cause (*upathambhaka*) 234
supreme Buddha 54, 312
supremely enlightened 98, 210
supreme net 3
supreme punishment (Brāhmadaṇḍena) 96
surgery 13, 73, 107
surpassing the dhamma of ordinary laymen 263
swell the king's coffers 64

T

tacapancaka 235
takkī vimansī 48, 50
talks about kings, robbers 70
taṇhā (craving) 331
taṇhā (craving) and *diṭṭhi* (bias) 39
taṇhā-diṭṭhiparāmāsa 211
tathāgata 5, 6, 13, 14, 16, 17, 21, 23, 26, 27, 28, 29, 30, 31, 32, 33, 35, 37, 38, 43, 65, 94, 98, 99, 155, 190, 191, 192, 193, 212, 243, 327
teacher of gods and men 65
Devas and men 88
teachings 14
temporary 265
tenfold wholesome course of action of ordinary laymen 263
ten precepts 352
ten thousand world systems shook 44
the fire of lust 220, 221
themselves, means for adorning and beautifying 103
third jhāna 52, 78
thirty-two bodily marks 90, 124
thought-conception and discursive thinking 342
three jewels (Buddha, Dhamma and Saṅgha) 252
thrift and economy 280
through the Process of Becoming arises Rebirth 42
throwing dice 8, 102
tirokuṭṭa 316
Tissabhūtitthera 238
tittle-tattle 9, 70, 103
tongue-consciousness 181
toy bows 8
toy pipes 68, 102
train yourselves in this manner 279
tranquillity 12, 14
tranquillity of mind 14, 15, 18
tranquillizing 14
trickeries and deceptions 10, 71
tricksters 10, 70, 104
trifling matters 13
tumba 265
turbid 139, 262, 265
turbid state of mind 262
turning somersaults 8, 68, 102
two bodily marks 90, 124

U

uccheda-diṭṭhi (annihilation-belief) 45
uccheda-vāda (7 views) 45
uccheda-vāda (annihilation-belief) 51
unadaptable 253
unbounded is consciousness 34
unbounded is space 34
uncalmed mind 233
unconscious beings 27
understand wholesome volitional action in its real sense 24
unguarded 257, 258
unpleasant object 234, 239, 242
unrestrained 258
untamed 257
unwholesome deeds 300
unwholesome volitional action 24
upadāna (grasping) 25
upādānakkhandhas 177

upādānaṃ (clinging) 341
Upālitthera 251
upāsaka 235, 283
upāyāsa (Despair) 347
upekkhā bhāvanā (development of equanimity) 159
uposatha day 359, 362
upside down 86, 128, 156, 197
uttamapuriso (one who is the noblest personage 182

V

vāditaṃ (playing instrumental music) 7
Vajirapānī Yakkha 94
value, qualities of morality that are insignificant 5
vassa 157, 241
vaṭṭa and *vivaṭṭa* 255, 256
vedanā (feeling) 172
vedanā (sensations) 16, 21, 23, 27, 28, 29, 31, 32, 33, 35, 37, 38
veḷudvāra 207
Venerable Gotama 211, 268
verbal conduct 209, 210
vexation to my mind 24, 25
vibhava-taṇhā (Craving for Self-annihilation) 145
view of the inefficacy of action 269, 272
view of the uncausedness 58
views on this in sixteen ways 30
vigilance 14, 15, 18
vihāra (monastery) 90, 313
vihiṃsā vitakka 132
vijambhitā (trembling) 232
vijjā (knowledge) 98
  and *caraṇa* (conduct) 120
  vimmutti (Freedom) 151

vinaya-dhamma (bhikkhus' disciplinary code) 251
vinipātaṃ (the World of Perdition) 165
viññāṇa, -aṃ (consciousness) 167, 348, 341
viññāṇañcāyatana brahmā plane 34
vipassanā insight 229, 256
vipassanā-paññā (direct knowledge gained through Insight) 45
virulent serpents 199
Visākha 145, 314
viveka (detachment, i.e. Nibbāna) 149
volition-six kinds 333
vusitavā (one who has lived the Holy life) 182

W

wandering ascetic Susima 169
wear the yellow robes 63, 64
weeping or sorrowing 311, 323
well advanced in years 91, 94
well-trained noble disciple 168
whisks of the yak's tail 9, 69
woollen coverlets 69, 102
words are empty, false and idle 59
world are partly eternal and partly not 39
world is both finite and infinite 22
world is neither finite nor infinite 23, 49

ABOUT PARIYATTI

Pariyatti is dedicated to providing affordable access to authentic teachings of the Buddha about the Dhamma theory (*pariyatti*) and practice (*paṭipatti*) of Vipassana meditation. A 501(c)(3) nonprofit charitable organization since 2002, Pariyatti is sustained by contributions from individuals who appreciate and want to share the incalculable value of the Dhamma teachings. We invite you to visit www.pariyatti.org to learn about our programs, services, and ways to support publishing and other undertakings.

Pariyatti Publishing Imprints

Vipassana Research Publications (focus on Vipassana as taught by S.N. Goenka in the tradition of Sayagyi U Ba Khin)

BPS Pariyatti Editions (selected titles from the Buddhist Publication Society, copublished by Pariyatti)

MPA Pariyatti Editions (selected titles from the Myanmar Pitaka Association, copublished by Pariyatti)

Pariyatti Digital Editions (audio and video titles, including discourses)

Pariyatti Press (classic titles returned to print and inspirational writing by contemporary authors)

Pariyatti enriches the world by

- disseminating the words of the Buddha,
- providing sustenance for the seeker's journey,
- illuminating the meditator's path.

www.ingramcontent.com/pod-product-compliance
Lightning Source LLC
Chambersburg PA
CBHW022056150426
43195CB00008B/161
* 9 7 8 1 6 8 1 7 2 8 1 6 2 *